BURT FRANKLIN: RESEARCH & SOURCE WORKS SERIES 770
Selected Essays in History, Economics and Social Science 279

Slavery

AS AN INDUSTRIAL SYSTEM

Slavery

AS AN INDUSTRIAL SYSTEM

ETHNOLOGICAL RESEARCHES

BY

Dr. H. J. NIEBOER

SECOND, REVISED EDITION

BURT FRANKLIN
NEW YORK

HT 901
N5
1971
cop. 2

Published by LENOX HILL Pub. & Dist. Co. (Burt Franklin)
235 East 44th St., New York, N.Y. 10017
Originally Published: 1910
Reprinted: 1971
Printed in the U.S.A.

S.B.N.: 8337-25408
Library of Congress Card Catalog No.: 78-121216
Burt Franklin: Research and Source Works Series 770
Selected Essays in History, Economics and Social Science 279

Reprinted from the original edition in the Free Library of Philadelphia

PREFACE.

The present work is a revised edition of my book on slavery as it was published in 1900.

Preparing this second edition, I saw that the general plan of the book could remain the same. The details, however, wanted improvement in many respects. The chapter treating of the geographical distribution of slavery among savage tribes has been much enlarged, as the information of which I disposed was far more complete now than when the book was originally written. The theoretical part, I hope, has also much improved. A closer study of the subject has led me to alter some passages and make several additions.

I have also profited by the remarks of my critics, among whom I especially mention Professor Tönnies (in Professor Schmoller's *Jahrbücher*, Vol. XXV) and Dr. Vierkandt (in *Zeitschrift für Socialwissenschaft*, Vol. IV). To these I may add Professor Westermarck, who, in his work on the origin and development of the moral ideas (1906—08), discusses at some length the conclusions to which I have arrived.

The fact that the first edition has been kindly received by the periodical press has encouraged me to prepare this second edition. I was happy to notice that my study of some conditions of primitive culture was valued not only as a contribution to the knowledge of savage life, but as furthering the understanding of the structure of human society in general.

I will not conclude this preface without offering my sincere thanks to my teacher and friend Professor STEINMETZ of Amsterdam, under whose guidance the first edition was written and whose help in preparing the present edition has been very valuable to me.

ROTTERDAM, Holland.   H. J. NIEBOER.
December 1909.

CONTENTS.

PART I. — DESCRIPTIVE.

CHAPTER I. — DEFINITION AND DISTINCTION FROM KINDRED PHENOMENA.

PART II. — THEORETICAL.

CHAPTER I. — METHOD AND DIVISIONS.

CHAPTER III. — PASTORAL TRIBES.

CHAPTER IV. — AGRICULTURAL TRIBES.

GENERAL INTRODUCTION.

There exists an extensive literature on slavery. Many of these works are intended for philanthropic purposes, viz. to further the suppression of the African slave-trade, whereas many others contain historical investigations of slavery among ancient or modern nations.

The present volume will not rank among either of these categories, but deal with the general character of slavery as an industrial system. Slavery has played a great part in the social history of mankind. Social life among most of the ancient nations was based upon slavery, and in many colonies it subsisted until far into the 19th century. On the other hand, in the civilized countries of to-day all industrial operations are carried on with free labour. Whence this difference? Why have slavery and serfdom gradually declined in the course of European history, so that at the close of the Middle Ages they had already in a large degree lost their significance? These problems can only be solved if we know the conditions necessary for the success of slavery as an industrial system, and the inverse conditions under which slave labour must give way to free labour. We shall try to find these conditions, or at least some of them.

We shall use the comparative method, collecting facts and inquiring what regularities can be found in these facts, under what general rules they may be included. But before enlarging upon our method we must say a few words concerning a limitation we have put upon our subject.

Our book, as the title shows, contains ethnological researches. We confine ourselves to investigating the conditions which govern the existence or non-existence of slavery among savage tribes, and the materials we make use of are exclusively ethnographical materials, i. e. descriptions of savage tribes.

Ethnology has already made considerable progress, and is taking a conspicuous place among the Mental Sciences. Yet some ethnologists still proceed in a somewhat narrow and one-sided manner. They generally aim at reconstructing the early history of mankind with the help of ethnographical data. The savages representing primitive man, or at least man in a more primitive state than we can find by direct historical research, they draw inferences from the actual state of savage tribes as to the early state of mankind at large. This kind of study has been very useful, especially in removing narrow views on human development which existed at a time, when the traditions of a few ancient nations were still considered to be the only evidence as to early history. But this should not be the sole, nor even the main object of ethnological investigation. It is sociological laws that we want in the first place. It is certainly interesting to know what changes have taken place in early history; but it is far more important to know on what circumstances the existence of each social phenomenon depends. And for this purpose ethnology can be of considerable use. Among savages social life is much simpler than among civilized men; the factors which govern it are comparatively few, and so the effect of each of them can be traced without much difficulty. We can thus, by comparing the institutions of many savage tribes, find sociological laws, several of which will have a wider application and lead us to a clearer understanding of the conditions which govern the social life of civilized nations. For instance, the study of moral phenomena among savages has already given us a deeper insight into morality at large.

The conclusions we arrive at in this book are of two kinds. Some of them apply to savages only and cannot further our understanding of civilized life. For instance, we shall see that settled tribes are more likely to keep slaves than nomadic tribes; but civilized, and even semi-civilized peoples are hardly ever nomadic. Other conclusions, however, have a more general bearing. Thus we shall find that slavery is not likely to exist in those countries, where all land is held as property. And as this has been the case in Western Europe for some centuries, we discover one of the principal causes, perhaps the main cause, why slavery (and serfdom, which is a mitigated form of slavery), have long since disappeared in these countries.

We do not, however, make any systematic inquiry into the bearing of the laws found by investigating the phenomena of savage life on the study of social life among civilized and semi-civilized nations. Where phenomena of civilized life occur to us which bear a striking resemblance to what we find among savages, we mention them briefly, generally in a note. Only in one case we go farther. Where we find that the relation between land and population is a factor of the utmost importance in shaping the lot of the labouring classes, it is obvious that this factor must have played a great part in the social history of Europe, and therefore we adduce some statements of historians in corroboration of our view. Yet, even here, it is our object to claim attention for this factor that is commonly overlooked, and clear the way for future research, rather than to give a ready explanation of the decline of serfdom in Western Europe. We are thus justified in making use of only a small part of the literature on this subject.

As we have already said, we proceed by an inductive, comparative method. We first collect ethnographical materials. Then we critically determine the meaning and reliability of the statements of our informants. We thus see where slavery exists, and where it is absent. And finally we inquire what are the causes of the observed phenomena.

Some remarks have still to be made on the details of our proceeding. First as to the ethnographical literature.

We have collected our materials quite impartially, without any regard to our ultimate conclusions, which, indeed, rest upon a study of the facts, not upon any preconceived opinion. Though there is, of course, much ethnographical literature we have not used, our collection is rather extensive and contains most of the better works. All geographical groups are properly represented, least of all perhaps India, most of the literature on which country (so far as wild tribes are concerned) seems to be wanting in the Dutch libraries. We have greatly profited by being allowed to make use of Professor Steinmetz's schedules, being detailed extracts of hundreds of ethnographical books and articles, somewhat resembling Spencer's "Descriptive Sociology", but far more complete.

The ethnographical literature may not, however, be used without a thorough criticism. We shall often meet with very loose and inaccurate statements, and this book will afford many instances of the careless use of the terms "slave" and "slavery" by ethnographers. The zoölogist and the geologist have only to deal with accounts of their fellow-scientists; but the ethnologist is obliged always to rely on ethnographers, who often have no notion of ethnology, and sometimes no notion of science at all. Hence the very bad terminology; hence also the frequent omission of details which would have been very valuable. Yet, regarding the very little that has as yet been achieved in ethnology, we can hardly blame the ethnographers. It is true, if the ethnographical literature were better, ethnology would greatly profit by it; but, on the other hand, even with the help of the existing literature, which, after all, is not so very bad, much more might be attained than is actually done. And as long as ethnology is still in an unsettled condition, it is perhaps better that an ethnographer should have no ideas at all on ethnological subjects, than premature, quasi-scientific, and probably erroneous ideas. Montaigne, one of the most sensible men who have ever lived, speaking of his informant on the cannibals of America, says: "This man whom I had was a simple and rude man, which is a condition conducive to reliable testimony; for refined people observe more curiously and observe more things; but then they gloss them; and in order to force their interpretation on you, they cannot but change the story a little; they never represent you the pure facts; they warp and mask them according to the point of view from which they regard them; and in order to give credit to their judgment and make you accept their view, they readily add something to the matter on that side and exaggerate it. A man must be either very truthful, or so simple that he does not want to construct false inventions and give them a semblance of truth, and is not riveted to a theory." What we want is, as the same writer has it, *la matière de l'histoire nue et informe* [1]. An ethnographer should be taught what to observe and how to observe, and how to record his observations. But when this ideal cannot be attained, it is better to have an ethnographer who only knows that every correct statement of his will interest the men of science, than one whose perceptive faculties are troubled by preconceived opinions.

We have subjected our materials to a thorough criticism, externally by comparing in each case the descriptions of the same tribe by different writers, and internally by inquiring what importance is to be attached to the statements of each writer, considering the time in which he wrote, his more or less intimate acquaintance with the people described, the general character of his writings, etc.

We thus find where slavery exists or formerly existed, and where it does or did not exist. We always mention the exact numbers of the tribes with and without slaves in the several geographical groups, and afterwards also in the several economic groups. We do not intend these numbers as statistical materials, upon which to base mathematical rules. We only mean to express the results of our investigations in the exactest manner possible. Instead of stating: Slavery in such a group exists in many cases, it is much more accurate to state: Slavery in such a group exists, so far as our observations go, in, say, 80 cases. We thus simply follow the method (sometimes miscalled statistical method) first introduced by Professor Tylor in his article "On a method of investigating the development of institutions", and adopted by Professor Steinmetz in his "*Entwicklung der Strafe*".

We inquire next what conditions govern the occurrence of the observed phenomena. This part of our work is certainly the most difficult, and it is necessary here to proceed with the utmost caution. Many ethnologists adopt a rather curious method. They have some theory, found by deductive reasoning, and then adduce a few facts by way of illustration. This, however, is quite insufficient. It does not appear whether all existing facts agree with the theory; there may be many instances, not mentioned by the theorist, in which his rule does not hold. The only scientific method is impartially to collect facts and inquire whether they can be brought

---

1) Montaigne, Essais, Book I Chapter XXX and Book II Chapter X.

under any general rule. If we find a hypothesis that accounts for many, but not all, of the observed phenomena, our task is not finished until we have explained the rest by showing the influence of additional factors. Moreover, the negative instances must be accounted for as well as the positive. If we account for the existence of B by the coexistence of A, we must prove either that in those cases where B does not exist A too is absent, or that in such cases there are additional causes which neutralize the effect of A. Ethnological works should not be *causeries*, as they often are, but scientific researches.

But we must also be careful not to fall into the other extreme. We shall never be able to arrive at a true understanding of the facts without the help of leading ideas. The facts do not arrange themselves spontaneously; we must try to account for them by hypotheses which seem *a priori* plausible. When such a hypothesis occurs to us, we have to inquire how far it can go to account for the facts, and, of course, to abandon it if, however plausible it seemed, it proves to be erroneous. By judiciously selecting our hypotheses we can save ourselves much futile labour. For instance, when about to investigate the causes of slavery, it occurs to us that its existence will probably largely depend on the economic state of society, and we inquire whether this be really so. If we began with investigating the effect of some factor that *a priori* seems to have little connection with slavery, *e. g.* the development of aesthetic sentiments, we should be almost certain to do useless work.

The present volume endeavours to come up to the ideal we have set ourselves and developed here. A book of the same size as this might contain a survey of many more subjects connected with slavery. In the last paragraph it will be shown how very much remains unsaid. We treat only a small portion of the subject of slavery. But this portion is treated carefully, and by doing so we think we have arrived at some conclusions of scientific value, whereas, if we had superficially treated a wider subject, our work, though perhaps more agreeable from a literary point of view, would be nearly useless in a scientific sense.

Slavery among savages has never yet been made the subject of any special investigation. Letourneau's *"Évolution de l'Esclavage"* treats of slavery among all races of mankind, savages included. But he deals with his subject in quite an insufficient manner. His literature is rather scanty, and there is no question of any critical inquiry into the value of his materials. The theoretical part of his work consists of some entirely unproved assertions; not a single systematic investigation is to be found in it. Hence his general conclusion is very meagre and contains only the hackneyed evolutionary series of slavery, — serfdom, — wage-system, — socialist paradise, to which he adds "slavery of women" as the very first stage. The scientific value of this book is very little.

There is another book dealing with the general history of slavery, Professor J. K. Ingram's "History of slavery and serfdom". This writer confines himself to the historical nations of ancient and modern times; the savages are excluded. Though he makes many valuable remarks, of which, as the reader will see, we have availed ourselves, by far the greater part of his work is purely descriptive. A great difference between his book and ours is further that he writes "not for scholars, but for the mass of thoughtful and cultivated men and women" 1), whereas we appeal to the men of sience, not to the public at large. Yet it is an instructive little book. We only regret that the writer appears to agree with Comte's curious theory concerning the relation between slavery and religion 2).

The general history of slavery is also the subject of a book of Tourmagne's. "There are two volumes by A. Tourmagne," says Ingram "entitled respectively *Histoire de l'Esclavage Ancien et Moderne*, 1880, and *Histoire du Servage Ancien et Moderne*, 1879, which bring together many facts relating to slavery and serfdom; but they are somewhat loose and uncritical; the author, too, repeats himself much, and dwells on many topics scarcely, if at all, connected with his main themes" 3). We are not acquainted with Tourmagne book on serfdom: but as to his *Histoire de l'Esclavage* we fully agree with Ingram.

---

1) Ingram, p. VII. In our notes we always mention the name of the book referred to in the shortest way possible. The full titles will be found in our list at the end of the volume. — 2) Ibid., pp. 7—9. — 3) Ibid., p. XII.

PART I.

DESCRIPTIVE.

CHAPTER I.

§ 1. *Ordinary meaning of the term "slavery".*

In most branches of knowledge the phenomena the man of science has to deal with have their technical names; and, when using a scientific term, he need not have regard to the meaning this term conveys in ordinary language; he knows he will not be misunderstood by his fellow-scientists. For instance, the Germans call a whale *Wallfisch*, and the English speak of shell-fish; but a zoölogist, using the word fish, need not fear that any competent person will think he means whales or shell-fish.

In ethnology the state of things is quite different. There are a few scientific names bearing a definite meaning, such as the terms "animism" and "survival", happily introduced by Professor Tylor. But most phenomena belonging to our science have not yet been accurately investigated; so it is no wonder, that different writers (sometimes even the same writer on different pages) give different names to the same phenomenon, whereas on the other hand sometimes the same term (*e.g.* "matriarchy") is applied to widely different phenomena. As for the subject we are about to treat of, we shall presently see that several writers have given a definition of slavery; but no one has taken the trouble to inquire whether his definition can be of any practical use in social science. Therefore we shall try to give a good definition and justify it.

But we may not content ourselves with this; we must also pay attention to the meaning of the term "slavery" as commonly employed. There are two reasons for this. First, we must always rely upon the statements of ethnographers. If an ethnographer states that some savage tribe carries on slavery without defining in what this "slavery" consists, we have ask: What may our informant have meant? And as he is likely to have used the word in the sense generally attached to it, we have to inquire: What is the ordinary meaning of the term "slavery"?

The second reason is this. Several theoretical writers speak of slavery, without defining what they mean by it; and we cannot avail ourselves of their remarks without knowing what meaning they attach to this term. And as they too may be supposed to have used it in the sense in which it is generally used, we have again to inquire: What is the meaning of the term "slavery" in ordinary language?

The general use of the word, as is so often the case, is rather inaccurate. "Careless or rhetorical writers" says Ingram, use the words "slave" and "slavery" in a very lax way. Thus, when protesting against the so-called "Subjection of Women", they absurdly apply those terms to the condition of the wife in the modern society of the west — designations which are inappropriate even in the case of the inmates of Indian zenanas; and they speak of the modern worker as a "wage-slave", even though he is backed by a powerful trade-union. Passion has a language of its own, and poets and orators must doubtless be permitted to denote by the word "slavery" the position of subjects of a state who labour under civil disabilities, or are excluded from the exercise of political power, but in sociological study things ought to have their right names, and those names should, as far as possible, be uniformly employed" [1]).

But this use of the word we may safely regard as a meta-phor [2]); nobody will assert that these labourers and women are really slaves. Whoever uses the term slavery in its ordinary sense attaches a fairly distinct idea to it.

What is this idea?

We can express it most generally thus: a slave is one who

---

1) Ingram, p. 261. — 2) In the second Chapter and in the continuation of this we shall meet with more instances of this metaphoric (sometimes rather dangerous) use of the term "slavery".

is not free. There are never slaves without there being freemen too; and nobody can be at the same time a slave and a freeman. We must, however, be careful to remember that, man being a "social animal", no man is literally free; all members of a community are restricted in their behaviour towards each other by social rules and customs [1]). But freemen at any rate are relatively free; so a slave must be one who does not share in the common amount of liberty, compatible with the social connection.

The condition of the slave as opposed to that of the freeman presents itself to us under the three following aspects.

First, every slave has his master to whom he is subjected. And this subjection is of a peculiar kind. Unlike the authority one freeman sometimes has over another, the master's power over his slave is unlimited, at least in principle; any restriction put upon the master's free exercise of his power is a mitigation of slavery, not belonging to its nature, just as in Roman law the proprietor may do with his property whatever he is not by special laws forbidden to do. The relation between master and slave is therefore properly expressed by the slave being called the master's "possession" or "property", expressions we frequently meet with.

Secondly, slaves are in a lower condition as compared with freemen. The slave has no political rights; he does not choose his government, he does not attend the public councils. Socially he is despised.

In the third place, we always connect with slavery the idea of compulsory labour. The slave is compelled to work; the free labourer may leave off working if he likes, be it at the cost of starving. All compulsory labour, however, is not slave labour; the latter requires that peculiar kind of compulsion, that is expressed by the word "possession" or "property", as has been said before.

Recapitulating, we may define a slave in the ordinary sense of the word as a man who is the property of another, politically and socially at a lower level than the mass of the people and performing compulsory labour.

---

[1]) Bastian, Rechtverhältnisse, p. 14.

We shall inquire next, whether this notion is a practical one for the purpose of our investigation, or whether it requires any improvement. But it may be convenient first to examine, what our theoretical authors have to say on the subject.

§ 2. *Use of the term "slavery" in theoretical literature.*

Spencer remarks: "[The captives] fall into unqualified servitude.... They belong absolutely to their captors.... They become property, of which any use whatever may be made" [1]. Although this may not properly be called a definition of slavery, it appears that he uses "becoming property" and "falling into unqualified servitude" (or slavery) as synonymous expressions.

According to Ingram "the essential character of slavery may be regarded as lying in the fact that the master was owner of the person of the slave" [2].

Lippert remarks: "The fact, that one man becomes an object of possession by another, characterizes the nature of slavery" [3].

Sohm calls a slave "a man who is not regarded as a person, but as a thing. The slave is left to the discretion of the master, who has over him the right of property" [4].

Letourneau says: "The rights of the masters over their slaves were always excessive; they were those of a proprietor over his possession" [5].

According to Schmoller "the slave is the property of his master" [6].

In the same way, Meyer, speaking of slavery, says that ancient law recognised an unlimited right of property over men [7].

Jhering also remarks that "the master's *potestas* may be called property" [8].

In the first paragraph three principal features of slavery have been enumerated. We see that our theorists attach most importance to the first feature: "property" or "possession" [9].

---

1) Spencer, Pol. Inst., p. 291. — 2) Ingram, p. 262. — 3) Lippert, II p. 534. — 4) Sohm, p. 106. — 5) Letourneau, p. 492. — 6) Schmoller, Grundriss I p. 339. — 7) E. Meyer, Die Sklaverei im Altertum, p. 11. — 8) Jhering, II p. 167. — 9) This view is also held by Wagner and Puchta, whose ample expositions we shall make use of in the next paragraph.

Whether we can agree with them will be shown in the next paragraph.

§ 3. *Definition for scientific use.*

The present investigation is a sociological one; therefore our definition of slavery has to be sociologically relevant. We have to ask: What is the social value of slavery? Slavery is an organ in the social body performing a certain function, and we have to inquire: How is this organ developed, and how, in the various stages of its development, does it perform its function? But then we must know first what this organ and its function are. Thus only can we exclude from our inquiry organs somewhat resembling slavery, but functionally quite different from it, and organs wholly different from slavery, but performing the same function or nearly the same. And this is necessary; for the inclusion of such organs would create a confusion fatal to a right understanding.

What then is slavery and what is its function?

The great function of slavery can be no other than a *division of labour* [1]). Division of labour is taken here in the widest sense, as including not only a qualitative division, by which one man does one kind of work and another a different kind, but also a quantitative one, by which one man's wants are provided for not by his own work only, but by another's. A society without any division of labour would be one, in which each man worked for his own wants, and nobody for another's; in any case but this there is a division of labour in this wider sense of the word. Now this division can be brought about by two means. "There are two ways" says Puchta, "in which we can avail ourselves of the strength of other men which we are in need of. One is the way of free commerce, that does not interfere with the liberty of the person who serves us, the making of contracts by which we exchange the strength and skill of another, or their products, for other performances

---

[1] Wagner remarks that this is the main function of bondage in general (*Unfreiheit*). Wagner, pp. 374—376, 382.

on our part: hire of services, purchase of manufactures, etc. The other way is the subjection of such persons, which enables us to dispose of their strength in our behalf, but at the same time injures the personality, of the subjected. This subjection can be imagined as being restricted to certain purposes, for instance to the cultivation of the land, as with soil-tilling serfs; the result of which is that this subjection, for the very reason that is has a definite and limited aim, does not quite annul the liberty of the subjected. But the subjection can also be an unlimited one, as is the case when the subjected person, in the whole of his outward life, is treated as but a means to the purposes of the man of power, and so his personality is entirely absorbed. This is the institution of slavery" [1]. We have not much to add to this lucid description of slavery and its function. The function is a system of compulsory labour, and slavery is the absorption of the whole personality of the forced labourer to this end. As this absorption is properly expressed by the word "property" or "possession", we may define the slave as *a man who is the property or possession of another man, and forced to work for him.*

This definition, however, on further consideration will show itself capable of some simplification. For when one man is the property of another, this implies compulsory labour. The right of property in this case, the object of it being a man, is a power over that man's will too. The Romans recognised this: "The master has not only a right of property over the slave as over a lifeless thing, but also a power like that over his son, the *potestas dominica*, that is a power over the slave's will" [2]. The right of property, that is a legally unlimited power over a man, were useless, if the owner did not influence the man's will; and this influencing is equivalent to imposing labour upon him, labour being taken in the widest sense. A mere physical possession, such as the preserving of captives for cannibal purposes, which Letourneau and Spencer make so much of [3], is socially of little consequence. Possession of human beings, as a social institution, is that which gets hold

---

1) Puchta, II pp. 82, 83. Wagner (pp. 382, 395) arrives at the same conclusion, but does not state it so clearly. — 2) Sohm, p. 106. — 3) Letourneau, passim; Spencer, Pol. Inst. p. 291.

of the will of its object. Hence it follows, that *slavery is the fact that one man is the property or possession of another.*

This simplification of our formula has this advantage that, in inquiring whether in any country there are slaves, we need not ask whether there is labour imposed on subjected men. When this does not sufficiently appear, we need not say : We do not know whether slavery really exists here. When we are told that in such a country some men are the property of others (except of course the cases of mere physical possession we have hinted at, which are few and easy to recognise), we may be sure that they perform some kind of compulsory labour, and are justified in calling them slaves.

Further advantages of our definition are, that it is the definition given by many theorists, and that it lies within the limits of current speech.

In the following paragraphs we shall mark the distinction of slavery from some phenomena which somewhat resemble it. Of phenomena of this kind we shall consider only those that most frequently occur; other questionable cases will be examined in surveying the occurrence of slavery in the several parts of the globe.

§ 4. *Distinction of slavery from kindred phenomena.*
I. Wives in an abject condition.

In the first paragraph it has already been noticed, that the advocates of women's rights make very great use of the term "slavery". We shall see that this equally applies to some ethnographers and theorists describing the state of women, especially as wives, in some primitive societies. To give one instance of each of them : Bancroft says of the Northern Californians : "Although I find no description of an actual system of slavery existing among them, yet there is no doubt that they have slaves. We shall see .... that women entitled by courtesy wives, are bought and sold" [1]. The theorist we shall quote is Letourneau : "In all very primitive societies woman represents the domestic

---

[1] Bancroft, p. 349.

animals, the beasts of burden which the more advanced societies possess: she is indeed treated as a slave, and this certainly
is one of the reasons why slavery has been instituted so late
in the course of social evolution" [1]).

We may say that such authors use the word metaphorically
(as Letourneau certainly does); but this does not exempt us
from examining, whether the condition of wives in those cases,
where according to them it so much resembles slavery, is
really slavery. We must not, of course, inquire whether there
are instances of female slaves being the wives of their
owners, but whether in any case *the* wives as such are
slaves. In doing this, we may confine ourselves to observing
the condition of wives among the natives of Australia, as
this condition is commonly described as a striking instance of
an abject one. Letourneau remarks: "In the Australian clans
slavery, in the sense in which we use the word, did not
exist; but one half of the social group, the weaker half, was
reduced to servitude; the Australian woman, an indispensable
and despised helpmate, was during her whole life burdened
with work, ill-used, and in reward often eaten by those
whom her unavailing labour had fed" [2]). Schurtz states that
the treatment of the Australian wives is bad [3]). Ratzel
expresses the same view: "The position of the wife in such
circumstances is always a low one. That she is positively
considered to be the property of her husband (hence in the
Adelaide district "owner of a wife" means husband) is not
peculiar to Australia. But to this a number of customs are
added here, that, more than among other peoples to which
the notion of the wife as a commodity is equally familiar, place
her in the back-ground of public and even of family life" [4]).

Now let us cite some particulars about this abject state of
the Australian wives, as given by ethnographers. For the
purpose of enabling the reader to take a comprehensive view
of the matter, we shall arrange these particulars not according
to the different tribes each applies to, but according to the
several phenomena bearing on the object of our inquiry. This
gives the following result:

1) Letourneau, p. 27. — 2) Idem, p. 45. — 3) Schurtz, Katechismus, p. 139. —
4) Ratzel, Völkerkunde, II p. 66.

A. *The wife is acquired by the husband without her consent being asked.* So among the Dieri: "under no circumstances has a woman any say in the choice of a partner". Powell's Creek natives: "After being purchased or captured, the woman is generally taken away to a distance and kept more or less isolated with her husband for some months, until she contentedly settles down to the new order of things". Queenslanders on Herbert River: wives are acquired by bethrothal as children, by exchange for a sister or daughter or by capture. N. W. Central Queenslanders: the marriage can be proposed by the male relatives of the woman, or a man can exchange his true blood-sister, *i. e.* by the same mother, for another's blood-sister; in both cases the consent of the whole camp-council is required. Aborigines of N. S. Wales: girls are often betrothed in infancy, or else given away by their father or brother without their wishes being consulted; "the women are considered an article of property, and are sold or given away by the parents or relatives without the least regard to their own wishes". Natives of the Western District of Victoria: betrothal of children is very frequent. A girl when adult can be asked of her father, without any attention being paid to her wishes. When two young men have each a sister or cousin, they may exchange the young women and marry them; the women are obliged to obey. Southern Australians: the husband most often acquires his wife by means of a contract with her father. Southern Australians of Port Lincoln: girls are betrothed long before puberty; when adult they must follow their intended husbands whether they wish it or not. Tribes of Central Australia (described by Spencer and Gillen): the most usual method of obtaining a wife is that which is connected with the custom of *Tualcha mura, i. e.* an agreement between two men that the relationship shall be established between their two children, one a boy and the other a girl. S. W. Australians: "In no case is the girl asked for her consent". Natives of King George Sound (W. Australia): a girl is often promised to a man years before her birth, but generally she is acquired by capture. Northern Australians of Port Darwin and the W. Coast of the Gulf of Carpentaria: "Wives are obtained by gifts of parents; in the majority of cases female children when born are promised to men of all ages.... Some men obtain women by stealing them, generally from other tribes, or get them in exchange for a sister". Tasmanians: the girls are betrothed as children; before marriage they are the property of their father or brother. When the match is broken off, the girl is again betrothed, without her wishes being consulted. Brough Smyth, speaking of the Australians in general, remarks: "Men obtain wives by a convenient system of exchange, by conquest sometimes, and sometimes a woman is stolen. By what mode soever a man procures a bride, it is very seldom an occasion of rejoicing for the female". And Thomas says: "The process of acquiring a bride differs in different tribes; she may be exchanged for a sister, the simplest and perhaps the commonest form; she may be betrothed at, or even, provisionally, before, birth, but this is usually part of a process of barter; she may be obducted, either from an already existing, or a prospective husband, or from her relatives; or she may be inherited from a brother or tribal kinsman".

B. *The wife is entirely in the power of her husband, and treated accordingly.*

a. Sometimes such *general expressions* are found, as the wife being her husband's *"property"* or *"slave"*. So on Moreton Bay: wives are slaves. On Herbert River: wives are slaves. In N. S. Wales: "the woman is the absolute property of her husband". In S. W. Australia: "the state of slavery in which they [the women] are all held, is really deplorable." In Central Australia: the wife is desired by the husband only for a slave. In Tasmania: the women are slaves and do all the menial work. We may add Curr's statement about the Australians in general: The wife "is not the relative, but the property of her husband". "The husband is the absolute owner of his wife (or wives)". Brough Smyth too remarks that the husband is called the owner of the wife.

b. *He treats her with contempt.* In S. Australia women are despised. In the Moore River District of W. Australia the husband gives his wife only the offal of the chase. Central Australian men "eat alone, and throw what they can't eat to the women". In N. S. Wales "as her husband walks along, she follows him at a respectful distance.... If they sit down to

Kurnai the same custom prevails. In N. Australia "a widow belongs to her late husband's brother". We may add Curr's general statement that "when a man dies, his widows devolve on his eldest surviving brother".

C. *The husband makes his wife work for him.* As regards the Dieri we are told that "the more wives a man has, the more indolent he becomes; as they do not till the soil, each wife has to go daily in search of food, gather seeds, roots, and other vegetable products according to the seasons; the men with a plurality of wives stay at home making weapons, ornaments and fishing nets from rushes grown on the banks of the lakes". At Powell's Creek "polygamy is common, more so amongst the old men, who find a plurality of wives useful in hunting for them, and as carriers when shifting camp, etc.". On Herbert River the women procure the food, and for this often make long journeys; they do all the hard work. The husband makes the frame of the hut; she covers it. When travelling she carries all that is to be carried. The husband often keeps the animal food to himself; his hunting has rather the character of a sport; the procuring of food is entirely incumbent on the wife. According to Fraser the fate of the native wife in N. S. Wales is very pitiable. "Married at an early age, she has not only to bear and rear the children, but she does all the heavy work of the family; in camp, it is her duty to put up the rude windshelter of sticks and foliage which serves them as a home, to make a fire and keep it burning, and to cook the food; on the march, she carries in a bag, resting on her back and slung from her neck, all their portable property, and seated on this bag is her youngest child,... in this bag, in addition to the few utensils she requires for domestic labours, she has a yam-stick with which to dig up the numerous native roots which are used as food, a supply of these and other articles of food required for a meal, a quantity of native string and hooks for catching fish.... For the ready kindling of a fire, whenever it is required, she has to carry with her a smouldering piece of firewood; if she allows this to go out, and thus puts her lord and master to the labour of getting fire by friction, or if she in any other way gives him displeasure, he will beat her severely, even till her body is covered with bruises and her hair is matted with blood". At Victoria River Downs Station an old man generally has many wives, "probably to work and get food for him, for in their wild state the man is too proud to do anything except carry a *woomera* and spear." In Western Victoria "after marriage the women are compelled to do all the hard work of erecting habitations, collecting fuel and water, carrying burdens, procuring roots and delicacies of various kinds, making baskets for cooking roots and other purposes, preparing food, and attending to the children. The only work the men do, in time of peace, is to hunt for oppossums and large animals of various kinds, and to make rugs and weapons." In S.W. Australia "when, wandering through the woods, the savage observes that the sky threatens rain, he enjoins his wife to erect a hut at the place which he thinks most fit, and where he intends to pass the night". At King George Sound the women look very miserable; they do all the work. In the Moore River District the wife who has not yams enough for her husband is severely beaten (as quoted above). The Central Australian wife is the drudge of her husband. About the natives of Port Darwin we get this information: "The only reason I know of for the practice of polygamy is that, as the wives have to provide food for their lords and carry all their family possessions when travelling, the husband can lead a perfect life of indolence". Tasmanian women had to procure all sorts of food, except the kangaroo. Ling Roth quotes a description of a Tasmanian repast: "Hitherto we had had but a faint idea of the pains the women take to prepare the food requisite for the subsistence of their families. They quitted the water only to bring their husbands the fruits of their labour, and frequently returned almost directly to their diving, till they had procured a sufficient meal for their families". Curr, surveying the mode of life of the Australians in general, remarks: "Wives have to undergo all the drudgery of the camp and the march, have the poorest food and the hardest work". Brough Smyth enumerates as duties of the wife „building a new camp, getting firewood etc. and on journeys acting as a carrier for all the worldly goods of her husband. They are packed on her back, all excepting his war implements, which he himself deigns to carry".

This picture, surely, is very black. But, unlike Letourneau, we must not view the dark side only. We may remark, first that, as it appears from the foregoing survey, there are with regard to each of the Australian tribes but a part of the enumerated phenomena on record; the black picture is produced by blending the dark sides of each into a whole. And, secondly, the same writers relate some particulars, which prove that the life of the Australian wife is not all darkness. These too we shall arrange in the order observed above.

A. In some cases we are told, that *the girl's wishes* are to some extent *taken into consideration* as to the choice of her husband. On Herbert River the woman sometimes gets the man she loves; she is then very happy; sometimes she runs away with the beloved man. In N. W. Queensland, when a young man and a girl are in love with each other, and the camp-council is not opposed to it, they elope, live as husband and wife for some two months, and then return to the camp. In N. S. Wales a girl, to escape from the betrothed man (oftentimes an old one), may elope with her young lover; she is then brought back and beaten by her family, "but it may be that she elopes again and again, and, if at last they see that she is determined on it, they let her have her own way". In Tasmania the woman was stolen from her tribe, but not against her will. Most often the girl succeeded in getting from her father the man she wanted; otherwise she had to run away with him. Curr remarks: "In no instance, unless Mr. Howitt's account of the Kurnai be correct, which I doubt, has the female any voice in the selection of her husband." This may be true, if we take "voice" in the sense of a legally recognized right; virtually, however, she sometimes has a "voice", as appears from the instances given here. Howitt's account which Curr alludes to we have not been fortunate enough to meet with. According to Brough Smyth "a young man who has engaged the affections of a girl of a neighbouring tribe, agrees with her to run away at the first opportunity that offers". They are then persecuted by the members of her tribe, as custom and law require, but not energetically. After a few days the young man and his wife return to his tribe. Except at first some scolding and muttering his new state provokes little comment. "His young wife is treated well, and is soon familiar with all the women of the tribe, to which she has become attached".

B. a, b. Sometimes the ethnographers tell of much *affection* existing between husband and wife. At Moreton Bay there is often a great affection. On Herbert River "as a rule man and wife apparently get on very well". According to Eylmann, happy unions are not unknown among the natives of South Australia. Fraser remarks about the aborigines of N. S. Wales: "the *kuri* or black man is usually kind and affectionate to his *jiu*, wife"; "in spite of the hardness of their mode of life, married couples often live happily and affectionately together to a considerable age". On the river Darling, N. S. Wales, according to Bonney, "although young women are often compelled to marry a man of whom they know little and often nothing, they generally find happiness and contentment in their married lives. Quarrels between husband and wife are rare, and they show much affection for each other in their own way". In Central Australia "the women are not treated usually with anything like excessive harshness". "Taking everything into account.... the life of one of these savage women, judged from the point of view of her requirements in order to make life more or less comfortable, is far from being the miserable one that it is so often pictured". Dawson, after describing the work imposed on women in W. Victoria (as quoted above), adds: "But notwithstanding this drudgery and the apparent hard usage to which the women are subjected, there is no want of affection amongst the members of a family". Even Salvado, who so pities the S. W. Australian wife, remarks: "Sometimes I heard a betrothed man say: I love her and she loves me". Of the Tasmanians we are told that they "treat their women kindly". Brough Smyth makes this general statement: "It is hard to believe that even in a lower state the male would not have had the same feeling of affection for his mate and an equal jealousy of love as we see among the aborigines now". In the same sense Bonwick remarks on the Australian natives in general: "Home life there was not quite the dark scene some pictured.... Affection is witnessed between husband and wife, parent and child, tribesman and mate".

We may add, that the Tasmanian women, though overburdened with work, are described as a merry and laughter-loving kind of people. And Curr remarks about Australian women in general: "In every way the female's looks to us a hard lot; and yet, notwithstanding, I do not hesitate to say that they are, on the whole, fairly happy, merry and contented."

c. *The husband does not always enjoy such an entire freedom of action towards his wife.*

Sometimes, for punishing and divorcing her, *he must have the consent of the tribe.* So in N. S. Wales, in case of adultery "he may complain to the elders of the tribe, and they, on cause shown, decree a divorce; but not if she has children." According to another writer "the husband who suspects another of seducing his wife, either kills one or both. The affair is taken up by the tribe, if the party belongs to another, who inflict punishment on him." In W. Victoria "a man can divorce his wife for serious misconduct, and can even put her to death; but in every case the charge against her must be laid before the chiefs of his own and his wife's tribes, and their consent to her punishment obtained. If the wife has children, however, she cannot be divorced". Here we find also some slight traces of protection of the wife by her relatives: "A man is allowed to marry his brother's widow, or his own deceased wife's sister, or a woman of her tribe; but he is not permitted to do so, if he has divorced or killed his wife". In N. W. Central Queensland the wife is avenged by her relations. "In the case of a man killing his own *gin* [wife], he has to deliver up one of his own sisters for his late wife's friends to put to death, he personally escaping punishment.... A wife has always her "brothers" to look after her interests". At the initiation-feasts "each woman can exercise the right of punishing any man who may have ill-treated, abused or "hammered" her.... the delinquent not being allowed to retaliate in any way whatsoever". If these women are slaves, they at least have their *saturnalia* [1]).

---

1) Curr asserts that, if the husband killed his wife, "her death would be avenged by her brothers". But the information we get about the several tribes makes it probable, that this is not true regarding the majority of Australian tribes.

We even find cases of *the wife putting a check upon her husband*, especially in a sexual respect. On Herbert River the wife is furious if her husband is unfaithful to her. In N. S. Wales "a wife may similarly complain to them [the elders of the tribe] of the conduct of her husband, and they may order both the man and his paramour to be punished". In W. Victoria "if a husband is unfaithful, his wife cannot divorce him. She may make a complaint to the chief, who can punish the man by sending him away from his tribe for two or three moons; and the guilty woman is very severely punished by her relatives". "A chief who has been married under the law of betrothal, is not permitted to marry another woman for a long time; and should he do so without obtaining the consent of his wife, there would be constant quarreling". At Port Lincoln an old, former wife sometimes forces her husband to desist from taking a young, new one.

Finally we meet with instances of *the wife having a real ascendency over her husband*. On Herbert River the husband is sometimes led by his wife, and even beaten by her. A curious piece of information we get about W. Victoria. When a wife treats her husband with such persistent disrespect or unkindness as to make him wish to get rid of her, he goes away to some neighbouring tribe and tries to bring about her death by means of sorcery. The wife, being informed of this, repairs thither and entreats him to return, and so a reconciliation is effected.

In Tasmania the husband could divorce his wife; but she could also force him to do so.

d. *Exchange of wives* does not seem always to take place against their will. In W. Victoria wives may be exchanged only after the death of their parents and with the consent of the chiefs, but not if one of them has children. After the exchange both couples live peacefully together in one hut, each in a separate compartment. If a man knows that his wife is in love with another, and he is not opposed to it, she can be amicably transferred to the other man with the consent of the chief. At Port Lincoln the men frequently exchange wives; brothers and near relatives have their wives nearly in common. The wife calls the brothers of her husband by the name of husbands. This seems rather a kind of group-marriage than a bartering of wives as of commodities.

These two instances point to the possibility that in other cases too exchange of wives may be not so arbitrary an action as at first sight it seems.

As to the *lending of wives*, in some cases it appears that these offer themselves to strangers. In N. S. Wales the husband "is quite ready to bargain with a white man, and with her consent too; for a black woman considers it an honour to be thus courted by a man of a superior race". The Cammarray women prostitute themselves to Europeans for almost nothing, and among themselves without any shame. In Central Australia marriage does not impose any obligation of chastity; the wives always prostitute themselves. In S. Australia women give themselves to strangers with or without the consent of their husbands. On Moore River the wives often have connections with young men; the husbands do not seem to take much notice of it. Moreover, Spencer and Gillen warn us, that "in many cases in which apparently women are lent (in the sense in which we use the word, which is the sense in which it is generally used in this connection) indiscriminately, a knowledge of details would show that this was not so.... In the nine tribes examined by us we have found that intercourse of this nature is strictly regulated by custom".

e. The *levirate law* sometimes appears in the character of a duty rather than a right of the deceased man's brother. Fraser (describing N. S. Wales) calls it a "refuge" for the widow. Dawson, speaking of the aborigines of W. Victoria, states: "When a married man dies, his brother is bound to marry the widow if she has a family, as it is his duty to protect her and rear his brother's children". Salvado speaks of the philanthropy of the S. W. Australian, who takes upon himself the care of the wife of an absent friend or parent, or of a brother's widow.

C. Among the Kurnai *the man must hunt* for the sustenance of his wife and children, and fight for their protection. In Central Australia the women "have, as amongst other savage tribes, to do a considerable part, but by no means all, of the work of the camp, but, after all, in a good season this does not amount to very much, and in a bad season men and women suffer alike, and of what food there is they get their share". The last-cited cases of levirate law, too, show that the subsistence of the family does not depend on the wife only. Even the instances quoted under C (p. 15) provide us with evidence that the men perform some kind of work as hunting the larger animals, making weapons and fishing-nets, getting fire by friction, etc. And what is said here about the Kurnai certainly applies to all these tribes: the husband fights to protect his wife. This being his great and indispensable function, we must not wonder at his not liking to do other work that women can perform as well [1]).

The division of labour between the sexes is not always so unreasonable as at first sight it seems. Hore, speaking of the African Wajiji, very justly remarks: "Much has been said about the unfair division of labour in such circumstances, but when it is considered that a wild man finds scarcely anything to his hand, but must himself cut the wood and the grass to build his house, manufacture his spear and cooking vessels, take his part in tribal duties, and is frequently compelled to seek food in long and laborious hunting expeditions, it will be seen that he often gets his fair share of work" [2]). A similar division of labour is admirably described by Pinart, as existing among the Indians of Panama: "I may be allowed to make here a short digression on woman's place in the Indian household.

---

1) Literature referred to in surveying the state of the Australian wife. On the Dieri: Gason in Frazer's Notes, p. 170; Powell's Creek: The Stationmaster, ibid. pp. 177, 178; Victoria River Downs Station: Cranford, ibid. p. 181; Queensland and S. Australia: Matthews, ibid. pp. 187, 188; S. Australia: Eylmann, pp. 129, 130, 131; Moreton Bay: Lang, pp. 337, 338; Herbert River: Lumholtz, p.p. 100, 160—164, 213; N. S. Wales: Fraser, pp. 2,26—28, 35; Wilkes, II p. 205; River Darling (N. S. Wales): Bonney p. 129; Cammarray: Collins, pp. 559—562; Kurnai: Fison and Howitt, pp. 204, 206; N. W. Central Queensland: Roth, pp. 141, 176, 181; W. Victoria: Dawson, pp. 27, 28, 33—37; Port Lincoln: Woods, p. 223; S. Australia: Angas, I pp. 82, 93; S. W. Australia: Salvado pp. 313, 314, 349; King George Sound: Browne, Die Eingeborenen Australiens, pp. 450, 451; Moore River District: Oldfield, pp. 248—251; Central Australia: Spencer and Gillen, Native tribes, pp. 50, 93, 102, 558; Spencer and Gillen, Northern tribes, p. 33; Eyre II p. 322; Willshire, in Frazer's Notes, pp. 183, 184; Port Darwin, etc.: Foelsche, ibid. p. 194; Tasmania: Bonwick, Tasmania, pp. 56, 62, 66, 68, 73; Ling Roth, Tasmania, pp. 125, 46; Australia in general: Curr, I pp. 106—110; Brough Smyth, I pp. 76,79—82, 85, 86; Bonwick, Austr. Natives, p. 205; Thomas, pp. 151, 174, 177. — 2) Hore, p. 11.

It is commonly said by those who have not lived intimately with the Indians, that they consider woman as a beast of burden, that to her share falls a life full of troublesome and fatiguing work, and to the man's an easy and idle existence. It may, indeed, seem strange to the superficial observer to see the woman charged with heavy burdens and the man walking before her carrying nothing but his weapons. But if the observer will only reflect a little, he will understand that, whereas the man carries his weapons only, the responsibility and the safety of his wife and children are incumbent on him. The Indian's life is indeed surrounded with dangers; when traversing a savannah, or forest, a hostile Indian may appear at any moment; a tiger, a snake etc. may throw himself upon the travellers. Therefore it is the man's task to be continually on the alert, to have his hands and his movements free, in order to be able immediately to take his arms and defend those who are dear to him. How often have not I seen the Indian, when about to traverse a river, making his family stand still, entering into the water and reconnoitring whether it was not too deep or the stream too rapid; then inspecting the opposite bank to see whether all was right there; then crossing the river again, helping his wife and children to pass through, often even carrying the burdens, and several times re-crossing the river to transport on his back his wife and children. The river being crossed, the man again takes the lead with his arms, the wife and family resume their burdens, and the little caravan continues its way in the same order" [1]).

Another fact, proving that the Australian women are not in every respect regarded as slaves, is the great influence they often have in intertribal matters. "The peace-making influence of the women is very great, and has often been observed among many tribes". "The peace-making function of the women is also very characteristically shown by their being employed as international ambassadresses" [2]). Darwin justly remarks: We thus see that with savages the women are not in quite so abject a state in relation to marriage, as has often been supposed" [3]).

---

1) Pinart, pp. 44, 45. — 2) Steinmetz, Strafe, II p. 45. — 3) Darwin, Descent of Man, p, 593.

The question to be settled now is this: Are these Australian wives, and accordingly all the wives that live in an abject state, to be called slaves? Remembering the conclusion we arrived at in the third paragraph, we may put the question thus: are they objects of possession? Under B, a, we have quoted several statements of ethnographers calling them the slaves, or the property, of their husbands. We must not, however, forget Ingram's warning against taking a rhetorical use of the word "slave" too literally. The facts recorded under B, c, B, d, and C are of more interest to us. The husband may do with his wife as he likes: ill-use and kill her, overtax her with work, exchange and lend her. It is but seldom that her relations protect her; in but very few cases is the man's power interfered with by the chief or elders of the tribe. Therefore we cannot but admit that she is the property of her husband.

Yet there is a reason, why we are not to bring these wives under the denomination of slaves. We may refer here to the point of view we have taken in determining the nature of slavery. Slavery is an organ in the social body, that in a peculiar manner brings about a division of labour. The Australian wives share the character of this organ as an object of possession. Yet they are not the same organ; for besides being forced labourers they are wives; hence it follows that their relation towards their husbands is wholly bound up with the sexual and family life: it is their character as women, not as labourers, that prevails. We may remember here the mutual affection observed in so many cases by the ethnographers. As the mother of his children, too, the husband is likely to value his wife. We have seen (under B, c) that in a few cases she cannot be divorced or exchanged if she has children. Besides, it is frequently stated, that the Australian aborigines are very fond of their children [1]).

The Australian woman discharges the duties of a wife and a mother, and besides, to some extent, the work that among other peoples falls to the share of the slave; therefore she is not a slave. If she were, her place, in a slave-keeping society,

---

1) See Ploss, II pp. 333, 334, and Steinmetz, Das Verhältniss zwischen Eltern und Kindern, p. 613.

would be entirely occupied by the slave; but no one will doubt whether in any such society there are wives. In an evolutionary sense the slave and the Australian wife differ in this: the Australian wife is a not-yet-differentiated organ, performing two functions, which at a later stage of development will be incumbent on two quite distinct organs: the peculiar function of a wife, and the labour of a slave. This reasoning is not an assertion *a priori*, by a biological parallelism, of a development that must actually have taken place; it is only intended to show the fundamental difference existing between wives, however abject their condition, and slaves [1]).

We may even go farther and say: *Slavery proper does not exist, when there are none but female slaves.* For when females only are enslaved, the reason probably is, that they are valued as women, not only as labourers; otherwise males would be enslaved too. So, according to Meyer [2]), in the early stages of ancient history, most of the slaves were women and their chief function was a sexual one. And even where such women are not, all of them, actually treated as wives or concubines, but only kept as labourers, there is no slavery in the true sense of the word. In such cases, the husband keeps his wife or wives subjected; this leads to the keeping of numerous subjected females, who are scarcely to be called wives. But it is always women, as the weaker sex, who are subjected to the men; subjection of labourers, only in their quality of labourers, does not exist. The labourers have the name, if not the state, of wives; this proves that the subjection of labourers as such, *i. e.* slavery, is not yet developed.

We have dwelt at considerable length on this distinction between slaves and subjected wives. There are some more distinctions to be made between slavery and kindred phenomena; but these will not occupy so much space and time.

---

1) Lippert (II p. 535) distinguishes the wife, as mistress of the household, from the slave, who has no share in the authority wielded bij the master. This may be true, but it is only a small portion of the truth. — 2) Meyer, Die Sklaverei im Altertum, p. 18.

§ 5. *Distinction of slavery from kindred phenomena.*
II. Children subjected to the head of the family.

There was a time, the time of the good old patriarchal
theory, when the condition of children in the early stages of
social life was thought to be one of complete subjection to
the head of the family, the *pater familias,* who had over them
an unlimited power, extending to the power of life and death.
Carey, among others, holds this view, and very plainly expresses it. "By nothing is the progress of mankind in population and wealth made more manifest than by the change in
the relation of parent and child. In the infancy of cultivation
the one is a tyrant and the other a slave" [1]).

The adherents of the matriarchal theory have assigned to
the Roman-like agnatic family its place as a later product of
history; but to the question as to how children were treated
in an ante-patriarchal state of culture they have not given
much attention.

It is to Professor S. R. Steinmetz that we are indebted for the
first exact inquiry into the early history of the treatment of
children. His conclusions, based upon a large amount of ethnographical materials, are these:

With most savages rational education is out of the question,
the children soon growing independent, and when young being
either neglected or much petted and spoiled [2]); a lesser number of savage tribes show some slight beginnings of education
without or nearly without bodily castigation; in a few cases
the childeren are under strict discipline. In this last set of
cases there is to some extent a subjection of the children.
"With the power over the mother the father gradually acquired the power over the children." "The patriarch became
master of his children and, whenever circumstances required
and allowed it, introduced a strict discipline over them" [3]).

---

1) Carey, p. 275. See also Wuttke and Maine, as quoted by Steinmetz, Strafe II pp. 180, 181.
— 2) Chamberlain (p. 116) justly remarks: "Much too little has been made of the bright
side of child-life among the lower races." — 3) Steinmetz, Strafe II pp. 179—253, see
especially p. 252, and his article on: *"Das Verhältniss zwischen Eltern und Kindern bei
den Naturvölkern."*

We may therefore suppose, that there will be instances of children being treated in a somewhat slave-like manner. We shall presently see that there are a few such cases on record in Steinmetz's book.

Among the Apaches the father holds unlimited sway over his children up to the age of puberty [1]).

Tlinkit boys must render unbounded obedience to their parents and especially to their maternal uncle, to whom, according to the law of inheritance, they are almost more nearly related than to their own father. They have to perform the labour imposed upon them, without any claim to compensation [2]).

Of the Botocudos we are told, that the father, being stronger than his children, compels them to work for him [3]).

Among the Aeneze Bedouins the young girls work hard; they drive the cattle to the pasture-ground; if one out of the herd is lost, they are severely beaten by their father [4]).

Among the Assja Samoyedes the father has a patriarchal power, and punishes at his discretion and according to custom [5]).

In these few cases only is it clearly stated that the head of the family has an arbitrary power. The value of Zu Wied's statement about the Botocudos is much lessened by the same ethnographer telling us that the children enjoy much freedom [6]).

Considering now the state of the children in the cases referred to here, are we justified in calling it slavery?

The head of the family has power over the children; and so far as it appears from the particulars given by the ethnographers, this is a legally unlimited power, that may be called right of property, and is likely to lead to compulsory labour, as among the Tlinkits and Aeneze Bedouins it certainly does. The condition of these children may therefore be expressed by the word "possession", our criterion of slavery.

We may even go farther. The condition of slaves is not always very bad; but however kindly treated, they are slaves, are the property of their masters. So with children too. They may not be, as in the cases mentioned above, under strict discipline; yet the father's, or in a few cases the maternal

---

1) Steinmetz, Strafe II p. 190 (after Bancroft). — 2) Ibid., p. 194 (after Krause). — 3) Ibid., p. 196 (after Zu Wied). — 4) Ibid., p. 199 (after Burckhardt). — 5) Ibid., p. 201 (after Von Middendorf). — 6) Ibid., p. 196.

uncle's, power, however moderate a use he makes of it, may be legally unbounded, not restricted by social rules, not interfered with by the community. In such a case the head of the family may be called owner of the child, and is really called so in Roman law, so clearly distinct from Roman practice. "The *patria potestas* of ancient civil law means the full power of the father over the persons subjected to him (the child, the grand-child by the son, the wife *in manu*), the right of death and life (*ius vitae ac necis*) and the right to sell into slavery" [1]. "This *potestas* originally was equal to that over the slaves" [2].

We see that the term "possession" may well be used here. Yet there is a reason that induces us not to call these children slaves, a reason resembling that for which we have excluded the subjected wives. These children may be called the property of their fathers; but this is not the whole, nor even the main part of their condition. The relation between father and child, if it includes subjection, includes much more. There is mutual sympathy and in many respects a coincidence of interests; there is respect on the side of the child; there is on the side of the father a desire to promote the welfare of the child, however much bound up with egotistical motives. There is also physical and mental superiority on the side of the father and inferiority on the side of the child [3]); and this in some cases may bring about a somewhat slave-like condition of the latter; but this condition is not an essential part of the relation between father and child; *a fortiori* it is not coextensive with the relation, as in the case of the slave. Biologically expressed: the child is quite another organ, with quite another function, but in some cases performing in some degree

---

1) Sohm, p. 363. — 2) Puchta, II p. 384. As this is not the place to enter into a systematic description of the treatment of children among savages, we have confined ourselves to mentioning the results of Steinmetz's investigations. Yet we will quote here one ethnographical record, that clearly shows the high degree of development of the *patria potestas* possible among savages. "In Flores the sons even of rich families, as long as their father lives, at public feasts are dressed like slaves, and also at his funeral; this being apparently the external sign of a strict *patria potestas*, which remains in force till the funeral; until then the son is the father's slave." Von Martens, p. 117. — 3) Viz. as long as the child is really a child. Savage children are generally much sooner full-grown than those of civilized nations; see Steinmetz, Strafe, II pp. 215—217.

the function of a slave; therefore it is not a slave. We may add, that the child is only temporarily subjected; one day he will be a master himself [1]. This also bears upon the treatment of the child: the slave is brought up to servility, the child to authority. Children can never form a subjected class.

As for adopted children, it is not always easy to distinguish them from slaves. Sometimes they are rather severely treated, especially those captured in war or kidnapped. Tanner was thus adopted by an Indian of the Shahnee tribe. The youngest son of this Indian had lately died, and his wife had told her husband, she could not live if he did not restore her the child. The husband accordingly went off, and came back with Tanner whom he had kidnapped. Tanner was adopted on the grave of the deceased boy, and given an Indian name. But the adoptive father treated him not at all as a son. He had to do the hardest work, got but little food, and was often severely beaten. If the mother tried to protect him, she was beaten too. Finally the father, regardless of the mother's wishes sold him to an old Indian woman, who now became his adoptive mother. She treated him kindly, yet made him cut wood, carry water and meat, and perform other kinds of labour, which generally were not imposed upon children of his age. However, he was not a slave. When full-grown, he was considered by the Indians one of their tribe, and married an Indian girl [2].

In the second Chapter we shall meet with more instances of captives being adopted either into the tribe or into one of the families within the tribe. As long as such persons are children, it is often not easy to see whether they are slaves or adopted children, for it is not always stated, as in Tanner's case, that they are formally adopted. We must ask then, what becomes of them when full-grown. If they have still a master to serve, it is clear that they are slaves; for if they are adopted members of the community, they will be free when adult, excepting the (most often slight) moral obligations of full-grown children towards their parents. Other facts proving that the captives are slaves, are their not taking share in govern-

---

1) See Lippert, II p. 535. — 2) Tanner, pp. 8—17, 114; see also p. 315.

ment affairs, when the tribe is democratically organized, and their being excluded from marriage with native-born women. With the aid of these criteria we shall try, in every particular case, to decide whether the captives are slaves or adopted members of the community. What has been said here of captives, equally applies to purchased persons.

The last two paragraphs show that there is still something wanting in our definition. Not every state of possession is slavery; those arising from family relations are to be excluded. Thus only can we come to a true understanding of the signification of slavery.. For wives and children may accidentally be forced labourers and the like; the slave only is *ex definitione* a subjected person, a forced labourer, an object of possession. Wives and children there would be, and there are in many cases, without subjection; slaves there are not where there is not subjection and compulsory labour. A society that begins to keeps slaves, develops a new organ with a special, well marked function; and it is the evolution of this organ we are to trace in the following Chapters.

Our definition therefore wants an addition. We may now put it so: *Slavery is the fact, that one man is the property or possession of another beyond the limits of the family proper.*

§ 6.   *Distinction of slavery from kindred phenomena.*
III. Members of a society in their relation to the head of the community.

Bastian, after remarking that in a social community nobody is literally free, gives a great number of quotations, describing widely different kinds of subjection, and among these some few, where the subjects of a despot are called his slaves or his property. "The Siamese are all (even marked) slaves of their king." "The subjects of the king of Djagga are slaves, who may not marry without his consent." "In Usumbara all are slaves of the king." "The absolute rulers dispose of all their subjects as their property (even without having acquired a right by the subjects having transgressed the law), and even mark with their badge the different working-guilds, as is done by the king of Siam." "The princes and princesses on the Congo have the right to sell any one who is not a prince like themselves" [1]).

What Bastian means by heaping up these various quotations, without any order or attempt at an explanation, is not clear. We, however, must not follow his example, but inquire whether the word "slave" is rightly used here, whether the subjects of a despot may be called slaves. A few moments of consideration will show that they may not. For however great the power of the chief, the king, the despot, in a word the head of the community, over his subjects, they are not his property. "Property" supposes a power of the master, pervading the whole life, personal, domestic and social, of the slave; so great a power over his subjects a chief never has. The following reasoning will make this clear. Slavery would not be capable of much development, if it depended upon the master's personal superiority only; for slavery to become a social system, the master's power over the slave must be recognized by the society. The slave lives in a society that regards him as a slave; slavery cannot exist where there is not a society of freemen. Therefore the despot, however great his power, is not as such a master of slaves. The slave-owner has the community on his side; the chief has subjects who themselves compose the community. Looked at from the practical side, the chief's power contains much more of voluntary submission than the slave-owner's. A chief never has the whole person of the citizens subjected in his own behalf; he may exact some performances for his personal benefit, but the restrictions put upon the subjects, encroaching on their freedom in private life, will generally be measures taken in the (real or supposed) interest of the community, and approved of by the community. These restrictions are mutual, and arise from the social connection itself; this is not, as in slavery, using one person as a means to the purposes of another definite person. This yet more distinctly appears, where not a single man imposes these rules,

---

1) Bastian, Rechtsverhältnisse, pp. 15, 15 note 2, 187, 187 note 2. Post (Ethn. Jur., I p. 358) also speaks of subjects being the slaves of the king.

but the council of citizens. In a communistic society there would be an entire absence of personal freedom; yet there would be no slaves, as there would be no freemen whom they could serve.

It need hardly be said, that a chief may keep slaves like any other freeman. The public power as such, the state, also sometimes keeps slaves (*e. g.* the *servi publici* in Rome). But these slaves are quite distinct from the main body of citizens.

Sometimes it is stated, that the chief, or the public power, has slaves, whereas no mention is made of any other slaves. In such cases the slaves generally become such as a punishment for some offence. Where such a state of things exists, we may not speak of a slave-keeping people. For here the power of the government is so great, that it can avail itself of the labour of the citizens; whether this is done by imposing an equal amount of labour on all of them, or by selecting a few persons for this purpose and keeping them in a slave-like state, does not make much difference. Besides, slavery here cannot have the same influence on social life it generally has; for every freeman has to work for himself. This kind of slavery may be compared with the tread-mill and other kinds of penal servitude existing in more civilized societies. And we may not speak of a slave-keeping people, where the only slaves are criminals, who become the slaves of him who represents the public power, any more than we can say that slavery exists in those civilized countries, where penal servitude is still practised.

One more remark has to be added here. Hitherto we have used the terms "possession" and "property" synonymously as indicating the nature of slavery. In this paragraph it has been shown, that an essential feature of slavery is its being recognized by the community. Therefore we prefer the term "property", that, better than the other term, conveys the notion, not only of a virtual subjection, but of a subjection considered legal in those communities where it exists.

§ 7. *Distinction of slavery from kindred phenomena.*
IV. Subjected tribes; tributary provinces; lower classes; free labourers.

We shall meet with instances of tribes, the members of which are bound to perform some kind of labour for other tribes or for the members of the latter.

This is not slavery; for slavery is subjection of one individual to another, and a subjection that absorbs the whole personality of the subjected; and under such circumstances it is not possible that the subjected lead a tribal life. Therefore, where the subjected are described as forming a separate tribe, we may be sure that they are not slaves. Ingram justly remarks that "the lowest caste may be a degraded and despised one, but its members are not in a state of slavery; they are in collective, not individual, subjection to the members of the higher classes" [1]). What Ingram says here of the lowest caste, often applies to subjected tribes.

That conquered districts, bound to pay a tribute in kind or money, do not consist of slaves, is clear.

The foregoing remarks would be almost superfluous, were it not that some ethnographers in such cases spoke of "slave tribes" and "slave districts". This may partly be caused by the natives themselves making an incorrect use of the term "slavery". In North Africa the coast tribes call the inland tribes their slaves, because they keep them bound by a trade monopoly. In the same regions a chief calls himself the slave of another chief, to whom he has to pay a tribute [2]). As in some cases the slaves live together in separate villages [3]), it may be difficult to decide whether we have to deal with slave villages or with subjected groups. The criterion then is, whether the subjected people have each an individual master. When we are informed that such is the case, or that they are bought and sold, we may be certain that they are slaves.

Lower classes can be of different kinds. Where they are

---

1) Ingram, p. 3. Schurtz also remarks that pariah artisans, though despised, are not slaves. (Das afrikanische Gewerbe, p. 142). — 2) Goldstein, pp. 354, 355. — 3) See for instance Hutter, pp. 270, 271.

only considered inferior to the upper classes, or excluded from governmental functions, it is easy to see that they are not slaves. Greater difficulties are presented by some other cases. Sometimes a lower class consists of free labourers. Now theoretically free labourers are easy to distinguish from slaves: the slave is compelled to work, the free labourer voluntarily submits to it. But the accounts of the ethnographers do not always make it clear, which of these two kinds of labourers we have to deal with in any particular case. When a labourer lives in the house of his master and is wholly dependent on him, it may be rather difficult at first sight to decide whether he is free or a slave. Sometimes the details given are sufficient to settle the question; if not, we shall have to leave it undecided.

A lower class can also consist of serfs. What they are, and what is the difference between them and slaves, will be shown in the next paragraph.

§ 8. *Distinction of slavery from kindred phenomena. V. Serfs.*

What we have said of free labourers applies also to serfs: to draw the theoretical line of demarcation between them and slaves is not so very difficult; but practically it is not always easy to decide, whether a subjected class we get some information about consists of slaves or of serfs; sometimes even, because of the unstable terminology and the scanty information, it is quite impossible. But there are several unequivocal cases of serfdom, too, on record in history. Mentioning a few of these will suffice to give the reader a clear idea of its nature as distinct from slavery.

In Germany *Leibeigene* was, in the earliest times, synonymous with slave. The law placed the *Leibeigenen* on a level with the domestic animals. The master had the *ius vitae ac necis*, an unlimited right to sell them, the right to exact from them all possible services, to marry and divorce them. The owner of the *Leibeigene* was also owner of his goods and chattels. The lord was responsible for any damages caused by his servant, as for those caused by his horse, and might claim indemnity if any one injured his man. But gradually this slavery was mitigated into a state of subserviency. First the claim to unlimited services was waived, and on the *Leibeigene* were imposed definite *Roboten* (labour dues) and tributes. He had to work on fixed days, to perform fixed services, to pay fixed sums. His earnings legally still belonged to the lord, and the latter succeeded to his goods; but from the 13th century the lord's right of inheritance dwindled into a present (*mortuarium*). From the 14th century the serfs acquired a usufruct of the soil they tilled, and so their obligations assumed more or less the character of a quit-rent. Sometimes they were even allowed to choose another lord. In the Frankish empire the lords were already forbidden to sell them abroad; from the 13th century they lost the right to kill them, and afterwards also the right to whip them. The church took away from the lord the right to divorce his serfs, if the marriage had been contracted with his consent. The *ius primae noctis* remained longer. Moreover, the relations of the serfs towards others were gradually recognized by law, at first only as to unjust acts, later on as to contracts. And so, when at last serfdom was abolished, the only changes effected by this were: allowing of the right of emigrating, abolition of the marriage-consent and of the court-services and personal tributes.

Thus Siegel describes the development of serfdom in Germany [1]). Other writers come to nearly the same conclusions. According to Brunner, there was among the Western Germans a class between freemen and slaves, called *Liten* or *Aldien*, a hereditary class, whose position was secured by law. They had the right of acquiring property and making contracts; they could by emancipation become fully free, or purchase their own liberty. To marry they wanted the consent of their lord. They had the right of feud (*Fehderecht*), and when they were killed a *wergild* was paid, that fell partly to the lord. Their right of inheritance was originally not recognized [2]).

Schröder remarks, that the difference between freemen and subservients (*Hörigen*) consisted in this, that the landed pos-

---

1) Siegel, pp. 328—330. — 2) Brunner, I pp. 101, 102.

sessions of the latter were smaller and liable to tribute. Moreover, they had no *connubium* with freemen, nor any political
rights; the *wergild* paid for them was one half of that paid
for a freeman [1]).

In medieval France a similar state of things prevailed.
There were no longer slaves, but serfs. "Serfdom is a transitory stage between slavery and entire liberty. The serf of the
middle ages is not, like the ancient slave, indissolubly riveted
to his condition, deprived of rights by his very birth, placed
on a level with the beasts of burden of his lord's estate. Public opinion is favourable to him." "The facts agree with the
doctrine. The serf has some means of acquiring property; he
may marry and have legitimate descendants, who will succeed
to his goods; he may give evidence in the courts; he may
purchase his liberty by means of his *peculium*. By getting
some profits he is interested in the cultivation of the soil.
Giving his labour to the land, he may expect to enjoy the
fruits of it, by paying fixed tributes. By marrying his children to free women he secures the liberty of his offspring.
By paying an indemnity he acquires the succession to his
father's inheritance, and the right of property over his
savings.... He may dispute the tributes (*tailles et cens*)
which the lord levies on the tenement he cultivates, invoke
an enquiry of experts who attest his means, contract to pay
a fixed annuity and so know beforehand what profit he may
depend upon" [2]).

With these serfs may be compared the Roman *coloni*. "The
colonatus consists in this, that men are inseparably attached
to a landed property for the purpose of cultivating it....
This connection with a determinate estate, from which the
colonus might be severed only in some cases fixed by law,
brought about an approximation of the *colonus* to the slave
(as *servus terrae*), but also a difference between them, a security for the *colonus*, which protects him from the lord's arbitrary power. Hence the *colonus* stands with regard to the lord
on the free footing of one bound only to comply with the

---

1) Schröder, p. 41. He states that these *Hörigen* were also called *lati* or *aldio* (l. c.,
p. 40); so they are the same class as those described by Brunner. — 2) Gasquet, II,
pp. 281, 282.

yearly canon, *annua functio*, a tribute fixed by contract or custom, wich he has to pay to the lord, generally in products of the land" [1]).

The foregoing statements once more prove the sufficiency of our definition of slavery. As soon as the forced labourer is no longer entirely at the disposal of the lord, the latter being entitled to fixed services and tributes only, such a state of things is called serfdom, or *colonatus*, or subserviency, but not slavery. This agrees with our definition of slavery. The slave, as we have remarked above, is the property of his master, whose power is in principle unlimited, not restricted to fixed performances. Therefore, even if the writers referred to here called such institutions as serfdom and *colonatus* slavery, we are not to do so; but we may regard it as a corroboration of the conclusion we had arrived at before, that such writers, most of whom have not made any special research into the nature of slavery, when they meet with such an institution as serfdom, feel that they are not to call it slavery.

Now let us look what the theorists have to say on the subject.

Ingram remarks: "The transition to serfdom took place in civic communities, when the master parted with or was deprived of his property in the person of the slave, and became entitled only to his services, or a determinate portion of them. In rural life, where the march of development was slower, the corresponding stage was reached when, in accordance with the fundamental principles of feudalism, the relation between the lord and serf, from being personal, became territorial" [2])

The first words here perfectly express the truth: when the master loses "his property in the person of the slave", he is no longer a slave-owner. What follows, that the master "became entitled only to his services", is less correct; for he who is entitled to all the services of another is his owner; just the limiting of the master's right to "a determinate portion of them" is the change from slavery to something else. If I may require all the services a man can perform, I am his owner; if I am restricted to a determinate portion of them, I am not.

---

1) Puchta II p. 97. — 2) Ingram, p. 262.

Spencer says: "As the distinctions between different forms of slavery are indefinite, so must there be an indefinite distinction between slavery and serfdom, and between the several forms of serfdom. Much confusion has arisen in describing these respective institutions, and for the sufficient reason that the institutions themselves are confused" [1]).

This consideration, however true, will not prevent us from drawing a theoretical line of demarcation. Not a single social institution is practically strictly separated from kindred institutions; yet we cannot understand such institutions, unless we make a distinction, and not an "indefinite" one.

Letourneau, after describing the state of the *colonus*, adds: "In a word, he was not an object of possession, a slave, but only a proletarian attached to the soil." In another passage he remarks that slavery always undergoes some mitigation in the course of civilization: "Less and less is the person of the slave himself oppressed; one is contented with exploiting him, depriving him in a larger or smaller degree of the fruits of his labour, in a word the slave becomes a serf" [2]).

These quotations may suffice to show that our view of the matter is held by theorists as well as historians.

The serf, therefore, is not a slave, because he is not the property of his master, and the particulars of serfdom related by historians provide us with means of more clearly understanding the practical meaning of this notion "property". It means a power that, however leniently exercised in many cases, is in principle unlimited. Among many peoples the master may ill-use and even kill his slave, without the law taking any notice of it. And even where his power is restricted by social regulations, he may have a right of property, viz. if his authority be in principle unbounded, and any limitation put upon it suppose a special legal provision. The slave-owner may do with his slave whatever he is not by special laws forbidden to do; the master of a serf may require from his man such services and tributes only, as the law

---

1) Spencer, Ind. Inst., p. 472. — 2) Letourneau, pp. 423, 355, 356. In a letter we received from Mr. A. C. Kruyt, it is remarked that among the Dyaks and the Toradja of Celebes a slave in some cases rises to the position of a serf; he is then no longer continually in the service of his master, but only has to work at definite periods.

allows him to require. The slave-owner has a right of property; the master of a serf has, so to speak, a *ius in re aliena*. [1])

§ 9. *Pawns or debtor-slaves.*

In the course of our investigation it will be shown, that among some peoples a debtor, unable to pay a debt he has contracted, becomes the slave of his creditor. Sometimes such persons are ordinary slaves; but pawns or debtor-slaves in the restricted sense (who are of frequent occurrence in the Malay Archipelago, Dutch *pandelingen*) are a class whose slave-state is conditional; they become free as soon as the debt is paid by or for them; the creditor cannot refuse to accept the money. Because of this great difference between pawns and ordinary slaves (who generally have not a right to be ransomed), most ethnographers do not call the former slaves, but give separate descriptions of slavery and pawning.

The question arises, and has to be settled here, whether we for our purpose have to call these pawns slaves. We shall quote here one description of pawning. Among the Tshi-speaking peoples of the Gold Coast of West Africa "a pawn is a person placed in temporary bondage to another by the head of the family.... either to pay a debt, or to obtain a loan.... When a person is pawned on account of a debt, the services

---

1) Mr. Westermarck observes: "According to a common definition of slavery, the slave is the property of his master, but this definition is hardly accurate. It is true that even in the case of inanimate property the notion of ownership does not involve that the owner of a thing is always entitled to do with it whatever he likes; a person may own a thing and yet been prohibited by law from destroying it. But it seems that the owner's right over his property, even when not absolute, is at all events exclusive, that is, that nobody but the owner has a right to the disposal of it. Now the master's right of disposing of his slave is not necessarily exclusive; custom or law may grant the latter a certain amount of liberty, and in such a case his condition differs essentially from that of a piece of property. The chief characteristic of slavery is the compulsory nature of the slave's relation to his master" (Moral Ideas, I pp. 670, 671).

We are fully aware that a certain amount of liberty is often granted to the slaves. This was also the case in ancient Rome; yet we think the Roman legislators were correct in calling the slaves the property of their masters. For every check, put by custom or law upon the master's power over his slaves, is foreign to the nature of slavery; in principle the master's power is unlimited, just as the owner's power over his property. It is just in this that slavery differs from other relations of a compulsory nature.

of the pawn, even should they extend over a considerable number of years, count for nothing towards the liquidation of the debt; and a pawn has to serve his master, until the amount of the original debt with 50 per cent. interest, is paid by the person who pawned him" [1].

Here the debtor pawns one of the members of his family; among some other peoples (e. g. in the Malay Archipelago) he pawns himself; this is not essential. The main fact is that the pawn is in "bondage", however temporarily, that he "has to serve his master." Therefore, as long as the debt remains unpaid, the pawn is in the same condition as a slave. He has not to perform a fixed amount of labour, he must serve his master without any limitation; the master has over him a power that is, in principle, unlimited. Now we have to inquire: Is this pawn a slave, i. e. is he the property of his master? In a legal sense the creditor has not a right of property over his pawn; his right agrees with a kind of *pignus* which the Romans called *antichresis*, i. e. something yielding profit was handed over to the creditor, who utilized it instead of receiving the usual interest [2]. Yet the right of the holder of the pawn bore much resemblance to that of the owner: he had a *utilis in rem actio*, a *vindicatio pignoris* [3]. We, for our purpose, may classify the pawns among the slaves, if we can prove that sociologically a system of pawning performs the same function as a slave-system. And this certainly is the case. The same system of compulsory labour, the same subjection of the entire person exists, whether the subjected are perpetually slaves or temporarily pawns, viz. in those cases where, as among the Tshi-speaking peoples, the master's power is in principle unlimited. Where pawns have a fixed amount of work to do, they are temporary serfs; but where (as is most often the case) no limit is put to the amount of work the master may exact from them, they are temporary slaves, and as long as they are slaves, take the same place as other slaves in the social system.

---

1) Ellis, Tshi-speaking peoples, p. 294. — 2) Puchta, II p. 250; see also Wilken, Pandrecht, pp. 42—44. — 3) Puchta, II p. 264.

CHAPTER II.

---

§ 1. *Introduction.*

Having now determined what is the meaning of the term "slavery", we are about to inquire, what is its social signification, what place does it occupy in those societies where it formerly existed or still exists? As this book confines itself to ethnological investigations, we shall try to throw light on this problem with the help of the data supplied to us by the study of savage races. But then we must first know, whether slavery exists among all savage tribes, and, if not, whether it is confined to certain races of men or to certain parts of the world; and further, whether it is found on all levels of lower culture, or on some only, and if the latter, on which. The solution of these problems requires a survey of the occurrence of slavery among wild tribes in the several parts of the globe. This survey will occupy the present chapter.

A few words have still to be said about our method of ascertaining the existence or non-existence of slavery in every particular case.

To one unacquainted with our science the task to be performed now may seem very easy: we have only to consult the ethnographical literature bearing on any tribe, and to look whether slavery is mentioned; if it is mentioned in an affirmative sense, slavery exists; if in a negative sense or not at all, slavery does not exist. But every one familiar with ethnographical literature knows that it has not to be used in such a rough-and-ready manner. The statements of eth-

4

nographers are not to be accepted without much caution and a thorough criticism [1]).

The observance of the following rules will, so far as we can judge, give to our conclusions the highest possible degree of probability.

1°. If it is stated that slavery exists, is this sufficient evidence of its existence? Our definition, arrived at in the first chapter, lies within the limits of ordinary language; therefore it is probable that our informants have used the term in the same sense we attach to it. There are, however, many cases in which the words "slave" and "slavery" are applied to something quite different from their true meaning, as will be seen from our survey of the matter. Thus it is necessary to ask for more evidence than is given by the mere term "slavery".

a. If it sufficiently appears that in some tribe there are men considered to be the property of others, we need not doubt whether slavery exists.

b. If this is not clearly proved, there is still one particular, that being mentioned makes the existence of slavery very probable, viz. the fact that people are bought and sold within the tribe, except of course women sold for wives. For other kinds of subjected persons, serfs, lower classes, and subjects of a despot, are not bought or sold, at least not within the tribe. Beyond the limits of the tribe a man may be sold without previously having been a slave. Thus some African despots sell their subjects to Arabian slave-traders; such a sale does not prove that slavery exists within the tribe. But when a man is sold within the tribe, either he was already a

---

1) Dr. Tönnies, in his review of the first edition of this work, expresses a doubt as to whether slavery in the proper sense exists in every case in which, relying on the often superficial accounts of travellers, we conclude that slavery is present.

The foregoing passage and the whole of the present chapter are, we think, sufficient evidence that we have set ourselves the task of subjecting the accounts of travellers and other writers on savage tribes, on which our conclusions are to be based, to a critical examination. There may be particular instances in which we have failed in this respect; but we believe our conclusions on the whole rest upon a solid basis and Dr. Tönnies's objection, in corroboration of which he does not adduce a single fact, does not seem to us well founded.

slave, or he becomes such, *e.g.* as a punishment; in both cases slavery is practised by the tribe [1]).

c. If the particulars on record are quite insufficient to determine the nature of the alleged slave-state, the possibility of a mistake is much lessened by several writers, independently of each other, stating that slavery exists.

d. Finally, the general trustworthiness of the writer or writers must be taken into account.

2°. If we are told that there are no slaves, it is very probable that slavery really does not exist, for slavery is a phenomenon rather easy to observe, and the ethnographers are generally inclined to use the word in a too wide rather than in a too restricted sense. There is no need here for the extreme scepticism with which we have to receive an assertion of any tribe having no religion [2]). This does not prevent, of course, that if we find the existence of slavery denied by a writer who is generally badly informed, we may reject such an assertion.

3°. The greatest difficulties are presented by those cases in which no mention is made of slavery. Here the utmost caution has to be observed.

a. If it clearly appears from the description, that there are people considered to be the property of others, without the word "slavery" being used, the conclusion is evident.

b. Perhaps some facts are mentioned which make the existence of slavery highly improbable. We shall see that the main source of slavery is captivity in war; so, if it is stated that no captives are made, or that the lot of the captives is something else than slavery, the non-existence of slavery is probable. But even then it is not quite certain: there may still be slaves, acquired by other means. Further: if it is stated that there are no social classes, or if the classes are enumerated and slaves are not among them, there is a strong presumption that slavery does not exist. Yet here too there is no certainty; for slaves, among savage tribes, have not always the aspect of a social class. The description of the

---

1) Sometimes, however, children are sold to adoptive parents within the tribe. Such is the case in Greenland; see Crantz I, p. 178. But these are exceptional cases, so, when no particulars are given, we may suppose that the purchased persons become slaves and not adopted childern. — 2) See Tylor, Primitive Culture, I pp. 417 sqq.

division of labour between the sexes may also suggest to us the non-existence of slavery. When we are informed that the men do some kinds of work and the women some other kinds, we are inclined to think: if there were slaves, their special work would be mentioned too. But this argument is most dangerous; for the slaves very often have no special kind of work allotted to them.

We see that none of these criteria prove quite reliable. Yet, taken together, they give a high degree of probability. And it is not even necessary that all of them can be ascertained. If an ethnographer, know to be trustworthy, gives us an elaborate description, pretending to be a picture of the whole social life of the tribe he describes, it were a wonder if he had entirely omitted slavery, while it existed; the more so as this phenomenon is not so difficult to recognize. The same argument obtains *a fortiori*, when several such descriptions of the same tribe exist.

4°. In doubtful cases we may take into account the state of the group to which a particular tribe belongs. It may be that in the general descriptions of a group no mention is made of slavery; that, further, all tribes belonging to this group of which we are well informed prove to have no slaves. If, then, the information we get concerning a particular tribe belonging to the same group, is not complete enough to rely upon, there is a strong presumption that this tribe will be in the same state as the rest of the group, *i. e.* that it does not keep slaves. Under the same conditions we may suppose that a tribe belonging to a slave-keeping group keeps slaves. The term "group" has to be taken here in a sociological, not in an anthropological or linguistic sense, and its application must be somewhat restricted. It must consist of tribes, that live in somewhat similar conditions and the institutions of which closely resemble each other; *e. g.* Australia (the continent) is a group in this sense, North America is not. It is almost superfluous to add, that this group-argument may be used only to strengthen existing, but insufficient, evidence.

We confine ourselves here to the phenomena of savage life; therefore we shall exclude the semi-civilized peoples. An exact distinction, however, between these two classes of peoples has not yet been made [1]); so we are fully aware of the possibility of mistakes, made here in this respect. As we were not able to apply any exact criterion, we have more or less followed our general impressions, paying most attention to the development of political institutions. So for instance we have excluded the Kabyls of Northern Africa, because their detailed legal system, as described by Hanoteau and Letourneux [2]), proves that politically they have passed beyond the stage of savagery. And a developed political organization cannot exist without profoundly marking such an institution as slavery.

We shall find that several savage tribes have to a considerable extent been influenced by civilized or semi-civilized nations. In such cases the question arises: have we to deal here with phenomena of unadulterated savage life? This question is important and deserves full attention. We shall see that many savage tribes in their true aboriginal state have been acquainted with slavery, whereas many others when first discovered did not practise it; so neither the existence nor the non-existence of slavery must necessarily be due to foreign interference; either may be aboriginal, and must be supposed to be so wherever there is not a strong presumption to the contrary [3]). But there are also many cases in which foreign influence has undoubtedly been at work. We must, then, make a distinction. If the influence of the civilized or semi-civilized nation has led to a, so to speak, normal development, *i. e.* a development, which lies within the limits of primitive culture, we have to deal with a phenomenon of savage life. For instance, commercial intercourse with a nation of higher civilization has brought about an accumulation of wealth and a social differentiation, which render the existence of slavery possible. In such case we may safely speak of slavery as practised by savages, for it is the effect of trade in general, not of intercourse with a

---

1) The distinction between the several stages of culture will be enlarged upon in the second Part. — 2) Hanoteau et Letourneux, La Kabylie et les coutumes Kabyles. — 3) When similar phenomena are found among different peoples, modern ethnology supposes that they have spontaneously originated among each of them, viz. as long as the contrary is not made probable. See Steinmetz, Endokannibalismus, pp. 56, 57, and Darwin, Descent of Man, p. 141.

civilized nation as such, that we have to deal with here. If, on the contrary, there has been an abnormal development, i. e. a development which does not take place in countries inhabited by savages only, the present condition of the savage tribe has no interest to us. For instance, measures have been taken by a civilized nation on purpose to abolish slavery. Then we, for our purpose, must consider the savage tribe concerned as keeping slaves, and pay attention only to the descriptions of its institutions as they were before the abolition.

The ensuing paragraphs will show which savage tribes keep slaves and which do not keep any. The groups into which we have divided the several tribes are mainly geographical, not intended to answer any anthropological purpose. As long as the meaning of the term "race" is so unstable as at present, we think it better not to operate with it. Our groups are nearly the same as those given by Schurtz in his *Völkerkunde*.

At the end of each paragraph its result will be mentioned. The "positive cases" are the tribes which probably keep slaves, the "negative cases" those which probably do not keep slaves. Under the head of "no conclusion" we have given the cases in which the probability that slavery exists is nearly as great, or as little, as the inverse probability. The tribes, the names of which are printed in italics, are those which afford "clear cases", i. e. where the probability nearly amounts to certainty.

At the end of the chapter a brief recapitulation will show the occurrence of slavery among savages in the several parts of the globe.

When, in the following paragraphs, we say: "Such a tribe keeps slaves," or: "Such a tribe does not keep slaves," this does not imply that the same state of things still prevails. The tribe we speak of may have died out; or, where slavery existed, it may have been abolished. When we know that such a thing has taken place, we shall use the past tense. But in many cases the only information we have got concerning some tribe dates from many years back; and we do not know what has become of this tribe in the meantime. Then, not to be obliged always to use such tedious formulas as: "In Mr. X.'s time slavery existed among such a tribe," we shall simply say: "slavery exists." Whether it still exists is certainly of

much interest to a philanthropist; but to us, for the purposes
we have set ourselves in the present volume, it is quite immaterial.

§ 2. North America.

1. Eskimos.

Rink's account applies especially to Western Greenland at
the time of the first European settlement, but may be taken
as a general description of the Eskimos [1]). According to him
the family in the restricted sense comprehended foster-children,
widows, helpless persons adopted as relatives and more or
less treated as servants. They were regarded as subordinate
members of the family but never subjected to any corporal
punishment [2]). He then describes their social organization, but
makes no mention of slavery [3]). The question remains whether
these helpless persons are to be called slaves. This does not
very clearly appear; but, happily, we have more detailed
accounts of the several Eskimo tribes.

Crantz, in his description of the Greenlanders, gives many
particulars about their servants. Mothers of illegitimate
children are despised; sometimes a childless person buys
her children. When a married couple have no children
or no full-grown children, the husband adopts one or two
orphan boys, who help him in his work and must provide the
family with the neccessaries of life. The same is done by the
wife with daughters of others or with a widow. Although
the adopted youths are employed as servants, they are free
from any compulsion, and are regarded as the future lords
of the house. The adopted maid-servant or daughter can leave
when she likes. A man will never beat his man-servant, and
were he to touch a maid-servant, he would incur great disgrace [4]). We see that the condition of these servants is not
slavery. The boy is the future lord of the house, the girl may
leave when she pleases. Servants are only required to occupy
the place that in a normal household is taken up by the children.

---

1) Rink, p. 5. — 2) Ibid., pp. 24, 25. — 3) Ibid. pp. 24—34. — 4) Crantz I. pp. 178, 186.

Labour is not asked for. "If a man dies without leaving behind relatives, or full-grown sons, nobody cares for the children, unless one wants a maid-servant." A widow must try to get a lodging, in which she does not always succeed [1]). It is clear that to these Greenlanders slaves would not be of any use. Nansen, too, makes no mention of slavery [2]).

Boas, describing the Central Eskimos, states that among them too children are adopted and regarded by the adoptive parents as their own children; so "an elder adopted son has a preference over a younger son born of the marriage," viz. as to the right of inheritance. The following statement still more directly bears on our subject: "Sometimes men are adopted who may almost be considered servants. Particularly bachelors without any relations, cripples who are not able to provide for themselves, or men who have lost their sledges and dogs are found in this position. They fulfil minor occupations, mend the hunting-implements, fit out the sledges, feed the dogs, etc.; sometimes however, they join the hunters. They follow the master of the house when he removes from one place to another, make journeys in order to do his commissions, and so on. The position, however, is a voluntary one, and therefore these men are not less esteemed than the self-dependent providers" [3]). The last sentence clearly shows that these servants are not slaves. And as in no other place does Boas make any mention of slaves, it is certain that slavery does not exist.

Ribbach gives some notes on the Eskimos of Labrador. There is nothing on slavery in these notes. Describing their dwellings he says: "The principal family has of course the best place; the servants, widows or orphans, if there are such, have to content themselves with a place near the door, where the cold is most severe" [4]). This agrees so much with the foregoing descriptions, that we may suppose that the same state of things prevails here.

As little mention is made of slavery in the descriptions of some other Central Eskimo tribes, as the Frobisher Bay and

---

1) Ibid., pp. 211, 215. — 2) Nansen. — 3) Boas, Central, Eskimo, pp. 580, 581. — 4) Ribbach, p. 286.

Field Bay Eskimos [1]), the Kinipetu Eskimos [2]), the Tchiglit Eskimos [3]), the Eskimos of the Ungava district [4]).

Bancroft says of the Western Eskimos (or Eskimos of Alaska): "Slavery in any form is unknown among them". Elliott makes no mention of slavery [5]).

The describers of the Eskimos of Point Barrow, too, have not a word about slavery. Adoption is practised to a great extent [6]). So the same state of things probably prevails here as among the other Eskimos.

Some other tribes, belonging to the Eskimo group in the wider sense [7]), may also be treated here.

Amongst the Aleuts, according to Bancroft, the chief "is exempt from work, is allowed a servant to row his boat, but in other respects possesses no power" [8]). No more is added bearing on our subject. Petroff, however, gives a detailed account of slavery among them. The slaves were prisoners of war and their descendants. The master could punish the slave with death, could sell and liberate him. Any attempt to escape was severely punished. [9]). So the Aleuts had slaves.

The Athka Aleuts, according to Petroff, had also slaves [10]).

Among the Koniagas or Southern Eskimos "slavery" says Bancroft "existed to a limited extent." This is affirmed by Holmberg [11]).

2. Nootka group.

The Tlinkits formerly carried on slavery to a great extent. This is proved by the detailed accounts of several writers [12]).

The same applies to the Haidas [13]).

Krause, in a short note, speaks of a female slave of a Tsimshian chief. Niblack states that the Tsimshians acted as

---

1) Hall. — 2) Klutschak. — 3) Petitot. — 4) Turner, Ungava District. — 5) Bancroft, p. 65; Elliott. — 6) Ray, p. 44; Murdoch, p. 419. — 7) See Schurtz, Katechismus, p. 268. — 8) Bancroft, p. 92. — 9) Petroff, p. 152. — 10) Petroff, pp. 158, 159. — 11) Bancroft, p. 80; see also Holmberg, I pp. 78, 79. — 12) Krause, p. 152, etc.; Bancroft, p. 108; Dall, pp. 419—421; Petroff, p. 165 Elliott, p. 64; Niblack, p. 252; Holmberg, I pp. 50, 51, II pp. 43—46. — 13) Krause, p. 311; Bancroft, p. 168.

middlemen in the slave trade. Boas describes the legends of the Tsimshians; in these legends slaves and their occupations are frequently spoken of. Kane, in his census of Indian tribes states that among the Tsimshians there were slaves. [1]). Hence we may infer that slavery formerly existed among them.

Boas, speaking of the Kwakiutl Indians, writes: "All the tribes of the Pacific Coast are divided into a nobility, common people and slaves. The last of these may be left out of consideration, as they do not form part and parcel of the clan, but are captives made in war, or purchases, and may change ownership as any other piece of property" [2]). From this statement it appears that the Kwakiutl kept slaves.

Krause says of the Bilballas; "The chief possessed numerous wives and many slaves; also were these Indians much given to slave-stealing and the slave trade" [3]). As the Bilballas are reckoned by Bancroft among the Haidas, amongst whom, according to him, "slavery is universal", we may suppose, that slaves were kept by them for their own use, not for export only.

The many details, given in the works of Sproat and Brown, prove that slavery existed among the Ahts of Vancouver Island [4]).

The Nootkas, among whom, according to Bancroft, "slavery is practised bij all the tribes", seem to be the same as the Ahts [5]).

Bancroft informs us that "slaves are held by all the tribes" about Puget Sound, and gives several details of their slave system [6]).

Slavery also existed among the Fish Indians of British Columbia [7]).

3. Tinneh group.

According to Kane, who was well acquainted with this group, slavery in its most cruel form exists among the Indians of

---

1) Krause, p. 319; Niblack, p. 252; Boas, Die Tsimschian, pp. 237, 240, 244; Kane, Appendix A. — 2) Boas, Kwakiutl Indians, p. 338. — 3) Krause, p. 321. — 4) Sproat, pp. 89—92; Brown, adventures of John Jewitt, pp. 130, 131. — 5) Bancroft p. 195; Brown, ibid., pp. 19, 28, 35. — 6) Bancroft, p. 217. — 7) Mayne, pp. 242, 275, 253, etc.

the whole coast, from California to Behring's Straits, the stronger tribes making slaves of all the others they can conquer. In the interior, where there is but little warfare, slavery does not exist." Niblack, however, states that slavery existed among the interior Tinneh but they "had no hereditary slaves, getting their supply from the coast" [1]).

Of the Kutchins or Loucheux Jones says: "Slavery is practised among them. Any poor creature who has no friends is made a slave" [2]). Hardisty gives more détails; he tells us: "As a rule slavery does not exist, but the orphan and the friendless are kept in servitude and treated so harshly as to be really little better than slaves, until such time as they get big enough and bold enough to assert their independence, when they are allowed to shift for themselves" [3]). Such ill-treated children, who when full-grown are "allowed to shift for themselves", certainly are not slaves. Therefore we may safely infer, that slavery did not exist here, the more so, as the other authors [4]) make no mention of slaves.

Mackenzie, describing the Chepewyans or Athabascas, states that "they are constantly at war with the Eskimos, and kill as many of them as they can, as it is a principle with them never to make prisoners" [5]). Neither in his notes on the Chepewyans in general, nor in those on some single tribes belonging to the Chepewyan family, as the Slave and Dog-Rib Indians, Hare Indians, Beaver and Rocky-Mountain Indians, does our informant make any mention of slavery. Nor is there a word to be found about slaves in Russell's and Bancroft's accounts. Hearne speaks of Northern and Southern Indians, divisions of the Chepewyans. Among the Southern Indians a wife sometimes begs of her husband, who is going to war, to bring a female slave with him for her to kill. The chief Matonabbee was the son of a Northern Indian man and a Southern Indian slave [6]). Hearne does not speak of male slaves. So we may suppose that slavery proper does not exist.

On the Tacullies Bancroft remarks: "Slavery is common

---

1) Kane, pp. 214, 215; Niblack, p. 252. — 2) Jones, The Kutchin Tribes, p. 325. — 3) Hardisty, p. 316. — 4) Whymper; Kirby; Bancroft. — 5) Mackenzie, I p. 152. — 6) Hearne, II pp. 87, 179.

with them, all who can afford it keeping slaves. They use them as beasts of burden, and treat them most inhumanely" [1]).

Of the Atnas on Copper River, a division of the Kenai, Bancroft says: "Those who can afford it, keep slaves, buying them from the Koltschanes" [2]).

Mrs. Allison informs us that among the Similkameem Indians of British Columbia "slaves taken in war were well treated, but always had one eye blemished to mark them" [3]).

4. Algonquin group.

The authors we have consulted on the Algonquins in general [4]) make no mention whatever of slaves.

Loskiel, describing the Lenape or Delawares, states that captured boys and girls were received into their families, and employed as servants; sometimes, however, they were sold to Europeans. If such prisoners behaved well, they had nothing to complain of and were not overworked. If they ran away and were recaptured, they were generally killed. But the adult male prisoners, viz. those of them who were not killed, were adopted by families, instead of those who had been killed in war or had died in some other way, and from this moment were looked upon as members of the tribe to which they now belonged [5]). As these men became members of the tribe, it is not probable that the captive children were made slaves; we may safely suppose that as long as they were young they had to perform menial work, but when adult were on a level with the members of the tribe. And as neither Loskiel, in any other passage, nor Brinton refers to slavery, slaves were very probably not to be found among the Delawares. [6]).

In Le Jeune's account of the Montagnais no mention is made of slaves. Prisoners of war were cruelly put to death [7]).

The Ojibways or Chippeways, according to Keating, killed the captive warriors and old women; the marriageable women

---

1) Bancroft, p. 124. — 2) Bancroft, p. 135. — 3) Allison, p. 316. — 4) Roosevelt; Le Jeune in The Jesuit Relations; Sagard; Mackenzie. — 5) Loskiel, p. 195. — 6) Loskiel; Brinton, The Lenape. — 7) Jesuit Relations, V pp. 31, 55; VI p. 245.

became slaves and were very cruelly treated by the women of the victorious tribe; the children were adopted and treated fairly well [1]. Jones's account is somewhat different. Most often all enemies were killed. Sometimes they made a few prisoners, who were adopted by those who had lost a relative; then the adopted prisoner became a relative or slave; if not adopted he was burned alive. The relatives of a murderer sometimes paid large indemnities to those of the victim; the murderer had then to work for them in order to pay off the debt; he was reduced to a kind of servitude [2]. In these accounts slaves and servitude are mentioned. The servitude of the murderer very probably was not slavery. He had to work: but it is not stated that he was made a slave, *i. e.* the property of an individual person. The prisoners who became "relatives or slaves" were adopted; therefore they were not slaves in the proper sense of the word. And as for the female slaves Keating speaks of, we know that a slave system without male slaves is not slavery proper. We may suppose, that these female captives became an inferior kind of wives, to whom the women of the tribe were unkind through a very natural jealousy. Kohl, in his elaborate description of the Ojibways, makes no mention of slavery. Their wars, he states, did not bring them any profit [3]. According to Carver, "all that are captivated bij both parties, are either put to death, adopted, or made slaves of." "That part of the prisoners, which are considered as slaves, are generally distributed among the chiefs, who frequently make presents of some of them to the European governors of the out-posts, or to the superintendants or commissaries of Indian affairs. I have been informed that it was the Jesuits and French missionaries that first occasioned the introduction of these unhappy captives into the settlements and who by so doing taught the Indians that they were valuable" [4]. From all the foregoing we may infer that slavery was not an indigenous institution among the Ojibways.

This inference is strengthened by what Tanner tells us of the Ottawas, an Ojibway tribe. He was adopted by an Ottawa

---

1) Keating, II p. 168. — 2) Jones, Ojibway Indians, pp. 131, 109. — 3) Kohl, I p. 96. — 4) Carver, pp. 325, 326.

woman, but was not at first on a level with the other children. The first few years she made him do various kinds of manual labour: he had to cut wood, fetch water and do other kinds of work, which were not generally required from children of his age. Yet when grown-up he was on a level with the Indians into whose tribe he was admitted, and married an Indian girl [1]).

Before passing to the Ottawas, Tanner had been a captive amongst the Shahnees. He was very cruelly and ignominiously treated. Yet he was not a slave, for he had been adopted by a married couple on the grave of their youngest son, whose place he was to fill [2]). As this agrees with the general customs of this group, in which there are no slaves, we may suppose that here also slavery was unknown.

The Potawatomi also very probably had no slaves; for none of their describers make any mention of slavery [3]).

Amongst the Crees or Knisteneaux, according to McLean, adoption of aliens was practised. A missionary, who had unintentionally killed a Cree boy, offered himself in his stead, and was adopted. Kane speaks of "the universal custom of Indian mothers eagerly seeking another child, although it may be of an enemy, to replace one of her own, whom she may have lost ... This child is always treated with as great, if not greater, kindness than the rest." The existence of this custom, together with the fact that none of their describers makes mention of slaves, renders it most probable that they did not keep slaves [4]).

The Cheyennes very seldom captured adult males; when they did, they generally put them to death. Children were adopted and treated like their own children; women became the wives of their captors [5]). Slavery is not mentioned.

The Blackfeet nation consisted of four tribes: Piegans, Blackfeet, Bloods, and Gros Ventres. We are told that once when at war against the Crows, the Gros Ventres "rushed upon them and killed the whole number" [6]). Grinnell, speaking of a Piegan

---

1) Tanner, pp, 17, 112, 114. — 2) Tanner, pp. 11—16. — 3) Keating; Long, Ojibway Indians; Roosevelt. — 4) McLean, p. 64; Kane, p. 128; Mackenzie. — 5) Dodge, pp. 266, 267. — 6) Reports of Expl., Vol. XII Part I p. 99.

chief, says: "He told his men not to kill the captured women. They also captured .... many children. The chief selected a wife for himself from among these women." As a rule they spare none of their enemies, killing alike men, women and children. Sometimes they spare a captive for his bravery or from dread of sorcery; he is then provided with food and dismissed to his home [1]). These particulars being given, and no mention made of slavery by any of our informants [2]), we may safely infer that slavery did not exist among these tribes.

Among the Abenakies, according to Maurault, prisoners of war were either tortured to death or adopted into the tribe. Hence we may infer that slavery, of which this writer makes no mention, was unknown among them [3]).

Hoffmann, in his description of the Menomini Indians, referring to Grignon, says that he does not know whether they had captive slaves; but certainly they had purchased slaves. Our informant saw 6 male and 8 female slaves, most of whom had been enslaved when young. The female slaves had been sold for 100 dollars each. The slaves were called Pawnees, though some of them belonged to other tribes [4]). This statement sufficiently proves, that in the time of this description the Menomini had slaves. But in Hoffmann's time they were already very much under the influence of European civilization. Whether at the more remote period from which most of our information on the Algonquin tribes dates slavery existed among them, we do not know.

5. Iroquois group.

The Iroquois had no slaves. This is stated by Morgan, who was intimately acquainted with them. "Slavery", says Morgan, "which in the Upper Status of barbarism became the fate of the captive, was unknown among tribes in the Lower Status in the aboriginal period." And the Iroquois are his typical instance of this "Lower Status": "When discovered the Iroquois

---

1) Grinnell, pp. 115, 116, 123. — 2) Grinnell; Möllhausen; Mackenzie; Reports of Expl., Vol. I and Vol. XII Part I; Zu Wied, Nord-Amerika; Schoolcraft. — 3) Maurault, pp. 26—28. — 4) Hoffmann, p. 35.

were in the Lower Status of barbarism." Captives were either
put to death or adopted [1]). Charlevoix states, that "most of
their captives are condemned to death, or to a state of abject
slavery in which they were never certain of their lives" [2]).
But he gives no more particulars about this slave state, nor
do our other informants [3]). On the contrary, Lafitau informs
us, that the condition of prisoners, whose life is rather hard
amongst the Algonquin tribes, amongst the Iroquois and Hurons
is very easy [4]). The descriptions given by the authors of the
fate of captives justify Morgan's statement: they were either
killed or adopted [5]); and though Lafitau calls the prisoners
"*esclaves*", their state, as he describes it, is not at all like that
of slaves. So we may safely infer, that slavery did not exist
among them, and that Charlevoix's above quoted statement is
erroneous.

Among the Hurons or Wyandots, according to Powell, the
captives were either killed or adopted [6]). Lafitau's and Charlevoix's
accounts of the fate of captives among the Iroquois apply also
to the Hurons. So it is probable that they had no slaves.

6. Choctaw-Muskoghe group and neighbouring tribes.

Adair, speaking of the Katahba, Cherokee, Muskoghe, Choctaw
and Chickasaw Indians, states that they burned their prisoners.
Only if a prisoner succeeded in escaping to the house of the
high-priest or some other place of refuge, he was not burned;
but what his fate was in such a case we are not told. Young
prisoners were not killed; but it is not stated what became of
them. If warriors had offended a neighbouring tribe, and the
chiefs wished to prevent war, they sacrificed either one of the
offenders belonging to a weak family or some unfortunate
prisoner, who had been incorporated into a declining tribe [7]).

---

1) Morgan, Anc. Soc., pp. 80, 69. — 2) Charlevoix, Nouv. France, III p. 245. — 3)
Lafitau and Loskiel. Loskiel's account of the Delawares applies equally to the Iroquois,.
see Loskiel, p. 1. — 4) Lafitau, II p. 308. — 5) Lafitau, III pp. 264—290; Charlevoix, l.
c. pp. 242—252; Loskiel, p. 195; Mrs. Kinzie, pp. 214, sqq. — 6) Powell, Wyandot Gov., p. 68
— 7) Adair, pp. 303, 304, 287.

The last sentence seems to show, that the custom of adopting prisoners prevailed here too. At any rate, no mention is made of slaves.

Rochefort remarks that among the Apalaches (who, according to Roosevelt, included the Cherokees, Chickasaws, Choctaws, Creeks and Seminoles [1]) an enemy who surrendered during the fight, was taken to the conqueror's home with his wife and children, held in an honourable freedom and treated with as much leniency and care as their own servants [2]). Whether such persons were slaves does not clearly appear from this statement. But Adair's record tends to prove that slavery did not exist, at least as far as the three former divisions of the Apalaches are concerned.

Loskiel relates that a prisoner was once condemned to death by the Cherokees. He had already been tied to the stake, when a Cherokee woman arrived. She brought a basketful of commodities, which she deposed at the feet of the man to whom the prisoner belonged, and bade him leave this prisoner to her, a childless widow, who wanted to adopt him as a son. This was done [3]).

Bartram tells us that the Creeks formerly tortured their captives to death [4]).

The Seminoles, too, according to Roosevelt, used to burn their prisoners [5]).

From all the foregoing we may safely infer that slavery did not exist in the Apalache group.

Natchez warriors delivered their captives to the relations of those who had fallen in battle. The captives were always burned [6]).

Bossu speaks of slaves among the Attakapas; but it does not appear from his notes whether they made slaves for their own use or for sale abroad [7]).

Strachey describes the inhabitants of Virginia (several tribes). He makes no mention of slaves. It is stated in his account, that children and foreigners were sacrificed [8]); if there had been slaves, these probably would in the first place have been

---

1) Roosevelt, I p. 50. — 2) Rochefort, p. 412. — 3) Loskiel, p. 197. — 4) Bartram, p. 38. — 5) Roosevelt, I pp. 63, 64. — 6) Charlevoix, Nouv. France, III pp. 426; see also Lettres édif., XX pp. 132, 133. — 7) Bossu, pp. 241, 245, 249. — 8) Strachey, p. 83.

the victims. One of the objects of their wars was to capture women and children. Before the commencement of the battle it was announced that the conquered "upon their submission or comyng in, though two daies after, should live, but their wives and childrene should be prize for the conquerors" [1]). Another ancient writer gives a different description of the fate of their conquered enemies: "when they gain a victory, they spare neither men, nor women, nor children, in order to render revenge impossible" [2]). We cannot arrive at a definite conclusion here.

7. Dacotah group.

Owen Dorsey, describing the Dacotahs or Sioux, says: "There are no slaves among the Siouan tribes" [3]). This assertion is strengthened by the other authors [4]) making no mention of slaves. Mrs. E. G. Eastman tells us, that captive women and children were well treated and restored on the conclusion of peace; but often they preferred to remain with their new husbands and adopted parents. Copway and Neill also speak of captive children being adopted [5]).

Mathews states, that the Hidatsas generally adopt the children captured in war, and treat them like their own. When grown-up they sometimes return to their own tribe, but most often remain where they are [6]).

Owen Dorsey informs us that among the Omahas "Slavery was not known". "Captives were not slain by the Omahas and Ponkas. When peace was declared, the captives were sent home, if they wished to go. If not they could remain where they were, and were treated as if they were members of the tribe; but they were not adopted by any one" [7]). This positive statement is not weakened by James's assertion about captive women becoming slaves [8]).

---

1) Ibid., pp. 101, 108. — 2) Histoire de la Virginie, p. 261. — 3) Owen Dorsey, Siouan Soc., p. 215. — 4) Eastman, Dahcotah; Eastman, Indian Wars; Reports of Expl., Vol. I; Möllhausen; Ten Kate, Noord-Amerika; Schoolcraft. — 5) Eastman, Indian Wars, p 412; Copway, pp. 65, 66; Neill, pp. 340, 526. — 6) Mathews, p. 47. — 7) Owen Dorsey, Omaha Soc., pp. 364, 332. — 8) James, p. 299.

Hunter states that among the Osage and Kansas Indians prisoners were adopted into the conquering tribe, as husbands, wives and children [1]).

Of the Assiniboins we are told: "Chiefs never receive a gift, considering it a degradation to accept anything but what their own prowess or superior qualities of manhood acquire for them. Their hearts are so good and strong that they scorn to take anything, and self-denial and the power to resist temptation to luxury or easily acquired property is a boast with them" [2]). Where even the chiefs rely only on their own prowess, the existence of slavery is improbable.

Lewis and Clark, describing the Mandans, speak of prisoners living among them. One of their chiefs had been taken prisoner and adopted by them, "and he now enjoys great consideration among the tribe." In another place they tell us of a woman, who was sold as a slave to a Mandan chief, who brought her up and afterwards married her [3]). The evidence is not sufficient to decide, whether their prisoners were held as slaves or were adopted into the tribe.

8. Oregon group.

Gibbs describes the tribes of Western Washington and North-Western Oregon in general. The principal of these tribes are the Chinooks and the tribes about Puget Sound. "Slavery," says Gibbs, "is thoroughly interwoven with the social policy of the Indians of the coast section of Oregon and Washington Territory. East of the Cascades, though it exists, it is not so common.... Southward it ceases, so far as my observation has gone, with the Siskiou Mountains, which divide Oregon from California" [4]).

"By the Flatheads," says Bancroft, "captives are generally killed by their sufferings." McLean, speaking of their wars, remarks: "When one party lost more than the other, com-

---

1) Hunter, Gedenkschriften, pp. 268, 270, 271. — 2) Reports of Expl..Vol. XII Part I p. 76 — 3) Lewis and Clark, I pp. 175, 242; see also pp. 212, 233. — 4) Gibbs, p. 188.

pensation was made in slaves or some other kind of property" [1]).
This statement does not, however, prove that slavery existed
among them; these "slaves" might be members of the tribe,
delivered up either to be killed or adopted. So we are left in
doubt as to the existence of slavery [2]).

The Chinooks had slaves. Bancroft says: "Slavery, common
to all the coast families, is also practised by the Chinooks; ....
the slaves are obliged to perform all the drudgery for their
masters, and their children must remain in their parents'
condition, their round heads serving as a distinguishing mark
from freemen". Kane also gives many particulars about their
slave system [3]). Equally Swan, describing the Chinooks and
neighbouring tribes, makes mention of slavery as practised by
them [4]). Lewis and Clark speak of a war, in which the Killamucks took several prisoners. "These, as far as we could perceive,
were treated very well, and though nominally slaves, yet
were adopted into the families of their masters, and the young
ones placed on the same footing with the children of the
purchaser". This short note is not sufficient for us to arrive
at any definite conclusion, the less so, as these writers themselves declare that they had not the opportunity of making
a close study of the tribes of the Pacific Coast [5]).

"The Shushwaps," Bancroft remarks, "are said to have no
slaves" [6]). Among the Okanagans, a division of the Shushwaps,
according to Ross, "there are but few slaves .... and these
few are adopted as children, and treated in all respects as
members of the family" [7]). From this it would seem that
slavery proper does not exist.

Another division of the Shushwaps are the Atnahs on Fraser
River (not to be confused with the Atnas on Copper River).
Mackenzie describes a division of Indians, whom he does not
mention under a separate name; but they seem to be akin to
the Atnahs. "The Atnah and Chin tribe," says Mackenzie, "as

---

1) Bancroft, p. 269; McLean, p. 54. — 2) The Flatheads of Fort George, who in Kane's
time kept slaves, are described by him as consisting principally of Chinooks and
Klickataats. We are not sure whether these Flatheads are the same as those mentioned
by Bancroft and Mc.Lean. (See Kane, pp. 173, 175, 181). — 3) Bancroft, p. 240; Kane, pp.
181, 182. — 4) Swan, The Northwest Coast, pp. 166, 167, etc. — 5) Lewis and Clark, II
pp. 344, 345, 313, 314. — 6) Bancroft, p. 276. — 7) Ross, as quoted by Bancroft, l. c.

far as I can judge from the very little I saw of that people, bear the nearest resemblance to them." On these Indians he remarks: "The strangers who live among these people are kept by them in a state of awe and subjection" [1]. These strangers perhaps are slaves; but the lack of further details prevents our arriving at any positive conclusion.

Bancroft, after describing the manner in which some tribes put their prisoners to death, adds: "Among the Sahaptins some survive and are made slaves.... The Nez Percé system is a little less cruel in order to save the life for future slavery" [2]. So the Sahaptins or Nez Percés seem to have kept slaves, though we should wish for some more particulars that would exclude all doubt.

Powers states, that female slaves are more numerous among the Shastika than among the Californians [3]. This short note is the only evidence we have been able to collect on the subject.

Kane makes mention of slavery as practised by some other tribes, about which we could not collect further information (perhaps they are subdivisions of the tribes already enumerated) viz. the Macaws, Babines or Big-lips, Nasquallies and Kye-uses [4].

9. Californians.

Of the Northern Californians Bancroft tells us: "Although I find no description of an actual system of slavery existing among them, yet there is no doubt that they have slaves. Illegitimate children are the life-slaves of some male relative of the mother, and upon them the drudgery falls; they are only allowed to marry one in their own station, and their sole hope of emancipation lies in a slow accumulation of allicochick (shell-money), with which they can buy their freedom" [5].

Powers gives some more particulars about two North Californian tribes. Among the Karoks it is thought ignominious for a man to have connection with a female slave. When the

---

1) Mackenzie, II pp. 217, 263. — 2) Brancroft, p. 269. — 3 Powers, p. 248. — 4) Kane, pp. 237, 242, 248, 320. — 5) Bancroft, pp. 349, 351.

purchase-money for the wife has not been paid, the children are looked upon as bastards; they live as outcasts and marry none but persons of their own condition. Among the Hupas a similar system prevails. A bastard is much despised; when old enough he is taken from his mother and becomes the property of one of her male relatives; he is not a slave, and yet has no share in the privileges of the family. The produce of his labour belongs to his master; he may marry only a person of his own condition, and is treated with ignominy. What he wins by gaming is his own; when this amounts to 15 or 20 dollars, he is free. His children are of the same rank [1]).

Although these bastards present a close resemblance to slaves, Powers explicitly says that they are not slaves. Probably they are only a despised class; for social status, among these tribes, depends largely upon wealth. The chief "obtains his position from his wealth, and usually manages to transmit his effects, and with them his honours, to his posterity" [2]). "The ruling passion of the savage seems to be love of wealth; having it he is respected, without it he is despised" [3]). We may therefore suppose, that these bastards are despised because penniless, and as soon as they possess 15 or 20 dollars, respected for their wealth. And as we "find no description of an actual system of slavery existing among them," slavery probably does not exist [4]).

Gatschet, describing the Klamath Indians, makes mention of slaves. Once they attacked the Pit River Indians, "killed the men, abducted the women and children to their homes, or sold them into slavery at the international bartering place at The Dalles." According to Judge E. Steele "they had been selling to whites and others Indian children of their own and other tribes, and also squaws, the latter mainly for the purpose of prostitution" [5]). Whether all slaves were sold abroad, or any slaves were kept by them, does not appear. According to Bancroft "Mr. Drew asserts that the Klamath children of slave

---

1) Powers, pp. 22, 75, 76. — 2) Hubbard, as quoted by Bancroft, p. 348. — 3) Bancroft, p. 360. — 4) This conclusion of ours is strengthened by the following statement of Gibbs, which we have already referred to: "Southward it [slavery] ceases, so far as my observation has gone, with the Siskiou Mountains, which divide Oregon from California." (Gibbs, p. 188). — 5) Gatschet, pp. 59, 62; see also pp. 60, 16.

parents, who, it may be, prevent the profitable prostitution or sale of the mother, are killed without compunction" [1]). Altogether the notes given by our informants are insufficient for us to decide, whether slavery really exists here.

On the Central Californians Bancroft remarks: "Slavery in any form is rare, and hereditary bondage unknown." "They do not appear to have kept or sold prisoners as slaves, but to have either exchanged or killed them" [2]). Here "rare" is perhaps a synonym for "absent"; at any rate the existence of slavery here is doubtful.

As for the Southern Californians, according to Bancroft, "Hugo Reid affirms of the natives of Los Angeles County that all prisoners, after being tormented in the most cruel manner, are invariably put to death...... Female prisoners are either sold or retained as slaves" [3]). From Boscana's narrative also it would appear, that there were formerly slaves among them. "No quarter" he says "was ever given, and consequently, no prisoners were ever made among the men, excepting of such as were killed, or mortally wounded. These were immediately decapitated..... The women and children taken prisoners, were either disposed of by sale or detained by the captain as slaves..... The women and children were never released, — ever remaining as slaves to their enemies" [4]). But as no more details are added and as Boscana describes a state of things which in his time had already ceased to exist, we are not quite sure whether slaves were really kept by these Indians.

The Nishinam, according to Powers, killed their male prisoners. Women, after being flogged, were married; but sometimes they were also killed [5]). So it seems that they had no slaves.

10. New Mexicans.

On the Shoshones and Utahs we are not very well informed. "An act which passed the legislature of Utah in 1852....

---

1) Bancroft, p. 349. — 2) Ibid., pp. 388, 381. — 3) Ibid., p. 407.— 4) Boscana, in "Life in California", pp. 308, 309. — 5) Powers, p. 322.

set forth that from time immemorial slavery has been a customary traffic among the Indians." But we are not told who
bought and who sold the slaves. It is only stated that the
Utahs sold their wives and children into slavery to the Navajos [1]). It is not probable that the Shoshones and Utahs
themselves had slaves; for Bancroft states that prisoners of
war were killed, or in some cases dismissed unhurt, and Meline
tells us, that the Utes and Pueblos almost invariably sold their
prisoners to the Mexicans for slaves [2]).

Bancroft, describing the Apache family (including Apaches,
Comanches, Navajos, Mojaves, etc.), says: "All the natives of
this family hold captives as slaves" [3]). But his account of the
Comanches does not quite agree with this general statement:
"Prisoners belong to the captors and the males are usually
killed, but women are reserved and become the wives or
servants of their owners, while children of both sexes are
adopted into the tribe" [4]). According to Schoolcraft, "prisoners
of war belong to the captors and may be sold or released at
their will". Captive children are adopted and afterwards are
on a level with the members of the tribe [5]). Gregg speaks of
prisoners being enslaved and ill-treated by the conquerors.
But whether he means to say that they remained slaves is not
clear [6]). Cessac also speaks of slaves. "If, among the captives of
the deceased, one was particularly loved by his master, he is
sacrificed and buried with him." "If a favourite slave is sacrificed,
it is to give the master a fellow-traveller." No more particulars
about these slaves are given. In their wars against the Mexicans
they spare none but the children, whom they treat as their own.
"These captives forget their origin and later on, when full-grown,
become an integral part of the tribe" [7]). It is not clear whether
the slaves Cessac speaks of are identical with these adopted
children; he would not have used then the term "slave" in its
proper sense. Ten Kate, a careful observer, states that a
number of Mexican captives, altogether about fifty, live among
the Comanches and Kioways; they have almost entirely adopted

---

1) Bancroft, p. 436. — 2) Bancroft, p. 433; Meline, p. 120. — 3) Bancroft., p. 510. —
4) Ibid., p. 500. — 5) Schoolcraft, I pp. 232, 235. — 6) Gregg, II p. 243. — 7) Cessac,
pp. 115, 116.

the manners and customs of the Indians and are regarded by the latter as members of their tribes [1]). Another author tells us of a Mexican boy and girl, taken prisoners by the Comanches. The boy was afterwards sold to the Cherokees, the girl was married against her will by a Comanche. Another captive Mexican woman was married to a Comanche chief [2]). Comparing these several statements, we think it probable, though not quite certain, that the Comanches did not keep slaves, but adopted their prisoners.

Ten Kate's above-quoted statement applies also to the Kioways. Möllhausen met with two young Mexican prisoners among them, a man and a woman. The young man declared, that he did not want to exchange his present abode for another. The woman, though married to a chief and mother of a young chief, expressed the wish to return to her own country; but the chief would not let her and her child go [3]). We may suppose, that the same state of things prevailed here as among the Comanches.

Of the Apaches proper Bancroft (besides his above-quoted general statement) says: "They treat their prisoners cruelly; scalping them, or burning them at the stake; yet, ruled as they are by greediness, they are always ready to exchange them for horses, blankets, beads, or other property. When hotly pursued, they murder their male prisoners, preserving only the females and children, and the captured cattle" [4]). This is not very suggestive of slavery; and Bancroft's general statement about the Apache family appears rather strange. Schoolcraft tells us: "These [the chiefs] can have any number of wives they choose; but one .only is the favourite. She is admitted to his confidence, and superintends his household affairs; all the other wives are slaves to her; next come his *peons*, or slaves, and his wife's slaves, and the servants of his concubines; then the young men or warriors, most generally composed of the youth who have deserted other tribes on account of crimes, and have fled to the protection of the chief of this tribe .... Then come the herdsmen, and so on" [5]). These

---

1) Ten Kate, Noord-Amerika, pp. 382, 384. — 2) Reports of Expl., Vol. III Part I pp. 22, 31. — 3) Möllhausen, p. 137. — 4) Bancroft, p. 498. — 5) Schoolcraft, V p. 210.

"slaves", ranking even above the warriors, very probably were
not slaves in the true sense of the word. According to Bourke,
the Mexican captives, living among the Apaches, were treated
very kindly and often rose to positions of great influence. It
does not appear that these captives were kept in a slave-like
state. Fremont and Emory say: "Women, when captured, are
taken as wives by those who capture them, but they are treated
by the Indian wives of the capturers as slaves". It is evident
that we have not to do here with slaves in the true sense.
Taking into consideration all the foregoing statements, we may
suppose that slavery did not exist among the Apaches [1]).

In an above-quoted passage Bancroft states that the Utahs
frequently sell their wives and children as slaves to the
Navajos. According to Bent, the Navajos, "have in their possession many prisoners, men, women and children, ... whom
they hold and treat as slaves" [2]). But these statements are not
sufficient for us to go upon; these prisoners may be adopted,
or indended to be sold, as well as kept as slaves.

Miss Olive Oatman, who had been detained among the Mohaves
or Mojaves, says: "They invented modes and seemed to create
necessities of labour that they might gratify themselves by taxing
us to the utmost, and even took unwarranted delight in whipping
us on beyond our strength. And all their requests and exact-
ions were couched in the most insulting and taunting language
and manner, as it then seemed, and as they had the frankness
soon to confess, to fume their hate against the race to whom
we belonged. Often under the frown and lash were we compelled to labour for whole days upon an allowance amply sufficient to starve a common dandy civilized idler" [3]). Though
such prisoners are held in a slave-like state, yet evidently
the object of the masters in imposing disagreeable work upon
them is not to get useful labourers, but to "fume their hate".
This account may warn us against attaching too much value
to statements about slavery among similar tribes, especially
where the "slaves" are whites. For such tribes as the Apaches,
who are always ready to exchange their prisoners for some

---

1) Bourke, pp. 128, 129; Fremont and Emory, p. 150. — 2) Bent, as quoted by Bancroft,
p. 510. — 3) Stratton, as quoted bij Bancroft, p. 511.

property, will be very apt to take prisoners, especially whites, who are likely to offer a better ransom than Indians. In such cases the prisoners are not killed; for by killing them the Indians would lose their ransom ; but they may safely, as in Miss Oatman's case, be treated as slaves by way of vengeance. But where these are the only slaves existing, a regular slave-system does not prevail. As for the Mohaves, no more particulars being given, we do not know whether they have slaves.

In Bancroft's account of the Pueblo tribes no mention is made of slavery. On the Pimas he informs us: "If prisoners are taken, the males are crucified or otherwise cruelly put to death, and the women and children sold as soon as possible" 1).

In Parker Winship's article it is quoted from Mendoza's letter, that the Cibola Pueblo "keep those whom they capture in war as slaves" 2). This being the only reference made to slavery, we are unable to decide whether it really existed.

Ten Kate in his detailed account of the Zuñi (a Pueblo tribe) makes no mention of slavery; so they probably have no slaves 3).

Bancroft, describing the Lower Californians, has nothing about slavery. Although their battles are described at some length, no mention is made of captives; probably they took no prisoners 4). We may therefore safely infer, that slavery did not exist among them.

Result. Positive cases: *Aleuts,* 5)
Athka Aleuts,
Koniagas,
Tlinkits,
Haidas,
Tsimshian,
Kwakiutl,
Bilballas,
Ahts,
Tribes about Puget Sound,
Fish Indians,

---

1) Bancroft. p. 543; see also Meline's above-quoted statement about the Pueblos. — 2) Parker Winship, p. 548. — 3) Ten Kate, Noord-Amerika; see also Möllhausen, and Reports of Expl., Vol. III. — 4) Bancroft, p. 562. — 5) The names printed in italics contain the clear, the other the more doubtful cases (vide p. 46).

Tacullies,
Atnas on Copper River,
Similkameem,
Chinooks,
Atnahs on Fraser River and allied tribes,
Sahaptins or Nez Percés,
Southern Californians,
Klamaths,
Navajos,
Cibola Pueblos.

Negative cases: *Greenlanders,*
Central Eskimos,
Eskimos of Labrador,
Frobisher Bay and Field Bay Eskimos,
Kinipetu Eskimos,
Tchiglit Eskimos,
Eskimos of the Ungava District,
Western Eskimos or Eskimos of Alaska,
Eskimos of Point Barrow,
Kutchins or Loucheux,
Chepewyans or Athabascas,
Lenape or Delawares,
Montagnais,
Ojibways or Chippeways,
Ottawas,
Shahnees,
Potawatomi,
Crees or Knisteneaux,
Cheyennes,
Blackfeet nation,
Abenakies,
Iroquois,
Hurons or Wyandots,
Katahbas,
Cherokees,
Muskoghe,
Choctaws,
Chickasaws,
Creeks,

Seminoles,
Natchez,
Dacotahs or Sioux,
Hidatsas,
Omahas,
Osages,
Kansas Indians,
Assiniboins,
Hupas,
Apaches,
Pimas,
Zuñi,
Lower Californians,
Okanagans,
Karoks,
Central Californians,
Nishinam,
Shoshones,
Utahs,
Comanches,
Kioways.

No conclusion : Menomini,
Attakapas,
Inhabitants of Virginia,
Mandans,
Flatheads,
Killamucks,
Shastika,
Mohaves.

We may add here a short account of Negro-slavery among the Indians.

According to the census of 1860, several Indian tribes had Negro-slaves. Our informant enumerates the Choctaws, Cherokees, Creeks and Chickasaws. Slavery was carried on to a great extent; some owners had from 50 tot 200 slaves [1]). We may remember that all these tribes originally had no slaves.

The Creeks already in Bartram's time (1789) had slaves.

1) Boudin, pp. 826, 827. Gregg (II p. 195) also states that Negro slaves were to be found among these tribes.

He tells us of a chief who kept 15 Negroes; they were slaves
until they married Indian women, and then acquired the privileges of the tribe. Schoolcraft informs us that "if an Indian
should murder a Negro, the law is satisfied with the value
of the Negro being paid to the owner" [1]).

The Seminoles also had Negro-slaves, according to Roosevelt
and Gregg [2]). But Maccauley is not quite certain about it.
He observed a few Negroes living with them. It had been
said that they were slaves; but our informant is not of that
opinion [3]). Maccauley's account, however, dates from a later
period than the other statements.

The Shahnees in Gregg's time also kept a few Negro slaves [4]).

But these facts do not represent phenomena of unadulterated
savage life. These Indian tribes had already undergone great
changes by contact with the whites. Moreover, the Negroes
kept by them as slaves were in a very peculiar condition,
living in a foreign continent amongst foreign races. So we
are justified in omitting these cases from our list of slave-
keeping Indian tribes.

§ 3. Central and South America.

About the treatment of prisoners by the wild tribes of North
Mexico Bancroft remarks: "Seldom is sex or age spared, and
when prisoners are taken, they are handed over to the women
for torture, who treat them most inhumanly, heaping upon
them every insult devisable, besides searing their flesh with
burning brands, and finally burning them at the stake, or
sacrificing them in some equally cruel manner. Many cook
and eat the flesh of their captives, reserving the bones as
trophies" [5]). These particulars given, and no mention being
made of slaves, slavery probably does not exist among them.

Among the wild tribes of Central Mexico "the heads of the
slain were placed on poles and paraded through their villages
in token of victory, the inhabitants meanwhile dancing round
them. Young children were sometimes spared, and reared to

---

1) Bartram, p. 38; Schoolcraft, I p. 277. — 2) Roosevelt, I p. 59; Gregg, l. c. —
3) Maccauley, p. 526. — 4) Gregg, II p. 196. — 5) Bancroft, p. 581.

fight in the ranks of their conquerors, and in order to bru-
talize their youthful minds and eradicate all feelings of affection
toward their own kindred, the youthful captives were given
to drink the brains and blood of their murdered parents" [1]).
Whether these children became slaves is not quite clear;
we should think not, as they were "reared to fight in the
ranks of their conquerors"; but this may also be the case
with slaves [2]). The lack of further particulars prevents our
arriving at a positive conclusion.

Bancroft's notes on the wild tribes of South Mexico are very
scanty. They sacrificed their prisoners. The Mayas had female
slaves [3]).

Bancroft informs us that "one principal object of war among
the ancient nations of Honduras was to make slaves; but the
Mosquito Coast was free from this scourge, according to all
accounts." "When prisoners were taken they were usually
held as slaves, after having the nose cut off . . . . The coast
people . . . . usually kill their prisoners." Wickham, who gives
a detailed account of the Woolwa or Soumoo of the Mosquito
Coast, makes no mention of slavery [4]). So the inhabitants of
Honduras had slaves, whereas those of the Mosquito Coast had not.

Slavery, according to Bancroft, was in force among the
inhabitants of the Isthmus of Panama and Costa Rica, with
the exception of the Caribs. "The prisoner is the slave of the
captor; he is branded on the face and one of his front teeth
knocked out. The Caribs however used to kill and eat their
prisoners". Gabb, who gives several particulars about the
tribes of Costa Rica, makes no mention of slavery. According
to Pokalowsky, the Indians of Coctu in Costa Rica, when
conquered by the Spaniards in the 16th century, had slaves.
"They cut off the heads of their prisoners and preserve them
as trophies; the boys and girls of the enemies are enslaved
or sacrificed to their gods. If a master dies, his slaves are
killed and buried with him; this custom prevails here to a
greater extent than in any other part of India" [5]).

---

1) Bancroft, p. 629. — 2) So for instance among the Tlinkits; see Niblack, p. 252. —
3) Bancroft, pp. 656, 663. — 4) Bancroft, pp. 729, 723; Wickham. — 5) Bancroft, pp.
771, 764; Gabb; Pokalowsky, p. 50.

Bancroft's statement about the Caribs of the Isthmus is confirmed by the fact that Pinart, who has largely drawn upon ancient Spanish literature, makes no mention of slavery [1]).

Rochefort speaks of slavery existing among the Caribs of the Antilles. They believed, that the bravest warriors of their nation after death would live in happy islands, and have their enemies, the Arawaks, for slaves, whereas the cowards would be the slaves of the Arawaks. In their wars with the Spaniards they did not kill the Negro slaves, but took them with them and made them work. Sometimes slaves were killed after their master's death, to serve him in the other world. Male prisoners were killed and eaten after a few days. Captive women became slaves; their children were reared with those of the Caribs. Female prisoners were sometimes taken for wives; then the children were free, but the mothers remained slaves. In the isle of Saint Vincent there were in Rochefort's time English boys and girls, captured when very young; they had quite forgotten their parents, and would not even return with them, so accustomed were they to the mode of life of the Caribs, who treated them very kindly, just as if they were of their own nation. De la Borde makes no mention of slaves [2]). It seems to us very doubtful whether slavery really existed here. Rochefort's statement that captive children were reared with those of the conquerors is more suggestive of adoption of captives than of slavery, and the enslavement of Negroes by the Indians is something foreign to the aboriginal state of things, as has been said before. So we cannot arrive at a definite conclusion.

The Continental Caribs, according to Gumilla, killed all their prisoners, except the young women and children, whom they sold [3]). So slavery probably did not exist among them.

Ling Roth, in his article on Hispaniola or Hayti (inhabited by Arawaks), makes no mention of slavery; but this does not prove much, as his sources of information (early Spanish literature) were very incomplete. For instance, he has not been able to find anything bearing on the division of labour between the sexes [4]).

---

1) Pinart, see pp. 33, 48. — 2) Rochefort, pp. 430, 478, 512, 480, 489, 477; de la Borde. — 3) Gumilla, II p. 255. — 4) Ling Roth, Hispaniola; see especially p. 272.

The several describers of the Indians of Guiana [1]) make no mention of slavery. The tribes most fully described are the Arawaks, Warraus, Macusi and Roucouyennes. Martius however states that the Arawaks have slaves, who work in their houses and on the fields [2]). So we are not certain about the Arawaks; but we may safely suppose that among the three other tribes slavery does not exist.

The Saliva of Columbia, according to Gumilla, made war in order to acquire slaves to till their lands [3]).

In Sievers', Reclus' and Simons' descriptions of the Goajiro no mention is made of slaves [4]). According to De Brettes, however, "slavery exists; but the slave is a member of the family, though looked upon as an inferior being that may be killed if he refuses to obey". A few more details are added about these slaves [5]). Sievers, reviewing De Brettes' articles, remarks that this author is generally not very trustworthy, but that the ethnographical parts are the best of his work. Speaking of a photograph of Goajiro slaves given by De Brettes, he adds: "If there can be any question at all of slavery among them" [6]). On the same page, however, he translates De Brettes' ethnographical account of the Goajiro, in which it is stated that slavery exists, without any commentary. Considering all this, we cannot arrive at any accurate conclusion.

De Lery, speaking of the ancient Tupinambas, describes at considerable length the fate of their captives, who were killed and eaten; even the child of a captive and a woman of their own tribe was not allowed to live. Though an expert hunter or fisher, and a woman well able to work, were preserved somewhat longer than the rest, all were invariably killed after a few months. Nowhere in De Lery's book does it appear, that they made slaves by capture or by any other means [7]). According to another ancient writer, however, they kept prisoners as slaves. The slaves were kindly treated, allowed to

---

1) Im Thurn; Brett; R. Schomburgk; R. H. Schomburgk; Joest, Guyana; Bonaparte; Goudreau; Vidal; van Coll. — 2) Martius, p. 693. — 3) Gumilla, II p. 254. — 4) Sievers, Sierra Nevada; Reclus; Simons. — 5) De Brettes, pp. 94, 96, 78—80. — 6) Sievers, Des Grafen Josef de Brettes Reisen, pp. 381, 382. — 7) De Lery, pp. 225—242; see especially pp. 225, 236. Stade gives a similar account of the treatment of prisoners, quoted by Andree, pp. 85—88.

marry free women, but finally killed and eaten. They had to catch fish and game and to bring it to their master. Without the master's consent they were not allowed to work for others. If they tried to escape and were caught, they were killed. A slave, who died a natural death, was not buried but thrown away in the bush [1]). All this is very suggestive of slavery. But the fact, that D'Evreux got his information through an interpreter, prevents us from decidedly concluding, against the testimony of our other informants, that the Tupinambas kept slaves.

Martius remarks about the Indians of Brazil in general: "Many of these tribes keep slaves.... Captivity in war is the only cause by which one loses his freedom, especially' if a male; for the husband may sell his wife and children; but this is of rare occurence" [2]).

The Apiacas (a group of the Central Tupis), according to the same author, in their wars kill all adult prisoners, male and female, and eat them. Children they take with them and rear them with their own; they make them work in the plantations; but when about twelve or fourteen years old, these children are killed and eaten [3]). Though these children may be kept in a somewhat slave-like state, a tribe that kills its slaves when full-grown is not properly to be called a slave-keeping tribe.

The same author informs us, that the Mundrucus and Mauhés have slaves [4]).

Of the Miranhas we are told that they enslave their prisoners; but usually these prisoners are intended to be sold to the whites. It does not appear whether any of them are kept for the Miranhas' own use [5]).

Keane, von Tschudi and Ehrenreich make no mention of slavery among the Botocudos. According to Zu Wied "the conqueror persecutes the vanquished, and but seldom makes captives, at least among the Botocudos; but on the Belmonte there are said to be seen some who were used as slaves for all kinds of work" [6]). We do not know what this last second-hand information of Zu Wied's is worth; but we are justified

---

1) D'Evreux, pp. 21, 46, 52—54. — 2) Martius, pp. 71, 74. — 3) Ibid., pp. 206, 207. — 4) Ibid., p. 71. — 5) Ibid., p. 73. — 6) Keane; von Tschudi; Ehrenreich, Botocudos; Zu Wied, Brasilien, II p. 45. Martius (p. 326) apparently relies entirely on Zu Wied.

in inferring that the Botocudos in general (except those on Rio Belmonte) have no slaves.

Azara states that in his time (he travelled in South America from 1781 to 1801) the Guaycurù had nearly died out, only one man being left [1]). But according to Boggiani Guaycurù is a general name for the tribes that inhabit the Gran Chaco [2]), so this statement of Azara's seems to apply to a small division of the Guaycurù only. Southey and Martius give some particulars about the slave system of the Guaycurù [3]); but Colini, who has taken great pains to ascertain the identity of these tribes, quotes these descriptions as referring to the Mbayás. Of the ancient Guaycurù he says: "In their combats they gave no quarter to the adult males; but they spared the lives of the youths, whom they educated after their customs and gave in marriage to their daughters, so as to augment the number of their tribe. Full-grown women were sold to the neighbouring nations, who made them slaves" [4]). The only captives whom they kept among them, the youths, were not slaves; so slavery probably did not exist among them.

Two tribes inhabiting the Gran Chaco and so belonging to the Guaycurù in Boggiani's sense, are described by Thouar. Of the Chiriguanos he says: "The prisoners are the property of their captors and must serve the mistress of the hut." In his description of the Tobas he makes no mention of slavery [5]). Thouar, however, does not seem to be very well informed [6]).

The Mbayás, according to Azara, in his time had two kinds of slaves, one composed of the Guanás, the other of Indian and Spanish prisoners of war. But the former were no real slave class. The Guanás "used to repair in troops to the Mbayás, to obey and serve them and till their lands without any payment. Hence the Mbayás always call them their slaves. This slavery is indeed very mild, as the Guaná voluntarily submits to it, and leaves off whenever he likes." Such "slaves", who lead a tribal life and come and go when they like, certainly are not slaves. The others however were real slaves. They procured the fuel, cooked the food, took care of the horses

---

1) Azara, II p. 146. — 2) Boggiani, p. 80. — 3) Southey III, pp. 391, 392; Martius, pp. 232, 233, 71. — 4) Colini, in Boggiani, p. 297. — 5) Thouar, pp. 51, 60 sqq. — 6) See Steinmetz, Strafe, I p. 174 note 1.

and tilled the land. When Azara once offered a present to a Mbayá, the latter would not take it himself, but ordered his slaves to receive it for him. Even the poorest Mbayá had three of four slaves. During the mourning-time women and slaves were not allowed to speak or eat any meat. One place in Azara's book seems to show that they had no slaves: "They said they had received a divine command to wage war against all nations, kill the adult males and adopt the women and children, in order to augment their number." But where the recorded tradition and the description of the actual state of things disagree, we hold that the latter is to be accepted [1]). Colini refers to Azara and Martius, and then adds: "Serra however asserts that among the Mbayás slavery proper (*la schiavitù vera e propria*) did not exist; the slaves might rather be called servants." They fought together with the freemen and took part in the public council, even when it decided upon war and peace. They married free persons, but were themselves looked upon as slaves. On the master's death, the sons or next relations, according to the rules of inheritance, became masters of the slaves; but these rights were only nominal. The slaves gradually merged into the tribe. Yet it was always considered degrading to be a descendant of a slave; those who had in their ancestry none but members of the tribe were very proud of it. Generally the best slave girls were married to their masters; the boys of greatest promise were treated as sons, whereas the others were set to do the ruder work [2]). This account, however, does not prove that the captives were not slaves. Some of the boys only were treated as sons; what were the rest if not slaves? And even slaves may to a certain degree be treated as sons. The slaves gradually coalesced with the tribe (though not entirely); but we are told that this change took place "through personal merits and intermarriage." This shows that all captives were not on a level with the freemen; probably it was only the most deserving prisoners, and the offspring of slaves and freemen, who attended the public council and were on an equal footing with the main body of tribesmen. Slaves may be kindly treated and yet be slaves.

---

1) Azara II, pp. 96, 108—110, 119. — 2) Colini, in Boggiani, p. 316.

Our opinion is, that we have here a *schiavitù vera e propria*; the more so, as the description given by Azara leads to the same conclusion.

The present Caduvei, according to Boggiani, are the same people as the ancient Mbayás. Very probably he is right here. Yet we have seen how much confusion there is in the application of the terms Guaycurù and Mbayás; so we are a little sceptical. Moreover, there is a great lapse of time between the early descriptions of the Mbayás and Boggiani's travels, and during that time their state of culture has greatly changed; from nomadic hunters they have in the 19th century become settled agriculturists [1]). So we are justified in treating them separately. The Caduvei keep slaves. The slaves are well treated, but looked upon as an inferior race. The ruder kinds of work, and the tilling of the soil, fall to their share. As a rule they are kindly treated, without being allowed to forget their duties. The Caduvei exchange the slaves among them for horses, cattle and various commodities [2]).

Pohl states, that the Canoeiros had captured a young man and treated him well [3]). Nothing more being added, we cannot make out whether slavery exists.

Of the tribes of Central Brasil, visited by Von den Steinen, the principal are the Bakaïri, Paressi, Bororo, Suya and Yuruna. In his description of the Bakaïri, Paressi and Bororo he makes no mention of slavery. If it existed, this careful observer would certainly have mentioned it. Neither is a word about slaves to be found in Hensel's description of the Coroados, who are often identified with the Bororo [4]).

Among the Suya Von den Steinen observed Indians of other tribes, who were kept as slaves. The presents, which the author gave to one of these slaves, had to be delivered to his master [5]).

The same writer speaks of captives residing among the Yuruna; but his short remark on this subject cannot lead us to a safe conclusion as to the existence of slavery among them [6]).

The Karayas on Rio Araguaya keep captive women in a somewhat slave-like state. Prisoners of war, adopted into the

---

1) Boggiani, pp. 305, 310. — 2) Boggiani, p. 100. — 3) Pohl, p. 163. — 4) Von den Steinen, Unter den Naturvölkern; von den Steinen, Durch Central-Brasilien; Hensel. — 5) Von den Steinen, Durch Central-Brasilien, p. 211. — 6) Ibid., p. 265.

tribe, sometimes are made chiefs if they have distinguished themselves [1]). This is not very suggestive of slavery; but the details given are not sufficient for us to arrive at a clear conclusion.

On the Záparos we get this scanty information. They are always at war, killing many of the men, and stealing the women, children and chattels of the enemies, the children either for use as servants or for sale. A boy or girl stolen by them is commonly sold to traders [2]). Apparently the author himself is in doubt, whether any of these captives are kept as slaves.

Some savage tribes of Peru are treated of by Ordinaire. In his account of the Campas or Antis there is nothing bearing on slavery. He states that he met with a Lorenzo child living among the Campas; but it is not clear whether this was a slave; and the rest of his ample record makes the existence of slavery rather improbable [3]).

About the Conibas and kindred tribes the same writer remarks, that among their wives there are some slaves captured from neighbouring tribes. But as he states, that all the fatiguing work is incumbent on women, it would seem, that there are no male slaves and therefore no slavery proper. Prisoners of war are killed at their feasts [4]). From a description of about a hundred years ago we learn, that these tribes kept prisoners as slaves. Several of these slaves were observed among the Panos; the masters treated them with as much affection as their own children and married them to their daughters. The conquerors married the captive women in order to augment the number of their tribe [5]). The details given are not sufficient to decide, whether the prisoners merged into the tribe or constituted a slave class.

Smyth and Lowe, speaking of the Sencis of Peru, remark: "They give no quarter, and take no prisoners in the battle ... The women and children are taken for slaves, and if there are any in infancy, or much advanced in age, they are killed as useless." [6]). Whether the fate of the captive women and

---

1) Ehrenreich, Beiträge, pp. 28, 29. — 2) Simson, p. 505. — 3) Ordinaire, pp. 287, 270—273. — 4) Ibid., pp. 308, 309. — 5) Skinner, II pp. 113, 114. — 6) Smyth and Lowe, p. 226.

children was really slavery, is not clear from this short note.

The Guanas probably had no slaves. We are told that the head of the tribe "is obliged to work for his subsistence, as nobody serves him" [1]).

As little does it appear that the Yuracarés and Mocéténès are slave-keeping tribes. The former live in families, and even in these subordination is unknown. The latter are not war-like [2]). It is not, however, a first-rate authority to whom we owe these particulars.

The Chiquitos, according to the same author, in their wild state attacked their neighbours, and made prisoners, to whom they gave their own daughters as wives [3]). Whether these prisoners were slaves is not clear; we should rather think not.

The Chapacuras were very peaceable, and but seldom attacked their neighbours [4]). Whether slavery existed among them we are not told.

The Moxos, in D'Orbigny's time, had already long been civilized and christianized. What their political institutions were in their former wild state we do not know [5]).

Muratori, speaking of the Indians of Paraguay and some neighbouring districts, states that they kill and eat their pri-soners of war. Some tribes, however, he tells us, are more peaceful and take all pains to induce their prisoners to reside among them. Children of prisoners are sold by some of the tribes to other nations [6]). From all this it would seem that slavery did not exist. But we shall presently see, that the other information we have got does not entirely agree with Muratori's general statement.

The principal native tribe of Paraguay were the Abipones, described at large by Dobrizhoffer. The prisoners they made were very leniently treated. They gave them the best of their food, and tended them when ill. The prisoners had daily opportunity to run away, but they did not desire it, for they were very contented. They were never beaten, nor even reproved. They hunted and fought together with the Abipones. And yet they were not merged into the nation of the Abipones;

1) Azara, II p. 96. — 2) D'Orbigny, I pp. 360, 372. — 3) Ibid., II p. 166. — 4) Ibid., II p. 211. — 5) L. c. — 6) Muratori, pp. 29, 128, 129.

for the Abipone women generally would marry only a man
of their own people; and the men never married female
prisoners, nor had they any connection with them. It appears
that every captive was assigned to an individual master. So
we have here to deal with the fact, that one man is the property
of another beyond the limits of the family proper, *i. e.* slavery,
though slavery of an extraordinarily mild character [1]).

The Payaguas in their wars killed all adult men, and preserved
the women and children. What became of the latter does
not appear. The Payaguas were absolutely free and did not
recognize any difference of classes. From this it is probable,
though not certain, that they had no slaves [2]).

The Enimagas, according to Azara, were hunters; agriculture
among them was incumbent on slaves. No further particulars
are given about these slaves. The Enimagas are said formerly
to have held the Mbayas in a kind of slavery; but such a
subjection of a tribe as a whole is not slavery in the true
sense; slavery is subjection of individuals. If the "slaves" the
Enimagas had in Azara's time were of the same description,
they were not slaves [3]). So we cannot arrive here at any
definite conclusion.

D'Orbigny remarks, that the Charruas when at war killed
all the men, and preserved the women and children, whom
they made concubines and slaves [4]). As Azara's statement is
quite different, we shall translate it literally: "All are equal;
nobody serves another; or it must be some old woman who,
having no means of subsistence, joins some family, or assists
at the burying of the dead". In their wars they kill all they
meet, preserving none but the women and the children under
twelve years of age. They take their prisoners along with
them, and let them enjoy their freedom; most of them marry
there and get so much accustomed to this mode of life, that
they but rarely wish to return to their own people [5]). Although
such kind treatment is compatible with slavery, Azara's statement about nobody serving another is positive enough to
exclude all notion of slavery. Heusser and Claraz, who seem

---

1) Dobrizhoffer, II pp. 148—152. — 2) Azara, II pp. 145, 132. — 3) Ibid., pp. 159,
157. — 4) D'Orbigny, II p. 89. — 5) Azara, II pp. 15, 19, 20.

to be well informed, make no mention of slavery [1]). This fact, together with the above-quoted positive statement of Azara, who on the whole seems to be better informed than D'Orbigny [2]), and who also treats this matter much more fully, leads us to conclude that they had no slaves. The lapse of time between Azara's and D'Orbigny's travels (from about 30 to 50 years) might account for the difference of their descriptions; but it seems to us that so much importance need not be attached to the latter's short remark.

The Minuanes, according to Azara, resemble the Charruas in their mode of warfare, and in acknowledging no social classes [3]). We may therefore suppose them to have had no slaves.

The Patagons or Tehuelches, according to Musters and Falkner, have slaves. The same is stated by Letourneau on the authority of Guimard [4]). And as these authors not only assert that there are slaves, but also give some particulars about them, we may be sure that slavery really exists.

About the Puelches we get some information from Azara, who calls them Pampas. "In war they kill all adult males, preserving none but the women and young boys; these they take home and treat in the same manner as the Charruas do. It is true, that they impose some kinds of work upon them, and use them as slaves or servants until they marry; but then they are as free as the others" [5]). Such men, who as soon as they marry are on a level with the members of the tribe, certainly are not slaves.

The Araucanians, according to D'Orbigny, kill their male enemies and enslave the women and children [6]). Molina says: "The prisoners of war, as is the custom of all semibarbarous nations, become *tavaichi, i. e.* slaves, until they are exchanged or ransomed" [7]). In his dètailed description of Araucanian social life he makes no further mention of slaves, nor do the

---

1) Heusser and Claraz. — 2) Azara travelled in South America for 20 years, D'Orbigny for only 7. The former was commissary and commander of the Spanish frontiers in Paraguay; the latter made a journey for scientific purposes, mainly zoölogical. — 3) Azara, II p. 32. — 4) Musters, p. 217; Falkner, pp. 122, 123, 126; Letourneau, p. 123. — 5) Azara, II p. 38. — 6) D'Orbigny, I p. 401. — 7) Molina, p. 74.

other authors [1]). So we may suppose that the prisoners are always exchanged or ransomed, and that slavery is unknown among them.

About the Fuegians we have this positive statement of Hyades and Déniker: "They have no chiefs, no labourers who work for pay, and no slaves" [2]. This statement, already valuable in itself, is corroborated by the fact, that none of the other authors we have consulted on the subject make any mention of slavery [3]).

Result. Positive cases: *Ancient nations of Honduras,*
Inhabitants of Panama and Costa Rica,
Mundrucus,
Mauhés,
Mbayas,
Caduvei,
Suya,
Abipones,
Tehuelches,
Arawaks,
Saliva,
Goajiro,
Tupinambas,
Chiriguanos,
Yuruna,
Sencis,
Enimagas.

Negative cases: *Wild tribes of North Mexico,*
Natives of the Mosquito Coast,
Caribs of the Isthmus,
Warraus,
Macusi,
Roucouyennes,
Apiacas,
Botocudos,
Bakairi,

---

1) Von Bibra; Ochsenius; Smith; Musters. — 2) Hyades et Déniker, p. 242. — 3) Parker Snow; Darwin, Voyage; Vincent; O'Sullivan.

> *Paressi,*
> *Bororo,*
> *Guanas,*
> *Charruas,*
> *Minuanes,*
> *Puelches,*
> *Araucanians,*
> *Fuegians,*
> Wild tribes of Central Mexico,
> Continental Caribs,
> Guaycurû,
> Tobas,
> Karayas,
> Zaparos,
> Campas,
> Conibos,
> Yuracarès,
> Mocéténès,
> Chiquitos,
> Chapacuras,
> Payaguas.

No conclusion: Caribs of the Antilles,
> Wild tribes of South Mexico,
> Natives of Hispaniola,
> Miranhas,
> Canoeiros,
> Moxos.

§ 4. *Australia.*

The Australian tribes, as they are marked on the map in Mr. Thomas's book on the "Natives of Australia", are the following:
In Western Australia: *Yerkla-mining,*
In South Australia: *Eucla,*
> *Arunta,*
> *Urabunna,*
> *Dieri,*
> *Narrinyeri,*

> *Booandik,*
> *Wotjoballak,*
In South Australia (N. Territory): *Mara,*
> *Anula,*
> *Worgaia,*
> *Warramunga,*
> *Kaitish,*
In Victoria: *Wolgai,*
> *Wurinyeri,*
> *Kurnai,*
> *Bangerang,*
In N. S. Wales: *Tongaranka,*
> *Euahlayi,*
> *Kamilaroi,*
> *Wiimbaio,*
> *Geawegal,*
> *Yuin,*
> *Murring,*
In Queensland: *Otati,*
> *Pitta Pitta,*
> *Kiabara,*
> *Kabi,*
> *Turribul.*

The extinct *Tasmanians* also belonged to the Australian group.

Nowhere in all the books and articles we have consulted on the Australian tribes is any mention made of slaves [1]). Now it is true that, whereas on many of these tribes we are well informed, there are others on which we have little information or no information at all. But here our group-argument may be brought to bear. We have to deal here with an isolated district, inhabited by tribes living in similar conditions and physically and psychically resembling each other, so much so, that some ethnographers [2]) and theorists [3]) speak of the Australians as if they were one people, as if all Australians were in exactly the same state of culture. This really is erroneous:

---

1) The literature used is the same as that quoted on p. 22, Chapter I, and besides: Howitt, South-East Australia; Stokes; Mitchell; Hale; Grey; Taplin, as quoted by Woods. — 2) Curr Brough Smyth. Gerland's survey of Australian social life is much better. — 3) *E. g.* Grosse and Letourneau.

there are many differences in several respects between the Australian tribes [1]. But that they can be treated in this manner, proves that the differences are not so very great; it is unimaginable, that Grosse would have spoken in the same way of the American Indians or the Negroes. What we mean to say now is this: our information on some Australian tribes is not sufficient to prove that just in that district which each particular account relates to, slavery does not exist. But then the several accounts strengthen each other; for taking into consideration the great likeness existing between the Australian tribes, it is *a priori* unlikely that some of these tribes would have and others would not have slaves. Moreover, if in any part of Australia slavery existed, our informants probably would have found this too remarkable a fact to leave it unnoticed.

As little mention is made of slaves by those ethnographers who speak of the Australians in general [2]. According to Brough Smyth, "each of the principal men and priests seeks for his food, and ministers to his own wants (with such help as he gets from his wives); and has no one whom he can call servant" [3]. Gerland states that the Australians make no captives, except women sometimes [4].

All this makes it sufficiently clear that the Australians have no slaves [5]. The 30 tribes we have enumerated here may therefore rank as clear cases of savage tribes without slaves.

§ 5. *Melanesia.*

Rochas, describing the New Caledonians, writes: "Slavery does not exist in the New Caledonian society" [6]. Lambert tells us that the only division into social classes is that between the chief and his parents and the common people. Captive children are adopted and enjoy all the privileges of their adoptive

---

1) Comp. Steinmetz's treatment of the problem of Australian chieftainship, Strafe, II pp. 20—42. See also Spencer and Gillen's statement that „whilst undoubtedly there is a certain amount in common as regards social organisation and customs amongst the Australian tribes, yet, on the other hand, there is great diversity" (Native tribes, p. 34). — 2) Curr; Brough Smyth; Gerland. — 3) Brough Smyth, I p. 127. — 4) Waitz-Gerland, VI p. 764. — 5) Letourneau (pp. 26, 35) arrives at the same conclusion. — 6) De Rochas, p. 252.

parents' own children [1]). Brainne informsus, that there are two social classes: chiefs of various kinds, and serfs; the latter term probably means the common people. De Vaux and Legrand make no mention whatever of slaves [2]). According to Glaumont there are four classes, the fourth of which is composed of slaves (*en-dji-dio*) [3]). But no further particulars are given about these slaves in his rather long article. Taking all this in consideration, we are justified in concluding that slavery does not exist.

On the state of things in the Solomon Islands we are well informed by several authors. Elton says: "If a man is married and has got a little money and a few slaves, he calls himself a chief, but does not exercise any power over his slaves; they do pretty well as they like" [4]). Guppy gives this general description of slavery in the Solomon Islands: "In the larger islands the bush-tribes and the coast-natives wage an unceasing warfare, in which the latter are usually the aggressors and the victors — the bushmen captured during these raids either affording materials for the cannibal feast or being detained in servitude by their captors. But there prevails in the group a recognized system of slave-traffic, in which a human being becomes a marketable commodity — the equivalent being represented in goods either of native or of foreign manufacture. This custom, which came under the notice of Surville's expedition, during their visit to Port Praslin in Isabel, in 1769, obtains under the same conditions at the present time. These natives were in the habit of making voyages of ten and twelve days' duration with the object of exchanging men for "fine cloths covered with designs", articles which were manufactured by a race of people much fairer than their own, who were in all probability the inhabitants of Ontong Java. The servitude to which the victims of this traffic are doomed is not usually an arduous one. But there is one grave contingency attached to his thraldom which must be always before the mind of the captive, however lightly his chains of service may lie upon him. When a head is required to satisfy the offended honour of a

---

1) Lambert, pp. 79, 177. — 2) Brainne, p. 239; de Vaux; Legrand. — 3) Glaumont, p. 74. — 4) Elton, p. 98.

neighbouring chief, or when a life has to be sacrificed on the completion of a tambu house or at the launching of a new war-canoe, the victim chosen is usually the man who is not a free-born native of the village. He may have been bought as a child and have lived amongst them from his boyhood up, a slave only in name, and enjoying all the rights of his fellow natives. But no feelings of compassion can save him from his doom; and the only consideration which he receives at the hands of those with whom he may have lived on terms of equality for many years is to be found in the circumstance that he gets no warning of his fate" [1]).

The notes of the other ethnographers relate to single parts of this group. Verguet states that in St. Christoval (in the southeastern part of the group) the slaves "are treated as adopted children; the slave cultivates the master's fields together with the master himself; he helps him to prepare the food and accompanies him when hunting or fighting; he shares in his pleasures as well as in his work; when the tribe celebrates a feast, the slaves are not excluded from it. When full-grown, they marry into their master's tribe, erect their houses next to their master's house or share the latter. Sometimes the master does not disdain to marry his slave" [2]). Codrington, whose notes mainly relate to the same parts of the group, remarks: "There is no such thing as slavery properly so called. In head-hunting expeditions prisoners are made for the sake of their heads, to be used when occasion requires, and such persons live with their captors in a condition very different from that of freedom, but they are not taken or maintained for the purposes of service. In the same islands when a successful attack and massacre enriches the victors with many heads, they spare and carry off children, whom they bring up among their own people. Such a *seka* will certainly be killed for a head or for a sacrifice before any native member of the community; but he lives as an adopted member, shares the work, pleasure and dangers of those with whom he dwells, and often becomes a leading personage among them. A refugee or a castaway is not a slave but a guest; his life is naturally

---

1) Guppy, p. 33. — 2) Verguet, p. 205.

much less valued than that of a man of the place, and useful services are expected from him, while he mixes freely and on equal terms with the common people" [1]. Guppy says: "I will turn for a moment to the subject of slavery in the eastern islands of the group. In Ugi it is the practice of infanticide which has given rise to a slave-commerce regularly conducted with the natives of the interior of St. Christoval. Three-fourths of the men of this island were originally bought as youths to supply the place of the natural offspring killed in infancy. But such natives when they attain manhood virtually acquire their independence, and their original purchaser has but little control over them.... Connected in the manner above shown with the subject of slavery is the practice of cannibalism. The completion of a new tambu-house is frequently celebrated among the St. Christoval natives by a cannibal feast. Residents in that part of the group tell me that if the victim is not procured in a raid amongst the neighbouring tribes of the interior, some man is usually selected from those men in the village who were originally purchased by the chief. The doomed man is not enlightened as to the fate which awaits him, and may perhaps have been engaged in the erection of the very building at the completion of which his life is forfeited". On the neighbouring small island of Santa Anna the natives are reputed to abstain from human flesh; but "the war-chief has acquired a considerable fortune, in a native's point of view, by following the profitable calling of purveyor of human flesh to the man-eaters of the adjacent coasts of St. Christoval..... I am told that there is a faint gleam of tender feeling shown in the case of a man who, by long residence in the village, has almost come to be looked upon as one of themselves. He is allowed to remain in ignorance of the dreaded moment until the last; and, perhaps, he may be standing on the beach assisting in the launching of the very canoe in which he is destined to take his final journey, when suddenly he is laid hold of, and in a few moments more he is being ferried across to the man-eaters of the opposite coast" [2].

From the foregoing statements it appears that the so-called

---

1) Codrington, The Melanesians, p. 46. — 2) Guppy, pp. 35, 36.

slaves are kept either for cannibal purposes or to strengthen the number of the tribe into which they are incorporated. Hence we may safely infer, in accordance with Codrington, that slavery proper does not exist in the south-eastern part of the group.

Somerville, describing the New Georgia group (in the centre of the Solomon Islands), remarks: "Slavery certainly exists, but it is in so mild a form that it is scarcely possible to detect master from man. I have never been able to elicit any facts concerning its introduction, propagation or limits, or even if (in so many words) it existed at all." "I was informed that slaves are kept chiefly for their heads, which are demanded whenever any occasion necessitates them, such as the death of the owner" [1]. Ribbe, too, speaks of slaves in the New Georgia group. On the isle of Wella-La-Wella the household commonly consists of the man with his wives, slaves and unmarried daughters. On Rubiana the master treats his slaves like his equals, but may at any time kill and eat them [2]. The following statement of Woodford's also relates to New Georgia: "On their expeditions it is not heads alone that they bring back, but slaves as well. These are either bought or captured alive, and it is from among these slaves that the victims are selected in case a head is required. They appear to be well treated in other ways, and to have as much liberty as they please; in fact, seem to be on a perfect footing of equality and familiarity with their captors. But any day a head may be wanted to celebrate the completion of a new canoe or other work, and one of the luckless slaves is unexpectedly called upon to furnish it. Mercifully for the victim, the blow falls from behind and unexpectedly. These slaves are often employed as guides to lead a party of head-hunters unexpectedly upon the mountain villages on Ysabel, whence they originally came" [3].

These details do not make it quite clear whether the condition of the "slaves" in the New Georgia group is not yet slavery or slavery in an incipient stage. We should rather think the latter; but we are not certain about it.

---

1) Somerville, New Georgia, pp. 402, 400. — 2) Ribbe, pp. 248, 276. — 3) Woodford, pp. 154, 155.

Parkinson's description of the north-western part of the group applies mainly to the isles of Bouka and Bougainville. In Bougainville individuals belonging to the inland tribes are sometimes enslaved by the coast people. Male slaves are not allowed to marry. (This has probably reference to both Bouka and Bougainville). At the death of a person of rank a slave was formely, and in some parts still is killed [1]). Ribbe also states that in Bougainville slavery exists, though in a mild form, most of the slaves being children captured in war. In the Shortland Islands (to the south of Bougainville) slaves are prisoners of war, most of them being imported from Bougainville. They are well treated and not seldom attain power and consideration and even can marry the chief's relations. Those slaves, however, who are not so fortunate, run the risk of being sacrificed at funeral feasts, at the building of a house or the launching of a canoe. On the fields the roughest work falls to the share of the slaves [2]). Guppy, speaking of the small isle of Treasury (near Bougainville), says: "There are in Treasury several men and women who, originally bought as slaves from the people of Bouka and Bougainville, now enjoy apparently the same privileges and freedom of action as their fellow islanders. It is sometimes not a matter of much difficulty to single out the slaves amongst a crowd of natives. On one occasion I engaged a canoe of Faromen to take me to a distant part of their island; and very soon after we started I became aware from the cowed and sullen condition of one of the crew that he was a slave. On inquiry I learned that this man had been captured when a boy in the island of Bougainville, and I was informed that if he was to return to his native place — a bush-village named Kiata — he would undoubtedly be killed. Although in fact a slave, I concluded from the bearing of the other men towards him that his bondage was not a very hard one; and he evidently appeared to enjoy most of the rights of a native of the common class. Sukai, however, for such was his name, had to make himself generally useful in the course of the day; and when at the close of the excursion we were seated inside the house of a man who provided us with a meal of

---

1) Parkinson, N. W. Salomo-Inseln, pp. 2 note, 8, 9, 10. — 2) Ribbe, pp. 100, 138, 139, 110.

boiled taro, sweet potatoes, and bananas, he was served with his repast on the beach outside" [1]).

We see that the difference between slaves and free men is more marked here than in the other parts of the Solomon group. Neither with regard to their work nor with regard to their social position are the slaves on a footing of equality with the free men. The conclusion is that in the north-western part of the group slavery certainly exists.

In the Nissan Islands, lying between the Solomon group and the Bismarck Archipelago, there are no slaves. Prisoners of war are killed and eaten [2]).

Several describers of the Fijians speak of slaves, but it is not easy to say what they mean by the term. According to Wilkes, there are five social classes, viz. kings, chiefs, warriors, landholders and slaves (*kai-si*). "The last have nominally little influence; but in this group, as in other countries, the mere force of numbers is sufficient to counterbalance or overcome the force of the prescriptive rights of the higher and less numerous classes. This has been the case at Amban, where the people at no distant period rose against and drove out their kings." In another place the same writer speaks of "the *kai-si* or common people." [3]). We see that "slaves," "people" and "common people" are synonymous terms with him. Williams equally states that the lowest class was composed of slaves, but gives no particulars about the condition of these slaves. Prisoners of war were barbarously tortured [4]). In a legend told by Seemann mention is made of a woman who had female slaves. But in another place the distinction into social classes is drawn between the chiefs and gentry and the common people [5]). Waterhouse does not speak of slaves [6]). In Jackson's narrative, published by Erskine, we read: "The lowest condition of all, the consequence of some late total defeat, or conquest, is absolute slavery, the districts where such a state exists being called *vanua kaisis* or slave lands". "I visited nearly all the *vanua kaisis* ... the meaning of *vanua kaisi* being slave-places, the

---

1) Guppy, p. 34. — 2) Sorge, in Steinmetz's Rechtsverhältnisse, p. 414. — 3) Wilkes, III, pp. 81, 108. — 4) Williams, pp. 32, 53. — 5) Seemann, pp. 196, 179, 180. — 6) Waterhouse.

inhabitants of which are supposed to supply Tanoa's and Tha-
kombau's [two chiefs'] houses with daily food, and build the
houses and keep them in repair;... they also pay tribute
periodically." Evidently we have to deal here with subjection
of districts as such, not with enslavement of individuals. In
another place of this narrative, *kaisi* is translated with "slave
or poor man". But the same writer gives some details suggestive
of real slavery. An enemy, whose life I had saved, he says,
"called and considered himself my *kaisi* (slave)". "Mara's
mother was saved when Tanoa conquered Lakemba, and was
considered as a prisoner, and consequently as a slave" [1]).

Though some of the details given seem to prove that there
were formerly not only people of the lowest class and inhabitants of conquered districts, but also slaves in the proper sense,
we are not quite certain about it.

Codrington's above quoted statement, that "there is no such
thing as slavery properly so called", applies also to a part of
the New Hebrides. Meinicke, after speaking of the chiefs, adds:
"The rest of the people are free men" [2]). Our other informants [3])
making no mention of slavery, we may safely infer that it
does not exist here.

The Bismarck Archipelago consists of Neu Pommern, Neu
Mecklenburg and a number of smaller islands. Danks gives an
elaborate account of marriage customs in this group, in which
there is not a word to be found about slaves. Pfeil's description
also applies to the whole archipelago. According to him, debtors
have to work for their creditors, but their condition is not
that of slaves. Slavery, in the sense we attach to it, does not
exist. Sale of full-grown people, as well as unrewarded labour,
is unknown. Children are bought, but only for the purpose of
adoption, and are not sold again. Boys, who run away to some
other tribe, are equally adopted. [4])

The information we have got about the separate islands does
not wholly agree with these general statements.

The best known part of Neu Pommern is the Gazelle Penin-

---

1) Erskine, pp. 456, 457, 420, 438, 458. — 2) Meinicke, Die Inseln des stillen Oceans,
I p. 202. — 3) Hagen and Pineau; Inglis; Somerville, New Hebrides. — 4) Danks;
Pfeil, p. 78.

sula. According to Hahl, slavery, in the country about Blanche
Bay, is known by name, but practically absent. On the north
coast, however, it is general. The Baining (an inland tribe) are
kidnapped or captured in battle and sold by the coast people,
who prefer taking children. The slaves are not allowed to
marry; they have to perform female labour, especially to cultivate the plantations, and always run the risk of being killed
and eaten at feasts. In the districts surrounding Mount Varzin
some Taulil (another inland tribe) are kept as slaves. Parkinson, in his splendid work on the German possessions in the
South Sea, also speaks of slaves. Great numbers of Baining
were formerly enslaved by the coast people, who sold them to
remote parts of the peninsula. The Taulil also were victims
of the slave raids; men and youths were killed, women and
children were made captives [1]).

It is remarkable that Parkinson, describing the social organisation of the several tribes, does not make any mention of
a slave class or of the work imposed on slaves. The social
signification of slavery therefore seems to be small. Yet the
foregoing statements must lead to the conclusion that slavery
exists, at least in some parts of the peninsula.

In his description of Neu Mecklenburg and neighbouring
islands, Parkinson also makes mention of slaves. On the isle
of Lir or Lihir, the chief, when about to give a cannibal repast,
gathers around him his whole tribe, inclusive of the slaves, who
have been captured in war. And on St. John's Island slaves
are said formerly to have been boiled in the hot springs. These
short notes do not seem to prove sufficiently the existence of
slavery, the less so, as Romilly, in his account of Neu Mecklenburg, has not a word about slaves [2]).

Speaking of the tribes inhabiting the Admiralty Islands,
Parkinson states that among the Usiai prisoners of war are
allowed to buy their liberty; if unable to do so, they are made
slaves. Further particulars are not given. Among the Moanus
the retinue of the chief consists of his nearest relations, further
of servants or soldiers whom he has attached to his person by
payment of shell-money, and finally of youths and boys captured

---

1) Hahl, p. 77; Parkinson, Dreissig Jahre, pp. 159, 172, 173. — 2) Parkinson, Dreissig
Jahre, p. 264; Romilly, Western Pacific.

in battle. The servants fight and work for their lord, but enjoy a rather independent position. We are not sure whether we have to deal here with slavery or with a voluntary submission. So the existence of slavery in the Admiralty group, though probable in some degree, does not seem to us to be proved as yet. As little is a positive conclusion warranted by Parkinson's statement, that in the group of small islands to the west of the Admiralty group wars between the separate islands were formerly frequent, owing to the slave stealing propensities of the natives [1]).

In the islands of Torres Straits, according to Meinicke, there is no government and no social division, except the division into tribes. Haddon, describing the western tribes of Torres Straits, says: "I never heard of slavery being practised" [2]). So slavery is probably unknown here.

The rest of this paragraph will be taken up with a survey of New Guinea and in the first place of the Dutch part of the island.

Bink and Krieger both state the Papuans of Humboldt Bay have no slaves, neither are slaves mentioned in Koning's account [3]).

In the district of Tabi some men were observed, who had their hair cut short; according to a Dorey interpreter, they were slaves [4]). This short note is not, however, sufficient to go upon.

The inhabitants of Seroei are much given to the kidnapping of slaves, whom they sell. Whether they keep any slaves themselves, does not appear [5]).

The Papuans near Lake Sentani keep neither slaves nor pawns [6]).

The natives of Ansus purchase many slaves, and sell slaves to Ternate traders [7]). In this case, too, we are not told, whether all the purchased slaves are sold abroad, or any of them are kept by the natives.

The aborigines of Windessi in their raids make prisoners

---

1) Parkinson, Dreissig Jahre, pp. 380, 396—398, 443. — 2) Meinicke, Die Torresstrasse, p. 116; Haddon, p. 355. See also Hunt's Ethnogr. notes on the Murray Islands, Torres Straits, in which no mention is made of slaves. — 3) Bink, p. 325; Krieger, p. 413; Koning. — 4) Robidé, p. 109. — 5) Ibid., p. 262. — 6) Moolenburgh, p. 180. — 7) Robidé, p. 235.

"to whom they give the name of *woman*, slave" [1]). This short note does not enable us to arrive at a clear conclusion.

Goudswaard says of the Papuans of Geelvinck Bay generally: "The Papuan steals men, makes them slaves, and despises them." "The wars of the Papuans are little more than raids, in which they burn the houses of their enemies, destroy their gardens, and if possible make women and children prisoners, to restore them later on for an edequate ransom, or else to keep them as slaves or exchange them" [2]).

The accounts, given by Van Hasselt and De Clercq, prove that slavery exists among the Nuforese [3]).

The inhabitants of Dorey and Roon belong to the Nuforese. Rosenberg gives some particulars about slavery in Dorey, and Robidé has a few notes on slaves kept by the inhabitants of Roon [4]).

Slavery also exists among the natives of Arfak [5]).

The Hattamers, however, who live in the Arfak mountains, have no slaves. "The Hattamers," says Robidé, "keep no slaves; in their wars with neighbouring tribes they do not enslave the prisoners, but cut off their heads, which they bring home as trophies" [6]).

The Karons, according to Bruijn, capture slaves from their neighbours, but whether they keep them for their own use is not quite clear. Another author tells us that they eat their prisoners [7]).

The existence of slavery among the Papuans of the Gulf of Maccluer is made probable by De Clercq's and Strauch's notes [8]). Another author observed slaves in some districts at the southwest side of this gulf; the population of these districts is a mongrel race of Buginese, emigrants from Serang, and Papuans [9]).

Slavery exists on the isle of Adie and along the Gulf of Kaimani [10]).

The Papuans of Ayambori have no slaves [11]).

---

1) Van der Roest, p. 157. — 2) Goudswaard, pp. 27, 51; see also Ottow and Geissler, pp. 115, 118. — 3) Van Hasselt in Z. E. VIII, pp. 191 sqq.; Van Hasselt in Tijds. XXXI, pp. 583, 584, XXXII, pp 270, 272; De Clercq, Nieuw-Guinea, p. 619. — 4) Rosenberg, Mal. Arch., pp. 454, 456; Robidé, pp. 64, 65, 76, 94, 228; see also Nieuw-Guinea, p. 149. — 5) Rosenberg, Mal. Arch., p. 532; Rosenberg, Nieuw-Guinea, p. 90. — 6) Robidé, p. 242. — 7) Bruijn, pp. 103, 104; Robidé, p. 59. — 8) De Clercq, Nieuw-Guinea, p. 459; Strauch, p. 30. — 9) Robidé, pp. 300, 305, 306. — 10) Nieuw-Guinea, pp. 116, 128. — 11) Ibid., pp. 158, 163.

In Krieger's elaborate account of the natives of British and German New Guinea there is not a word about slaves. Hence it would appear that they are unacquainted with slavery and we shall presently see that this conclusion is strengthened by the information we get about the separate tribes.

Thomson states that several tribes of British New Guinea in warfare kill alike men, women and children [1]), and in the descriptions of single tribes: Motu, Mowat, Toaripi, natives on the mouth of the Wanigela River, no mention is made of slavery [2]).

As for German New Guinea, Maclay does not speak of slaves and Finsch says that every Papuan warrior considers it an honour to kill women and children [3]).

Among the Yabim slavery does not exist [4]).

The same is the case among the natives of the Tami Islands [5]).

Slavery is equally unknown among the Tamoes of Bogadjim [6]) and the natives of the adjacent Dampier Island [7]).

Result.   Positive cases: *North-western Solomon Islanders,*
Natives of the Gazelle Peninsula,
Nuforese,
Papuans of Arfak,
          „   on the Gulf of Maccluer,
          „   of Adie,
          „   on the Gulf of Kaimani,
Central Solomon Islanders,
Fijians,
Natives of Neu Mecklenburg and
    neighbouring islands,
Admiralty Islanders,
Papuans of Tabi,
          „   „ Ansus.

Negative cases: *New Caledonians,*
South-eastern Solomon Islanders,
Nissan Islanders,

---

1) Thomson, British New Guinea, pp. 52, 63, 157, 158. — 2) Turner, Motu ; d'Albertis ; Beardmore; Romilly, Verandah; Chalmers, see especially p. 326; Guise. — 3) Maclay ; Finsch, Samoafahrten, p. 80. — 4) Vetter, p. 91. — 5) Kohler, Das Recht der Papuas, p. 389 (on the authority of Bamler). — 6) Hagen, Unter den Papuas, p. 220; see also Vallentin, p. 634. — 7) See Kunze's minute description, in which slavery is not mentioned.

New Hebridians,
Natives of Torres Straits,
Papuans of Humboldt Bay,
     „   *near Lake Sentani,*
Hattamers,
Papuans of Ayambori,
Motu,
Mowat,
Toaripi,
Papuans on the mouth of the Wanigela
     river,
Yabim,
Natives of the Tami Islands,
Tamoes,
Natives of Dampier Island.

No conclusion: Papuans of Seroei,
             „   „ Windessi,
     Karons.

§ 6. *Polynesia.*

All authors agree that the Maori of New Zealand had slaves ; and the many details they give prove that slavery really existed [1]).

The Tongans, according to Meinicke, had slaves, partly prisoners of war, partly condemned criminals [2]). Gerland, referring to a missionary report, speaks of slaves, *tamaiveiki* [3]). But in his very minute description of Tongan government and social classes [4]) he gives no more particulars about these slaves; and Mariner who, according to Gerland, is very reliable [5]), makes no mention of slavery. Mariner enumerates five social classes; the lowest class were the *tooas*, the bulk of the people, consisting of *a.* a few warriors, *b.* professed cooks in the service of the chiefs, *c.* those who tilled the soil and had no

---

1) Thomson, New Zealand, pp. 149, etc.; Polack, I pp. 35, 36, etc., II pp. 52—59, etc. ; Tregear, p. 113; Waitz-Gerland, VI p. 206; Meinicke, Die Inseln des stillen Oceans, I p. 326; Letourneau, pp. 173—182; Weisz, pp. 22, 24, 28, 30 ; Taylor, pp. 165, 167, 185, 189, 191 etc.; Brown, New Zealand, pp. 29, 30; Yate, pp. 120, 121. — 2) Meinicke, l. c. II. p. 185. — 3) Waitz-G erland, VI p. 170. — 4) Ibid., pp. 170—185. — 5) Ibid., p. 185

other occupation [1]). Mariner only makes mention of captive women, so it is probable that no men were taken prisoners in their wars [2]). West states that there was a monarchical despotism, supported by an hereditary aristocracy. The people were divided into several, strictly separated, classes. The lowest class where the *tuas,* common people, subdivided into different trades: carpenters, fishermen, etc. The feudal principle, that the whole country belonged exclusively to the king, made the people slaves [3]). Such "slavery" of a whole people is not, however, slavery in the true sense of the word. Of slavery proper West makes as little mention as Mariner. We may, therefore, safely suppose that Meinicke and Gerland have been mistaken, and that slavery did not exist here.

With reference to Samoa Gerland speaks of two political parties who were always at war, "but they do not destroy their adversaries", he says, "nor enslave them, as frequently members of the same family belong to different parties" [4]). According to Meinicke the prisoners were at different times differently disposed of; but among these modes of treatment slavery is not mentioned [5]). Wilkes states that their wars "were attended with great cruelty, and neither old or young of either sex were spared" [6]). Turner, a good authority, remarks : "Prisoners, if men, were generally killed; if women, distributed among the conquerors" [7]). We are not told whether these women were married, or kept in a slave-like state; but even in the last case this would be slavery of women only, and therefore not slavery in the proper sense. Krämer is the only author who speaks of slaves. The conquered party had to ask the pardon of the conquerors and to bring firewood as if to show that they considered themselves worth to be eaten like pigs. Often also they had to perform degrading work as slaves *(pologa),* to pay a tribute or even to furnish human flesh for cannibal purposes [8]). It would seem that this degrading work was imposed upon the conquered as a temporary punishment and that we have not to deal here with a permanent system of forced labour as among slave-keeping tribes. This being the only

---

1) Mariner, II pp. 153, 349, 350. — 2) Ibid., p. 237. — 3) West, pp. 260, 262. — 4) Waitz-Gerland, VI p. 170. — 5) Meinicke, l. c. II p. 122. — 6) Wilkes, II p. 159. — 7) Turner, Samoa, p. 192. — 8) Krämer, Die Samoa-Inseln, II p. 341.

reference to slavery in Krämer's very detailed description of the Samoans, and slavery not being mentioned by any of our other informants [1]), we may safely infer that it did not exist.

Gardiner, in his excellent article on Rotuma, says: "Slaves as such did not properly exist" [2]).

Gerland and Meinicke, enumerating the social classes in the Rarotonga group (or Hervey Islands, or Cook's Islands), make no mention of slaves. According to Meinicke, the lowest class are the common people [3]). So slavery seems to have been unknown here.

In Tahiti, according to Ellis, "the lowest class included the *titi* and the *teuteu*, the slaves and servants; the former were those who had lost their liberty in battle, or who, in consequence of the defeat of the chieftains to whom they were attached, had become the property of the conquerors. This kind of slavery appears to have existed among them from time immemorial. Individuals captured in actual combat, or who fled to the chief for protection when disarmed or disabled in the field, were considered the slaves of the captor or chief by whom they were protected. The women, children and others who remained in the districts of the vanquished, were also regarded as belonging to them; and the lands they occupied, together with their fields and plantations, were distributed among the victors.... If peace continued, the captive frequently regained his liberty after a limited servitude, and was permitted to return to his own land, or remain in voluntary service with his master" [4]). Though the second kind of slaves Ellis enumerates, the subjects of vanquished chiefs, probably were not slaves, and the frequent liberating of captive slaves proves that slavery was not of great significance, it would seem from Ellis's account that to a limited extent it was present. Another ancient writer, however, tells us that the lowest class were the common servants, called *toutou*, or, when they were in the service of women, *tuti*. Nobody was obliged to serve longer than he liked. The *manahoune* or peasants, who worked for the nobility, were also free to change their master or remove to another district. Hence we should infer that slavery did not

---

1) Gerland; Meinicke; Turner; Von Bülow. — 2) Gardiner, p. 429. — 3) Meinicke, l. c., II p. 148; Waitz-Gerland, VI p. 199. — 4) Ellis, Pol. Res., III p. 95.

exist [1]). Moerenhout says: In the Society Islands there were no slaves; the people served the chiefs voluntarily. Prisoners of war, men, women, and children, were almost always mercilessly murdered [2]). Considering the details given by Ellis, who was very well informed, we are inclined, notwithstanding the contrary statements of the other writers, to conclude that slavery existed in Tahiti, but we are not quite certain about it.

Of Hawaii Ellis says: "The wives and children of those whom they had defeated were frequently made slaves, and attached to the soil for its cultivation, and, together with the captives, treated with great cruelty." Captives were sometimes spared, "though perhaps spared only to be slaves, or to be sacrificed when the priests should require human victims. The persons of the captives were the property of the victors, and their lives entirely at their disposal." But in enumerating the social classes he makes no mention of slaves. "In the fourth [lowest] rank may be included the small farmers, who rent from ten to twenty or thirty acres of land; the mechanics .... indeed, all the labouring classes, those who attach themselves to some chief or farmer, and labour on his land for their food and clothing, as well as those who cultivate small portions of land for their own advantage" [3]). In the accounts of the other writers, who knew the ancient institutions of Hawaii by observation or personal information, we do not find anything tending to prove that slavery existed. Wilkes, in his very detailed account of government and land tenure, does not speak of slaves. "The authority" he says "descended in the scale of rank, rising from the lowest class of servants to tenants, agents, landholders, land-owners, petty chiefs, high chiefs, and the king" [4]). Chamisso expressly states that slavery was absent. The common people were entirely subjected to the chiefs, but there were no slaves or serfs. Peasants and servants were allowed to remove to any place they liked. The people were free; they could be killed, but not sold or retained [5]). Remy tells us that the common people were heavily oppressed by the chiefs. Slaves are not mentioned by him. Prisoners were sacrificed [6]). All this renders the existence

---

1) J. Wilson, III pp. 127—129. — 2) Moerenhout, II pp. 8, 47. — 3) Ellis, Pol. Res., IV pp. 161, 160, 413. — 4) Wilkes, IV p. 35. — 5) Chamisso, in Kotzebue, p. 149. — 6) Remy, pp. LXI—LXVI, XL.

of slavery in ancient Hawaii very improbable and so we think we are justified, notwithstanding the second-hand information, furnished by Meinicke, that there were a few slaves [1]), and Marcuse's short remark, that "to allure the sharks, they occasionally made human sacrifices, especially among the slaves" [2]), in concluding that slavery did not exist.

Hale states that in the Marquesas Islands there were no slaves [3]). The same follows from Radiguet's description. According to this writer, the natives were divided into the nobles and the common people. The latter served the nobles, but were free at any time to leave their employers [4]). According to Meinicke prisoners were either sacrificed and eaten, or spared and adopted into the conquering tribe [5]). De Rocquefeuil also states that the prisoners were eaten, unless, by the priests' intervention, they were buried; at any rate they were killed [6]). Moerenhout tells us that the sole object of their wars was to obtain a cannibal repast [7]). From all this we may safely infer that there were no slaves and that Gerland, stating that "slaves were rare; like the foreigners, who were always regarded as enemies, they had no rights, could be quite arbitrarily treated and even killed" [8]), has mistaken for slaves persons intended to be sacrificed. Letourneau holds the same view of the matter: "Everything seems to indicate, that slavery did not exist in the Marquesas Islands" [9]).

The natives of Tukopia, according to Gerland, formerly kept slaves, who were prisoners of war [10]). No more details are given.

Wilkes, speaking of the Paumotu group, observes that Anaa or Chain Island "is said to contain five thousand inhabitants, which large number is accounted for by the conquest of the other islands, and taking their inhabitants off as captives". The influence of the missionaries caused a change in "the treatment of their captives, whom they allowed to return, if they chose, to their own island; but very many of them had married at Anaa, and became permanent residents there, and

---

1) Meinicke, l. c., pp. 303, 304. — 2) Marcuse, p. 116. On p. 114, however, he states that they spared the lives of their captives only when they intended them to be sacrificed later on to their gods. — 3) Hale, p. 36. — 4) Radiguet, p. 156. — 5) Meinicke, l. c., II p. 254. — 6) Andree, p. 64. — 7) Moerenhout, II p. 31. — 8) Waitz-Gerland, VI p. 216. — 9) Letourneau, p. 183. — 10) Waitz-Gerland, V, 2 p. 194.

few have taken advantage of the permission to return" [1]). Whether the captives mentioned here were kept as slaves is not clear. Moerenhout tells us that the natives of the Paumotu group often preserved their prisoners to eat them later on at feasts [2]). We cannot arrive at a definite conclusion here.

Geiseler states that on Easter Island male prisoners of war were formerly eaten. Captured women and girls, however, were not killed, but given to young warriors. Slaves are not mentioned. The king had absolute power over the common people [3]). It would seem that slavery was absent here; but we are not quite certain about it, as Geiseler describes a state of things existing long before his visit to the island.

In the Abgarris, Marqueen and Tasman groups, according to Parkinson, there are three social classes, the chiefs and their parents, the nobles and priests, and the common people [4]). Hence we may safely infer, that slavery does not exist.

> *Result*. Positive cases: *Maori,*
> *Tahitians.*
> Negative cases: *Tongans,*
> *Samoans,*
> *Rotumians,*
> *Rarotonga Islanders,*
> *Hawaiians,*
> *Marquesas Islanders,*
> *Abgarris, Marqueen and Tasman Is-*
> *landers,*
> Easter Islanders.
> No conclusion: Tukopia Islanders,
> Paumotu Islanders.

§ 7. *Micronesia.*

According to Meinicke none of the describers of the Marshall Islands make mention of slaves. Gerland, too, does not speak of slaves [5]). According to Hernsheim the lowest class is com-

---

1) Wilkes, I p. 357. — 2) Moerenhout, II p. 191. — 3) Geiseler, pp. 30, 31, 41. — 4) Parkinson, Dreissig Jahre, p. 528. — 5) Meinicke, Die Gilbert- und Marshall-Inseln, p. 409; Waitz-Gerland, V, 2 p. 122.

posed of the poor, the *armidwon* or *kajur*. They are forbidden to take more than one wife. The next class is that of the *leadagedag*, who own property, have in most instances three wives, and are provided with food by the *kajur* [1]). Kubary says: "The common people are called *armij kajur* and form the greater part of the subjects. They have no property, except the land allotted to them by the chief, who can take it from them at his pleasure. Every week they have, each of them, to provide the chief with prepared food, the quantity and quality of which are determined". These people, according to Kubary, form the lowest class [2]). Hager quite agrees with Kubary, to whom he frequently refers [3]). Senfft states that sale or pawning of men is unknown. Captives, domestic slaves, debt-slaves etc. are not found. The lowest class are the *armidj kajur* or common people, who own no property. Hence we might infer that slavery does not exist. But in another place the same writer remarks that only the upper classes (kings, relations of kings and chiefs of districts) are free, the rest of the population being unfree and presenting all the characteristics of slaves. The *armidj* has no rights, everything he acquires is the property of his chief. The chief has over him the right of life and death. Yet we do not think the writer means to say that these people of very low standing are really slaves, *i. e.* the individual property of the chiefs. They are not bought and sold, as is generally the case with slaves. The *armidj* do not become such through captivity in war or indebtedness, the common manners in which people are made slaves. So some of the ordinary features of slavery are wanting. This already renders the existence of slavery doubtful. But we think the following passage in Senfft's description clearly shows that the *armidj* are not slaves: "The *armidj* cannot leave the tribe without the consent of his chief, but as most often he belongs by birth to several chiefs, he can go over from the tribe of one of his chiefs to that of another, *i. e.*, he can place himself under the immediate control of the other chief by rendering him services, especially by tilling his land. He commonly does so, when he is badly treated." From this it appears that the *armidj* is not

---

1) Hernsheim, p. 80. — 2) Kubary, Die Ebongruppe, pp. 36, 37. — 3) Hager, p. 96.

the individual property of his chief; else he would not be able to change his condition so easily. We think his relation to the chief is rather that of a subject to a petty despot [1]). This conclusion is strengthened by what we learn from other recent descriptions. Krämer makes no mention of slaves. The lowest class, according to him, are the *kadjur* or common people [2]). In a report regarding the isle of Jaluit it is equally stated that the lowest class are the *armidj kadjur* or common people, who own no land. They have to work for the landowners and to provide them with food. This is more suggestive of tenancy than of slavery. It is true that the writer calls them unfree; but then he says, that their becoming free was synonymous with their rising to the rank of a chief, so it seems that by "unfree" he means people whose condition is below that of the chiefs and nobles [3]). Taking all this into consideration, we think we may safely infer that there are no slaves in the Marshall group.

Though the isle of Nauru is often regarded as belonging to the Marshall group, its situation is rather isolated and the social organisation of the population is different from that on the other islands of the group, so we think we must treat it separately. Krämer remarks that there are three classes: chiefs, middle class and slaves. The chiefs have unlimited power over the slaves, who are not allowed to marry without their consent. A murderer in most cases has to yield his land to the parents of his victim, but when there are attenuating circumstances, he is allowed to give slaves as a compensation [4]). Jung gives more details. He speaks of serfs or slaves, but what he tells about them is not very suggestive of slavery. The serfs, unlike the other classes, own no land. A native who is supposed to have killed another by means of sorcery becomes the serf of the parents of his victim and his property is taken away. Many families stand in the relation of serfs to the chiefs and other people of rank. The power of the lords over these slaves is said formerly to have been very great. The origin of serfdom was this. In their wars, families belonging to the conquered party were driven from their lands and had to seek their sub-

---

1) Senfft, in Steinmetz's Rechtsverhältnisse, pp. 431, 442, 439, 441, 443. — 2) Krämer, Hawaii etc., p. 430. — 3) Kohler, Das Recht der Marschallinsulaner, Z. V. R. XIV pp. 427, 428, 431. — 4) Krämer, Hawaii etc., pp. 450, 451.

sistence elsewhere. They then applied to a powerful chief, put themselves under his protection and became entirely dependent on him. In later times these serfs were placed by the chief as agents on their own former property on condition of delivering the produce to him. It then sometimes happened that these agents or their children behaved as owners of the lands they lived upon and so came into conflict with the chief [1]. From this account it appears that the so-called serfs nowadays are not in a slave-like condition. Whether in former times they were really slaves is not clear; we should rather think their state was one of voluntary submission to a landowner; but we cannot arrive at a definite conclusion.

Gerland, minutely describing the social classes on the several Caroline Islands, only in one passage speaks of slaves. According to him, on the isle of Ponape there are three classes: chiefs, freemen, and slaves. Christian also makes mention of slaves. "After the chief ruler come twelve orders of chiefs, Chaulik being the smallest title of all, and after these the Aramach-mal, or common folk, and the Litu, or slave-class" [2]. But the only details given about these slaves are that the land "belongs exclusively to the two upper classes; the third class are attached to the soil on which they live" [3]. We are inclined to think that these so-called "slaves" are really free people of low standing, the more so as on the isle of Kusaie, also belonging to the Caroline group, the common people are subjected to the higher classes who own all the land [4]. Kubary, describing the Mortlock Islands (belonging to the same group), says: "Except the division into tribes, there is no social division in the Caroline Islands, such as into classes, ranks, secret societies, etc.; and I believe that all suppositions of former observers relating to such a state of things result from ignorance of tribal government. With these natives the notions of "noble", "gentleman", "commoner" have but a relative value; and special titles such as "king", "chieftain", "prince", etc. depend wholly upon the individual pleasure of the observer" [5]. The same writer tells us that on the isle of Ruk in warfare

---

1) Jung, pp. 67—70. — 2) Christian, p. 144. — 3) Waitz-Gerland V, 2 p. 118. — 4) Ibid., pp. 120, 121. — 5) Kubary, Mortlock-Inseln, p. 246.

"such captives as may accidentally be taken are killed," which statement is not very suggestive of slavery [1]). Gräffe, compiling Tetens and Kubary's notes on the inhabitants of Yap, speaks of slaves: "The population is composed of three classes, chiefs, freemen, and slaves or *pomilingais*. The latter live together in separate villages and are obliged daily to provide the freemen with agricultural products, and whenever the chiefs require it to aid in constructing houses and canoes. Everything the slaves possess, even their wives and daughters, may at any time be required by the freemen and used at their pleasure. As we have already hinted, the slaves are not allowed to wear the head-ornaments that the freemen are in the habit of wearing, not even the combs worn in the hair; and when waiting upon the chiefs, they must approach them in a creeping, bowing attitude. One would, however, fail in supposing, that all labour is exclusively incumbent on the slave-class. They are only bound to definite taxes, viz. to a tribute of food, and of mats and other materials for housebuilding; and their slave-state consists rather in a low and dependent condition than in being taxed with labour" [2]). From this last sentence we should infer, that these people are not slaves, but only a despised lowest class. A slave always has an individual master, whereas these people are subjected to the higher classes *en bloc*. Krämer, in his short description of the isle of Yap, equally speaks of slaves (*milingai*). They live in separate villages. "Their villages, however, differ little from those of the free inhabitants of Yap, and yet the *milingai* are a kind of slaves or at least derive their origin from slaves." Their social position is lower than that of the other natives. This description, in which no mention is made of the *milingai* serving individual masters, is little suggestive of slavery [3]). According to Volkens, there are two classes, the *pilun*, who are free and the *pimlingai*, who are slaves. "There are no domestic slaves, the dwellings of the free people and those of the slaves being strictly separated. Generally speaking, to each *pilun* country belong one or more *pimlingai* countries; the former are on the coast, the latter in the less

---

1) Kubary, quoted by Schmeltz and Krause, p. 373. — 2) Gräffe, p. 94. — 3) Krämer, Studienreise, p. 179.

fertile interior". "The slaves do not pay any tribute, but are obliged to perform in the *pilun* country without payment public and private works, such as thatching roofs, building roads and dams, etc." [1]). From this account also we may infer that the so-called slaves, who work for the governing districts, not for individual masters, are not really slaves. Slavery therefore seems to be unknown in the Caroline Islands.

In Gerland's detailed account of government and social classes among the ancient inhabitants ot the Marianne Islands no mention is made of slavery; and as this author uses this word in a too wide rather than in a too restricted sense, we may safely suppose that there were no slaves [2]).

Kubary tells us, that "among the Pelau Islanders there can be no question of a division of the people into ranks or classes, of a nobility in our sense of the word" [3]). In another place he states that a chief's wants are generally provided for by the work of dependent relatives, who are a kind of adopted children. If their work does not suit them, they leave their employer [4]). Semper speaks of a class of bondmen (*Hörigen*); but in another place he states that they work for wages; so they are neither slaves nor serfs, but a despised working class [5]). We may safely conclude that slavery does not exist here [6]).

In the Kingsmill or Gilbert Islands, according to Wilkes, there are three classes: chief (*nea*), landholders (*katoka*), and slaves (*kawa*). "The *katokas* are persons who possess land, but are not of noble birth; many of these were originally slaves, who have obtained land by acts of bravery, or through the favour cf their chiefs. The *kawas* are those who possess no land, and no one from whom they can claim support". "They have no term to designate a poor man, except that of slave. Anyone who owns land can always call upon others to provide him with a house, canoe, and the necessaries of life; but one who has none is considered as a slave, and can hold no property

---

1) Volkens, Ueber die Karolinen-Insel Yap. — 2) Waitz-Gerland, V, 2 pp. 112—114. — 3) Kubary, Soc. Einr. der Pelauer, p. 72. — 4) Kubary, Die Palau Inseln, p. 232. — 5) Semper, Die Pelau-Inseln, pp. 36, 79. — 6) This is also proved (if any further proof were needed) by Kubary's detailed description of fishing and agriculture: the former is carried on by the men, the latter by the women; nowhere is any mention made of slaves. Kubary, Industrie der Pelau-Insulaner, pp. 123 sqq., 156 sqq.

whatever" [1]). It is evident that these *kawas*, as described by Wilkes, are not slaves, but a subjected and despised class of people destitute of land. Meinicke enumerates the following classes: chiefs (in Tarawa: *nea* or *oamata*, in Makin: *jomata*), free landholders (in Tarawa: *katoka*, in Makin: *tiomata*), and the common people (in Tarawa: *kawa*, in Makin: *rang*); and he adds: "There are also slaves, who originally were captives, and whose children have remained such" [2]). So the *kawa*, called slaves by Wilkes, are called freemen by Meinicke, according to whom there is a class of slaves still below them. Behm asserts that on Makin there are slaves besides the three other classes [3]). The best description is given by Parkinson. According to him there are kings (these only on some islands); further great landholders; then the class of small landholders. Then there are two subjected classes. One is the class of the *te torre*, who live as vassals on the lands of the great landholders; they get a small piece of land for their own use; they must provide their lord with men when in war, and bring him the number of cocoanuts he desires, and what he needs for his household. The lowest class are the *te bei* or *kaungo*. They have no property, no land to live upon; they live with the great landholders by whom they are maintained; they on their part must work for their lord, *i. e.* fish, prepare food, etc. The lord, by giving them a piece of land, can raise them to the class of the *te torre*. These two classes have no voice in government matters; they follow their lord without grumbling; his will is their will; an offence against the lord is regarded by them as a personal offence, and avenged as such. Generally no one marries outside his class. In ordinary life there is no difference between master and vassal; they often sleep on the same mat; they drink, dance and play together; they wear the same kind of dress. When a poor man dies, a wealthy inhabitant of the village generally provides for his family; but they must labour for him and are, so to speak, his slaves [4]). We have to examine now, whether these two lowest classes are slave-classes. We may remark, first, that, whereas most ethnographers make a large use of the word "slave", Parkinson does not use it, except in

---

1) Wilkes, pp. 88, 95. — 2) Meinicke, Die Inseln des stillen Oceans, II p. 340. — 3) Waitz-Gerland, V, 2 p. 124. — 4) Parkinson, Gilbertinsulaner, pp. 98, 99, 39.

the last sentence, and there with the qualification "so to speak". Moreover, some particulars are not mentioned, which we should expect to find in such an elaborate description, if slavery really existed; *e. g.* it is not stated that the subjected persons are bought and sold; nor that care is taken that they do not run away; nor that the master is not at all, or only to a limited extent, responsible for his behaviour towards the person who serves him. As little does it appear, that these vassals become such in the same manner in which men generally become slaves. It is only stated that the family of a deceased poor man fall into a state of dependence upon a rich inhabitant of the village; but it is not clear, whether they voluntarily or involuntarily join the rich man's family. The principal objects of property, says Parkinson, are houses, lands, and canoes [1]). Were there slaves, they would have been mentioned here too. Krämer states that there are chiefs, a nobility (*aomata*), a middle class (*te vau*), and slaves (*te kanua*). A noble may not marry a girl of the middle class or a slave girl, nor is he allowed to have any connection with a female slave who is his own subject [2]). Krämer's use of the word slave, without any particulars suggestive of slavery, cannot impair the inference, to which Wilkes's notes and Parkinson's detailed account lead us, that there are no slaves on the Gilbert Islands.

Result. Negative cases: *Marshall Islanders,*
Caroline Islanders,
Marianne Islanders,
Pelau Islanders,
Kingsmill Islanders,
Natives of Nauru

Schurtz asserts that in Polynesia and Micronesia slaves are found everywhere; and Gerland is of the same opinion regarding Polynesia [3]). Our survey of both these groups shows that these writers are wrong: in Micronesia slavery is probably quite unknown; in Polynesia absence of slavery is the rule, slavery the exception.

---

1) Parkinson, Gilbertinsulaner, p. 43. — 2) Krämer, Hawaii, etc., p. 333. — 3) Schurtz Katechismus, p. 230; Waitz-Gerland, V, 2 p. 124.

§ 8. *Malay Archipelago.*

I. Malay Peninsula.

The savage tribes of the Malay Peninsula are divided into the Semang, the Sakai and the Jakun.

Among the Sakai, according to De Morgan "the debtor and his family work for the creditor during one or two moons, according to the decision of the panghulu (village-chief)". This certainly is a commencement of debt-slavery; but such compulsory labour, limited beforehand to one or two months, is not yet slavery in the true sense.

Skeat and Blagden state that, among the Benua-Jakun, crimes of all kinds might be expatiated by the payment of fines. If the offender failed to pay the fine, he became the slave of his victim. No more details being added, the existence of slavery does not seem to us to be quite certain.

As neither in Skeat and Blagden's exhaustive work, nor in the other books and articles we have consulted, any further mention is made of slaves, we are justified in concluding that these tribes, with the exception perhaps of a division of the Jakun, do not practise slavery [1]).

II. Sumatra and neighbouring islands.

Brenner and Junghuhn speak of the Battas of Sumatra in general as keeping slaves [2]).

The existence or former existence of slavery is sufficiently proved with regard to the following divisions of the Battas:

Battas on the Pane and Bila rivers [3]),
     ,,   of Mandheling [4]),
     ,,   of Pertibie [5]),

---

1) De Morgan, Exploration, divisions: Linguistique (see especially p. 17), and: Ethnographie; Skeat and Blagden, I p. 515; Vaughan Stevens; Montano; Borie; Favre; Newbold; Hervey. — 2) Brenner, pp. 341, 342; Junghuhn, II pp. 150—152. — 3) Neumann T. A. G. 2nd series, part IV, pp. 26—41. — 4) Heijting, pp. 246—249; "Résumé's", pp. 55, 56; Willer, pp. 43—47; see also Meerwaldt, p. 541. — 5) Willer, l. c.

Karo Battas [1]),
Raja Battas [2]),
Battas of Angkola [3]),
    ,,   of Simelungun [4]),
    ,,   of Singkel and Pak-pak [5]),
    ,,   of the country of Panei [6]).

Among the Battas of Silindung slavery has never existed, according to Meerwaldt [7]). Whether he means only slavery in the restricted sense, or also pawning, is not clear.

The Toba Battas, according to Meerwaldt, formerly had slaves; but now slavery is dying out under Dutch influence. Van Dijk, who visited the Habinsaran district in the Toba-lands, states that in some parts of the district there were slaves, in others there were not. Whether the latter fact is to be accounted for by Dutch influence, does not appear from his very short notes [8]).

On the Lubus we have found only two short articles, in which slavery is not mentioned; but this does not prove very much [9]).

None of the describers of the Kubus make any mention of slaves; so we may suppose, that slavery does not exist among them [10]).

De Groot gives a detailed account of slavery and pawning in the Lampong districts [11]).

In Nias slavery certainly exists [12]).

The Mentawei Islanders very probably have no slaves. None of their describers make any mention of slavery [13]). "Their whole warfare consists of treacherous attacks, in which nobody's life is spared" [14]).

---

1) Westenberg, Verslag, p. 76; Westenberg, Nota, pp. 113, 114. — 2) Van Dijk, Si Baloengoen, p. 158; Westenberg, Nota, p. 107; Mededeelingen, etc., pp. 580, 585. — 3) Meerwaldt, p. 541. — 4) Kroesen, Bataklanden, pp. 259, 260. — 5) Ypes, pp. 496—499, 542—545. — 6) Mededeelingen etc., pp. 567, 573, 575. — 7) Meerwaldt, p. 541. — 8) Meerwaldt, l. c.; Van Dijk, Nota, pp. 483, 491; see also Müller, Batak-Sammlung, p. 14. — 9) Van Ophuijsen; Van Dijk, Loeboe. — 10) See Mohnicke; Boers; Forbes, Kubus, and especially Dr. Hagen, who makes use of an extensive literature. — 11) De Groot. — 12) Modigliani, Nias, pp. 520—536; Rosenberg, Mal. Arch., pp. 157—163. — 13) Rosenberg, Mal. Arch.; Rosenberg, Mentawei-eilanden; Mess; Maass; Severijn, Poggi-eilanden. — 14) Rosenberg, Mal. Arch., p. 193.

On the Anambas, Natuna and Tambelan Islands, belonging to the Lingga-Riouw group, there are debtor-slaves [1].

Most of the writers on Enggano make no mention of slavery [2]. According to Walland, the Engganese wear ornaments in their ear-laps, which are pierced for that purpose. If anybody's ear-lap is broken, he incurs great disgrace; he is no longer listened to in any deliberation, nor considered a notable in his tribe, and becomes the slave of his relatives, for whom he is obliged to work. And Rosenberg says: "If a criminal does not pay the fine, this is done by his kindred; but if they are unable to pay, they sell him as a slave. So slavery exists; but it is of a very mild kind, and the number of slaves is very small" [3]. The fact that both authors speak of slavery only in connection with these particular cases, whereas the others do not speak of it at all, makes us doubt, whether what Walland and Rosenberg call slavery is slavery in the true sense. So we cannot come to a clear conclusion.

III. Borneo.

Among the Hill- or Land-Dyaks (Orang Gunong) slavery in the restricted sense and slave-trade did not exist, but, says Low: "the system of slave-debtors is carried on, though to a very small extent". Later on this kind of slavery also disappeared [4].

The Dyaks on the Barito have slaves and pawns [5].

The Sea-Dyaks also keep slaves, but not many [6].
Slavery equally exists among the

>Dyaks on Rejang river [7],
>Biadju-Dyaks [8],
>Ot-danoms [9],
>Olo-ngadju [10],

---

1) Kroesen, Anambas, p. 244. — 2) Modigliani, Engano; Oudemans; Severijn, Engano; Rosenberg, Engano; "Verslag eener reis". — 3) Walland, p. 301; Rosenberg, Mal. Arch., p. 216. — 4) Low, pp. 301, 302. — 5) Schwaner, I pp. 167, 168. — 6) Low, pp. 200, 201; Spencer St. John, I p. 83; Brooke Low, in Ling Roth, Sarawak, II p. 210. — 7) Brooke Low, l. c., pp. 210—213. — 8) Perelaer, pp. 152—160. — 9) Schwaner, I pp. 80, 195; Grabowsky, p. 199. — 10) Grabowsky, l. c.

Dyaks of Tompassuk [1]),
Kayans on the Mendalam [2]),
Kayans on the Upper Mahakam [3]),
Muruts [4]),
Dyaks of Sambas [5]),
Kindjin Dyaks [6]),
Dyaks of Pasir [7]).

Denison informs us that the Dusuns have no slaves [8]).

Von Dewall, in his notes on the Dyaks of Matan or Kaping, speaks of slaves of the chief. Whether these are the only slaves does not appear [9]).

Of the Dyaks of Simpang he says the same, and adds that pawning is unknown amongst them. Here too we cannot arrive at a clear conclusion [10]).

The Rambai- and Sebruang-Dyaks probably have no slaves; for it is stated, that their chiefs have no privileges; only, when some accident, illness for instance, prevents them from cultivating their own rice-fields, this is done by the people [11]). If there were slaves, the chiefs would not have to cultivate their own rice-fields. Moreover our informant, in his fairly detailed description, would probably have mentioned slavery, if it existed.

IV. Celebes.

Slavery is proved by good authorities to exist or have existed in several parts of this island. Such is the case

in the Minahassa [12]),
in Bolaäng Mongondou [13]),
in Lipu lo Holontalo [14]),

---

1) Treacher, in Ling Roth, l. c., pp. 213, 214. — 2) Nieuwenhuis, Quer durch Borneo, I pp. 58, 59, 65—67. — 3) Nieuwenhuis, l. c. II pp. 95, 96. — 4) Denison, as quoted by Ling Roth, l. c. — 5) Van Prehn, pp. 29—32. — 6) Engelhard, p. 468. — 7) Beschrijving van het landschap Pasir, pp. 541, 542. — 8) Denison, in Ling Roth, p. 210. — 9) Von Dewall, pp. 23, 24. — 10) Ibid., p. 80. — 11) Tromp, Rambai, p. 111. — 12) Graafland, Minahassa, I pp. 285, 286; Riedel, Minahasse, p. 502. — 13) Wilken and Schwartz, pp. 382—384. — 14) Riedel, Holontalo, pp. 65—67.

in Buool [1]),
among the Toradja of Central Celebes [2]),
among the Tomori (East-Central Celebes) [3]),
in the district of Sandjai [4]),
in Bangkala [5]),
among the Kailirese of Donggala or Banawa [6]),
in Saleyer, an island near the South Coast of Celebes [7]).

V. Little Sunda Islands and Moluccas.

Slavery on these islands seems almost universal. About the
following islands and groups of islands we have been able to
obtain some information:

Sumbawa [8]),
Sumba [9]),
Flores [10]),
Solor group [11]),
Bonerate and Kalao [12]),
East Timor [13]),
West Timor [14]),
Savu [15]),
Rote or Rotti [16]),
Wetar [17]),
Keisar [18]),
Leti [19]),
Dama [20]),

---

1) Riedel, Boeool, pp. 197, 204. — 2) Kruijt, N. Z. G. XXXIX pp. 121—123, 126—128;
XL pp. 141, 142; Adriani, pp. 240, 241. See also the description given by Riedel, who
calls them Topantunuazu; Riedel, Topantunuazu, pp. 82—84, 90. — 3) Kruijt, Toboengkoe en Tomori, pp. 233, sqq. — 4) Bakkers, Sandjai, p. 287. — 5) van Hasselt, Bangkala, p. 367. — 6) Het landschap Donggala, pp. 520, 521. — 7) Donselaar, Saleijer,
pp. 296—299. — 8) Ligtvoet, p. 570. — 9) de Roo, pp. 582—585; see also Bieger, p. 153.
— 10. Von Martens, p. 117 (on the whole island); Ten Kate Timorgroep, p. 212 (on
Sika); and especially Roos, pp. 488—491 (on Endeh). — 11) Ten Kate, Timorgroep, p. 242.
— 12) Bakkers, Bonerate, pp. 248—250; Vink, pp. 340, 341. — 13) De Castro, pp. 484, 485;
Forbes, Timor, p. 417. Zondervan mostly relies on De Castro. — 14) Ten Kate, l. c., p. 343.
— 15) Donselaar, Savoe, pp. 295, 296. — 16) Graafland, Rote, pp. 364, 365. — 17) Riedel,
Rassen, pp. 434 sqq. — 18) Ibid., p. 406. — 19) Ibid., p. 384; Van Hoëvell, Leti, p. 212.
— 20) Riedel, Rassen, p. 463.

Luang-Sermata group [1]),
Babar group [2]),
Tenimber and Timorlao Islands [3]),
Aru Islands [4]),
Kei Islands [5]),
Watubela Islands [6]),
Seranglao-Gorong group [7]),
Serang [8]),
Ambon and the Uliase [9]),
Sangi and Talauer Islands [10]).

In all these cases it is clear, that slavery either formerly existed or still exists.

Slaves are also employed by the Galela and Tobelorese on Halmaheira[11]), and by the inhabitants of the district of Kau on the same island [12]).

Riedel states, that on Buru there were formerly slaves, and gives some details about slavery as it was carried on here. Wilken however says that there are neither slaves nor pawns[13]). Whether the latter means to say, that slavery did not exist at the time at which he was writing (1875), or that it had never existed, is not clear. Van der Miesen, writing in 1902, states that, if a man is unable to pay his debt, he is obliged to serve his creditor till his parents have collected the required sum[14]). No further mention of slavery or pawning is made in his detailed description. So we are left in doubt as to the former existence of slavery here.

VI. Philippines.

The Tagals and Visayas, at the time of the conquista, already practised slavery on a large scale[15]).

---

1) Ibid., p. 320. — 2) Ibid., p. 346. — 3) Ibid., p. 293; Van Hoëvell, Tanimbar, p. 174; Forbes, Timorlaut, pp. 15, 18. — 4) Riedel, l. c., p. 251; Rosenberg, Mal. Arch., pp. 338, 344. — 5) Riedel, l.c., pp. 226, 228, 231; Van Hoëvell, Kei-eilanden, p. 120; Pleijte, p. 567. — 6) Riedel, l. c., p. 194. — 7) Ibid., p. 154. — 8) Ibid., pp. 101—103; Boot, p. 1171. — 9) Riedel, l. c., p. 49; Van Hoëvell, Ambon, p. 47. — 10) Hickson, p. 141; see also pp. 137, 139, 142; van Dinter. — 11) Riedel, Galela, pp. 64—66. — 12) Campen, p. 285. — 13) Riedel, Rassen, pp. 18, 19; Wilken, Boeroe, p. 3. — 14) Van der Miesen, p. 449. — 15) Blumentritt, Conquista, pp. 53—59; Blumentritt, Tagalen, pp. 12—17.

Slavery certainly exists among the Bagobos [1]), Manobos [2]), Maguindanaos and inhabitants of the Sulu islands [3]), and Samales [4]).

Among the Subanos slaves are sacrificed at funerals [5]). But whether these so-called slaves are really slaves, or persons captured or purchased for sacrificing purposes only, does not appear.

The Kiangans sell their debtors as slaves; whether within the tribe or abroad we are not told [6]).

In Blumentritt's rather short article on the Bungians no mention is made of slaves [7]).

From Venturillo's and Miller's descriptions it appears that slavery is unknown among the Bataks of Palawan [8]).

Jenks, in his minute account of the Bontoc Igorot of Northern Luzon, gives a full description of the division of labour among them. The poor serve the rich for wages. Slaves are not mentioned. Under the heading of "conquest" he remarks: "Certain Igorot, as those of Asin, make forcible conquests on their neighbours and carry away persons for slavery. But Bontoc has no such conquests". Schadenberg, too, does not speak of slaves among the Bontoc people [9]). Hence we may safely infer that the Bontoc Igorot do not keep slaves.

About the other divisions of the Igorot we are not so well informed. From Jenks's above-quoted incidental remark it would appear that some of them practise slavery. But as in the other sources [10]) we do not find anything strengthening this presumption, we cannot arrive at a positive conclusion.

Reed, describing the Negritos of Zambales (along the western coast of Luzon), says: "Notwithstanding the statements of Montano that the Negritos have no slaves and know nothing of slavery, the reverse is true, in Zambales at least; so say the Negritos and also the Filipinos who have spent several years among them. The word "a-li-pun" is used among them to

---

1) Schadenberg, Süd-Mindanao, pp. 9, 12, 28; Blumentritt, Mindanao, p. 281. — 2) Blumentritt, Ethnographie, p. 49; Blumentritt, Mindanao, pp. 293, 294. — 3) Blumentritt, Ethnographie, pp. 53, 54; Blumentritt, Maguindanaos, p. 891; Jansen, pp. 219, 224, 225. — 4) Schadenberg, Süd-Mindanao, p. 47. — 5) Blumentritt, Mindanao, p. 297. — 6) Blumentritt, Kianganen, p. 132. — 7) Blumentritt, Bungianen. — 8) Venturillo, see especially p. 142; Miller. — 9) Jenks, pp. 136—138; Schadenberg, Nord-Luzon. — 10) Blumentritt, Ethnographie; Meijer, Igorroten; Jagor, Philippines.

express such social condition. As has been stated, a man caught steeling may become a slave, as also may a person captured from another rancheria, a child left without support, a person under death sentence, or a debtor. It was also stated that if a man committed a crime and escaped a relative could be seized as a slave. It will take a long acquaintance with the Negritos and an intimate knowledge of their customs to get at the truth of these statements". From this last sentence, together with the fact that the other writers on the Negritos we have consulted do not make any mention of slavery, we must infer that it is doubtful whether slavery exists among the Negritos [1]).

VII. Madagascar.

The Hovas and kindred tribes are considered by many investigators to be Malays. Schurtz also classifies them among the Malays in the widest sense of the word [2]). The anthropologists do not yet agree about the origin of the Hovas; but as the divisions of this chapter are only intended to give the reader a clear survey of the matter, and not to answer any anthropological purpose, we may treat them here as well as elsewhere.

The existence of slavery among the Hovas is proved by the statements of several good authorities [3]).

Sibree, describing the Betsileo, Betsimisaraka, Bara, Tankay or Bezanozano, Sihanaka and Tanala, makes no mention of slavery; but his notes are not detailed enough to make its non-existence certain [4]).

Hildebrandt and Grandidier speak of slaves among the Antankarana [5]). As, however, in their short notes only slaves of the king are mentioned, we may put this down as a doubtful case.

---

1) See Reed, p. 63; Semper, Philippinen ; Mallat; Blumentritt, Negritos; Schadenberg, Negritos. — 2) Schurtz, Katechismus, p. 221. — 3) Sibree, pp. 181, 182; Hartmann, p. 75; Ellis, Madagascar, pp. 146—149. — 4) Sibree. — 5) Hildebrandt, Ambergebirge, p. 276; Grandidier, p. 217.

Result. Positive cases: *Battas on the Pane and Bila rivers,*
„   *of Mandheling,*
„   *of Pertibie,*
Karo Battas,
Raja Battas,
Battas of Angkola,
„   *of Simelungun,*
„   *of Singkel and Pak-pak,*
„   *of the country of Panei,*
Toba Battas,
Lampongs,
inhabitants of Nias,
„   „ *Anambas, etc.,*
Hill-Dyaks,
Dyaks on the Barito,
Sea-Dyaks,
Dyaks on Rejang river,
Biadju-Dyaks,
Ot-danoms,
Olo-ngadju,
Dyaks of Tompassuk,
Kayans on the Mendalam,
„   *on the Upper Mahakam,*
Muruts,
Dyaks of Sambas,
Kindjin-Dyaks,
Dyaks of Pasir,
inhabitants of the Minahassa,
„   „ *Bolaäng,*
„   „ *Holontalo,*
„   „ *Buool,*
Toradja,
Tomori,
inhabitants of Sandjai,
„   „ *Bangkala,*
Kailirese,
inhabitants of Saleyer,
„   „ *Sumbawa,*
„   „ *Sumba,*

inhabitants of Flores,

   "   " *the Solor group,*

   "   " *Bonerate and Kalao,*

   "   " *East Timor,*

   "   " *West Timor,*

   "   " *Savu,*

   "   " *Rote,*

   "   " *Wetar,*

   "   " *Keisar,*

   "   " *Leti,*

   "   " *Dama,*

   "   " *the Luang-Sermata group,*

   "   " *the Babar group,*

   "   " *the Tenimber and Timorlao Islands,*

   "   " *the Aru Islands,*

   "   " *the Kei Islands,*

   "   " *the Watubela Islands,*

   "   " *the Seranglao-Gorong group,*

   "   " *Serang,*

   "   " *Ambon and the Uliase,*

   "   " *the Sangi and Talauer Islands,*

Galela and Tobelorese,

inhabitants of Kau,

Tagals and Visayas,

Bagobos,

Manobos,

Maguindanaos,

inhabitants of Sulu,

Samales,

Hovas,

Jakun,

Dyaks of Matan,

  "   " Simpang,

Subanos,

Negritos,

Antankarana.

Negative cases: *Semang,*
Sakai,
Kubus,
Mentawei Islanders,
Dusuns,
Rambay and Sebruang Dyaks,
Bataks of Palawan,
Bontoc Igorot,
Battas of Silindung,
Lubus.

No conclusion: Enganese,
inhabitants of Buru,
Kiangans,
Bungians,
Igorot (except the Bontoc Igorot),
Betsileo,
Betsimisaraka,
Bara,
Tankay,
Sihanaka,
Tanala.

We shall add here a few notes on some Malay peoples, that have attained to a too high degree of civilization to be quoted here as instances of savages having or not having slaves. The purpose of this addition is only to complete this survey of the Archipelago, and to show what literature exists on these peoples.

In Java slavery has not prevailed for centuries. "In Mohammedan law a large place is taken up with regulations of slavery, of the rights of masters and slaves, and of the manner in which the latter can acquire their freedom. The peculiar state of the aboriginal Javanese society prevented the application of nearly all precepts relating to this matter. Before the introduction of Islam slavery proper seems to have been unknown; the universal subjection of the mass of the people, as Sudras, to the members of the higher castes, had made slavery superfluous. Nor has Islam introduced slavery into Java; for although in later times Javanese chiefs in a few cases kept slaves, this

was done in imitation of the Europeans, and the legal status
of these slaves depended on Roman-Dutch law, not on Mohammedan law." The *desas* or villages, that did not accept Islam,
were conquered; yet their inhabitants were not enslaved,
but the whole villages *en bloc* were reduced to a subjected
state: they had to pay extraordinary tributes and to perform
services to the Sultans. This ancient state of things remained
in force, even when gradually the whole population accepted
Islam. Even the concubines of the chiefs are not captured or
purchased slaves, but women taken from among the people [1].
This passage from Veth's book does not, however, inform us
as to whether there were slaves before the Hindu invasion
and some time after. In the "Encyclopaedie voor Nederlandsch
Indië" it is stated [2], that in old times Africans were imported
as slaves into Java, as appears from an inscription of 800 A. D.
The continued investigation of Javanese history will probably
throw more light on the subject.

In Bali slavery certainly exists, or at least formerly existed;
but, according to Liefrinck, only the chief and his family have
slaves [3]. Waanders, however, who gives a detailed account of
the Balinese slave-system, asserts that even Sudras ave slaves,
though he speaks but incidentally of this [4]. Perhaps the slaves
kept by the common people are only debtor-slaves; for, according to Liefrinck, debtors serve their creditors, and are sometimes sold by auction [5]. Tonkes, who has (rather deficiently)
collected the literature on the Balinese, does not solve the
question. At any rate, slavery here is not a fundamental institution. The chief has great power, and the Hindu caste-system
prevails, so that the social classes are widely separated; the
Sudras are at the mercy of the upper castes [6]. Slavery, though
discountenanced by the Dutch government, still prevailed as
late as 1877 [7].

Liefrinck states that in Lombok there were imported slaves
and native-born slaves or serfs; the condition of the latter was
much better than of the former, but they could be sold for
debts and then became slaves in the strict sense [8]. Van Eck

---

1) Veth, IV pp. 410—413. — 2) I, p. 11. — 3) Liefrinck, Nota etc., p. 184. — 4) Waanders, p. 133. — 5) Liefrinck, ibid., p. 185. — 6) Waanders, pp. 107, 123—125; Tonkes,
pp. 54—58. — 7) Tonkes, p. 61. — 8) Liefrinck, Slavernij op Lombok, pp. 508, 514, sqq.

has also some notes on Lombok. According to him, Sasaks and Balinese of the Sudra-caste frequently become slaves of the rich, as a punishment or in payment of debts [1]).

Van Hasselt gives a detailed account of slavery among the Malays of Menangkabao. In 1876 the slaves and pawns on the West Coast of Sumatra were emancipated by the Dutch government. But in the territories which are not under Dutch control slavery in van Hasselt's time was still carried on to a great extent. In the little independent states a chief's power depended upon the number of his slaves, who tilled his lands and strengthened his force in warfare. The slaves in the restricted sense were purchased and captured persons and their offspring. Besides these there were pawns [2]). Several further particulars are given in Van Hasselt's valuable book. Willinck, in his recent work on the laws of the Malays of Menangkabao, describes their slave system in details [3]).

In many other Malay districts of Sumatra slavery exists or formerly existed [4]).

Particular mention has to be made of Atjeh, where slavery prevails to a great extent [5]). Slaves are equally kept by the Gajos, whose country borders on Atjeh [6]).

Matthes gives some details on slavery among the Makassars and Bugis of South Celebes [7]).

In Tidore slavery formerly existed, many slaves being procured from New Guinea [8]). It has, however, been abolished by the Dutch government [9]).

---

1) Van Eck, p. 356. — 2) Van Hasselt, Volksbeschrijving van Midden-Sumatra, pp. 190, 191. — 3) Willinck, pp. 130—144. — 4) Among the Rejangs: Marsden, pp. 252, 255; in Semindo: Pauw ten Kate, pp. 537—542, Gramberg, pp. 458, 459; in Blalauw: Gramberg, pp. 471, 472; in Palembang: Gersen, pp. 136, 137; Singkel: Rosenberg, Singkel, p. 413, Rosenberg, Mal. Arch., p. 45; Pangkallan: Holle, pp. 382, 383; Labuan-Batu: Neumann, Laboean-Batoe, pp. 478, 479, Korte beschrijving van het landschap Bilu, p. 553; Karintji, Serampas and Sungai Tenang: Klerks, p. 89; Upper Asahan: Van den Bor, p. 410; Batubarah: de Scheemaker, pp. 471—473; Siak: Nieuwenhuijzen, pp. 412—414; the Rokan states: Quast, pp. 416—418. In Glugur "serfdom does not exist; all men have the same human rights" (Van Delden, p. 169). Whether this is the original state of things, or due to Dutch interference, does not appear. — 5) Snouck Hurgronje, De Atjehers, I pp. 21—25. Concerning the West Coast of Atjeh, see also van Langen, pp. 478, 479. — 6) Snouck Hurgronje, Het Gajoland, pp. 62—64. — 7) Matthes, pp. 3, 5, 136, 137, etc. On the Bugis of Tanette and Barru, see also Bakkers, Tanette, p. 257, and on those of Boni: Bakkers, Boni, pp. 60, 98, 153. — 8) Robidé, pp. 53, 218, 221, etc. — 9) De Clercq, Ternate, p. 74.

Among the Moros of Mindanao "slavery is such an established custom and institution of the land that it is generally sanctioned and supported in the Luwaran [laws]" [1]).

§ 9. *Indo-Chinese Peninsula.*

Some tribes of this group undoubtedly have slaves. These are the Kakhyens [2]), the Shans of Zimmé [3]), the Lawas and the Hill-tribes of North Aracan [4]), one of these hill-tribes being the Khyoungtha of Chittagong [5]).

The Lethtas have no slaves [6]).

The Steins, according to Colquhoun, sometimes seize a slave in order to sacrifice him [7]). No more particulars being given, we cannot make out whether the word slave is used here in its true sense, or means a captive taken to be sacrificed.

Mason remarks on the Karens: "In war they kill without regard to age or sex... The head of the war keeps the captives a considerable time, when, if none of their friends come to redeem them, he sells them off to other districts for oxen or buffaloes if practicable, that he may have an ox or a buffalo to give to each village that came to his aid" [8]). So the Karens seem to prefer oxen and buffaloes to captives. There are, however, many debtor-slaves among the Karen-Nees [9]). They are also noted for their kidnapping propensities; but it seems that the kidnapped are only intended for sale abroad [10]). At any rate there are debtor-slaves, and so slavery exists.

Wehrli, in his study on the Chingpaws (Sing-Phos or Kachins) of Upper Burma, gives many details, which sufficiently prove that slavery exists, or till recently existed among them [11]).

We may add here the inhabitants of the Andaman and Nicobar Islands in the Bay of Bengal.

Although Man does not explicitly state that the Andamanese have no slaves, his elaborate account of their social life suffi-

---

1) Saleeby, p. 65. — 2) Colquhoun, p. 189; Harper Parker, pp. 88, 100. — 3) Colquhoun, pp. 189, 258. — 4) St. John, Aracan, pp. 240—242. — 5) Lewin, p. 85. — 6) Colquhoun, p. 77. — 7) Ibid., p. 155. — 8) Mason, p. 159. — 9) Colquhoun, p. 69. — 10) Ibid., pp. 40, 69, 70. — 11) Wehrli, pp. 36, 37; see also Dalton, p. 10; Rowney, p. 167.

ciently proves that they are unacquainted with slavery. Social status is dependent on relationship, on skill in hunting, fishing etc., and on a reputation for generosity and hospitality. A child captured in war "would meet with kindly treatment, in the hope of his or her being induced ultimately to become a member of the captor's tribe" [1])

Of the Nicobarese Svoboda says: "All writers agree that nowhere in these islands is there subordination, all inhabitants being of the same rank. Only older and more experienced people have somewhat more influence than the rest" [2]). Hence we may infer that slavery does not exist.

Result. Positive cases: *Kakhyens,*
                             Shans of Zimmé,
                             Lawas,
                             Hill-tribes of North Aracan,
                             Karens,
                             Chingpaws,
                             Steins.

      Negative cases: *Lethtas,*
                             Andamanese,
                             Nicobarese.

§ 10. *India, Afghanistan, Himalaya.*

Several authors state that the Meshmees have slaves [3]).

The Hill-tribes near Rajamahall have no slaves [4]).

Dalton gives several particulars about slavery among the Garos. Eliot also affirms that they have slaves [5]).

The Kookies, according to Macrae, "at times .... make captives of the children, and often adopt them into their families, when they have none of their own; and the only slaves among them are the captives thus taken" [6]). What our informant means is not quite clear. The children who have been adopted certainly are not slaves. Perhaps a part only of the captured

---

1) Man, pp. 109, 356. — 2) Svoboda, p. 191. — 3) Cooper, p. 238; Dalton, p. 15; Spencer, Descr. Soc., V p. 15. — 4) Shaw, p. 89. — 5) Dalton, p. 58; Eliot, p. 28. — 6) Macrae, p. 188.

children are adopted, the rest constituting the slave-class of the Kookies; but this is not clearly stated. Lewin asserts that all the hill-tribes (Toungtha, divided into Lhoosai, Tipperah and Kookies) formerly had debtor-slaves [1]); but as none of our other authorities make any mention of this, we doubt whether this general remark applies to the Kookies, the more so as, according to Macrae, "the only slaves among them are the captives". So it becomes very doubtful whether the Kookies have slaves. Dalton's statement that "all the enemies he [the Kookie] has killed will be in the happy hunting-fields in attendance on him as slaves" [2]) is not sufficient to decide the question. One thing only is certain: the Rajah has slaves. According to Dalton, murderers and thieves become slaves of the Rajah. Stewart affirms the same of those guilty of theft, burglary or arson, and Butler of thieves [3]). But if only the Rajah, who represents the public power, has slaves, the Kookies are not properly to be called a slave-keeping people. Whether there are other slaves, besides those of the Rajah, is not sufficiently clear.

The Todas very probably have no slaves. Neither Metz, nor the writers quoted by Spencer, make any mention of slavery, though they fully describe their social life [4]).

The Santals also very probably are unacquainted with slavery. According to Hunter "caste is unknown among the Santals". "The classification of the Santals depended not upon social rank or occupation, but upon the family basis." Dalton, describing the Santals, does not speak of slaves [5]).

The Khonds formerly offered human sacrifices. The victims were purchased, and often kept for many years before being sacrificed. Our informant adds: "I may just allude here to another class of persons who are purchased by the Khonds, or procured by them for adoption into their families as helps in household affairs, and in field labours. These are called Possia Poes, and are usually obtained when young. They run little or no risk of being sacrificed, and very often marry into the families of their purchasers, and in the course of time merge

---

1) Lewin, p. 89. — 2) Dalton, p. 46. — 3) Dalton, p. 45: Stewart and Butler, as quoted by Spencer, l. c., p. 14. — 4) Metz; Spencer, Descr. Soc., V. — 5) Hunter, Rural Bengal, I pp. 200, 202; Dalton, pp. 207—218.

into the general population." In another passage these Possia Poes are called serfs: "These serfs are well treated, and in no immediate danger; but there is always a remote probability of their sacrifice" [1]. As it is stated that these Possia Poes are absorbed into the general population, we may safely conclude that they are not slaves.

The Lushais, according to Dalton, enslave women and children [2].

Of the Manipuris Dalton says that "slavery is an institution amongst them", and he gives some details besides. So we need not doubt its existence, though Watt makes no mention of it [3].

Among the Jyntias and Kasias the Rajah has slaves [4]. Whether there are any other slaves does not appear.

"There is no such thing as slavery among the Oraons", according to Dalton [5].

The Korwas also very probably have no slaves. In their raids they kill all they meet [6].

The Kafirs have slaves, according to several writers [7].

Among the Padam Abors slavery undoubtedly exists [8].

Dalton says of the Dophlas: "They have normally the same Mongolian type of physiognomy, but from their intercourse with the people of the plains and the number of Asamese slaves, which they have by fair means or foul acquired, it is much modified and softened" [9]. Nothing more is added about slavery. Perhaps these "slaves" are simply captured women, no other slaves being ever taken. Whether slavery really exists is not clear.

The Nagas keep slaves, if we are to believe Grange who "saw many Muneeporees who had been thus seized whilst young, and sold both amongst Kookies, Cacharees and Nagas". "The children of slaves are slaves." Miss Godden remarks: "Slavery was unknown among one or more tribes [of the Nagas] according

1) Campbell, pp. 53, 79. — 2) Dalton, p. 114. — 3) Dalton, p. 51; Watt. — 4) Dalton, p. 57. — 5) Ibid., p. 254. — 6) Ibid., p. 230. — 7) Ujfalvy, Aryens, pp. 352, 359; Robertson, pp. 78, 79; Rousselet, p. 223. — 8) Dalton, p. 24. Letourneau (p. 305) is in doubt whether slavery really exists here, first because the Padam Abors are organized in republican and even communistic clans, in which slavery is hardly possible (why?); secondly because the young slaves live together with the young freemen in communal long-houses. This last remark proves that Letourneau is not very familiar with the character of primitive slavery. — 9) Dalton, p. 36.

to Dr. Brown." "Among the Aos [one of the Naga tribes] it is said to have been universal" [1]).

Among the Bodo and Dhimals "there are neither servants nor slaves, nor aliens of any kind" [2]).

The Veddahs of Ceylon, according to Sarasin, are unacquainted with slavery [3]).

Result. Positive cases: *Meshmees,*
Garos,
Lushais,
Manipuris,
Kafirs,
Padam Abors,
Nagas,
Kookies,
Jyntias and Kasias,
Dophlas.
Negative cases: *Hill-tribes near Rajamahall,*
Todas,
Santals,
Khonds,
Oraons,
Korwas,
Bodo and Dhimals,
Veddahs.

§ 11. *Central Asia.*

The Kazak Kirghiz, according to Pallas, "much preferred the securing of a slave to the killing of a man. They did not treat their slaves cruelly, as long as the latter behaved well". But the information we get from other sources shows that they were not a slave-keeping people. Boutakoff says nothing about slavery. According to Ujfalvy the poor serve the rich; he calls this a real serfdom. But he adds that, if the poor do not wish to serve, they must borrow from the rich at 100 per cent.

---

1) Grange, as quoted by Spencer, l. c., pp. 7, 11; Godden in J. A. I. XXV p. 184. —
2) Hodgson, as quoted by Spencer, l. c., p. 7. — 3) Sarasin, p. 488.

interest. So these poor are compelled to serve by hunger, not by any social rule. Chambers says: "They . . . . have well earned for themselves the title of the "Slavehunters of the Steppes" by seizing upon caravans, appropriating the goods, and selling their captives at the great slave-markets at Khiva, Bokhara, etc. Their wealth consists of cattle, sheep, horses, and camels" [1]. This is clear: the captives are sold abroad, and do not serve as slaves among the Kirghiz themselves; therefore they are not enumerated as forming part of their wealth. The best describer of the Kazak Kirghiz that we know of, Levchine, agrees with Chambers. "Slavery is unknown among them." "The Turks, the Persians, and nearly all other sectaries of Mohammed keep slaves . . . . The Kirghiz, on the contrary, have no slaves" [2]. In several passages of his book, however, he makes mention of slaves [3]. But this will be understood, if we pay attention to two other statements of his. "They do not kill their prisoners, but sell them to the Bokharians, Khivians, and other neighbouring nations." They buy many commodities from their neighbours, and "in exchange . . . . provide them with slaves captured on the Russian frontiers" [4]. So the Kirghiz in Levchine's time made slaves; they did not, however, themselves employ them; they were only slave-traders and not a slave-keeping people. Radloff, who many years after Levchine visited the Kazak Kirghiz, supposes that they formerly kept slaves. He says: "The former serfs and slaves of the sultan, who have been for many decades emancipated, always try still to nomadize in the vicinity of the sultans, and, though at present entirely on a level with the other Kirghiz, are still called *telenguts*." "The denominations *kul* (male slave) and *küng* (female slave) now mean male and female servant" [5]. But we may compare this with a statement of Levchine's: "We do not arrange in a separate class the *telenguts* or servants of the khans, nor the *kuls* or slaves. The former are taken from among the Kirghiz and enjoy the same rights; the latter are looked upon as personal property or commodities and are not Kirghiz. They are

---

1 Pallas, Reise, I p. 338; Boutakoff; Ujfalvy, Expéd. scient., p. 112 ; Chambers, as quoted by Spencer, Descr. Soc., V p. 15. — 2) Levchine, pp. 341, 354. — 3) Ibid., pp. 305, 331, 368, 369, 399, 502. — 4) Ibid., pp. 347, 430. — 5) Radloff, Aus Sibirien, I p. 526. Finsch (West Sibirien, p. 150) speaks in the same way.

Russian, Persian, Kalmuck, etc. prisoners" [1]). We see that Radloff's "serfs or slaves", the *telenguts*, were not slaves, and the *kuls* were captured slaves intended to be sold. Our inference is that the Kazak Kirghiz in their former independent state did not keep slaves.

About the Kara Kirghiz we have got but little information. Radloff, in a short article on them, says: "In the regions of their winter-quarters (on the Issik-köl) they cultivate very large pieces of land, on which they leave behind labourers or slaves (of whom there are but few) whilst the tribe repairs *en masse* to the western mountains. These labourers get no wages, but a part of the produce in kind" [2]). Although this receiving of a part of the produce is not incompatible with slavery, their being left behind without any supervision, and Radloff's calling them labourers or slaves and in the latter sentence labourers only, makes us doubt whether these people are really slaves, the more so as in his book slavery among the Kara Kirghiz is not mentioned [3]).

Koehne, in his article on Kalmuck law, referring to Pallas and Bergmann, asserts that the Kalmucks had slaves [4]). But the particulars he gives are not sufficient for us to decide, whether the so-called slaves were slaves proper or retainers of the chiefs; and if slaves, whether they were employed by the Kalmucks, or intended for sale abroad. Spencer refers to a statement of Pallas' (but from which of his books does not appear), according to which slavery was inflicted as a punishment [5]); but whether the person so punished was kept as a slave among the Kalmucks or sold abroad, we are not told. The only book of Pallas' to which we have access does not throw much light on the subject. "Adultery and fornication" he says "which are voluntarily [?] committed with female slaves .... are liable to punishment". In another place he states that the Torguts (a division of the Kalmucks) had much changed in physical appearance, probably by their intercourse with females captured abroad. As a punishment for some offences

---

1) Levchine, p. 305. — 2) Radloff, Beobachtungen über die Kirgisen, p. 168.
3) Radloff, Aus Sibirien. The Kara Kirghiz are described I pp. 526—534. — 4) Koehne, pp. 458, 459. — 5) Spencer, Descr. Soc., V p. 16.

the culprit lost one or more of his children; but what was done with these children does not appear [1]). Nothing more definite on slavery is found is his detailed description of the Kalmucks. In an article on the Kalmucks of the Black Irtysch Valley we read: "Horrible is the state of the unfortunate people who are reduced to slavery; they are bartered and sold like cattle" [2]). Here probably slaves intended for sale abroad are meant; for such horrible treatment of slaves is more common with slave-dealers than with those who employ slaves. Radloff has nothing on slavery; but his description of the Kalmucks is too short to draw any inference from [3]). So we are left in doubt as to the existence of slavery, though we are inclined to think that it does not exist.

Much more fully than the Kalmucks proper Radloff describes the Altaians or Altaian Mountain-Kalmucks. Slaves not being mentioned, and it being stated in many places that the menial work is done by servants and by the poor who are fed by the rich [4]), it is certain that slavery does not exist. The word "slave" occurs in one place only, viz. in the mourning-song of the widow, who complains that "now she wears a leathern dress like base slaves; now she eats coarse food like slaves" [5]). If we have not here to deal with an inaccurate translation, this mourning-song might be a reminiscence of formerly existing slavery. Slavery would then have disappeared spontaneously, not through Russian influence, for the Altaians have maintained their position in the mountain-valleys of the Southwest Altai, least accessible to Russian colonization. So we may safely consider the Altaians as a savage tribe keeping no slaves.

Radloff's notes on the Teleuts, Tatars on the Kondoma and Abakan Tatars are too short to draw any safe inference from [6]).

Many Central Asiatic tribes have been described by Vambéry. The description of each of them fills many pages, but the information we get about social facts is rather incomplete. Therefore, though in most of his descriptions slavery is not

---

1) Pallas, Reise, I pp. 264, 233, 265. — 2) Die Bewohner des schwarzen Irtyschthales, p. 67. — 3) Radloff, Aus Sibirien, II pp. 327—330. — 4) Radloff, l. c., I pp. 270, 286, 287, 293, 295, 312, 315. — 5) Ibid., I p. 320. — 6) Ibid., I pp. 330—343, 353—357, 374—405.

mentioned, we may not infer that it does not exist. The positive cases have of course more value.

The Usbegs, according to Vambéry, till their land aided by Persian slaves [1]). No more details being given, we may put this down as a positive case, though not a clear one.

The Kara Kalpaks, in the beginning of the 18th century, were given to slave-stealing [2]), whether for their own use or for sale does not appear.

The Turkomans, according to Vambéry, sell foreigners as slaves [3]). In another book the same author tells us that in their internal wars they made slaves; and he speaks of their keeping female slaves [4]). Stein and Weil make no mention of slavery [5]). Letourneau, referring to Burnes, remarks: "The Persian captives are for the Turkomans a source of large profit; but the captors do not as a rule keep them for themselves, except sometimes the women, of whom they make concubines or wives" [6]). So we may safely infer that slavery does not exist here.

The Mongols have hired herdsmen who tend their camels [7]). Whether they have any slaves does not appear.

Ujfalvy informs us that among the Tadjiks of Hissar slavery was recently abolished by an order from Bokhara [8]).

According to the same writer "all Galtchas are free; for slavery does not exist and has never existed in their inaccessible valleys" [9]).

The Kurds of Eriwan probably have no slaves. They keep hired herdsmen. All members of the community, rich and poor, enjoy the same rights [10]).

Result. Positive cases: Usbegs,
Tadjiks of Hissar.

Negative cases: *Kazak Kirghiz,*
Altaians,
Turkomans,
Galtchas,
Kara Kirghiz,

---

1) Vambéry, Das Türkenvolk, p. 356. — 2) Ibid., p. 380. — 3) Ibid., p. 410. — 4) Vambéry, Skizzen, p. 64. — 5) Stein; Weil. — 6) Letourneau, p. 227. — 7) Obrutschew, I p. 37. — 8) Ujfalvy, Expéd. scient., p. 84. — 9) Ujfalvy, Aryens, p. 145. — 10) Von Stenin, Kurden, p. 221.

Kalmucks,

Mongols,

Kurds of Eriwan.

No conclusion: Teleuts,

Tatars on the Kondoma,

Abakan Tatars,

Kara Kalpaks.

§ 12. *Siberia.*

Pallas in the 18th century visited many Siberian tribes; but most of his notes are too short to draw any inference from as to the existence of slavery.

Of the Ostyaks he gives a detailed account. They probably had no slaves; for it is stated that the chiefs, like the common people, had to live by their own labour [1]). But in Pallas' time they were already entirely under Russian control [2]), so it is not certain that in their aboriginal state they had no slaves.

The Samoyedes were not nearly so much under Russian influence. The details given by Pallas make it nearly certain that slavery did not exist. "Every Samoyede keeps his reindeer and tends them himself with the help of his family, except the richest, who hire poor men as herdsmen" [3]). Islawin and Finsch also make no mention of slavery [4]). And the account of Samoyede customs given by Von Stenin, who has largely drawn upon Russian literature, makes the non-existence of slavery quite certain [5]).

"The Ghiliaks" says Déniker in a valuable article "are all equal, and never have there been slaves among them" [6]).

Müller gives a somewhat minute description of the Tunguz, in which slavery is not mentioned, so it very probably does not exist [7]).

Sieroshevski, who lived more than 12 years among the Yakuts, concludes from their traditions, that they formerly kept slaves. "In ancient times, the Yakuts had a name for a man whom a

---

1) Pallas, Reise, III p. 51. — 2) Ibid., pp. 25, 26. — 3) Ibid., pp. 72—74. — 4) Islawin; Finsch, West-Sibirien. — 5) Von Stenin, Samojeden, see especially p. 187. — 6) Déniker, Les Ghiliaks, p. 309. — 7) Müller, Unter Tungusen und Jakuten.

defeated hero gave to his conqueror as a compensation for sparing his own life. Such persons later were in fact slaves and were included in the gifts with a bride. If they were females, they became concubines of the master. Such a slave person was called an *enne*, and this word has new come to be used as an adjective for whatever is given with a bride". However this may be, it appears from his detailed and excellent description, that now they have no slaves [1]).

Laufer, describing the Gold of that part of the Amoor lying between Chabarovsk and Sophisk, makes no mention of slavery. But as their whole mode of life is strongly influenced by the Russians, we are not certain whether in their aboriginal state t ey kept slaves [2]).

Steller's statements about slavery among the Italmen or Kamchadales are not very clear. Speaking of their wars he says: "The victorious party enslaved the prisoners, made the women and girls concubines, and slaughtered all males they could to be henceforward safe from them." In another place he states: "They do not steal anything from each other but women and dogs, which was the cause of their former wars." In his survey of Kamchadale history he speaks of a chief who, in order to augment his power, exacted from his enemies a tribute of girls and boys. The Italmen of the Kurile Islands attacked those of the Kamchadale peninsula, and carried off many girls and boys into servitude. In a note he states: "The prisoners and slaves were employed in various rough and domestic labours.... If a prisoner behaved well, he was sometimes dismissed to his home after a two or three years' imprisonment" [3]). In his chapters on male and female labour and on marriage he makes no mention of slaves. In Steller's time Kamchatka had already been brought under Russian control; so he could not any more observe their warfare and taking of prisoners, but got his information about these matters from hearsay. This probably is the reason why this information is not more clear. As he gives some particulars about slaves kept by the Italmen of the Kurile Islands, we may suppose that these at least had slaves. The author of the "Histoire de Kamt-

---

1) Sumner, p. 85; see also Müller, l. c. — 2) Laufer, see especially p. 318. — 3) Steller, pp. 356, 293, 235, 235 note.

schatka", who consulted Steller's manuscript, says: "The end of their wars was to take prisoners in order to make the men work and to take the women as concubines" [1]). But he adds no details.

The Tuski or Chukchi are to be divided into the inland Tuski, who keep reindeer, and the Tuski of the coast, who are fishers. Nordenskiöld remarks: "According to some Russian authors there are slaves, undoubtedly descendants of war-captives, on the inland settlements. Amongst the natives of the coast, on the contrary, the most perfect equality prevails" [2]). A statement of Wrangell's, referred to by Erman, gives some more particulars. Wrangell, having lived already some time with the Tuski, perceived to his great amazement that there were serfs (*Leibeigenen*); he saw some families that did menial work; they had no property, and were not allowed to go away from the rich on whom they were dependent. They received clothing and lodging from their employers, and did the hardest work; for instance they ran by the side of the sledges to urge on the dogs. The Tuski said that this state of things had always existed. Wrangell supposes that these serfs were the offspring of war-captives. It does not appear what this supposition is founded upon [3]). This record is worth more than Nordenskiöld's vague reference to "some Russian authors." But it is not easy to decide whether these subjected people are slaves. They might simply be poor men dependent on the rich without being slaves, such as are also found among the Eskimos. But the fact, that the poor Tuski are obliged to stay with their employers is more suggestive of slavery. Georgi however states that among the Tuski the poor serve the rich as herdsmen; and Dall, Hooper, and Kennan make no mention of slaves [4]). In the "Histoire de Kamtschatka" it is stated that they made raids on the tribes subjected to Russia, "killing or taking prisoners all they meet" [5]). But we are not told what was the fate of these captives. So we must leave this question undecided. At any rate this alleged slavery has been useful; for it led to Nordenskiöld's positive

---

1) Hist. de Kamtschatka, II p. 156. — 2) Nordenskiöld, II p. 124. — 3) Erman, pp. 379, 380. — 4) Georgi as quoted by Hildebrand, Recht und Sitte, p. 36; Dall; Hooper; Kennan. — 5) Hist. de Kamtschatka, II p. 218.

statement that among the Tuski of the coast, whom he had visited himself, slavery was unknown.

The Koryakes are to be divided into nomadic Koryakes and settled Koryakes. The former with their herds roam from one place to another, the latter live along the rivers. The languages of these two divisions differ so much, that they cannot understand each other. "The nomadic Koryakes consider them [the settled Koryakes] as slaves, and treat them accordingly" says our informant. But we know that such slavery of a tribe as a whole is not slavery in the true sense of the word. No other mention is made of slaves. The nomadic Koryakes "before they were subjected by the Russians, had neither government nor magistrates; only the rich exercized some authority over the poor" [1]). So we may infer that slavery is unknown among both nomadic and settled Koryakes.

Melnikow, minutely describing the Buriats, makes no mention of slaves; but as they have been long under Russian influence [2]), we are not certain whether slavery was not formerly an institution among them.

The Ainu, though not inhabiting Siberia, may find a place here, as they live nearer to this than to any other group. Batchelor, describing the raids which the several divisions of the Ainu made on each other, says: "On such occasions the whole of the male population were murdered during sleep, whilst the women and children were carried off as slaves to work in the gardens, and were called *usshui ne guru*. The women however were kept as concubines" [3]). Landor refers to this and some other remarks of Batchelor's and then adds: "From my own experience — and I may add I am the only foreigner who has seen these Tokachi, or as others call them, Tokapchi Ainu — I came to a conclusion very different from this. I found that not only were they not cannibals, but that, taken altogether, they were the most peaceable, gentle, and kind Ainu I came across during my peregrinations through the land of the hairy people" [4]). Hitchcock also describes the Ainu as peaceable. Speaking of some cruel punishments in vogue amongst them, he remarks: "H. von Siebold has supposed from

---

1) Ibid., pp. 82, 223, 239. — 2) Melnikow, pp. 194, 206. — 3) Batchelor, p. 288. — 4) Savage Landor, p. 59.

these old customs, that the Ainos were once a savage and
warlike people. They may have been so, as one might infer
from Japanese tradition, but it seems to me unsafe to make
the assumption on the grounds suggested by von Siebold.
Their present character does not sustain it in any way" [1].
Some other describers of the Ainu we have consulted make
no mention at all of slaves [2]. So we cannot arrive at a definite
conclusion.

Result. Positive case: *Kamchadales.*
            Negative cases: *Samoyedes,*
                            Ghiliaks,
                            Tunguz,
                            Yakuts,
                            Tuski of the coast,
                            nomadic Koryakes,
                            settled Koryakes,
                            Ostyaks,
                            Gold.
      No conclusion: inland Tuski.
                     Ainu.

§ 13. *Caucasus.*

Slavery undoubtedly exists among the Ossetes [3] and Circassians [4].

The Shahsewenses, according to Radde, consist of two social
classes, the nobles and the common people [5]. So they probably
have no slaves.

According to Bodenstedt "every Suane who is not able to
provide for his daughters and sisters, may sell them as slaves" [6].
This is the only reference made to slavery by any of our
informants [7]. Telfer states that the independent Suanes

---

1) Hitchcock, p. 467. — 2) Joest, Weltfahrten; St. John, The Ainos; Holland. —
3) Morgan, Ossetes, pp. 374, 377, 408; Klaproth, II pp. 595, 615; Pallas, Neue Nord.
Beitr., VII p. 69; Kovalewsky, Coutume contemp., pp. 78, 189, 196, 203, 347. — 4) Bell,
I pp. 163, 169 etc., II pp. 97 etc.; Klaproth, I pp. 564—573. — 5) Radde, pp. 425, 426.
— 6) Bodenstedt, I p. 283. — 7) See Von Haxthausen; Telfer.

acknowledge neither king nor nobility, consider all men equal, despise all authority and have no laws [1]). Therefore it does not seem probable that they keep slaves; perhaps the daughters and sisters of whom Bodenstedt speaks are sold abroad.

In Klaproth's detailed description of the Charachai no mention is made of slavery; so probably it does not exist [2]).

Chantre gives a few short notes on some Caucasus tribes. Gourien nobles, according to him, export slaves to Turkey [3]). Whether they also employ slaves, we do not know.

Among the Kabards of Asia Minor the families consist of about twelve persons, slaves included [4]).

The Abchases were formerly slave-traders. They coupled their prisoners, and sold the children born of these unions [5]). Whether these slave-breeders kept their slaves only for the sake of reproduction or for anything beyond this, does not appear.

The Tchetchenes "say: We are all equal. There were never slaves among them. Only the captives were not members of the tribe; but even these often married their master's daughters and so became their equals" [6]). These captives bear a strong resemblance to slaves; and we should be very much inclined to call them such, were it not that Chantre positively asserts that there never were slaves in this tribe. The lack of further details prevents our coming to any definite conclusion.

Result. Positive cases: *Ossetes,*
Circassians,
Kabards of Asia Minor.
Negative cases: *Charachai,*
Shahsewenses.
No conclusion: Suanes,
Tchetchenes,
Gouriens,
Abchases.

---

1) Telfer, p. 113. — 2) Klaproth. — 3) Chantre, IV p. 79. — 4) Ibid., p. 129. — 5) Ibid., p. 136. — 6) Ibid., p. 192.

§ 14. *Arabia.*

The Aeneze Bedouins have slaves. "Slaves, both male and female, are numerous throughout the desert; there are but few sheiks or wealthy individuals who do not possess a couple of them" [1].

Doughty makes no mention of slavery among the Fejir Bedouins; but his description is not elaborate enough for us to infer that slavery does not exist [2].

Regarding the Larbas, a tribe of pastoral Arabs living in North Africa, we have got a very good description by Geoffroy. They keep Negro slaves [3].

Result. Positive cases: *Aeneze Bedouins,*
                         Larbas.
     No conclusion: Fejir Bedouins.

§ 15. *Africa. A. Bantu tribes.*

Theal remarks about the Bantu tribes in general that, when first discovered by the Portuguese, the coast tribes had no slaves, but in the inland there were heartless slave-owners [4].

1. Caffres.

Tromp and Macdonald, describing the Caffres in general, make no mention of slavery [5]. Waitz remarks: "The poor join the rich as their "children", live in servitude, and are often exposed to heavy oppression and arbitary treatment; but they are not slaves in the true sense: slavery proper does not exist." "The conquered are not enslaved, the conqueror requires only subjection; whereas often the object of their wars is the capturing of cattle rather than of men" [6].

---

1) Burckhardt, I p. 356; see also pp. 158, 175. — 2) Doughty. — 3) Geoffroy, p. 428. — 4) Theal, p. 72. — 5) Tromp, De Kaffers; Macdonald, South African tribes. — 6) Waitz-Gerland, II pp. 391, 398.

The Ama-Xosa are described by Fritsch. War is seldom sanguinary, its main object being cattle-stealing; but if the attacked defend their cattle energetically, a general slaughter ensues; women and children are killed without discrimination. Fugitive enemies are mercilessly slaughtered. When a chief has great renown, he gets many followers, who crowd towards him from all sides and contribute to the enlargement of his power; for it is a custom among the Caffres never to deliver up a fugitive whatever the reason of his fleeing from his native country. The chiefs punish insurgents by taking away their cattle; then they are poor men without any influence in the tribe. These particulars make the existence of slavery improbable: no prisoners are taken, fugitives and insurgents are not enslaved. In one place, however, Fritsch speaks of slaves. The Fengu, remnants of destroyed tribes, fell into the hands of the Ama-Xosa, who spared the lives of these fugitives, but kept them in wretched bondage. "In 1835, after this slave-state had lasted for more than ten years, when the Caffres were at war with the colony, the Fengu begged the Governor Sir Benjamin d'Urban to liberate them. The Governor, complying with the request, sent troops to enable them to depart, and so at once 16800 men, women and children with what little cattle and other property they had, established themselves in the colony" [1]). It is clear that these Fengu were not slaves. That they could depart in such large numbers from the country of the Ama-Xosa, proves that they lived more or less separate. They were weaker tribes subjected by a stronger one; we shall see that this occurs very often in South Africa. The tribes were subjected as tribes, not the individuals as such; therefore they were not slaves. Kropf, who lived among the Ama-Xosa as a missionary for 42 years, describes them as they were some 70 years ago. In his detailed account he does not speak of slaves. Male prisoners were killed, women and children were sometimes left alive. We are not told what was the fate of these women and children. There were no social classes, the whole people, from the chief down to the last of his subjects, regarding themselves as one family [2]). From all this we may safely infer that slavery did not exist among the Ama-Xosa.

1) Fritsch, pp. 79, 80, 93, 97, 147. — 2) Kropf, pp. 180, 170.

In his description of the Ama-Zulu Fritsch makes no mention of slavery. Livingstone says: "Zulus do not usually destroy any save the old, and able-bodied men. The object of their raids in general is that the captured women and children may be embodied into the tribe, and become Zulus. The masters of the captives are kind to them, and children are put on the same level as those of any ordinary man. In their usual plan, we seem to have the condition so bepraised by some advocates for slavery. The members of small disunited communities are taken under a powerful government, obtain kind masters, whom they are allowed to exchange for any one else within the tribe, and their children become freemen.... The Zulus are said never to sell their captives" [1]). These captives who are "embodied into the tribe, and become Zulus," and are never sold, certainly are not slaves.

The Matabele are a division of the Zulus, who in 1820 separated from the mother-country. Their mode of life still bears much resemblance to that of the Zulus [2]). Livingstone remarks: "Among the coast tribes a fugitive is almost always sold, but here [*i. e.* among the Zulus] a man retains the same rank he held in his own tribe. The children of captives even have the same privileges as the children of their captors. The Rev. T. M. Thomas, a missionary now living with Moselekatse, finds the same system prevailing among his Zulu or Matabele. He says that "the African slave, brought by a foray to the tribe, enjoys, from the beginning, the privileges and name of a child and looks upon his master and mistress in every respect as his new parents. He is not only nearly his master's equal, but he may, with impunity, leave his master and go wherever he likes within the boundary of the kingdom: although a bondman or servant, his position, especially in Moselekatse's country, does not convey the true idea of a state of slavery; for, by care and diligence, he may soon become a master himself, and even more rich and powerful than he who led him captive." The practice pursued by these people, on returning from a foray, of selling the captives to each other for corn or cattle, might lead one to imagine, that slavery existed in all its intensity among the

1) Livingstone, Zambesi, pp. 385, 386. — 2) Fritsch, pp. 145, 146.

native Africans; but Mr. Thomas, observing, as we have often done, the actual working of the system, says very truly: "Neither the punctuality, quickness, thoroughness, nor amount of exertion is required by the African as by the European master. In Europe the difficulty is want of time, in Africa, what is to be done with it. Apart from the shocking waste of life, which takes place in these and all slave forays, their slavery is not so repulsive as it always becomes in European hands" [1]. Kerr states, that the masters must pay for the offences committed by their slaves [2]. Holub's account throws quite another light on the subject. The captured boys are given to warriors in order to be instructed by them in warfare; those already accustomed to the use of weapons are instantly enrolled into the army. Female captives are lent to warriors. The king used yearly to make raids on the neighbouring countries; on these occasions thousands were slaughtered. Besides the men, old women no longer able to work, infants and young children were killed. When Mackenzie in 1863 visited Matabeleland, he found but a few Zulu-warriors. Most men in the prime of life were Bechuanas, whom the king had either captured or exacted as a tax. The regiments of young men consisted mainly of Makalaka and Mashona youths. In time of peace they had to tend the cattle, and on their return home to exercise themselves in the use of weapons [3]. Can these statements be brought to agree? It may be, that Holub's account relates to a period of strong but short-lived despotism, such as so often occurs among these tribes, and Livingstone's description to a more peaceful time. It may also be, that both relate to the same period, Livingstone not mentioning their military organization. Though Thomas (quoted by Livingstone) speaks of slaves, it is not easy to make out, whether the captives were really slaves; we should rather think not, as they were allowed to leave their masters and go wherever they liked. At any rate slavery, if it exists, is not much developed, the chief function of slaves probably being reinforcement of the tribe in warfare.

The Bechuana group consists of several tribes, the principal being, according to Schurtz [4], the Basuto, the Makololo, the

1) Livingstone, Zambesi, pp. 262, 263. — 2) Kerr, I p. 20. — 3) Holub, Süd-Afrika, II pp. 432, 434. — 4) Schurtz, Katechismus, p. 169.

Bamangwato, the Bakwains and the Bakalahari. Fritsch, describing the Bechuanas in general, makes no mention of slaves. According to Holub, however, they have Makalahiri slaves [1]). But from some particulars it appears that these Makalahiri are rather a tribe subjected as a whole than individual slaves. "These Makalahiri have to live in the more western parts, where game is plentiful, and have to kill the game and bring the spoil to their masters, who live in parts where the water is more abundant." They are employed as hunters or herdsmen. "If a Makalahiri servant behaves well and kills a good many ostriches for his master, he is allowed to marry a Bechuana woman" [2]). Conder describes the Makalahiri as "nomadic hunters, living chiefly in the west, and considered in the light of serfs of the chief" [3]). It is clear that these hunters, living away from the Bechuanas, and considered as "serfs of the chiefs," are a subjected tribe and not individual slaves. There are two other tribes subjected to the Bechuanas: the Barwa or Masarwa, and the Madenassana. That these are servile tribes and not slaves, appears still more clearly than with the Makalahiri [4]). Hence we should infer that the Bechuanas have no slaves. We shall presently see whether this conclusion agrees with the information we get about the single tribes belonging to this group.

According to Casalis, who was intimately acquainted with the Basutos, slavery was unkwown among them, the servile work being performed by the women and children. Prisoners of war were admitted to be ransomed [5]).

The Batauana are described by Passarge. Though he calls them a division of the Basutos, the state of things among them, as regards slavery, is quite different from that among the Basutos. Passarge speaks of slaves kept by them and also of tribes subjected by them, but living in separate settlements and leading a tribal life. Whether the so-called slaves are identical with the members of the subjected tribes or whether they are slaves in the proper sense, is not clear [6]).

---

1) Holub, Süd-Afrika, I p. 432. — 2) Holub in J. A. I. 1881, p. 10. — 3) Conder, p. 89. — 4) Holub, Süd-Afrika, I p. 432. — 5) Casalis, pp. 197, 236. — 6) Passarge, Okawango-sumpfland, pp. 704, 705, 710 711.

Livingstone tells us that the Makololo never make slaves. In another work he relates, how once a troop of Matabele was starving on an island; the Makololo finding them killed the adult people and adopted the rest. Formerly there was no slave-trade; now captured children are the object of it [1]). The Makololo therefore have no slaves.

As to the Bakwains, Livingstone speaks of a woman who, as a punishment for theft, became the property of the injured party [2]). But we do not know, whether she was intended to be sold abroad or to be kept as a slave. Holub speaks of Barwa and Makalahiri in a servile condition; but these are probably subjected tribes and not slaves [3]).

Joest informs us that among the Barolong there are descendants of slaves, though not treated as such, who live with most of their families. They tend the cattle; their name "Bakhalahari" vouches for their western origin [4]). Perhaps they are a division of the same Makalahiri we have met with as a tribe subjected to the Bechuanas. But the statement that they live with Barolong families is more suggestive of slavery; they may, however, be free labourers. We cannot arrive here at any definite conclusion.

The Angoni are great slave-traders, but also keep domestic slaves. Wiese and Kerr give some particulars regarding their slave-system [5]).

Junod gives a detailed description of the Baronga, living near Delagoa Bay. Slaves were formerly sold on a large scale to the coast people. Whether the Baronga themselves kept slaves does not appear [6]).

Among the Vawenda the children of sorcerers are sold as slaves; whether at home or abroad we are not told [7]). No more particulars being given, we do not know whether slavery exists here.

Theal, describing the Makalanga or Makaranga, tells us of a chief who offered female slaves to the whites [8]). But this short note is by no means sufficient for us to go upon.

---

1) Livingstone, Zambesi, p. 125; Livingstone, Miss. Trav., pp. 88, 93. — 2) Ibid., p. 235. — 3) Holub, Süd-Afrika, I p. 397. — 4) Joest, Weltfahrten, I p. 253. — 5) Wiese, pp. 188-197; Kerr, II p. 129. — 6) Junod, p. 96. — 7) Beuster, p. 239. — 8) Theal, p. 161.

2. South-West Bantus.

The Ovampo, according to Galton, have members of foreign
tribes living among them in a state of subjection; but whether
these people are slaves in the true sense is not clear. "I cannot
speak with certainty" he says "of the exact standing in which
the Damaras and the Bushmen severally live among the Ovampo.
The first are employed principally as cattle-watchers; the second,
who are even more ornamented than the Ovampo themselves,
are a kind of standing army; but I have great reason to doubt
whether either one or the other class is independent. The
Ovampo, as I have mentioned, looked down with much contempt on the Damaras; and there is not a single instance, so
far as I could learn, of any Ovampo woman marrying a Damara,
and settling in Damaraland, but the reverse is a very common
case. The Bushmen appear to be naturalised among the negro
tribes, and free in the border-lands between them to a distance
very far north of Ondonga" [1]).

Rautanen, in his description of the Ondonga, states that
there are neither serfs nor slaves. But at the same time he
repeatedly makes mention of slaves. Slaves have no rights of
inheritance. The master is responsible for damages caused by
his slaves. Nobody but the chief has the right to sell slaves [2]).
These contradictory statements do not allow us to arrive at a
definite conclusion.

The Ovaherero or Damaras, according to Andersson, have
slaves. The men are lazy; all their work is done by women
and slaves. The slaves are the offspring of impoverished families, and captured Bushmen. The former are enslaved when
children and mainly employed as herdsmen [3]). It is strange
that Fritsch, who often refers to Andersson, makes no mention
whatever of slavery. Hahn and Haarhoff also have nothing on
slavery [4]), which is very puzzling, as according to Andersson
slavery holds so large a place in their social life. Perhaps the
children of impoverished families whom Andersson speaks of

---

1) Galton, p. 142. — 2) Rautanen, in Steinmetz's Rechtsverhältnisse, pp. 336, 335, 342.
The Ondonga are perhaps identical with the Ovampo, see Steinmetz, ibid., p. 326. —
3) Andersson, I pp. 247, 248. — 4) Hahn, Die Ovaherero; Haarhoff.

are not slaves but free labourers compelled to serve only by poverty; for "among all South-African natives the rich oppress the poor, who in the hope of filling their stomachs, submit to a state of dependence that is not authorized by law [1]".

Viehe remarks, that slavery in the proper sense does not exist among the Ovaherero. But captive children are reared among them and regarded as making part of the low domestics, so to speak as serfs. These serfs are, most of them, Damaras of the mountains. They do the same kind of work as the Ovaherero. Many of them, when full-grown, acquire wealth and are on a footing of equality with the Ovaherero themselves. "The serfs live entirely without supervision and can at any time return to their free compatriots." The serfs, as well as the servants of Ovaherero origin, are designated by a native name, originally meaning foreigner, but that has become to mean servant. In another place our informant states, that every individual is called a servant, when compared with a person of higher standing [2]).

It is not easy to decide, whether this description is indicative of real slavery. Only some of the captives, when full-grown, arrive at a position equal to that of the free people; so it would seem that the others remain slaves. But if they are allowed at any time to return to their own country, their position is a voluntary one.

Kohler's authorities, viz. the German magistrate Bensen and the missionaries Meyer and Büttner, all affirm that the Ovaherero keep slaves and give several details. Slaves are captives or children of such; but slavery can also take its origin in voluntary submission. Most of the slaves are Damaras of the mountains. All the goods of the slave belong to his master. The master is responsible for any crime committed by the slave and has the right of life and death over him. Slaves are bought and sold and inherited. They cannot be manumitted. Children of slaves are slaves [3]).

From this it would appear that slavery really exists.

The seeming contradiction between Viehe and Kohler's autho-

---

1) Fritsch, p. 364; see also Waitz-Gerland, II p. 391. — 2) Viehe, in Steimetz's Rechtsverhältnisse, pp. 304, 305, 302. — 3) Kohler, Das Recht der Herero, pp. 311, 312.

rities might be solved, if we attend to the following remark, made by Kohler on Büttner's authority: "The practical possibility for the slaves of escaping from their master is the best warrant for good treatment [1])." We may infer from this that, when Viehe says that the slaves can at any time return to their own country, it is only meant that it is easy from them to do so (as among a pastoral and nomadic nation it is likely to be), not that they are permitted to do so by law or custom.

The conclusion is that the Ovaherero keep slaves.

Among the Batoka the slave-trade had in Livingstone's time been lately introduced [2]). We are not told whether they kept slaves themselves.

The Barotse have slaves; this is proved by the statements of several writers [3]).

In the descriptions of the Makalaka no mention is made of slavery, so they probably have no slaves [4]).

The Manansa are not fond of fighting [5]), so they probably make no prisoners. They might have purchased slaves; but as nothing is told us of slavery amongst them, the probability is against this.

The Kimbunda have an elaborate slave-system, minutely described by Magyar [6]).

The Lovalé people have the reputation of being harsh taskmasters. Slaves are procured by exchange from abroad [7]). These short notes are all the evidence we know of, bearing on the existence of slavery among them.

The people of Lunda are great slave-traders. Several details given by our informants prove that they also keep slaves for their own use [8]).

In the neighbouring country of Cazembe there are two social classes: the nobility and the Muzias or servants, including peasants, artisans, etc. Both classes are called slaves of the Muata (king); this of course is not slavery proper. All men able to fight must go to war; but this does not affect the

---

1) Ibid., p. 312. — 2) Livingstone, Zambesi, p. 322; Livingstone, Miss. Trav., p. 597. — 3) Holub, Süd-Afrika, II pp. 331, 348, 350, etc.; Livingstone, Miss Trav., p. 318; Serpa Pinto, II p. 42. — 4) Holub, Süd-Afrika; Livingstone, Miss. Trav.; Mauch. — 5) Holub, l. c. II p. 241. — 6) Magyar, I pp. 286—290, etc. — 7) Cameron, II pp. 164, 167. — 8) Pogge, Muata Jamwo, pp. 165, 134, 226, etc.; Livingstone, Last Journ., I p. 237.

cultivation of the land, which is carried on by the women only [1]). These statements make the existence of slavery improbable.

Among the Kioko slavery certainly exists [2]).

The Selles, according to Magyar, have also slaves [3]).

3. East-African Bantus.

Macdonald remarks that the East-Central African tribes in general have slaves [4]).

The Manganja suffer much from slave-stealing tribes, but also keep slaves themselves [5]).

Slavery also exists among the following tribes:

> Banyai [6]),
> Wagogo [7]),
> Washambala [8]),
> Wapare [9]),
> Wajao [10]),
> Makonde [11]),
> Wahehe [12]),
> Wachagga [13])
> Wanyamwesi [14]),
> Azimba [15]),
> Wajiji [16]),
> Wapokomo [17]),
> Bondei [18]).

Among the Wasiba or Basiba slavery is practised, though not to a great extent. "There are few slaves in the country,

1) Peters, pp. 395, 394. — 2) Pogge, Muata Jamwo, pp. 45, 46, 51. — 3) Magyar, I p. 80. — 4) Macdonald, East Central African Customs, pp. 101, 102. — 5) Livingstone, Zambesi, p. 396. — 6) Livingstone, Miss. Trav., p. 618. — 7) Beverley, in Steinmetz's Rechtsverhältnisse, p. 213. — 8) Lang, ibid., pp. 240—242; Storch, p. 319. — 9) Storch, p. 323. — 10) Weule, pp. 55, 56. — 11) Weule, pp. 123, 124. — 12) Von Schele, pp. 71, 72. — 13) Kohler, Das Banturecht, pp. 42—45 (after Merker). — 14) Baumann, p. 237; Kohler, Das Banturecht, pp. 42—45 (after Puder). On the Msalala, a division of the Wanyamwesi, see also Desoignies, in Steinmetz's Rechtsverhältnisse, p. 278. — 15) Angus, pp. 317, 323. — 16) Hore, p. 11. — 17) Kraft, in Steinmetz's Rechtsverhältnisse, p. 291. — 18) Dale, p. 230.

most of them being women; a male slave generally runs away and joins another chief as a free man [1])."

The Wanyakynsa, according to Fülleborn, do not keep slaves [2]).

Slavery is equally unknown among the Wambugu [3]).

The Wazaramo have no weapons of war; warfare seems unknown among them. They formerly suffered much from the slave-trade [4]). We do not know, whether they have slaves; probably they have not.

Peters, in his account of the Maravis, gives some particulars about slaves; but they are not sufficient to decide, whether there is domestic slavery or slave-trade only [5]).

The Wasinja and Wakerewe export slaves; but slaves are also imported into their country by caravans [6]). Probably the latter are kept among them; but this short note is not sufficient to draw a positive inference from.

The Wafipa are said never to make slaves or to sell them to traders. When a slave succeeds in arriving at the town of Kapufi, he is considered free. They never make war, though they defend themselves when attacked [7]).

Among the Wanyaturu slavery is unknown [8]).

Von Höhnel, visiting the country of the Wakikuyu, found two men, who some years before had joined a caravan and had been left behind because they were ill; from that time they had lived as slaves among the Wakikuyu [9]). This statement shows, that the Wakikuyu keep slaves for their own use, not for export only.

Of the Wawira we have a detailed description by Emin Pasha. As there is not a word about slaves in it, it is almost certain that slavery does not exist among them [10]).

Slavery is also very probably not to be found among the Wataveta, minutely described by Thomson, Johnston and Von Höhnel [11]).

---

1) Hermann, p. 55. — 2) Fülleborn, p. 383. — 3) Storch, p. 326. — 4) Thomson, Centr. Afr. Lakes, I pp. 102, 139. — 5) Peters, pp. 284, 285. — 6) Baumann, p. 214. — 7) Thomson, Centr. Afr. Lakes, II p. 222. — 8) Baumann, p. 237. — 9) Von Höhnel, p. 318. — 10) Stuhlmann, pp. 492—529. — 11) Thomson, Massai; Johnston; Von Höhnel.

4. Tribes on the Congo and in Lower Guinea.

Ward and De Bas, speaking of the Congo tribes in general, state that slavery exists [1]).

On the Lower Congo, according to Phillips, the family consists of "the head man or patriarch, his wives, family proper, dependents and slaves." There are also debtor-slaves [2]).

Slavery certainly exists among the following tribes:

> Bihés [3]),
> Minungo [4]),
> Mpongwe [5]),
> Orungu [6]),
> Mbengas [7]),
> Apinchi [8]),
> Duallas [9]),
> Fiotes [10]),
> Bayanzi [11]),
> Bangala on the Congo [12]),
> Baluba [13]),
> Manyuema [14]),
> Kabinda [15]),
> Ininga and Galloa [16]),
> Wangata [17]),
> Bondo [18]),
> Camas [19]),
> Bakundu,
> Banyang,
> Batom,

---

1) Ward in J. A. I. 1895, p. 287; De Bas, p. 173. — 2) Phillips, pp. 223, 224. — 3) Magyar, I pp. 213—216, etc. — 4) Schütt, pp. 115, 139, 140. — 5) Buchholz, p. 178; Lenz, pp. 21, 218; Compiègne, Okanda, pp. 194, 195; Winwood Reade, p. 259. — 6) Lenz, pp. 39, 40. — 7) Duloup, p. 222. — 8) Compiègne, Okanda, pp. 93, 95, 96. — 9) Buchholz, pp. 96, 97, 190, 200, 201, 85; see also Kohler, Negerrecht, pp. 10, 24, 25, 34. — 10) Coquilhat, pp. 500—502. — 11) Coquilhat, pp. 85, 86, 122; Ward, Cannibals, pp. 105, 106, 302; Dupont, pp. 210, 231—233; Johnston, The river Congo, p. 396; Torday and Joyce, Congo Free State, p. 139. — 12) Coquilhat, pp. 232, 296, 297, 365, 366; Ward, Cannibals, p. 132. — 13) Wissmann, Im Inneren Afrikas, pp. 82, 158. — 14) Livingstone, Last Journ., II pp. 131, 132, 29, 62, 63. — 15) Wolff, pp. 206, 207. — 16) Lenz, pp. 53, 218; Compiègne, Okanda, pp. 62, 65. — 17) Coquilhat, pp. 149, 157, 169. — 18) Schütt, pp. 38, 41. — 19) Compiègne, Gabonais, pp. 114, 130, 141.

> Mabum [1]),
> Bali tribes [2]),
> Bambala [3]).
> Bayaka [4]),
> Bahuana [5]),
> Bakwese [6]),
> Yaunde [7]),

Hoesemann gives several particulars about the slave system of some tribes of Cameroon, the principal of which are the Indikki [8]).

Regarding the Bakwiri, who are related to the Duallas, we are told that, unlike their neighbours, they do not keep slaves. On the death of a king a slave is bought from abroad and killed [9]).

The describers of the Mundombe make no mention of slavery; so they probably have no slaves [10]).

The writers on the Quillengue also are silent on this subject; but here the descriptions are not minute enough for us to arrive at any accurate conclusion [11]).

The natives of Angola have slaves; whether for export only or also for their own use, does not appear [12]).

The same applies to the Bangala on the Kuango, who are great slave-traders [13]).

The Songo or Masongo use slaves as articles of exchange, and wherever the chief goes, he is accompanied by slaves; but whether they can rightly be called a slave-keeping people, is not clear from Pogge's short notes [14]).

Several authors inform us that the Fans have no slaves [15]).

In a monography on the Banaka and Bapuku many particulars

---

1) On the Bakundu, Banyang, Batom and Mabum, see Hutter, pp. 259 sqq. — 2) Hutter, pp. 341 sqq. — 3) Torday and Joyce, Ba-Mbala, p. 411. — 4) Torday and Joyce, Ba-Yaka, p. 46. — 5) Torday and Joyce, Ba-Huana, p. 286. — 6) Torday and Joyce, Congo Free State, p. 150. — 7) Zenker, pp. 48, 49, 67. — 8) Hoesemann, pp. 176, 177. — 9) Leuschner, in Steinmetz's Rechtsverhältnisse, p. 21; Schwarz as quoted ibidem. — 10) Magyar; Serpa Pinto; Capello and Ivens. — 11) Serpa Pinto; Capello and Ivens. — 12) Pogge, Muata Jamwo, pp. 5, 7. — 13) Schütt, pp. 79, 90, 113; Livingstone, Miss. Trav., p. 435; Capello and Ivens, pp. 314, 325, etc. — 14) Pogge, Muata Jamwo, pp. 35, 36, 39, 40. — 15) Buchholz, p. 178; Lenz, p. 256; Compiègne, Gabonais, p. 159. Bennett, in his article on the Fans, makes no mention of slavery.

are given about their slave system [1]). Hence we infer that slavery exists among them, though Winwood Reade's short remark that among the Bapuka the men are equal would seem to point to a contrary conclusion [2]).

Buchholz, in a short note, speaks of slavery among the Bakele [3]).

The slave-trade is almost the only trade of the Okota. On the death of a distinguished person slaves are killed [4]). This information is not, however, sufficient to put this case down as a clear one.

None of our informants on the Bateke make any mention of slavery. According to Guiral they sometimes eat their prisoners, when they find no occasion to sell them [5]). So they probably keep no slaves.

The Wagenia are stated to throw the corpses of slaves, and perhaps of all the dead, into the river [6]). This short note being the only evidence, we are not certain that slavery really exists.

Among the Warua at the funeral of a chief slaves are killed [7]). But this does not prove that slavery is a social institution here.

The Bakuba have slaves, according to Wissmann [8]). But the same author states in another place, that male slaves are bought only to be killed at funerals [9]). So slavery proper probably does not exist.

When Wissmann visited the Tuchilangue, they had no male slaves; but on a later visit he found that male slaves had been introduced among them. Pogge also observed male slaves [10]). So at present slavery exists here.

Of the Tupende we are told, that slaves have for two hundred years been exported from their country. They buy female slaves, and make them their wives [11]). Probably they keep no male slaves; but it is not certain.

---

1) Steinmetz, Rechtsverhältnisse, pp. 42, 43; see also pp. 41, 51, 54 ibidem. — 2) Winwood Reade, p. 259. — 3) Buchholz, p. 178. — 4) Compiègne, Okanda, p. 84; Lenz. p. 240. — 5) Coquilhat; Ward, Cannibals; Dupont; Wissmann, im Inneren Afrikas; Guiral. p. 150. — 6) Coquilhat, p. 424. — 7) Cameron, II pp. 110, 111. — 8) Wissmann, Im Inneren Afrikas, pp. 240, 241. — 9) Wissmann, Zweite Durchquerung, p. 115. — 10) Wissmann, Unter deutscher Flagge, I p. 93; l. c. note; Pogge's Aufenthalt, pp. 381, 382. — 11) Wissmann, Im Inneren Afrikas, pp. 141, 145, 146.

The Aduma and Oschebo are slave-traders; but of domestic slavery no mention is made [1]).

The same applies to the Hollo [2]) and Milembue [3]).

5. Natives of the Wahuma states.

Among the Waganda slavery is carried on to a great extent [4]).

The describers of the Wanyoro [5]) make no mention of slavery; but their notes are not detailed enough to infer that it does not exist.

The Bahima of Enkole keep slaves [6]).

Slavery also exists among the natives of Bukoba [7]).

Result. Positive cases: *Angoni,*
  Ovaherero,
  Barotse,
  Kimbunda,
  Lunda people,
  Kioko,
  Selles,
  Manganja,
  Banyai,
  Wagogo,
  Washambala,
  Wapare,
  Wajao,
  Makonde,
  Wahehe,
  Wachagga,
  Wanyamwesi,
  Azimba,
  Wajiji,
  Wapokomo,

---

1) Lenz, pp. 281—283. — 2) Wissmann, Im Inneren Afrikas, p. 36. — 3) Wissmann, Unter deutscher Flagge, I p. 147; Pogge's Aufenthalt, p. 309. — 4) Wilson and Felkin, I pp, 161, 186, 193; Baskerville, in Steinmetz's Rechtsverhältnisse, pp. 193, 194. — 5) Chaillé Long; Junker; Wilson and Felkin. — 6) Roscoe, p. 100. — 7) Richter, Der Bezirk Bukoba, p. 87.

Bondei,
Wasiba,
Wakikuyu,
Bihés,
Minungo,
Mpongwe,
Orungu,
Mbengas,
Apinchi,
Duallas,
Fiotes,
Bayanzi,
Bangala on the Congo,
Baluba,
Manyuema,
Kabinda,
Ininga and Galloa,
Wangata,
Bondo,
Camas,
Bakundu,
Banyang,
Batom,
Mabum,
Bali tribes,
Bambala,
Bayaka,
Bahuana,
Bakwese,
Yaunde,
Indikki,
Banaka and Bapuku,
Tuchilangue,
Waganda,
Bahima,
natives of Bukoba,
Batawana,
Lovalé people,
Bakele,

> Wagenia,
> Warua.

Negative cases: *Ama-Xosa*,
> *Ama-Zulu*,
> *Basutos*,
> *Makololo*,
> *Makalaka*,
> *Wanyakynsa*,
> *Wambugu*,
> *Wafipa*,
> *Wanyaturu*,
> *Wawira*,
> *Wataveta*,
> *Bakwiri*,
> *Mumdombe*,
> *Fans*,
> *Bateke*,
> Matebele,
> Manansa,
> Cazembe people,
> Wazaramo,
> Bakuba,
> Tupende.

No conclusion: Bakwains,
> Baronga,
> Ovampo,
> Barolong,
> Vawenda,
> Makalanga,
> Batoka,
> Maravis,
> Wasinja and Wakerewe,
> Quillengue,
> Angola,
> Bangala on the Kuango,
> Songo or Masongo,
> Okota,
> Aduma and Oschebo,
> Hollo,

Milembue,
Wanyoro.

§ 16. *Africa. B. Soudan Negroes.*

1. Coast of Guinea.

Among several tribes here slavery certainly exists. These
are the

> Calabarese [1]),
> inhabitants of Bonny [2]),
> Brass people [3]),
> inhabitants of Benin [4]),
> Ewe [5]),
> inhabitants of Dahomey [6]),
> Geges and Nagos of Porto-Novo [7]),
> Yorubas [8]),
> inhabitants of Ashanti [9]),
> Fanti [10]),
> Gallinas [11]),
> Mandingoes [12]),
> Wolofs [13]),
> Saracolays or Soninkays [14]),

---

1) Bastian, Geogr. and Ethn. Bilder, p. 143; Hutchinson, pp. 133, 141—145; Compiègne, Gabonais, p. 87; Lander, III p. 321; Walker, pp. 120—123. — 2) Bastian, l. c. p. 166; Köler, pp. 84, 153—155, 164; Compiègne, l. c. p. 78; De Cardi, in Kingsley, West African studies, pp. 516, 517, 522—526. — 3) Hutchinson, p. 99; De Cardi, ibid., pp. 471—476. — 4) Bosman, II p. 228; Bastian, l. c. p.175; De Cardi, ibid., pp. 452—454. — 5) Zündel, pp. 387, 407, 408; Herold, pp. 168—170. On the slave system of the Ewe-speaking peoples in general, see Ellis, Ewe-speaking peoples, pp. 218—221. — 6) Burton, II pp. 74, 248. — 7) Hagen, Porto-Novo, p. 97. — 8) Lander, I p. 37; Staudinger, p. 16. On the slave system of the Yoruba-speaking peoples in general, see Ellis, Yoruba-speaking peoples, pp. 178, 182. — 9) Bowdich, pp. 151, 157, 159, 205, 209. The natives of Ashanti belong to the Tshi-speaking peoples of the Gold Coast. On slavery among these peoples in general, see Ellis, Tshi-speaking peoples, pp. 289—295, and Bosman, I pp. 126, 187. — 10) Finsch, Goldküste, pp. 359—361. — 11) Harris, pp. 27—30. — 12) Bérenger-Féraud, p. 211 ; Tautain, Mandingues, pp. 347—350. On slavery among the tribes of Liberia in general, see also Büttikofer in T. A. G. pp. 72, 73; Büttikofer in I. A. E. pp. 81—83. — 13) Bérenger-Féraud, pp. 44, 58—60; Tautain, Sénégal, p. 67. — 14) Bérenger-Feraud, p. 365. See also Fama Mademba's general description of the Sansanding States, inhabited, among others, by the Saracolays and Bambaras, in Steinmetz's Rechtsverhältnisse, p. 83 ; Nicole's notes on the Diakité, a subdivision of the Saracolays, ibidem, pp. 118—120; Arcin, pp. 269—276.

Kagoros [1]),
Bambaras [2]),
Toucouleurs or Torodos [3]),
Jekris [4]),
Malinkays [5]),
Susu,
Landuma,
Limba [6]).

Among the Ibo or Eboe in the hinterland of the Niger delta criminals are sold abroad as slaves [7]). Whether they keep slaves themselves does not appear.

Several writers affirm that the Krus keep slaves. Miss Kingsley, however, who seems to be well acquainted with them, speaks of "the Krus being a non-slave-holding tribe" [8]). So we cannot arrive at a positive conclusion.

"The Bobo" says Tautain "make no slaves; they hold slavery greatly in abhorrence.... It seems that the Bobo are very industrious; as they have no slaves, they probably have to work much harder than the Mandingoes and other neighbouring peoples" [9]).

Corre informs us that "slavery exists among the Sereres. However, the inhabitants of Fadiouth are said to have had captives during the last few years only, imitating what they saw amongst the Wolof traders, most of whom are subjects of France. Independent persons, such as a woman without a husband or family, may sell themselves to any one who is willing to buy them" [10]). This case may well be called a doubtful one.

---

1) Tellier, in Steinmetz's Rechtsverhältnisse, pp. 168—172; Tellier, Autour de Kita, pp. 98 sqq. — 2) Bérenger-Féraud, p. 236; Fama Mademba (see above, p. 155, note 14); Tellier (see note 1). — 3) Bérenger-Féraud, p. 269; Tellier, Autour de Kita, pp. 98 sqq. — 4) Granville and Roth, pp. 117, 118. — 5) Tellier (see note 1); Arcin, pp. 269—276. — 6) On the Susu, Landuma and Limba, see Madrolle, pp. 91—93. — 7) De Cardi, Ju-Ju Laws etc., p. 52. — 8) Lenz, pp. 233, 234; Köler, pp. 57, 58; Hutchinson, p. 48; Staudinger, p. 9; Kingsley in J. A. I. p. 62. — 9) Tautain, Bobo, pp. 230, 233. — 10) Corre, pp. 15, 16.

2. Haussa states.

3. Central Soudan.

The nations inhabiting these parts, such as the Haussa, Borgu, etc., are perhaps not properly to be called savage tribes, so we shall leave them out of regard here [1]).

4. Upper Nile.

Chaillé Long tells us that among the Chillooks the sheikh of each tribe detains as slaves those who do not possess at least one cow [2]). No more particulars being given about slavery, we may put this down as a very doubtful case.

The Diour tribes make raids on each other. A large number of slaves are carried off every year by the Arabian slave-traders [3]). Whether domestic slavery exists or not, we are not told.

Among the Dinka every man has on an average three head of cattle, but there are also poor people, who are the slaves or servants of the rich [4]). These "slaves or servants" very probably are not slaves. We may not, however, infer that slavery does not exist here; for the notes our informants [5]) give on their social life are very short.

The Bari are themselves victims of the slave trade [6]). Whether they keep slaves, we are not told.

Very minute descriptions are given in Stuhlmann's book of the Latuka [7]), Alur [8]) and Lendu [9]). No mention being made of slavery, we may be sure that it does not exist among them.

Junker speaks of a chief of the Abukaja or Amadi, who made raids and divided the booty, consisting of captured women and girls, with the allied chiefs and his subjects. Such is the

---

1) In the first edition of this book we had counted such peoples as the Fulbe, the Haussa and the Tuareg among the savages. Dr. Vierkandt, in his article on "Die Ver-breitung der Sklaverei und ihre Ursachen", rightly remarks that they are rather to be regarded as semi-civilized peoples. — 2) Chaillé Long, p. 29. — 3) Wilson and Felkin, II pp. 163, 162. — 4) Schweinfurth, I p. 164. — 5) Schweinfurth; Junker. — 6) Junker, I p. 531; Wilson and Felkin, II p. 96. — 7) Stuhlmann, pp. 774 sqq. (by Emin Pascha). — 8) Stuhlmann, pp. 492—529. — 9) Ibid., pp. 530 sqq.

custom, says Junker, and therefore the men like to go to war. In another place he speaks of captured women with children and infants, and girls [1]). Whether these captured persons are kept among the Abukaja or exported, and if the former, whether they are made slaves, we do not know.

The same author speaks of slaves among the Makaraka; but it is not clear, whether they keep these slaves or sell them to the Arabians, who carry on the slave-trade on a large scale in these regions [2]).

The Niam-Niam in their wars capture many women. Schweinfurth supposes, that they retain the captured women as slaves, but kill the men. Junker also speaks of female slaves. According to him male slaves are sometimes sacrificed; but it is not clear, whether the latter are ordinary slaves or only bought or captured to be sacrificed [3]). Our information does not admit of any accurate conclusion.

Schweinfurth's description seems to show, that the Mombuttus have male slaves. Junker speaks only of female slaves [4]). Burrows says: "Between the chief and the people are a race of freed men, who do not engage in manual labour of any kind. From the term freed men it must not be inferred that the people below them are slaves; they are equally free, but are without the hereditary rank of the so-called freed men, who are generally relations of the chief or in some way connected with him [5])." Hence it would appear that slavery does not exist among them. These conflicting statements do not allow us to arrive at a safe conclusion.

The Wagungo proper, says Junker, do hardly any work themselves; they leave it all to their slaves, the Schuli and Tschappu [6]). These Schuli and Tschappu seem to be subjected tribes rather than slaves; but as further particulars are wanting, we feel unable to decide.

Among the Warundi slavery is unknown [7]).

---

1) Junker, II pp. 477, 462. — 2) Junker, I pp. 331, 411, 428. — 3) Schweinfurth, II pp. 164, 190; Junker, III pp. 4, 292. — 4) Schweinfurth, II, pp. 45, 82; Junker, II pp. 265, 266, 317; III p. 129. — 5) Burrows, p. 45. — 6) Junker, III p. 507. — 7) Baumann, p. 224.

The same applies to the Wafiomi [1]), Wataturu [2]), and Wambugwe [3]).

The several describers of the Bongos, who give many details
of their social life, make no mention of slavery; hence we
may infer that it does not exist among them [4]).

5. Appendix. African Islands.

The Boobies of Fernando-Po, according to Compiègne, have
numerous slaves. Hutchinson states, that in their wars they
spare neither age nor sex [5]). So the slaves are probably purchased foreigners.

Sibree, describing the Sakalavas of Madagascar, speaks of a
kind of temple, which slaves may not enter, for should they
do so they would become free [6]). According to Hildebrandt the
occupations of the Sakalavas are not multifarious. The men tend
the cattle and now and then sell a beast, and sometimes help
the women in the little plantations. In the rice district
of North Sakalavaland, where rice is cultivated for export,
more labour is wanted on the fields; therefore in this
district many slaves are kept [7]). It is not clear, whether our
informant means to say, that in the other districts of Sakalavaland there are no slaves; at any rate we may conclude, that
among the Northern Sakalavas slavery exists.

Slavery also exists among the inhabitants of the small
islands of Nossi-Bé and Mayotte, many of whom belong to the
Sakalavas [8]).

The other tribes of Madagascar have found a place in § 8
(Malay Archipelago).

Result. Positive cases :   *Calabarese,*
                             inhabitants of Bonny,
                             Brass people,

---

1) Baumann, p. 179. — 2) Ibid., p. 173. Kannenberg's statement, that captives are made
slaves, does not seem to prove anything. These slaves may be sold abroad (see Kannenberg, p. 167, and below p. 164). — 3). Baumann, p. 187 .— 4) Schweinfurth ; Junker; Wilson and Felkin. — 5) Compiègne, Gabonais, p. 92 ; Hutchinson, p. 191. — 6) Sibree, p. 227.
— 7) Hildebrandt, West-Madagascar, p. 113. — 8) Walter, in Steinmetz's Rechtsverhältnisse, pp. 381, 387.

inhabitants of Benin,
Ewe,
inhabitants of Dahomey,
Geges and Nagos,
Yorubas,
inhabitants of Ashanti,
Fanti,
Gallinas,
Mandingoes,
Wolofs,
Saracolays,
Kagoros,
Bambaras,
Toucouleurs,
Jekris,
Malinkays,
Susu,
Landuma,
Limba,
Boobies,
Northern Sakalavas,
Sakalavas of Nossi-Bé and Mayotte,
Sereres,
Niam-Niam,
Mombuttus,
Wagungo.

Negative cases: *Bobo,*
Latuka,
Alur,
Lendu,
Warundi,
Wafiomi,
Wataturu,
Wambugwe,
Bongos.

No conclusion: Ibo or Eboe,
Krus,
Chillooks,
Diours,

Dinka,
Bari,
Abukaja,
Makaraka.

§ 17. *Africa. C. Light-coloured South Africans and African pigmy-tribes.*

Fritsch, at the beginning of his description of the Hottentots or Koi-Koin, states that in his time these tribes had already been much changed from their aboriginal state; so he had to rely on the statements of ancient writers, several of which bear a rather fantastic character [1]).

Of the Namaqua, one of the Hottentot tribes, he says, that the state of women is not so bad as among most South African tribes. The men assist their wives in the hard work; moreover a class of servants or slaves exists here. "This lowest class of people — one might object to our calling them "slaves", as there is no established law distinguishing slaves from freemen — among the Namaqua mainly consists of individuals belonging to the despised tribes of Mountain-Damara and Bushmen. These people are looked upon as inferior by their very birth, and (like the Vaalpenz among the Bechuanas) regard bad treatment as inevitably connected with their origin, without being slaves by law. Serfs (*Leibeigenen*) in the proper sense of the word may be called those only who, as prisoners of war, or by surrendering at discretion (like the Fengu among the Caffres), become subjected to men of power; of these there are but few among the Namaqua tribes, but among all South African natives the rich tyrannize over the poor who, in the hope of filling their stomachs, comply with a state of dependence which is not authorized by law." According to Th. Hahn, he who ill-treats or even barbarously murders a slave, is not punished [2]). This statement is not very clear. Fritsch speaks here of three kinds of "servants or slaves": *a.* poor dependent on the rich; these certainly are servants and not slaves; *b.* individuals belonging to despised tribes; of these Fritsch

---

1) Fritsch, p. 261. — 2) Fritsch, p. 364.

says, that they are not slaves by law, and as no more details are given, we cannot make out what they are; *c.* prisoners of war and those who have surrendered at discretion. These, according to Fritsch, are the only *Leibeigenen* in the proper sense; but he compares them to the Fengu, who, as we saw in § 15, are subjected tribes rather than slaves [1]). Galton remarks: "Though no slaves are exported from the countries in which I travelled, yet there is a kind of slavery in the countries themselves. It is not easy to draw a line between slavery and servitude; but I should say that the relation of the master to the man was, at least in Damara and Hottentotland, that of owner rather than employer. The Namaqua Hottentots and Oorlams, in all their plundering excursions, capture and drive back with them such Damara youths as they take a fancy to, and they keep them, and assert every kind of right over them. They punish them just as they please, and even shoot them, without any one attempting to interfere. Next in the scale of slavery are those Damaras, Ghou Damup, or Bushmen, who place themselves under Hottentot "protection", and on much the same footing as those among the Hottentots, are the paupers thaᴊ are attached to different werfts among the Damaras [2])". We see that Galton, like Fritsch, is uncertain as to whether the subjected classes among the Namaqua are to be called slaves. According to Wandrer, whose description applies to a later period than the foregoing accounts, there are no slaves, but a kind of serfs, most of them Herero, who were formerly prisoners of war [3]). Considering all this, we cannot arrive at any definite conclusion.

In his description of the other Hottentot tribes, viz. the Griqua, Korana, and Colonial Hottentots, Fritsch makes no mention of slavery. Holub remarks: "Where a well-to-do Korana can afford to keep some Makalahiri and Masarwa as servants and slaves, the soil is tilled to a small extent [4])". We have before met with these Makalahiri and Masarwa as tribes subjected to the Bechuanas; this makes us doubt, whether the "slaves" Holub speaks of are not divisions of the same tribes subjected to the

---

1) See above, p. 139. — 2) Galton, p. 142. — 3) Wandrer, in Steinmetz's Rechtsverhält-nisse, p. 323. — 4) Holub, Süd-Afrika, I, p. 112.

Korana, rather than slaves in the proper sense; the more so as he speaks of "servants and slaves".

The describers of the Bushmen [1]) make no mention of slavery. Fritsch tells us that they adopted parts of the declining Hottentots into their hordes [2]), so we may safely infer that slavery did not exist among them.

None of the describers of the Akkas [3]) speak of slaves. Burrows tells us that they "purchase their implements, such as spears, arrow-heads, and knives, from their neighbours, in exchange for dried meat, or for captives they have taken in the bush." But as the same writer states that "each village is ruled by a chief or head man, but among the people there is no variation of rank [4])", we may safely suppose that they sell abroad all captives they have made, and do not keep any of them as slaves.

Of the Abongos we know little, far too little to make out whether slavery exists among them [5]).

The Mucassequere, according to Serpa Pinto, sell the captives they make in their wars as slaves to the Ambuella, who transmit them to Bihé caravans [6]). We may therefore suppose that they do not keep slaves.

Result. Negative cases: *Bushmen,*
  Akkas,
  Mucassequere.

No conclusion: Namaqua,
  Griqua,
  Korana,
  Colonial Hottentots,
  Abongos.

§ 18. *Africa. D. Hamitic peoples.*

Munzinger, in his excellent books, describes several of these

---

1) Livingstone, Miss. Trav.; Fritsch; Theal; Passarge, Die Buschmänner. — 2) Fritsch, p. 444. — 3) Schweinfurth, II pp. 107—126; Emin Bey; Burrows. — 4) Burrows, pp. 39, 38. — 5) Lenz has some notes on the Abongos. — 6) Serpa Pinto, I p. 322.

tribes, all of which keep slaves: Beduan [1]), Takue [2]), Marea [3]),
Beni Amer [4]), Barea and Kunama [5]), Bogos [6]).

The Gallas practise slavery to a great extent [7]).

The Somal and Danakil also have slaves, though not so many
as the Gallas [8]).

Amongst the Massai slavery is unknown [9]).

Kannenberg, in his short notes on his journey through the
country of the Warangi, remarks that captives are made slaves.
But in Baumstark's elaborate description of this tribe no mention
is made of slavery [10]). We may therefore conclude, that the
Warangi do not keep slaves. If Kannenberg's statement is correct,
the prisoners certainly become victims of the slave trade, which
in his time was carried on to a great extent in German East
Africa [11]).

The Wandorobo have been described by several authors [12]),
who do not make any mention of slaves. They are themselves
subjected to the Massai [13]). We may safely conclude that they
have no slaves [14]).

The Wakwafi also probably have no slaves; for none of their
describers [15]) say a word about slavery.

Result. Positive cases: *Beduan,*
Takue,
Marea,
Beni Amer,
Barea and Kunama,
Bogos,
Gallas,
Somal,
Danakil.

---

1) Munzinger, Ostafr. Stud., pp. 154, 155. — 2) Ibid., p. 207. — 3) Ibid., pp. 231, 239,
244, 245. — 4) Ibid., pp. 279, 308—311 etc.; see also Junker I p. 180; von Müller, p.
428. — 5) Munzinger, Ostafr. Stud., pp. 483, 484, 497. — 6) Munzinger, Bogos, pp. 42,
43, 48—56. — 7) Paulitschke, I pp. 261, 262; II pp. 139—141. — 8) Paulitschke, I pp.
260, 263; II pp. 138, 139. Concerning the Somal see also Bottego, pp. 422—425; Hildebrandt, Somal, p. 4. — 9) Baumann, p. 165; Kallenberg, p. 93; Merker, pp. 96, 97, 118,
208. — 10) Kannenberg, p. 155; Baumstark. — 11) Kandt, p. 254. — 12) Thomson, Through
Massailand; Johnston; Baumann; Kallenberg; von Höhnel. — 13) Thomson, l. c. p. 448;
Johnston, p. 402. — 14) On Kannenberg's statement that the Wandorobo enslave captives
the same may be remarked as above with regard to the Warangi (See Kannenberg
p. 170). — 15) Thomson, l. c.; Johnston; von Höhnel.

Negative cases: *Massai,*
Warangi,
Wandorobo,
Wakwafi.

Several North-African peoples, such as the Fulbe, the Tuareg, the Kabyls, etc., being semi-civilized rather than savages, have been excluded here [1]).

§ 19. *Recapitulation.*

In the preceding paragraphs we have tried to find, which savage tribes have, and which have not, slaves. But we suppose that our enumeration of positive and negative cases has not yet given the reader a clear idea of the occurrence of slavery in the several geographical districts; probably he does not see the wood for trees. So we shall take here a short survey, serving, so to speak, as a map and showing in which parts of the globe slave-keeping savage tribes are found.

In North America slavery exists along the Pacific Coast from Behring Strait to the Northern boundary of California (15 clear positive cases). Beyond this district it seems to be unknown (42 clear negative cases).

In Central and South America we find 9 positive and 17 negative cases [2]). The positive cases are scattered over the whole continent; there are no large positive or negative districts. Such, at least, is the result we arrive at with the aid of our rather incomplete literature; a better literature would perhaps show that such districts exist.

In Australia slavery is unknown (30 negative cases).

In Oceania, *i. e.* Melanesia, Polynesia and Micronesia, slaves are only found in New Zealand, the North-Western Solomon Islands, the Gazelle Peninsula of Neu Pommern and the Western part of New Guinea (altogether 8 pos. cases). In the rest of this group (except a few uncertain cases) slavery does not exist (30 neg. cases).

---

1) See above, p. 157, note 1.— 2) In this paragraph we speak of "positive" and "negative cases", meaning only the clear cases.

In the Malay Archipelago slavery very frequently occurs (69 pos. cases). The 8 negative cases are scattered over the group.

India and the Indo-Chinese Peninsula, taken together, afford 13 positive and 11 negative cases, the former being found in the Northern parts of both groups.

In Central Asia and Siberia slavery seems to be unknown, except among the Kamchadales (in Central Asia 4 neg. cases, in Siberia 1 pos. case and 7 neg. cases).

The Caucasus yields 3 positive cases, 1 negative case, and several doubtful cases. Our literature on this group is rather scanty.

The Arabian Aeneze Bedouins, as well as the Arabian Larbas who live in North Africa, keep slaves (2 positive and no negative cases).

As for Africa, the Northern part of this continent, being inhabited by semi-civilized peoples, is excluded from our survey. Among the savage Africans slavery very frequently occurs. There are only two districts, in which scarcely any clear positive cases are found, viz. South Africa to the South of the Zambesi, and the country about the Upper Nile, to the South-West of Abyssinia. Large agglomerations of slave-keeping tribes are found on the Coast of Guinea, and in the district formed by Lower Guinea and the territories bordering the Congo. A few negative cases, however, are interspersed among the members of both groups, especially of the latter. There are altogether 90 pos. and 31 neg. cases in Africa.

All over the globe, there are, among the savage tribes on which we are sufficiently informed, 210 with slaves and 181 without slaves.

PART II.

THEORETICAL.

CHAPTER I.

METHOD AND DIVISIONS.

§ 1. *Method.*

The results of the first Part will be utilized in this. We have seen that slavery exists or formerly existed among many savage tribes, whereas many others have always, as far as we know, been unacquainted with it. The present Part will be taken up with an inquiry into the causes of these phenomena. We shall try to find out, what kinds of tribes have slaves, and what kinds have not.

To this end it would seem best to divide the several tribes according to their general culture, and then to inquire at which stages of culture slavery is found. But such a division cannot be made here incidentally; for it would require years of labour. And a good division, that we could adopt, has not yet been made. Morgan distinguishes three periods of savagery, three of barbarism, and one of civilization [1]. But his system rests on the unproved supposition, that the stage of culture a people has attained to entirely depends on its technical ability in the arts of subsistence. Dr. Vierkandt has made another distinction. Besides the civilized and semi-civilized peoples he has two categories: migratory tribes (*unstete Völker*), and primitive peoples proper (*eigentliche Naturvölker*). The former are the Australians, Tasmanians, Andamanese, Veddahs, Negritos, Kubus, Bushmen, African pigmy-tribes, Fuegians and Botocudos; the latter the American Indians, Arctic races,

---

[1] Morgan, Anc. Soc., see especially, pp. 10—12.

Northern Asiatics, Caucasus tribes, hill-tribes of India, Negroes
to the South of the Soudan, inhabitants of the Malay Archipelago
and Oceanic Islands [1]). But this division cannot be of any use
to us. It is not the result of an extensive and accurate exam-
iration of the facts; the writer himself admits that he has
followed his general impressions [2]). Now the impressions of a
capable sociologist, as Vierkandt undoubtedly is, may count for
something; they give a hint as to the direction, in which the
investigation has to be carried on; but they do not themselves
afford a scientific basis to rely upon. His *unstete Völker* are
simply those generally known as the "lowest type of man",
whether justly or unjustly we do not know [3]). And his *eigentliche Naturvölker*, as Professor Steinmetz rightly remarks [4]),
comprehend savages of widely different degrees of development.
Moreover, although he says his criterion is the psychical state
of man, the economic side of social life comes always prominently
into view [5]); but the author does not even try to prove that
the psychical state of man depends upon the stage of economic
development.

Yet, as it can be easily done here, we may inquire whether
Vierkandt's *unstete Völker* have slaves. It will be seen from
the second Chapter of our first Part that all of them, with the
exception perhaps of the Negritos, are unacquainted with
slavery [6]). This conclusion, however, is not of much use to us,
as we do not know whether they have been justly or unjustly
classified under one catagory.

As little can the other attempts, which have been made, to
classify the savages according to their general culture, serve
our purpose [7]). So the method of investigation that would seem
the best is not applicable here. Therefore we are also unable

---

1) Vierkandt, Culturtypen, pp. 67, 69. — 2) Vierkandt, l. c., p. 61. — 3) Peschel (pp.
144, 145) has already given nearly the same list. Vierkandt adds to Peschel's list the
Negritos, Kubus and African pigmy-tribes. The earliest enumeration of "lowest races" we
know of is that given by Malthus (Population, pp. 15—20). He mentions as such the
Fuegians, Tasmanians, Andamanese and Australians. — 4) Steinmetz, Classification, p. 133. —
5) Vierkandt, l. c., pp. 67, 69, 71, 72. His distinction of nomadic and settled semi-civilized
peoples is entirely an economic one. — 6) We may leave out of the question Zu Wied's
uncertain statement about the Botocudos. Of the pigmy-tribes we do not know very much;
but nowhere is it stated that any of them have slaves. — 7) On the different systems of
classification, see Steinmetz's "Classification", from which it clearly appears that a good
division of the peoples of the earth according to their general culture is still wanting.

to ascertain whether, as some writers assert, slavery at a certain stage of social development is universal. Bagehot says of slavery: "There is a wonderful presumption in its favour; it is one of the institutions which, at a certain stage of growth, all nations in all countries choose and cleave to" [1]. Grünberg expresses the same view: "No people has always and in all phases of its development been unacquainted with slavery" [2]. According to Spencer "observation of all societies in all times shows that slavery is the rule and freedom the exception" [3]. And Tourmagne exclaims: "This almost universal scourge, going back to the very origin of the nations and affecting all of them, is it not to be regarded as a social stage that every people has to traverse, as an evolution which it is obliged to undergo, before it can attain to the higher degrees of civilization" [4]? If we had an ascending series of stages of culture, we might inquire whether, within the limits of savagery (for the civilized and semi-civilized peoples fall beyond the scope of the present volume) there is a stage at which slavery is universal. But, as we have already remarked, this is not yet possible.

The best method we can use now will be to take into view one prominent side of social life, that may reasonably be supposed to have much influence on the social structure, especially on the division of labour; and to inquire whether this one factor may entirely, and if not to what extent it may, account for the existence or non-existence of slavery in every particular case. Here the economic side of life comes in the first place into consideration. We are not among the adherents of the materialistic theory of history; it is quite unproved and seems to us very one-sided. But we may suppose that the division of labour between the several social groups within a tribe, and therefore also the existence or non-existence of slavery, largely depends on the manner in which the tribe gets its subsistence. Whether, and to what extent, this supposition is true, will be shown by the examination of the facts. If this hypothesis fails to account for all the facts, we shall try, with the aid of other hypotheses, to explain the rest.

The opinion that the existence of slavery mainly depends

---

1) Bagehot, p. 72. — 2) Grünberg, Article "Unfreiheit", in Handwörterbuch der Staats-wissenschaften, 2nd edition. — 3) Spencer, Ind. Inst., p. 456. — 4) Tourmagne, p. 3.

on the mode of subsistence is also held by many theorists.
According to Morgan "slavery, which in the Upper Status of
barbarism became the fate of the captive, was unknown among
tribes in the Lower Status in the aboriginal period". This
Lower Status of barbarism begins with "the invention or practice of the art of pottery". Anterior to the art of pottery
was "the commencement of village life, with some degree of
control over subsistence". It ends with "the domestication of
animals in the Eastern hemisphere, and in the Western with
cultivation by irrigation and with the use of adobe-brick and
stone in architecture" [1]). So slavery, according to Morgan, does
not exist before a rather advanced period.

Several writers assert that hunters and fishers never have
slaves. Schmoller was formerly of the opinion that "no people
unacquainted with cattle-breeding and agriculture has slaves" [2]).
In his handbook, however, he informs us, that some highly
developed tribes of fishers also keep slaves [3]). Ingram expresses
the view formerly held by Schmoller: "In the hunter period
the savage warrior does not enslave his vanquished enemy, but
slays him; the women of the conquered tribe he may, however,
carry off and appropriate as wives or as servants, for in this
period domestic labour falls almost altogether on the female
sex. In the pastoral stage slaves are captured only to be sold,
with the exception of a few who may be required for the care
of flocks or the small amount of cultivation which is then
undertaken. It is in proportion as a sedentary life prevails, and
agricultural exploitation is practised on a larger scale, whilst
warlike habits continue to exist, that the labour of slaves is
increasingly introduced to provide food for the master, and at
the same time save him from irksome toil. Of this stage in
the social movement slavery seems to have been a universal
and inevitable accompaniment." But he makes an exception in
the case of those communities where "theocratic organisations
established themselves" [4]). Flügel says: "Hunting tribes can
neither feed nor employ the prisoners; generally they kill them" [5]).
According to Schurtz "among tribes of migratory hunters there

---

1) Morgan, Anc. Soc., pp. 80, 10, 13, 11. — 2) Schmoller, Die Thatsachen der Arbeitsteilung, p. 1010. — 3) Schmoller, Grundriss, I p. 339. — 4) Ingram, pp. 1, 2. — 5) Flügel,
p. 95.

is no room for slavery" [1]). Whether he means here all hunters or only Vierkandt's *unstete Völker* is not clear.

Pastoral nomadism especially is considered favourable to the growth of slavery. The nomadic herdsman, who had learned to domesticate animals, began also to domesticate men, *i. e.* to enslave them. According to Lippert, slavery "first arises in the patriarchal communities of pastoral peoples." "They [the slaves] were the object of an appropriation entirely similar to the appropriation of the domestic animals" [2]). Lamprecht also asserts that the prisoners, who formerly were either sacrificed or adopted into the community, in the pastoral stage were enslaved, because many hands were wanted to tend the cattle [3]). Dimitroff says that originally the captives were instantly killed like the game, as was the case amongst the hunting tribes of America, Australia and Africa. But as soon as man began to tame animals, he also learned to employ the captives as labourers [4]).

A few theorists, however, who are more familiar with ethnographical literature, know that it is not only among pastoral and agricultural tribes that slavery is found. So Peschel states. According to him hunters cannot employ slaves. Fishers, however, sometimes do so, as on the Northwest Coast of America, amongst the Koniagas, Koloshes, and Ahts of Vancouver Island. But only at the agricultural stage is slavery practised on an extensive scale [5]). Wagner is of the same opinion: "In the earliest economic state of society slavery is quite or nearly unknown; generally speaking slavery is coeval with a settled and agricultural life. This is to be accounted for by economic causes; for only in the agricultural stage can slave labour be of any considerable use. Therefore slavery is unknown among hunters, and occurs but seldom among fishers. Bondage (*Unfreiheit*) presents itself already under several forms among nomadic herdsmen; but only among settled agricultural peoples does it attain to its full development" [6]). Tylor remarks that slavery exists, as soon as the captives are spared to till the soil; but he adds that even among savage hunters and foresters absolute equality is not

---

1) Schurtz, Katechismus, p. 110. — 2) Lippert, II pp. 522, 535. — 3) Lamprecht, I p. 165. — 4) Dimitroff, p. 88. — 5) Peschel, p. 253. "Koloshes" is the Russian name for Tlinkits. — 6) Wagner, p. 375.

always to be found [1]). Spencer says: "Tribes which have not emerged from the hunting stage are little given to enslaving the vanquished; if they do not kill and eat them they adopt them. In the absence of industrial activity, slaves are almost useless, and indeed, where game is scarce, are not worth their food. But where, as among fishing tribes like the Chinooks, captives can be of use, or where the pastoral and agricultural stages have been reached, there arises a motive for sparing the lives of conquered men, and after inflicting on them such mutilations as mark their subjection, setting them to work" [2]). Bos is also aware of the fact, that the Tlinkits and similar tribes have slaves. He explains this in a curious way: slavery does not agree with the nature of hunting tribes; therefore it is probable that these tribes formerly were agricultural to a small extent [3]). Felix remarks that slavery already exists at the beginning of the agricultural stage [4]). Mommsen, however, asserts that in the oldest times (until when does not appear) slavery did not prevail to any considerable extent; more use was made of free labourers [5]).

Letourneau expresses his opinion very prudently: slavery was not carried on on a large scale before men applied themselves to cattle-breeding and especially to agriculture [6]). At the end of his book on slavery of over 500 pages he contents himself with this vague conclusion.

We see that the theories disagree very much. Whether any of them agree with the facts will appear from the investigation we are about to undertake.

§ 2. *Distinction of economic groups.*

This investigation will be carried on in the following manner. The tribes that afforded clear cases in the second chapter of the first Part will be divided into several groups according to their economic state. It will be seen then how many positive and how many negative cases there are in each group; and we

---

1) Tylor, Anthropology, p. 434. — 2) Spencer, Ind. Inst., p. 459. — 3) Bos, p. 191. — 4) Felix, II pp. 250. — 5) Mommsen, I p. 191. — 6) Letourneau, p. 491. See also Sutherland, I p. 379.

shall try to explain why the result is such as we shall find it. Perhaps we shall be able to account for this result entirely by economic causes; if not, we shall inquire what other causes there may be.

The following economic states will be distinguished:

1°. Hunting and fishing,
2°. Pastoral nomadism,
3°. First stage of agriculture,
4°. Second stage of agriculture,
5°. Third stage of agriculture.

It has to be remarked that this is not an ascending series òf stages of economic development. What the economic evolution has been we do not exactly know. Little credit is given to-day to the old division into the three successive stages of hunting, pastoral nomadism, and agriculture. This was not yet so in 1884, when Dargun could still write: "The evolutionary stages of hunting, pastoral, and agricultural life are so well established in science as stages of human evolution in general, that it seems rather audacious to object to this division. Taken in general, however, it is false; on the greater half of the globe pastoral life was not a transitory stage from hunting to agriculture; therefore the people concerned had not to pass through any regulation of property peculiar to herdsmen. They learned agriculture without having been pastoral. This phenomenon comprehends two parts of the world — America and Australia-Polynesia — completely, and two other parts — Asia and Africa — to a great extent, as the Malay Archipelago and the territory of the Negro tribes across Africa also are included. Therefore it will be necessary to leave off considering the three stages of hunting, pastoral and agricultural life as a rule of human progress. Moreover, nearly all pastoral tribes carry on agriculture, however negligently; and it is not at all certain that the origin of the latter does not go back to a more remote period than cattle-breeding; it is even probable that is does, for nomadic herdsmen are on the whole more civilized than the rudest agricultural tribes: cattle-breeding therefore is posterior to primitive agriculture" [1]). This

---

1) Dargun, pp. 59—61.

view of Dargun's is now generally accepted. But a new ascending series that would have any scientific value does not yet exist. And so we can only distinguish economic states, not stages of economic development.

A few remarks must still be made on each of our groups. These remarks will also serve to justify our division.

I. Hunting and fishing.

This group comprehends those tribes only that are entirely unacquainted with agriculture and cattle-breeding. Sometimes agriculture is carried on to such a small extent, that the tribe subsists almost entirely on hunting, fishing and gathering wild vegetable food. Such tribes bear much resemblance to true hunters; but if we called them hunting tribes it would be very difficult to draw the line of demarcation between them and other agricultural tribes; moreover, such tribes are not exactly in the same economic state as true hunters. So we have classified them under the agricultural groups.

Such tribes as use animals (especially horses) only as a means of locomotion, are hunters, viz. if they are unacquainted with agriculture; at any rate they are not pastoral tribes. This is the case with several tribes of North and South America.

II. Pastoral nomadism.

The tribes belonging to this group subsist mainly on the milk and meat of their cattle. Most of them also undertake a small amount of cultivation (see the above-quoted passage of Dargun's), whereas many agricultural tribes rear cattle. We shall draw the line of demarcation thus: this second group will contain those tribes only that depend so much on their cattle, that the whole tribe or the greater part of it is nomadic; whereas those who, although living for a considerable part on the produce of their cattle, have fixed habitations, will be classified under the agricultural groups.

III, IV, V. Agriculture.

Grosse makes a distinction between lower and higher agriculture; but as the former comprehends nearly all agricultural savages, this distinction cannot be of any use to us [1] Hahn, in his book on the domestic animals, distinguishes hoe-culture (*Hackbau*), agriculture proper (*Ackerbau*) and horticulture (*Gartenbau*) [2]. But hoe-culture is carried on by nearly all agricultural savages; besides, this division is purely technical and therefore cannot serve our purpose. What we want is a division according to the place agriculture occupies in social life. We must ask to what extent a tribe is occupied in and dependent for subsistence on agriculture. For on this, and not on the form of the agricultural implements, it will depend whether slaves are wanted to till the soil. A slave may be set to handle the hoe as well as the plough.

Perusing the ethnographical literature, we found such great differences between the several savage tribes in this respect, that we have thought it best to distinguish three stages of agriculture [3]. The principle according to which the distinction will be made is, as we have already hinted, the extent to which a tribe depends upon agriculture for its subsistence. The *first* agricultural group will contain those cases, in which agriculture holds a subordinate place, most of the subsistence being derived from other sources, viz. hunting, fishing or gathering wild-growing vegetable food [4]. The tribes of the *second* group carry on agriculture to a considerable extent, but not to the exclusion of hunting, etc. The *third*, or highest, agricultural stage is reached, when agriculture is by far the principal mode of subsistence, and hunting, etc. hold a very

---

1) Grosse, p. 28. — 2) Hahn, Die Haustiere, pp. 388 sqq. In a recent little book (Die Entstehung der wirtschaftlichen Arbeit, 1908, p. 92), Dr. Hahn, speaking of the first edition of the present work, observes that the result of our investigations amounts to very little, the reason being that we have confined ourselves to the study of those peoples among which the cultivation of the soil is of no consequence. The mere fact, that our chapter on agricultural tribes occupies more spaces than the chapters on hunters and fishers and on pastoral tribes taken together, proves the incorrectness of Dr. Hahn's remark. — 3) Whereas our 5 economic groups are not an ascending series, these 3 agricultural groups *are*. Primitive agriculture must be anterior to a more developed state of agriculture. — 4) This group is nearly identical with Dargun's *Jägerbauern;* see Dargun, p. 60 note 1.

subordinate place, so much so that, if the latter were entirely wanting, the economic state would be nearly the same.

But our information is not always very complete; and so it is not always clear to what extent subsistence is derived from agriculture. In such cases we shall make use of some *secondary characteristics*. Some facts may be recorded from which we can more or less safely draw conclusions as to the place agriculture occupies. The facts indicative of the first stage of agriculture are: 1. Women only are occupied in agriculture [1]), 2. The tribe is very mobile, habitations are often shifted. Those indicative of the second, as distinguished from the first, stage are: 1. The tribe has fixed habitations (except where this is due to an abundance of fish or fruit-bearing trees), 2. The lands are irrigated. Those indicative of the third stage are: 1. The lands are manured, 2. Rotation of crops is carried on, 3. Domestic animals are used in agriculture, 4. Agricultural products are exported.

It is not, of course, necessary that in every case a whole set of characteristics is found. Sometimes a part of them only are mentioned. Besides, there is much overlapping: a characteristic of the first stage may be found connected with one of the third. In all such cases we must not forget that these secondary characteristics have only signification as indications of the place occupied by agriculture, so they have not a fixed value; in every particular case the manner in which they are mentioned, the place they hold in the whole of the description, etc. will decide what importance we are to attach to each of them.

Hitherto we have supposed that agricultural tribes did nothing else besides tilling the soil, except hunting, fishing and gathering wild vegetable food. But it may also be that they subsist partly on agriculture, partly on cattle-breeding or trade [2]). In these cases we cannot apply the same principle of division. A tribe that subsists partly on agriculture, but chiefly on trade is not to be classified under the same category as a tribe that subsists partly on agriculture, but mainly on hunting. The latter

1) See Dargun, p. 110, and Hildebrand, Recht und Sitte, pp. 42, 43. — 2) Under "trade" we shall for the sake of convenience also comprehend industry.

is not yet agricultural, the former has perhaps passed beyond the agricultural stage. Here we may regard only the technical ability attained to in agriculture. Where agriculture is technically little developed, we have probably to deal with former *Jägerbauern* who have become traders. Where agriculture has reached a high perfection, but trade is one of the chief modes of subsistence, the tribe has probably passed through the higher stages of agriculture. What we say here of trade equally applies to cattle-breeding.

There are a few tribes that afforded clear cases in the second chapter of our first Part, but about the economic state of which we are not sufficiently informed. These will be left out here.

The literature used is the same as in Part I chap. II [1]). We have not thought it necessary to quote the pages relating to each tribe. In most ethnographical records the mode of subsistence occupies a conspicuous place, so any one wishing to verify our conclusions may easily find the passages concerned.

§ 3. *Hunting and fishing, pastoral, and agricultural tribes
in the several geographical districts.*

We shall give here a list of the tribes that afforded "clear cases" in the second chapter of Part I, stating, after the name of each tribe, the economic condition in which it lives. As we have said before, we shall omit a few tribes, about the economic state of which we are not sufficiently informed.

It will not perhaps be superfluous to remind the reader that, as our list contains only "clear cases", it gives no evidence as to the economic state of each geographical group. If, for instance, in our list some geographical group ¦contains as many hunting as agricultural tribes, this does not prove that in this group hunters and agriculturists are equally divided; for the group may contain many more tribes, which in our second chapter have not afforded "clear cases"; and what is the economic state of these tribes does not appear from our list.

---

1) About the Malay Archipelago we have also consulted De Hollander, and about Africa, Ratzel, Völkerkunde.

Among the agricultural tribes we have separately noted those, among which subsistence depends largely either on cattle-breeding or on trade, in addition to agriculture.

We shall make use of the following abbreviations.

h means hunting or fishing; the tribes so marked are hunters or fishers.

c means cattle-breeding; the tribes so marked are pastoral tribes.

a^1, a^2, a^3 means first, second, third stage of agriculture.

$a^1 + c$ means an agricultural tribe of the first stage, among which subsistence depends largely on cattle-breeding; similarly $a^2 + c$ and $a^3 + c$.

$a^1 + t$ means an agricultural tribe of the first stage, among which subsistence depends largely on trade; similarly $a^2 + t$ and $a^3 + t$.

$a^2 + c + t$ means an agricultural tribe of the second stage, among which subsistence depends largely both on cattle-breeding and trade; similarly $a^3 + c + t$.

	Positive cases.	*Negative cases.*
North America.	Aleuts h	The 9 tribes of Es-
	Athka Aleuts h	kimos proper, all of
	Koniagas h	them h
	Tlinkits h	Kutchins h
	Haidas h	Chepewyans h
	Tsimshian h	Delawares a^2
	Kwakiutl h	Montagnais h
	Bilballas h	Ojibways h
	Ahts h	Ottawas h
	tribes about Puget	Shahnees h
	Sound h	Potawatomi a^1 [1]
	Fish Indians h	Crees h
	Tacullies h	Cheyennes a^1
	Atnas h	Blackfeet nation h
	Similkameem h	Iroquois a^2
	Chinooks h	Hurons a^2
		Katahbas a^2
		Cherokees a^2

---

[1] Roosevelt calls them hunters; but in the Jesuit Relations it is stated, that they were not entirely unacquainted with agriculture.

	Positive cases.	Negative cases.
North America (continued).		Muskoghe a^2
		Choctaws a^2
		Chickasaws a^2
		Creeks a^2
		Seminoles a^2
		Natchez a^2
		Sioux h
		Hidatsas a^1
		Omahas a^1
		Osages a^1
		Kansas Indians a^1
		Assiniboins h
		Hupas h
		Apaches h
		Zuñi $a^3 + c$
		Lower Californians h
Central and South America.	Ancient nations of Honduras a^1	Wild tribes of North Mexico h
	inhabitants of Panama and Costa Rica a^1	natives of the Mosquito Coast a^1
	Mundrucus a^1	Caribs of the Isthmus a^1
	Mauhés a^1	
	Mbayas a^1	Warraus a^1
	Caduvei a^2	Macusi a^1
	Suya a^1	Roucouyennes a^1
	Abipones h	Apiacas a^1
	Tehuelches h [1])	Botocudos h [2])
		Bakairi a^1
		Paressi a^1
		Bororo a^1
		Guanas a^2
		Charruas h
		Minuanes h
		Puelches h
		Araucanians a^2
		Fuegians h

1) On Musters' authority. According to Charlevoix, agriculture was not entirely unknown amongst them. — 2) On Keane's authority. According to Zu Wied and Martius, there are some slight traces of agriculture.

	Positive cases.	*Negative cases.*
Australia.		The 30 tribes enumerated in chapter II of Part I, all of them h
Melanesia.	N. W. Solomon Islanders a^2	New Caledonians a^2
	natives of the Gazelle Peninsula a^1	S. E. Solomon Islanders a^1
	Nuforese $a^1 + t$	Nissan Islanders a^1
	Papuans of Arfak a^1	New Hebridians a^1
	„ of Adie $a^1 + t$	natives of Torres Straits a^1
	„ on the Gulf of Kaimani $a^1 + t$	Papuans of Humboldt Bay a^1
		Papuans near Lake Sentani a^2
		Papuans of Ayambori a^2
		Motu $a^1 + t$
		Mowat a^1
		Toaripi a^1
		Papuans on the mouth of the Wanigela River a^1
		Yabim a^1
		natives of the Tami Islands a^1
		Tamoes a^1
		natives of Dampier Island a^1
Polynesia.	Maori a^2	Tongans a^2
		Samoans a^2
		Rotumians a^2
		Rarotonga Islanders a^2
		Hawaiians a^2
		Marquesas Islanders a^2
		Abgarris, Marqueen and Tasman Islanders a^1

	Positive cases.	*Negative cases.*
Micronesia.		Marshall Islanders a^2
		Caroline Islanders a^2
		Marianne Islanders a^2
		Pelau Islanders a^2
		Kingsmill Islanders a^2
Malay Archipel-	Battas on the Pane and	Semang a^1
ago.	Bila Rivers a^3	Sakai a^1
	Battas of Mandhe-	Kubus h
	ling a^3	Mentawei Islanders a^1
	Battas of Pertibie a^3	Sebruang Dyaks a^2
	Karo-Battas a^2	Bataks of Palawan a^1
	Raja-Battas a^3	Bontoc Igorot a^3
	Battas of Angkola a^3	
	Battas of Simelun-	
	gun a^2	
	Battas of Singkel and	
	Pak-pak $a^2 + t$	
	Battas of Panei a^2	
	Toba-Battas a^2	
	Lampongs a^2	
	natives of Nias a^3	
	„ „ Anambas,	
	etc. a^1	
	Hill-Dyaks a^1	
	Dyaks on the Barito a^1	
	Sea-Dyaks a^2	
	Biadju Dyaks a^1	
	Kayans on the Men-	
	dalam a^2	
	Kayans on the upper	
	Mahakam a^2	
	Dyaks of Pasir a^2	
	inhabitants of the Mi-	
	nahassa a^2	
	inhabitants of Bolaäng	
	$a^2 + t$	
	inhabitants of Holon-	
	talo a^2	

	Positive cases.	*Negative cases.*
Malay Archipel-ago (continued).	inhabitants of Buool a^2	
	Toradja a^2	
	Tomori a^2	
	inhabitants of San-djai a^2	
	inhabitants of Bang-kala a^2	
	Kailirese a^2	
	inhabitants of Sa-leyer a^2	
	inhabitants of Sumba-wa a^3	
	inhabitants of Sum-ba a^2	
	inhabitants of Endeh on Flores $a^2 + t$	
	inhabitants of the So-lor group a^2	
	inhabitants of Bone-rate and Kalao $a^2 + t$	
	inhabitants of East Ti-mor $a^2 + t$	
	inhabitants of West Timor $a^2 + t$	
	inhabitants of Savu $a^2 + c$	
	inhabitants of Rote a^2	
	inhabitants of Wetar a^2	
	inhabitants of Keisar $a_2 + c$	
	inhabitants of Leti $a^2 + c$	
	inhabitants of Dama a^2	
	inhabitants of the Luang-Sermata group a^2	
	inhabitants of the Ba-bar group a^2	

	Positive cases.	*Negative cases.*
Malay Archipelago (continued).	inhabitants of the Tenimber and Timorlao Islands a^2	
	inhabitants of the Aru Islands a^1	
	inhabitants of the Kei Islands a^1	
	inhabitants of the Watubela Islands a^1	
	inhabitants of the Seranglao-Gorong group $a^1 + t$	
	inhabitants of Serang a^1	
	inhabitants of Ambon and the Uliase $a^2 + t$	
	inhabitants of the Sangi and Talauer Islands a^2	
	Galela and Tobelorese a^2	
	inhabitants of Kau a^1	
	Tagals and Visayas a^3	
	Bagobos a^1	
	Manobos a^1	
	Maguindanaos $a^2 + c + t$	
	inhabitants of Sulu $a^2 + c + \cdot t$	
	Samales a^2	
	Hovas a^3	
Indo-Chinese Peninsula.	Kakhyens a^2	Andamanese h
	Shans of Zimmé a^2	Nicobarese (central part) a^1
	Lawas a^2	
	hill-tribes of North Aracan a^2	Nicobarese (southern part) h
	Karens a^2	
	Chingpaws $a^3 + t$	

	Positive cases.	Negative cases.
India.	Meshmees a^1	Hill-tribes near Ra-
	Garos a^2	jamahall $a^1 + t$
	Lushais a^1	Todas c
	Manipuris a^2	Santals (a part) a^2
	Kafirs $a^2 + c$	Santals (a part) a^1
	Padam Abors a^2	Santals (a part) h
	Nagas a^2	Khonds (some divi-
		sions) a^2
		Khonds (other divi-
		sions) a^1
		Oraons a^2
		Korwas a^1
		Bodo and Dhimals a^2
		Veddahs h
Central Asia.		Kazak Kirghiz c
		Altaians c
		Turkomans c
Siberia.	Kamchadales h	Samoyedes c
		Ghiliaks h
		Tunguz c
		Yakuts c
		Tuski of the Coast h
		nomadic Koryakes c
		settled Koryakes h
Caucasus.	Ossetes $a^3 + c$	
	Circassians c	
	Kabards of Asia Mi-	
	nor c	
Arabia.	Aeneze Bedouins c	
	Larbas c	
Bantu tribes.	Angoni a^2	Ama-Xosa c
	Ovaherero c	Ama-Zulu c
	Barotse $a^2 + c$	Basuto $a^2 + c$
	Kimbunda $a^3 + t$	Makololo $a^2 + c$
	Lunda people $a^3 + t$	Makalaka $a^2 + c$
	Kioko $a^2 + t$	Wanyakyusa a^2
	Selles $a^2 + t$	Wambugu $a^1 + c$
	Manganja a^2	Wafipa $a^3 + c$

Bantu tribes (continued).	*Positive cases.*	*Negative cases.*
	Banyai a^2	Wanyaturu a^2
	Wagogo $a^2 + c$	Wawira a^2
	Washambala $a^2 + c$	Wataveta a^2
	Wapare $a^2 + c$	Bakwiri a^2
	Wajao $a^3 + t$	Mundombe (a part) c
	Makonde $a^3 + t$	Mundombe (a part) a^2
	Wahehe $a^2 + c$	Fans a^1
	Wachagga $a^2 + c$	Bateke $a^1 + t$
	Wanyamwesi $a^3 + t$	
	Azimba a^2	
	Wajiji $a^1 + t$	
	Wapokomo a^2	
	Bondei a^2	
	Wasiba $a^2 + t$	
	Wakikuyu a^3	
	Bondei a^2	
	Bihés $a^2 + t$	
	Minungo a^2	
	Mpongwe a^2	
	Orungu a^1	
	Mbengas $a^2 + t$	
	Duallas $a^2 + t$	
	Bayanzi $a^1 + t$	
	Bangala on the Congo a^2	
	Baluba a^2	
	Manyuema $a^2 + t$	
	Kabinda $a^2 + t$	
	Ininga and Galloa a^2	
	Wangata a^1	
	Bakundu a^2	
	Banyang a^2	
	Batom a^2	
	Mabum a^2	
	Bali tribes a^2	
	Bambala $a^2 + t$	
	Bayaka $a^2 + t$	
	Bahuana $a^2 + t$	

Bantu tribes (continued).	*Positive cases.*	*Negative cases.*
	Bakwese $a^1 + t$	
	Yaunde a^1	
	Indikki $a^3 + t$	
	Banaka and Bapu-ku a^1	
	Tuchilangue a^2	
	Waganda $a^2 + c$	
	Bahima c	
	natives of Bukoba $a^2 + c + t$	
Soudan Negroes.	Calabarese a^2	Latuka a^2
	inhabitants of Bonny $a^2 + t$	Alur $a^2 + c$
		Lendu a^2
	Brass people $a^1 + t$	Warundi a^2
	Ewe $a^2 + t$	Wafiomi $a^2 + c$
	inhabitants of Daho-mey $a^2 + t$	Wataturu $a^1 + c$
		Wambugwe $a^1 + c$
	Geges and Nagos $a^2 + c + t$	Bongos a^2
	Yorubas $a^3 + c + t$	
	inhabitants of Ashanti $a^2 + t$	
	Fanti a^2	
	Mandingoes $a^2 + c$	
	Wolofs a^2	
	Saracolays $a^2 + t$	
	Kagoros $a^2 + c$	
	Bambaras a^2	
	Toucouleurs a^2	
	Jekris $a^2 + t$	
	Malinkays $a^2 + t$	
	Susu $a^2 + c + t$	
	Landuma $a^2 + c + t$	
	Limba $a^2 + c + t$	
	Boobies of Fernando-Po a^1	
	Northern Sakalavas $a^2 + c$	

	Positive cases.	*Negative cases.*
Soudan Negroes (continued).	Sakalavas of Nossi-Bé and Mayotte $a^2 + c$	
Pigmies etc.		Bushmen h
		Mucassequere h
		Akkas h
Hamitic peoples.	Beduan c	Massai c
	Takue $a^3 + c$	Warangi $a^3 + c$
	Marea $a^2 + c$	Wandorobo h
	Beni Amer c	Wakwafi a^2
	Barea and Kunama a^2	
	Bogos $a^2 + c$	
	Gallas $a^3 + c$	
	Somal (some divisions) c	
	Somal (some divisions) a^2	
	Danakil c	

CHAPTER II.

---

§ 1. *Why slaves are not of much use to hunters.*

Among the "clear cases" of the second chapter of our first Part the following are hunting and fishing tribes.

Positive cases. North America: Aleuts,
Athka Aleuts,
Koniagas,
Tlinkits,
Haidas,
Tsimshian,
Kwakiutl,
Bilballas,
Ahts,
tribes about Puget Sound,
Fish Indians,
Tacullies,
Atnas,
Similkameen,
Chinooks.

15

South America: Abipones,
Tehuelches.

2

Siberia: Kamchadales.

1

18.

Negative cases. North America: the 9 tribes of Eskimos
proper,
Kutchins,
Chepewyans,
Montagnais,
Ojibways,
Ottawas,
Shahnees,
Crees,
Blackfeet nation,
Sioux,
Assiniboins,
Hupas,
Apaches,
Lower Californians.
___
22

South America: wild tribes of North Mexico,
Botocudos,
Charruas,
Minuanes,
Puelches,
Fuegians.
___
6

Australia: the 30 Australian tribes.
___
30

Malay Archipelago: Kubus.
___
1

Indo-Chinese peninsula: Andamanese,
Southern Nicobarese.
___
2

India: some Santal tribes,
Veddahs.
___
2

Siberia: Ghiliaks,
Tuski of the Coast,
settled Koryakes.
___
3

Pigmies, etc.:	Bushmen,
	Muscassequere,
	Akkas.

3

| Hamitic peoples: | Wandorobo. |

1

70.

So the great majority of the 88 cases we have got are negative. This fact agrees with the opinion of those theorists who assert that this economic state is unfavourable to the development of slavery. The existence of 18 positive cases, however, shows that those are wrong who hold that no tribe unacquainted with agriculture and cattle-breeding ever has slaves.

We have to explain now, why most hunters and fishers do not keep slaves. In a few cases the fact that they are inclosed between superior peoples and reduced to a dependent, powerless state, might afford sufficient explanation. So the Wandorobo, according to Thomson, are considered by the Massai as a kind of serfs; and Johnston calls them a helot race [1]). But with most of our hunters and fishers, who do not keep slaves, this is not the case, as is proved by their being often at war with their neighbours. It has been shown that the Ojibways and Sioux in North America, the Charruas, Minuanes and Puelches in South America either killed or adopted their prisoners, that the Andamanese also sometimes adopt captive children, that the Montagnais generally tortured their prisoners to death, that warfare is also known among the Botocudos [2]). And the most striking evidence is afforded by the Australians, an isolated group consisting entirely of hunters, in which slavery is altogether unknown. So the non-existence of slavery among the great majority of the hunters and fishers must be due on the whole to more general causes; and only if the latter fail to account for the absence of slavery among the

---

1) Thomson, Through Massailand, p. 448; Johnston, p. 402. — 2) See above, pp. 53, 58, 80, 81, 124, 52, 74. The Montagnais seem also sometimes to have adopted prisoners. Le Jeune observed a young Iroquois, whom they had adopted, Jesuit relations, VI p. 259.

Wandorobo or any other tribe in a similar subjected state, may we have recourse to an explanation by this state.

What general causes may there be? Spencer, speaking of hunters, says: "In the absence of industrial activity, slaves are almost useless; and, indeed, where game is scarce, are not worth their food" [1]. It is true, where food is more plentiful than it is among most hunters, slaves can be of more use; but we cannot think that the only cause why slavery does not exist, is that the slave is "not worth his food", *i. e.* that the produce of a man's labour cannot much exceed his own primary wants. For we meet with several instances, among these tribes, of people whose wants are provided for by the labour of others. In our first Part we saw, that the Australian men depend largely for their subsistence on the work of their wives. Some other statements are indicative of a similar state of things. Dawson says of the natives of the Western District of Victoria: "Great respect is paid to the chiefs and their wives and families. They can command the services of every one belonging to their tribe. As many as six young bachelors are obliged to wait on a chief, and eight young unmarried women on his wife; and as the children are of superior rank to the common people, they also have a number of attendants to wait on them.... Food and water, when brought to the camp, must be offered to them first, and reeds provided for each in the family to drink with, while the common people drink in the usual way. Should they fancy any article of dress, opossum rug, or weapon, it must be given without a murmur" [2]. And of the chiefs of the Andaman Islanders we are told: "They and their wives are at liberty to enjoy immunity from the drudgery incidental to their mode of life, all such acts being voluntarily performed for them by the young unmarried persons living under their headship" [3].

So there are people here whose wants are provided for by the work of others; therefore scarcity of food cannot be the only cause why slavery does not exist, and we have to examine what other causes there may be [4].

---

1) Spencer, Ind. Inst., p. 459. — 2) Dawson, p. 5. — 3) Man, p. 109. — 4) Another instance of people providing for the wants of others is the marriage by service, the young man serving the parents of his bride, sometimes for several years. This even occurs among the Ainu, Bushmen, and Fuegians; see Westermarck, Human marriage, pp. 390, 391.

The reader will remember, from the details given in the first Part, that slaves are frequently acquired from without the community to which the slave's owner belongs, by war, kidnapping or trade. It may be convenient to give this phenomenon the technical name of *extratribal slavery*, whereas we shall speak of *intratribal slavery* in those cases where the slave remains within the same community to which he belonged before being enslaved, *e. g.* a debtor-slave. Now the keeping of extratribal slaves must be very difficult to hunters. Hunting supposes a nomadic life; and the hunter, who roams over vast tracts of land in pursuit of his game has not much opportunity to watch the movements of his slave, who may be apt to run away at any moment. And if the slave himself is set to hunt, the difficulty amounts nearly to impossibility. Moreover, the hunting slave will be much more inclined to run away than a soil-tilling slave; for the latter, during his flight, has to live in a make-shift way on the spontaneous products of nature; whereas the former continues hunting, as he has always done; his flight has not the character of a flight.

Another cause is the following. Primitive hunters generally live in small groups. Hildebrand remarks that at the lowest stage of culture men live together in families or small tribes. Several instances are given in his book. "The Nilgala Veddahs are distributed through their lovely country in small septs or families." The Indians of the Rocky Mountains "exist in small detached bodies or families." The Fuegians "appear to live in families, not in tribes." The same applies to the Indians of Upper California, the Woguls of Siberia, the Kubus, the Negritos, the Bushmen, etc. [1]. And Sutherland remarks: "The middle savages, on the average of six races, reach about 150 as the social unit." "The upper savages, as typified by the North American Indians, would average about 360 to an encampment" [2]. Now it is easy to understand, that such small communities would not be able to develop much coercive power over slaves introduced into the tribe from foreign parts. A fugitive slave would be very soon beyond the reach of the tribe; and a comparatively small number of slaves would be dangerous to

---

1) Hildebrand, Recht und Sitte, pp. 1, 2. — 2) Sutherland, I p. 360.

the maintenance of power by the tribesmen within the tribe.

But the nomadic life of hunting tribes does not prevent the existence of intratribal slavery; such slavery might even be compatible with living in small groups. There are however other, more internal causes.

If there were slaves, *i. e.* male slaves, for slavery proper does not exist where all slaves are women, they would have to perform either the same work as free men, or the same work as free women. One might object, that sometimes slaves have separate kinds of labour assigned to them, which are performed by slaves only. This is true; but when slaves were first kept it must have been otherwise. It is not to be supposed that men, convinced of the utility of some new kind of work, began to procure slaves in order to make them perform this work; or that, finding some work tedious, they invented slavery to relieve themselves of this burden. Modern psychology does not account for psychical and social phenomena in such a ratio- nalistic way [1]). Differentiation of slave labour from free labour cannot have existed in the first stage of slavery. Therefore two problems are to be solved: 1°. why are there no slaves performing men's work? 2°. why are there no slaves performing women's work?

Men's work, besides warfare, is hunting. Now hunting is never a drudgery, but always a noble and agreeable work. Occupying the whole soul and leaving no room for distracting thought; offering the hunter a definite aim, to which he can reach by one mighty effort of strength and skill; uncertain in its results like a battle, and promising the glory of victory over a living creature; elevating the whole person, in a word intoxicating; it agrees very well with the impulsiveness of savage character [2]) Therefore it is not a work fit to be imposed upon men who are deprived of the common rights of freemen and are the property of others.

For, first, good hunters are highly respected. This appears from several statements. Ottawa women respected a man if he was a good hunter [3]). Tasmanian fathers took care to give their

---

1) Social institutions are sometimes made; but this is the exception: generally they grow. — 2) See Ferrero's beautiful exposition of this character. — 3) Tanner, p. 112.

daughters to the best hunters [1]). Among the Dumagas (a Ne-
grito tribe) a man who wishes to marry must show his skill
in shooting [2]). Ojibway parents tried to give their daughters
to good hunters. If the husband was lazy the wife had a right to
leave him [3]). In Western Victoria "if a chief is a man of ability,
exhibiting bravery in battle or skill in hunting, he is often
presented with wives from other chiefs" [4]). Among the Andaman
Islanders social status is dependent "on skill in hunting, fishing
etc. and on a reputation for generosity and hospitality" [5]). Le
Jeune tells us of a Montagnais, who was laughed at because
he was a bad hunter. This was a great disgrace among the
savages; for such men could never find or keep a wife [6]). A
describer of Kamchatka says of the dangerous sea-lion hunting: "This chase is so honourable, that he who has killed most
sea-lions is considered a hero; therefore many men engage in
it, less for the sake of the meat, that is looked upon as a
delicacy, than in order to win renown" [7]). In W. Washington
and N. W. Oregon "a hunter is, in fact, looked upon with
respect by almost every tribe in the district" [8]). An ancient
describer of the Indians of Paraguay tells us that skill and
bravery were the only qualities they valued. A would-be son-in-
law had to bring game to the hut of the girl's parents.
"From the kind and the quantity of the game the parents
judge whether he is a brave man and deserves to marry their
daughter" [9]). Among the Northern Athabascans "none but a
successful hunter need aspire to the hand of a chief's daughter" [10]).
Among the Attakapas, if a young man aspired to the hand of
a girl, her father asked him whether he was a brave warrior
and a good hunter and well acquainted with the art of making
harpoons [11]). Even among the pastoral Colonial Hottentots those
who had killed a savage animal were highly respected by their
countrymen [12]). Personal qualities, among such tribes, are the
only cause of social differentiation. Wealth does not yet exist [13]);
and hereditary nobility is unknown. So a good hunter cannot

---

1) Bonwick, p. 62. — 2) Blumentritt, Negritos, p. 65. — 3) Jones, Ojibway Indians,
pp. 79, 80. — 4) Dawson, p. 35. — 5) Man, p. 109. — 6) Jesuit Relations, VII p. 173. —
7) Histoire de Kamtschatka, I p. 287. — 8) Gibbs, p. 193. — 9) Muratori, pp. 28, 33. —
10) Russell, p. 164. — 11) Bossu, p. 247. — 12) Fritsch, p. 324. — 13) As to Australia,
see Steinmetz, Strafe, I pp. 430, 431.

be regarded by public opinion as a slave, the more so as a good hunter is also a good warrior, and without the aid of public opinion the master is not able to keep him subjected. And a bad hunter would be of little use as a hunting slave [1]).

This prevents the growth of intratribal slavery: no member of the tribe is so superior to any other member, that he can reduce him to a state of complete subjection; except perhaps where the latter is physically or psychically much weaker; and then he would not be of any use as a hunting slave. But it also prevents extratribal slavery. Enemies are hated, but not despised. In Central North America prisoners are either killed or adopted, and in the latter case entirely considered and treated as members of the tribe. Sometimes a captive is spared for his bravery; he is then provided with all necessaries and dismissed to his home [2]). Even those who are intended to be killed, are in the meantime treated with all due honours, sometimes even provided with wives [3]). Enemies, at least fullgrown men, if allowed to live, are on a footing of equality with the tribesmen; another state of things is not yet thought possible [4]).

But even if the idea of subjecting tribesmen or enemies had entered the minds of these hunters, hunting slaves would not be of any use. For hunting requires the utmost application of

---

1) Members of despised classes are often excluded from the occupations considered noble by the community. So the Jews in the Middle Ages were not allowed to hold real property (except in some periods in the South of France and Spain), nor to enter into corporations and trades. (Nys, p. 136). Mr. A. C. Kruijt tells us that, in Central Celebes, slaves who excel in those qualities which are highly valued in free men, *i. e.* bravery or oratorical power, are practically no longer regarded as slaves. — 2) Grinnell, p. 123. — 3) See Charlevoix, Nouv. France, III p. 246 (about the Hurons and Iroquois); in the same sense Lery, p. 225, about the Tupinambas of Brazil. These tribes are not hunters proper, but *Jägerbauern*; but this is rather a proof *a fortiori*. — 4) Mr. Westermarck observes: "The prevalence of slavery in a savage tribe and the extent to which it is practised must also depend upon the ability of the tribe to procure slaves from foreign communities and upon its willingness to allow its own members to be kept as slaves within the tribe. It may be very useful for a group to have a certain number of slaves, and yet they may not have them, for the reason that no slaves are to be had" (Moral Ideas, I p. 674). It will be seen from what we have just said, that we fully agree with this. For some hunting tribes it might be very useful, in an economic sense, to keep slaves; but there is a series of social and psychical factors that render the subjection of men as slaves impossible. We do not think, therefore, that Mr. Westermarck is quite right in remarking that in our book "the influence of economic conditions upon the institution of slavery has perhaps been emphasised too much at the cost of other factors" (Ibid).

strength and skill; therefore a compulsory hunting system cannot
exist. If a man is to exert all his faculties to the utmost, there
must be other motives than mere compulsion. It is for the
same reason that in countries where manufactures are highly
developed, a system of labour other than slavery is required.
"It remains certain" Stuart Mill remarks "that slavery is incompatible with any high state of the arts of life, and any
great efficiency of labour. For all products which require much
skill, slave countries are usually dependent on foreigners ....
All processes carried on by slave labour are conducted in the
rudest and most unimproved manner" [1]. And Cairnes says that
the slave is "unsuited for all branches of industry which require
the slightest care, forethought, or dexterity. He cannot be made
to co-operate with machinery; he can only be trusted with
the coarsest implements; he is incapable of all but the rudest
forms of labour" [2]. Mr. Kruijt, describing the natives of Central
Celebes, speaks in the same way: "The free Alifur works as
hard as his slave and even harder; for during the hours that
there is nothing to do in the gardens, the freeman has to mend
the furniture, plait baskets, and cut handles from wood or horn
etc., all which work the slave does not understand" [3]. And
Schurtz, in his most valuable essay on African industry,
remarks: "Slavery has little to do with the development of
industry. Among the Negroes of Africa only free people
spend most of their time in industrial pursuits, the slaves performing at most subordinate functions. In the Soudan there
are slaves who work on their own account and pay only a
tribute to their master; but it scarcely ever happens that
slaves are made to work in large numbers for the purpose of
manufacturing goods. Those artisans who belong to pariah tribes
are despised, but are not slaves, and the unwritten law defends
them from arbitrary treatment" [4]. A freeman may give his
whole mind to his work, because he knows he will enjoy the
fruits of it, and still more because he will win a reputation
by it among his fellow-men. The slave has not these motives;

---

1) Mill, p. 302. — 2) Cairnes, p. 46. — 3) Kruijt, N. Z. G. XXXIX p. 122. — 4) Schurtz,
Das Afrikanische Gewerbe, p. 142.

he works mainly on compulsion [1]). And as both hunting and higher industrial labour require much personal application, neither can be well performed by slaves. Here extremes meet, if hunting and manufactures are to be considered as extremes, which we are inclined to doubt, at least regarding those tribes that have brought the art of hunting to a high perfection; such hunting probably supposes more development of cerebral power than the lowest stage of agriculture [2]). But there is a difference between hunting and manufacturing nations. In manufacturing countries, besides the higher kinds of labour, there are also many sorts of ruder work to be done, that can be done by slaves as well. Moreover, slavery among a manufacturing nation may date from a former period and have passed into the laws and customs; then social life is based upon it; and so it remains for a long time after its economic basis has fallen. Slavery in such cases, by a gradual mitigation, is made to agree with changed economic conditions: the slave is given a proportionate share in the produce of his labour; he is allowed to buy his freedom by means of his savings; or his obligations are restricted to fixed tributes and services, and so the slave becomes a serf [3]). But the Australians and other hunting tribes have not probably ever done anything but hunting; and so neither present wants induce them to make slaves, nor do the traditions of the past maintain slavery [4]). We may add, that supervision of the work of a hunting slave would be nearly impossible. An agricultural slave can work in the presence of and surveyed by his master; but hunting requires rather independent action.

So slaves cannot be employed in hunting. They might, however, be set to do women's work, *i. e.* "erecting habitations, collecting fuel and water, carrying burdens, procuring roots and delicacies of various kinds, making baskets for cooking roots and other

---

1) See Wagner, p. 389. Schmoller (Grundriss, I p. 340) also remarks that slaves have no interest in the result of their work. — 2) See Bücher, p. 9, and Fritsch's beautiful description of Bushman hunting, Fritsch, pp. 424 sqq. — 3) See the exposition of the causes and development of this mitigation by Wagner, pp. 390—405. — 4) The assertion of some writers (*e. g.* Waitz-Gerland, VI pp, 767, 796), that the Australians have declined from a higher state of culture, seems to us quite unfounded.

purposes, preparing food, and attending to the children" [1]). But, first, nomadic life and the requirements of the work would, in this case too, very much facilitate the escape of the slave, the more so, as the slaves, when the men are engaged in hunting, would be under the supervision of the women only. Moreover, the men are not likely to take the pains of procuring slaves for the sole benefit of their wives. We must also take into consideration, that these small tribes are very much in need of the forces of every man in hunting and still more in warfare; therefore an able-bodied boy will be brought up to be a hunter and warrior, rather than given to the women as a slave. And finally, where war is frequent, such slaves, not being able to fight, would soon be eliminated in the struggle for life, whereas women are often spared because they are women [2]). Therefore it is only among tribes which either live in peaceful surroundings, or are so powerful as not to have to fear their neighbours very much, that men performing women's work are to be found. Crantz speaks of a young Greenlander who was unable to navigate, because when a child he had been taken too much care of by his mother. "This man was employed by other Greenlanders like a maid-servant, performing all female labour, in which he excelled" [3]). Among the Central Eskimos, according to Boas, "cripples who are unable to hunt do the same kind of work as women" [4]). Tanner tells us of an Ojibway, who behaved entirely as a woman, and was kept as a wife by another Ojibway. He excelled in female labour, which he had performed all his life. Such men, according to Tanner, are found among all Indian tribes; they are called *agokwa* [5]). But in all these cases the men who perform female labour are not slaves. Crantz's young Greenlander probably was glad to earn his livelihood in this way. Domestic labour among the Greenlanders is not generally wanted. Widows and orphans are sometimes taken as servants; but this is done rather as a favour;

---

1) This description, given by Dawson (p. 37) of female labour in Western Victoria, may be taken as a fair type of female labour among hunters in general. — 2) See Steinmetz, Strafe, II pp. 96 sqq. — 3) Crantz, I p. 185. — 4) Boas, Central Eskimo, p. 580. — 5) Tanner, p. 98.

for else they would have to starve [1]). Among the Central Eskimos only those who are unable to hunt do the same work
as women; a man able to hunt will never be compelled to
do female work. And the men of Tanner's narrative are entirely treated as women and somehow perform the sexual
functions of wives; the performing of domestic labour only
would not probably be sufficient for them to get their subsistence [2]). Only where either peaceful surroundings or a fighting power much superior to that of the neighbours makes the
existence of men performing female labour possible, and where
at the same time female labour is so much valued that the
more labourers can be got to do it the better, can there be
male slaves performing women's work [3]). Whether these requirements are fulfilled in any of our positive cases, will appear
from our investigation of these cases.

The non-existence of slavery among most hunters and fishers now being accounted for, we shall proceed to an inquiry
into the causes of the existence of slavery among 18 hunting
and fishing tribes.

§ 2. *The slave-keeping tribes of the Pacific Coast of North America.*

Going on to account for our 18 positive cases, we may remark
in the first place, that what we have said about the causes
preventing the existence of slavery, applies much more to
hunters than to fishers. Fishers are not necessarily so nomadic
as hunters; and where a sedentary life prevails, there is more
domestic work to be done, and the slaves cannot so easily
escape. Moreover it is not so very difficult to control a fishing
slave, who is in the same boat with the master. The slave may
also be used to row the boat. Therefore it may be of some
use to inquire, how many hunting and how many fishing tribes

---

1) Crantz, I p. 211, 215. — 2) Such men, treated as wives and performing female labour,
were very numerous in Kamchatka; see Steller, p. 350 note. — 3) Sutherland (I p. 379)
remarks that "when a slave has to be fed by the huntsman skill of his master, he is a
burden rather than a help, and amid roving habits it is difficult to see how there can be
enough of drudgery to made it convenient to feed him."

are to be found among our positive and negative cases. Fishing in our sense includes the killing of water-animals besides fish: whales, seals, etc. Where a tribe lives by hunting and fishing, we shall call it a hunting or a fishing tribe, according to the predominating mode of subsistence.

One difficulty arises here. Some tribes, especially Australian, subsist largely on wild fruits, roots, berries, grasses, etc., shell-fish and lower land-animals, such as beetles, lizards, rats, snakes, etc.; so that neither hunting in the true sense nor fishing prevails [1]. For our purpose it will be most convenient to classify them under the head of hunters; for the peculiar features of fishing tribes which we have enumerated: fixed habitations, easy supervision of the work of slaves, drudgery such as rowing, are not found among them. Moreover, the gathering of wild-growing vegetable food and the catching of the lower animals, in Australia too, are chiefly incumbent on women, whereas the men hunt; so the division of labour is the same as among other hunters regarding the quality of the work of each sex; only the quantity of male labour is less and of female labour greater here.

Of our positive cases the following are hunters: some tribes about Puget Sound, Atnas, Similkameem, Abipones, Tehuelches. The rest are fishers.

Of our negative cases the following are fishers: Eskimos (9 tribes), Hupas, Fuegians, Southern Nicobarese, Tuski, Ghiliaks, Koryakes. The rest are hunters, with the exception of the Chepewyans, of whom Bancroft says: "Their food consists mostly of fish and reindeer, the latter being easily taken in snares. Much of their land is barren, but with sufficient vegetation to support numerous herds of reindeer, and fish abound in their lakes and streams" [2]. So we are not able to ascertain whether hunting or fishing predominates among the Chepewyans.

We see that 5 hunting and 14 fishing tribes have slaves; 54 hunting and 15 fishing tribes have no slaves [3]. In other words: *of the*

---

1) The Germans call such people *Sammler*. — 2) Bancroft, p. 118; see also Mackenzie, I p. 151. — 3) The positive cases here are 5 + 14 = 19, instead of 18, because the Indians about Puget Sound count double, some of them being hunters and others fishers. The negative cases are 54 + 15 = 69, instead of 70, because we have omitted the Chepewyans.

hunting tribes 8½ per cent., of the fishing tribes 48 per cent. have slaves.

We may say now, that hunting is very unfavourable, and fishing not nearly so much so, to the existence of slavery. But it remains to be explained, why a few hunting tribes keep slaves, and why among the fishers the tribes with and without slaves are nearly equally divided.

Now it is worth noticing, that the great majority of our positive cases (all except the Abipones, Tehuelches and Kamchadales) belong to one geographical group: they all live on or near the Pacific Coast of North America, from Behring Strait to the Northern boundary of California. Therefore we may suppose that the existence of slavery among all these tribes is due to the same or nearly the same causes; and a survey of the economic state of this group will probably enable us to find these causes. We shall examine then, whether slavery among the three tribes outside this group can be accounted for by the same causes, or if special causes are at work there.

The circumstances that may be considered favouring the existence of slavery on the Pacific Coast are the following:

1°. *Abundance of food.* The Aleuts eat only the best parts of the dried fish; the rest is thrown away [1]. Bancroft tells us that "although game is plentiful, the Haidas are not a race of hunters, but derive their food chiefly from the innumerable multitude of fish and sea animals, which, each variety in its season, fill the coast waters" [2]. The Tacullies, "are able to procure food with but little labour" [3]. Our informant also speaks of the "abundant natural supplies in ocean, stream, and forest" of the Puget Sound Indians [4]. The Tlinkits, according to Holmberg, do not take great pains to secure their food; the ebbing tide leaves a multitude of sea-animals ashore, which they can gather without difficulty [5]. Kane remarks: "Salmon is almost the only food used by the Indians on the Lower Columbia River, the two months' fishing affording a sufficient supply to last them the whole year round" [6]. About the tribes

---

1) Wemiaminow, p. 214. — 2) Bancroft, p. 161. — 3) Ibid., p. 122. — 4) Ibid., p. 213. — 5) Holmberg, I p. 17; see also p. 22. — 6) Kane, p. 314.

of W. Washington and N. W. Oregon Gibbs remarks: "With all these sources of subsistence, the greater part of which is afforded spontaneously by the land or water, nothing but indolence or want of thrift could lead to want among a population even greater than we have reason to believe at any time inhabited this district" [1]). The salmon fishery "has always been the chief and an inexhaustible source of food for the Chinooks, who, although skilful fishermen, have not been obliged to invent a great variety of methods or implements for the capture of the salmon, which rarely if ever have failed them" [2]). The Aths also, in Jewitt's time, could procure an immense quantity of salmon with the greatest facility [3]). Several other tribes on the Pacific Coast have fixed habitations and live together in large groups, as we soon shall see; therefore amongst them too food must be abundant, though this is not explicitly stated.

The consequence is, that the produce of labour exceeds the primary wants of the labourer much more than for instance in Australia, and the use of slaves is greater.

2°. Most of these tribes *live chiefly by fishing* (see above). Moreover, there is a great *variety of food*. The Koniagas catch salmon, haddock, whales, seals, deer, reindeer, waterfowls, a small white fish and grizzly bears [4]). The Tlinkits eat fish, various kinds of meat and plants, and shell-fish; formerly they also killed whales [5]). The Haidas have abundance of game and fish. They eat also birds, and various kinds of vegetables. Shell-fish are gathered by the women [6]). Of some tribes about Puget Sound we are told: "Fish is their chief dependence, though game is taken in much larger quantities than by the Nootkas" [7]). The Ahts eat fish, roots and berries, and hunt the deer [8]). The Tacullies eat fish (chiefly salmon), herbs and berries and small game [9]). The Similkameem eat fresh and dried game of all kinds, the seed of the sunflower, various roots, edible fungi, berries, wild onions [10]). The tribes of W. Wash-

---

1) Gibbs, p. 197. — 2) Bancroft, p. 232. — 3) Brown, Adventures of John Jewitt, p. 151. — 4) Ibid., pp. 76—78. — 5) Krause, pp. 155, 159, 181. See also Holmberg, I pp. 22—24. — 6) Bancroft, pp. 161—163. — 7) Ibid., pp. 212, 213. — 8) Sproat, pp. 53, 89. — 9) Bancroft, p. 123. — 10) Allison, p. 308.

ington and N. W. Oregon live on fish, roots, berries and a little game. "The roots used are numerous." "Besides the salmon sturgeon is taken in the Columbia, and a variety of other fish." Seals and whales are also occasionally killed. "Shell-fish in great variety exist in the bays and on the coast" [1]). The basis of the Chinooks' food is salmon; but besides this they eat sturgeon, wild-fowl, deer, rabbits, nuts, berries, wild fruits and roots [2]).

We do not attach very much importance to this circumstance; for even the Australians have a great variety of food, and yet they are poorly off [3]). But together with the other causes it may have some influence; for where various kinds of food are available, there is a good chance, that the procuring of one or more of them will be a work fit to be performed by slaves.

3°. They generally have *fixed habitations* and live in *rather large groups;* they are enabled to do so by *preserving food* for winter use. The Koniagas "build two kinds of houses; one a large, winter village residence, ... and the other a summer hunting hut.... Their winter houses are very large, accommodating three or four families each." "The *kashim* or public house of the Koniagas is built like their dwellings, and is capable of accommodating three or four hundred people." During the summer great quantities of fish are dried for winter use, which they lay up in their houses [4]). The Tlinkits during the winter dwell in villages, regularly built and consisting of solidly constructed houses. The greater houses lodge up to 30 persons. "For winter they dry large quantities of herring, roes, and the flesh of animals" [5]). Haida houses are similar to those of the Tlinkits, but larger, better constructed and more richly ornamented. "Fish, when caught, are delivered to the women, whose duty it is to prepare them for winter use by drying" [6]). Among the Nootkas "each tribe has several villages in favourable locations for fishing at different seasons." Each house accommodates many families. Fish and shell-fish are preserved by

---

1) Gibbs, pp. 193—195. — 2) Bancroft, pp. 232—234. — 3) See Waitz-Gerland, VI p. 724. — 4) Bancroft, pp. 74, 75; Holmberg, I p. 90. — 5) Krause, pp. 123, 155; Bancroft, p. 104. See also Holmberg, I pp. 22, 24. — 6) Krause, p. 307; Bancroft, p. 163.

drying; some varieties of seaweed and lichens, as well as various roots, are regularly laid up for winter use [1]. In Jewitt's narrative mention is made of divisions of the Ahts, consisting of 500—1000 warriors. They used to preserve various kinds of fish for the winter [2]. In W. Washington and N. W. Oregon acorns, some kinds of berries, and especially salmon and whaleblubber, are stored for winter use [3]. About Puget Sound "the rich and powerful build substantial houses". "These houses sometimes measure over one hundred feet in length, and are divided into rooms or pens, each house accommodating many families." "In the better class of houses, supplies are neatly stored in baskets at the sides" [4]. "During a portion of every year the Tacullies dwell in villages." "In April they visit the lakes and take small fish; and after these fail, they return to their villages and subsist upon the fish they have dried, and upon herbs and berries" [5]. The Chinooks, according to Bancroft, do not move about much for the purpose of obtaining a supply of food. They have permanent winter dwellings. "Once taken, the salmon were cleaned by the women, dried in the sun and smoked in the lodges; then they were sometimes powdered fine between two stones before packing in skins or mats for winter use". Swan also states that they preserve fish and berries for the winter [6]. Similar accounts are given of the Similkameem [7].

These circumstances greatly tend to further the growth of slavery. A settled life makes escape of the slaves more difficult [8]. Living in larger groups brings about a higher organization of freemen, and therefore a greater coercive power of the tribe over its slaves. And the preserving of food requires additional work; and this work is very fit to be performed by slaves, as it does not require overmuch skill, and has to be done in or near the house, so that supervision of the work is very easy. Moreover, the hope of partaking of the stored food is a tie that binds the slave to his master's house, in

1) Bancroft, pp 183—187. — 2) Brown, Adventures of John Jewitt, pp. 132, 134, 151. See also Sproat, p. 37. — 3) Gibbs, pp. 194—196. — 4) Bancroft, pp. 211—213. — 5) Ibid., p. 123. — 6) Ibid., pp. 231, 233; Swan, The Northwest Coast, p. 161. — 7) Allison, p. 309. — 8) Gibbs remarks: "East of the Cascades, though it [slavery] exists, it is not so common; the equestrian habits of the tribes living there probably rendering it less profitable or convenient than among the more settled inhabitants of the coast." (Gibbs, p. 188).

much the same manner as a modern workman is bound by having a share in the insurance fund of the factory.

4°. *Trade and industry* are highly developed along the Pacific Coast. Kane speaks of the *ioquas*, "a small shell found at Cape Flattery, and only there, in great abundance. These shells are used as money, and a great traffic is carried on among all the tribes by means of them" [1]. Among the Aleuts "whalefishing is confined to certain families, and the spirit of the craft descends from father to son" [2]. The Koniagas are "adapted to labour and commerce rather than to war and hunting". They make very good boats and men as well as women excel in divers trades. They got slaves by means of exchange from other tribes [3]. Among the Tlinkits there are professional wood-carvers, smiths and silversmiths. The women are very skilful in plaiting. Very good canoes are made. Formerly they hunted whales with harpoons. Trade was already highly developed before the arrival of the whites; they traded even with remote parts of the coast and with the tribes of the interior. The trade in slaves was formerly carried on on a large scale [4]. The large and ingeniously built canoes of the Haidas are widely celebrated; they often make them for sale. They have a standard of value: formerly slaves or pieces of copper, now blankets. Their houses are richly ornamented. They are "noted for their skill in the construction of their various implements, particularly for sculptures in stone and ivory, in which they excel all the other tribes of Northern America" [5]. The Tsimshian formerly acted as middlemen in the slave-trade. The southern tribes kidnapped or captured slaves, sold them to the Tsimshian, and these again to the Tlinkits and interior Tinneh. "Each chief about Fort Simpson kept an artisan, whose business it was to repair canoes, make masks, etc." [6]. The Atnas "understand the art of working copper, and have commercial relations with surrounding tribes". They buy their slaves from the Koltschanes [7]. Gibbs states that in W. Washington

---

1) Kane, p. 238. — 2) Bancroft, p. 90. — 3) Ibid., p. 86; Holmberg, I pp. 99—103, 79. — 4) Krause, pp. 159, 173, 181,|183, 186. See also Holmberg, I pp. 26—29. — 5) Krause, pp. 306, 307, 313; Swan, Haidah Indians, pp. 2, 3; Bancroft, p. 165. — 6) Niblack, p. 252; Bancroft, p. 166. — 7) Bancroft, p. 135.

and N. W. Oregon the Indians of the interior preserve some
kinds of salmon, "which after a stay in the fresh water have
lost their superfluous oil, and these are often actually traded
to those Indians at the mouth of the river or on the Sound.
The Dalles was formerly a great depot for this commerce".
Some wild-growing roots "were formerly a great article of trade
with the interior". The slave-trade is carried on here too.
"Many of the slaves held here are .... brought from California,
where they were taken by the warlike and predatory Indians
of the plains, and sold to the Kallapuia and Tsinuk." "Many
of them [the slaves] belong to distant tribes" [1]. The tribes
about Puget Sound have canoes, beautifully made, painted and
polished. The houses of the rich are made of planks split from
trees by means of bone wedges. "In their barter between the
different tribes, and in estimating their wealth, the blanket is
generally the unit of value, and the *hiaqua,* a long white shell
obtained off Cape Flattery at a considerable depth, is also
extensively used for money, its value increasing with its length.
A kind of annual fair for trading purposes and festivities is
held by the tribes of Puget Sound at Bajada Point." "Slaves
are obtained by war and kidnapping, and are sold in large
numbers to northern tribes" [2]. Of the Nootkas Bancroft says:
"Trade in all their productions was carried on briskly between
the different Nootka tribes before the coming of the whites."
"The slave-trade forms an important part of their commerce."
Harpooners are a privileged class [3]. The several divisions of the
Ahts mutually exchange the fish that each of them catches.
They also sell mats and baskets manufactured by the women.
According to Jewitt's narrative, they made very good canoes.
A kind of shell, strung upon threads, formed a circulating
medium among them, five fathoms of it being the price of a
slave, their most valuable species of property. "The trade of
most of the other tribes with Nootka was principally train-oil,
seal or whale's blubber, fish fresh or dried, herring or salmon
spawn, clams and mussels, and the yama, a species of fruit which
is pressed and dried, cloth, sea-otter skins, and slaves" [4].

1) Gibbs, pp. 195, 193, 188, 189. — 2) Bancroft, pp. 211, 216—218. — 3) Ibid., pp. 192,
187, 194. — 4) Sproat, pp. 38, 97; Brown, Adventures of John Jewitt, pp. 123, 115, 137.

Among the Makah (a Nootka tribe) the whale-oil "is used as an article of food as well as for trade.... The Makah were till lately in the habit of purchasing oil from the Nittinat also, and have traded in a single season, it is said, as much as 30,000 gallons." A division into different trades also exists among them. "A portion of them only attain the dignity of whalers, a second class devote themselves to halibut, and a third to salmon and inferior fish, the occupations being kept distinct, at least, in a great measure" [1]). Among the Tacullies *hiaqua* shells up to 1810 were the circulating medium of the country [2]). The Chinooks, says Bancroft, "were always a commercial rather than a warlike people, and are excelled by none in their shrewdness in bargaining. Before the arrival of the Europeans they repaired annually to the region of the Cascades and Dalles, where they met the tribes of the interior, with whom they exchanged their few articles of trade — fish, oil, shell and Wapato — for the skins, roots and grasses of their eastern neighbours." "Their original currency or standard of value was the *hiaqua* shell." They obtain their slaves "by war, or more commonly by trade". According to Swan, the Chinooks "manage, during the course of the winter, to make a great many articles, which are disposed of to the whites". A species of small shell passes as money among them. "Their slaves are purchased from the Northern Indians, and are either stolen or captives of war, and were regularly brought down and sold to the southern tribes" [3]).

This development of trade and industry furthers the growth of slavery in several ways:

a. The slave-trade facilitates the keeping of slaves. Prisoners of war usually belong to a neighbouring tribe; they have much more opportunity to escape to their native country than purchased slaves, who have been transported from a great distance. The latter, if escaping from their masters, would instantly be recaptured by some other slave-keeping tribe of the Pacific Coast. So among the Nootkas "a runaway slave is generally seized and resold by the first tribe he meets" [4]). We can

---

1) Gibbs, p. 175. — 2) Bancroft, p. 122. — 3) Ibid., pp. 238—240; Swan, The Northwest Coast, pp. 164, 158, 166. — 4) Bancroft, p. 195.

therefore easily understand why the Koniagas did not keep
full-grown captive men as slaves, but acquired their male slaves
by means of exchange [1]). Similarly, a chief of the Cowitchins
(near Vancouver Island), according to Kane, "took many captives,
whom he usually sold to the tribes further north, thus diminishing their chance of escaping back through a hostile country
to their own people" [2]).

b. Where the fishing implements are brought to a high
perfection (canoes, nets, harpoons), fishing becomes more remu-
nerative; the produce of a fishing slave's labour exceeds his
primary wants more than where fishing is carried on in a
ruder manner.

c. The more the freemen devote themselves to trade and
industry, the more need there is for slaves to do the ruder
work (fishing, rowing, cooking, etc.). The trade itself may
also require menial work: carrying goods or rowing boats on
commercial journeys, etc. [3]).

d. Another effect of intertribal trade, together with a settled
life and abundance of food, is probably this, that these tribes
are not so warlike as most hunters. So they need not employ
all available forces in warfare; they can afford to keep male
slaves who do not fight. We have seen that the Koniagas are
"adapted to labour and commerce rather than to war and hunting", and that the Chinooks "were always a commercial rather
than a warlike people". Regarding the other tribes it is not
clearly stated, whether war is very frequent [4]); but our impression, on perusing the ethnographical literature, is, that it
is not nearly so frequent as among the Sioux, Ojibways, and
similar tribes.

5°. *Property and wealth* are also highly developed. Schmoller
remarks: "We know now, that there are some instances of
settled hunting and fishing tribes with villages, with some development of the means of conveyance, with dog-sledges, reindeer,

---

1) Holmberg, I p. 79. — 2) Kane, p. 220. — 3) Trading itself is not a drudgery, but
a highly agreeable occupation. "Most of the Africans" says Livingstone (Zambesi, p. 50) "are
natural-born traders; they love trade more for the sake of trading, than for what they make
by it." Bücher decidedly underrates the significance of trade among savages. — 4) So
Bancroft (p. 91) says of the Aleuts: "Notwithstanding their peaceful character, the occupants
of the several islands were almost constantly at war." This is far from clear; for we can
hardly imagine peaceful people being always at war with each other.

etc., with a certain social organization of the chase and fishery, with ornaments and slaves, with rich and poor people; such is the case in Northern California, in Northern Asia, in Kamchatka" [1]). Among the Koniagas "when an individual becomes ambitious of popularity, a feast is given". A man's wealth, among them, formerly depended on the number of sea-otter skins he owned [2]). Among the Tlinkits private property comprises clothes, weapons, implements, hunting territories and roads of commerce. Nobility depends on wealth rather than on birth [3]). Of the Haidas Bancroft says: "Rank and power depend greatly upon wealth, which consists of implements, wives and slaves. Admission to alliance with medicine-men, whose influence is greatest in the tribe, can only be gained by sacrifice of private property". Swan speaks of wooden pillars, placed before the houses of the rich. They are elaborately carved at a cost of hundreds of blankets, and fetch up to 1000 dollars. Only the very rich are able to purchase them [4]). Kane speaks of a Cowitchin chief who "possessed much of what is considered wealth amongst the Indians, and it gradually accumulated from tributes which he exacted from his people. On his possessions reaching a certain amount, it is customary to make a great feast, to which all contribute. The neighbouring chiefs with whom he is in amity are invited, and at the conclusion of the entertainment, he distributes all he has collected since the last feast, perhaps three or four years preceding, among his guests as presents. The amount of property thus collected and given away by a chief is sometimes very considerable. I have heard of one possessing as many as twelve bales of blankets, from twenty to thirty guns, with numberless pots, kettles, and pans, knives, and other articles of cutlery, and great quantities of beads, and other trinkets, as well as numerous beautiful Chinese boxes, which find their way here from the Sandwich Islands. The object in thus giving his treasures away is to add to his own importance in the eyes of others, his own people often boasting of how much their chief had given away, and exhibiting with pride such things as they had received themselves from

---

1) Schmoller, Grundriss, I p. 195. — 2) Bancroft, p. 84; Holmberg, I p. 112. — 3) Krause, pp. 167, 122. — 4) Bancroft, p. 167; Swan, p. 3.

him" [1]). Among the Nootkas "private wealth consists of boats and implements for obtaining food, domestic utensils, slaves, and blankets". "The accumulation of property beyond the necessities of life is only considered desirable for the purpose of distributing it in presents on great feast-days, and thereby acquiring a reputation for wealth and liberality" [2]). In Jewitt's narrative it is stated, that among the Ahts the king is obliged to support his dignity by making frequent entertainments, otherwise he would not be considered as conducting himself like a king, and would be no more thought of than a common man [3]). A wealthy Fish Indian may also win renown by giving away or destroying property [4]). Boas, describing the Kwakiutl Indians, speaks of "the method of acquiring rank. This is done by means of the potlatch, or the distribution of property. The underlying principle is that of the interest-bearing investment of property". He gives an elaborate account of this institution [5]). Among the Makah "the larger class of canoes generally belong to a single individual and he receives a proportionate share of the booty from the crew" [6]). Among the Tacullies "any person may become a *miuty* or chief who will occasionally provide a village feast" [7]). Of the tribes of W. Washington and N. W. Oregon Gibbs says: "Wealth gives a certain power among them, and influence is purchased by its lavish distribution." They have pretty clear ideas about the right of property in houses and goods. The men own property distinct from their wives. The husband has his own blankets, the wife her mats and baskets [8]). Bancroft tells us of the Puget Sound Indians: "I find no evidence of hereditary rank or caste except as wealth is sometimes inherited" [9]). Among the Chinooks "individuals were protected in their right to personal property, such as slaves, canoes, and implements". Each village was ruled by a chief "either hereditary or selected for his wealth and popularity" [10]).

The effects of this development of property and wealth are:

a. Social status depending mainly upon wealth, a slave may be a good hunter or fisher and valued as such, and yet be despised as a penniless fellow.

1) Kane, pp. 220, 221. — 2) Bancroft, p. 191. — 3) Brown, Adventures of John Jewitt, p. 216. — 4) Mayne, p. 263. — 5) Boas, Kwakiutl, p. 341. — 6) Gibbs, p. 175. — 7) Bancroft, p. 123. — 8) Gibbs, p. 185, 187. — 9) Bancroft, p. 217. — 10) Ibid., pp. 239, 240.

b. The accumulation of property beyond the necessities of life requires more labour than would otherwise be wanted. Moreover, slaves are the more desired, as the keeping of many slaves is indicative of wealth and therefore honourable. We may quote here Kane's account of a chief of the Pacific Coast, "who having erected a colossal idol of wood, sacrificed five slaves to it, barbarously murdering them at its base, and asking in a boasting manner who amongst them could afford to kill so many slaves". And Holmberg remarks that among the Tlinkits the consideration which the nobles enjoy depends only on their wealth, *i. e.* on the number of the slaves they own [1]).

The five causes we have enumerated here are not at work independently of each other. Abundance of food enables a tribe to have fixed habitations, to live in larger groups, to preserve food. Any greater development of trade and industry would be impossible if food were not abundant; for else all time and energy would be occupied by the seeking of food; and a settled life tends greatly to further the growth of industry. Wealth would scarcely exist if there were no trade and industry. The industrial development again facilitates the procuring of food. What is the primary cause of this relatively high state of economic life is not easy to say, and an investigation into this matter falls beyond the scope of the present volume.

It must also be remembered, that this economic state is not only the cause, but also to some extent the effect of slavery.

The development of trade and industry, of property and wealth, is undoubtedly much furthered by slavery. By imposing the ruder work upon slaves, the slave-owner can give more of his time and mind to trade and industry. "Leisure" as Bagehot remarks "is the great need of early societies, and slaves only can give men leisure" [2]). And that the keeping of slaves furthers the accumulation of wealth need hardly be said. The slave-trade, which enriches the traders, is even quite impossible where slavery does not exist. Hence we may infer that slavery must already have existed here at a somewhat lower stage of economic life.

On the other hand, there is a circumstance tending to acce-

1) Kane, p. 216; Holmberg, I p. 14. — 2) Bagehot, p. 72.

lerate the growth of slavery on the Pacific Coast. These tribes form a somewhat homogeneous group, and have much intercourse with each other. So we may suppose that some of them, that were not yet in such an economic state as spontaneously to invent slavery, have begun to keep slaves, imitating what they saw among their neighbours; the more so, as the slave-trade made this very easy. For our group is not quite homogeneous. The picture we gave of their highly developed economic life does not equally apply to all these tribes. The summer and winter dwellings of the Similkameem are rather primitive. They depend on hunting for a large portion of their food. Trade and industry, property and wealth are not mentioned; it is only stated that at a later period they had horses and cattle [1]. Niblack tells us that the Tsimshian sold slaves to the Tlinkits and interior Tinneh; but "the last-named had no hereditary slaves, getting their supply from the coast" [2]. No more particulars are given; but we may suppose that among these interior Tinneh slavery existed in a rather embryonic state, and would not have existed at all but for the slave-trade. The early ethnologists overrated the influence of imitation and derivation of social institutions; but we must not fall into the other extreme and underrate it. An institution may be derived and thereby its growth accelerated, of course within restricted limits.

If the information we have got on the *work imposed on slaves* were more complete, it would perhaps have been better first to survey this information, and thence to infer what place slavery occupies among the tribes of the Pacific Coast. But the statements of our ethnographers regarding slave labour are rather incomplete. A survey of them may, however, be of some use. In the first place it will be seen, whether they can be brought to agree with the exposition given above of the causes of slavery; and, secondly, our survey will perhaps provide us with new valuable data, which may give us a clearer understanding of the significance of slavery on the Pacific Coast of North America.

The occupations of slaves mentioned by our ethnographers are the following:

---

1) Allison, pp. 309, 306, 315. — 2) Niblack, p. 252.

1°. In a few cases the *slaves strengthen their master's force in warfare*. Aleut slaves always accompany their masters, and have to protect them [1]. "Kotzebue says that a rich man [among the Tlinkits] purchases male and female slaves, who must labour and fish for him, and strengthen his force when he is engaged in warfare" [2]. We may suppose that the last part of this sentence applies to male slaves only. Tsimshian slaves guard the house, when the master is absent [3]. Among the Ahts, the slaves were obliged to attend their masters in war and to fight for them [4].

This military function of slavery, as we shall see, also exists among several pastoral and agricultural peoples. The industrial part of society, in such cases, is not quite differentiated from the military part. As for the Tlinkits, Tsimshian and Ahts, the employing of slaves for protecting the master or his property is facilitated by the slave-trade: a purchased slave, brought from a great distance, may be made to fight, where it would not be safe to employ in warfare a slave captured from a neighbouring tribe; for the latter will probably be much inclined to go over to the enemies, who often are his own kindred. But the example of the Aleuts, whose slaves are prisoners of war and their descendants [5], shows that even captive slaves may be employed in warfare. We shall not very much wonder at this, if we take into consideration, that prisoners of war are sometimes soon forgotten, and even repelled, by their former countrymen. So "if a Mojave is taken prisoner he is forever discarded in his own nation, and should he return his mother even will not own him" [6]. The expectation of such treatment may induce captive slaves to fight on their masters' side against their own tribesmen rather than join the latter.

2°. Slaves are sometimes employed in *hunting, fishing and work connected with fishing,* such as rowing, etc. From a statement of Dunn's, quoted by Niblack, we learn that at Fort Simpson, British Columbia (in the country of the Tsimshian), a full-grown athletic slave, who is a good hunter, will fetch nine blankets, a gun, a quantity of powder and ball, a couple

---

1) Petroff, p. 152. — 2) Bancroft, p. 108; see also Niblack, p. 252. — 3) Boas, Die Tsimshian, p. 244. — 4) Brown, Adventures of John Jewitt, p. 130. — 5) Petroff, p. 152. — 6) Bancroft, p. 499.

of dressed elk skins, tobacco, vermilion paint, a flat file, and
other little articles" [1]). And Boas tells us, that Tsimshian slaves
row the boats, bring the killed seals to land, and cook them [2]).
Tlinkit slaves, as it appears from Kotzebue's above- quoted statement, must fish for their masters. Among the Nootkas "the
common business of fishing for ordinary sustenance is carried
on by slaves, or the lower class of people; while the more
noble occupation of killing the whale and hunting the sea-otter
is followed by none but the chiefs and warriors" [3]). According
to Jewitt's narrative, Aht slaves had to supply their masters
with fish. The author, on his wedding an Aht girl, got two
young male slaves presented to him to assist him in fishing [4]).

Dunn's statement about hunting slaves is very valuable. It
proves that hunting is here no longer the chief and noble
occupation of freemen. Among such people as for instance the
Ojibways a good hunter is held in high esteem, not bought at
a high price as a valuable slave. [5]). What we have said in the
last paragraph about hunting not being fit to be performed by
slaves, is not impaired by this statement; for hunting among
these traders is not the most honoured occupation; moreover,
the abundance of game along the Pacific Coast makes it very
easy; it does not require nearly so much skill and application
as among the Ojibways and similar tribes. This statement also
contains a most striking refutation of Bos' assertion, that slavery
here exists only as a reminiscence of a hypothetical former
agricultural state [6]). If this were true, there might be traces
of an ancient slave system; slaves might even still be kept by
rich men as a luxury; but the slave's ability in hunting would
not enter as a determining factor into his price. Slavery exists
here in full vigour, and is not in any way, as Bos will have
it, foreign to the economic state in which these tribes live [7]).

1) Niblack, p. 252. — 2) Boas, Die Tsimshian, p. 237. — 3) Meares, as quoted by
Bancroft, p. 188. — 4) Brown, Adventures of John Jewitt, pp. 130, 201. — 5) See above,
p. 196. — 6) See above, p. 174. — 7) Letourneau also seems to consider slavery foreign
to the way of life of these tribes. He has not, however, recourse to a hypothetical former
agricultural state, but to the great ethnological *pons asinorum*, derivation (pp. 132, 134).
But he does not inform us whence slavery can have been derived. Perhaps from the
inland tribes who, as Letourneau himself proves to be aware, have no slaves? Or from
the Siberians, who are rather in a lower than in a higher economic state as compared
with the Indians of the Pacific Coast? Or from the Hindus or any other mythical early
visitors of America?

What Meares tells us of the Nootkas is also instructive. The drudgery for daily sustenance, fishing, is left to the slaves; whereas the chiefs and warriors reserve to themselves the less productive and (partly therefore) more noble occupation of killing whales and sea-otters. It is remarkable that fishing is carried on by "the slaves or the lower class of people". Those who cannot afford to buy slaves must themselves perform the drudgery that others leave to slaves. The formation of social classes among freemen is furthered by slavery.

3°. The slaves of the Ahts, in Jewitt's time, were obliged to *make the canoes* and to *assist in building and repairing the houses* [1]). This proves, that slavery among them discharged an important economic function.

4°. We are often informed, that slaves do *domestic work*. Tsimshian slaves cook the killed seals and cut wood [2]). Among the Nootkas "women prepare the fish and game for winter use, cook, manufacture cloth and clothing, and increase the stock of food by gathering berries and shell-fish; and most of this work among the richer class is done by slaves". Our informant speaks also of "the hard labour required" from the slaves [3]). Among the Ahts, slaves, as Sproat tells us, serve the family. When a man of rank is going to remove, the new house is prepared in advance by his slaves. According to Jewitt's narrative, "all the menial offices are performed by them, such as bringing water, cutting wood, and a variety of others". "The females are employed principally in manufacturing cloth, in cooking, collecting berries, etc" [4].) Among the Fish Indians old women and slaves prepare the food [5]). Chinook slaves "are obliged to perform all the drudgery for their masters.... But the amount of the work connected with the Chinook household is never great" [6]). The last sentence here proves that "drudgery" means household work.

Some general expressions we find on record with our ethnographers seem to bear the same meaning. For instance, Tlinkit slaves, according to Kotzebue (quoted above), must "labour" for their masters; and Niblack, evidently referring to

1) Brown, Adventures of John Jewitt, p. 130. — 2) Boas, Die Tsimschian, pp. 237, 240. 3) Bancroft, pp. 196, 195. — 4) Sproat, pp. 90, 39; Brown, Adventures of John Jewitt, pp. 130, 131. — 5) Mayne, p. 253. — 6) Bancroft, p. 240.

the same statement, says that "slaves did all the drudgery" [1]. The Tacullies use their slaves "as beasts of burden", which perhaps also means imposing household labour upon them [2]. Holmberg states that the Koniagas employed their slaves as labourers or servants [3]. And Niblack remarks about the Coast Indians of Southern Alaska and Northern British Columbia in general: "When slavery was in vogue, this class performed all the menial drudgery" [4].

It is remarkable, that slaves in so many cases are stated to perform household, *i. e.* female, labour. These statements are even more numerous than those about fishing and similar work; so it would seem (we may not speak more positively, as our information is rather incomplete), that household work is the chief occupation of slaves along the Pacific Coast. Now it is easy to understand, that fixed habitations and the preserving of food for winter use require a large amount of domestic labour. But this does not solve the question, why slaves are employed for this work; why the men purchase or capture slaves not for their own private use, but in order to relieve their wives of a part of their task. In Australia women are overworked, and beaten into the bargain; why are the men of the Pacific Coast so anxious to give the women assistance in their work?

It might be, that female labour is valued by the men, because articles of trade are prepared by the women. Unfortunately the ethnographers most often content themselves with remarking that a brisk trade is carried on, or that some tribe is commercial rather than warlike, without specifying the articles of commerce. Yet a few statements tend to verify our hypothesis. The articles of trade of the Chinooks before the arrival of the Europeans were: fish, oil, shells, and Wapato. "The Wapato, a bulbous root, compared by some to the potato and turnip, was the aboriginal staple, and was gathered by women" [5]. Lewis and Clark also state that this bulb, which "is the great article of food, and almost the staple article of commerce on the Columbia", is collected chiefly by the women [6].

---

1) Niblack, p. 252. — 2) Bancroft, p. 124. — 3) Holmberg, I p. 78. — 4) Niblack, p. 253. — 5) Bancroft, pp. 239, 234. — 6) Lewis and Clark, III p. 38.

The Tlinkits export to the interior basket-work, dancing clothes, train-oil prepared from the *ssag* (a kind of fish), a sort of cakes made of Alaria Esculenta (a sea-weed). The women manufacture basket-work, dancing clothes, mocassins and other clothes. In the fishing season they are from morning to night engaged in preparing the fish. In the autumn they gather berries, bark, leaves and other vegetable by-meat; in other seasons they gather shells and sea-urchins on the beach [1]. Here all articles of trade are products of female labour. Among the Ahts baskets and mats, manufactured by the women, are sold; the women may keep the proceeds, and also get a little portion of their husbands' earnings. Our informant, speaking of the several divisions of the Ahts mutually exchanging the fish that each of them catches, probably also means fish prepared by the women [2]. In W. Washington and N. W. Oregon the *kamas*, a root which was "formerly a great article of trade with the interior", is dug by the women [3]. What articles are exported by the other tribes we do not know.

There is another fact strengthening our hypothesis: women are often consulted in matters of trade. Among the Tlinkits "the men rarely conclude a bargain without consulting their wives" [4]. Nootka wives too "are consulted in matters of trade" [5]. About Puget Sound the females "are always consulted in matters of trade before a bargain is closed" [6]. Chinook women "are consulted on all important matters" [7], which matters, among these commercial people, necessarily include the trade. Among the Haidas, the trade, in Jewitt's time, was even principally managed by the women, who were expert in making a bargain [8].

This need not, however, be the only cause; for women here enjoy a rather high position; so it might be that the men wish to alleviate the task of their wives, quite apart from the occupation of the latter in preparing the articles of commerce. Aleuts, if not addicted to drinking, are good husbands, and help their wives in everything [9]. Among the Tlinkits, according to Krause, "woman's position is not a bad one. She is not the

---

1) Krause, pp. 186, 159. — 2) Sproat, pp. 97, 38. — 3) Gibbs, p. 193. — 4) Bancroft, p. 112; see also Krause, p. 161. — 5) Brancroft, p. 196. — 6) Ibid., p. 218. — 7) Ibid., p. 242. — 8) Brown, Adventures of John Jewitt, p. 241. — 9) Elliott, p. 164.

slave of her husband; she has determinate rights, and her
influence is considerable"; and Bancroft remarks that "there
are few savage nations, in which the sex have greater influence
or command greater respect" [1]. Nootka wives "seem to be
nearly on terms of equality with their husbands, except that
they are excluded from some public feasts and ceremonies" [2];
and Sproat tells us that among the Ahts slaves only are pro-
stituted; women are not badly treated; a wife may leave her
husband with the consent of her relatives [3]. Among the
Koniagas, according to Holmberg, the women did not hold a
subordinate place as among other savage tribes of North America,
but enjoyed high consideration [4]. In W. Washington and
N. W. Oregon, according to Gibbs, "the condition of the woman
is that of slavery under any circumstances." But the particulars he gives prove that the women here are not so very
badly off. In their councils "the women are present at, and
join in the deliberations, speaking in a low tone, their words
being repeated aloud by a reporter. On occasions of less ceremony, they sometimes address the audience without any such
intervention, and give their admonitions with a freedom of
tongue highly edifying. In a few instances, matrons of superior
character, "strong minded women", have obtained an influence
similar to that of chiefs." The men own property distinct from
their wives. "He has his own blankets, she her mats and baskets,
and generally speaking her earnings belong to her, except those
arising from prostitution, which are her husband's." Sometimes
"the courtship commences in this way — the girl wishing a
husband, and taking a straightforward mode of attracting one."
"The accession of a new wife in the lodge very naturally pro-
duces jealousy and discord, and the first often returns for a
time in dudgeon to her friends, to be reclaimed by her husband
when he chooses, perhaps after propitiating her by some
present" [5]. Yet the condition of women seems not to be quite
as good as among the other tribes. "A man sends his wife away,
or sells her at his will." "An Indian, perhaps, will not let his
favourite wife, but he looks upon his others, his sisters, daughters,

1) Krause, p. 161; Bancroft, p. 109. — 2) Bancroft, p. 196. — 3) Sproat, p. 95. — 4) Holmberg, I p. 119. — 5) Gibbs, pp. 198, 185, 187.

female relatives, and slaves, as a legitimate source of profit" [1]).
But we must take into consideration, that Gibbs gives a
general description of inland tribes and coast tribes together.
That among the latter the condition of women is not so very
bad, is proved by Bancroft's statements about the tribes on
Puget Sound and Chinooks. About Puget Sound "women have
all the work to do except hunting and fishing, while their
lords spend their time in idleness and gambling. Still the
females are not ill-treated; they acquire great influence in
the tribe" [2]). And among the Chinooks "work is equally
divided between the sexes.... Their [women's] condition is
by no means a hard one. It is among tribes that live by the
chase or by other means in which women can be of little
service, that we find the sex most oppressed and cruelly
treated" [3]) This statement is strengthened by Swan writing
that "with these Indians the position of the women is not so
degraded as with the tribes of the Plains" [4]). The Tacullies
"are fond of their wives, performing the most of the household
drudgery in order to relieve them" [5]). Mackenzie, speaking of
an Indian tribe, probably related to the Atnahs on Fraser
River, amongst whom strangers are kept "in a state of awe
and subjection," states that they live upon the products of the
sea and rivers and are to be considered as a "stationary people."
"Hence it is that the men engage in those toilsome employments,
which the tribes who support themselves by the chase leave
entirely to the women" [6]).

Our information, here again, is not very complete; but as
far as it goes it tends to prove that the condition of women
on the Pacific Coast is not a bad one.

This good condition of women here, as compared with for
instance that of Australian women, may for a great part be
due to the settled life of these tribes. While the men are on
fishing, hunting, or trading expeditions, the women enjoy much
liberty; whereas Australian women are continually marching
along with their husbands [7]). The men must also be aware

1) Ibid., p. 199. — 2) Bancroft, p. 218. — 3) Ibid., p. 242. — 4) Swan, The Northwest
Coast, p. 160. — 5) Elliott, p. 164. — 6) Mackenzie, II p. 268. — 7) A writer of the 18th century
tells us of the women of the Dutch isle of Ameland (the men being fishers and mariners):
"They are generally somewhat imperious, and by their foolish cleanliness most men are

that domestic comfort, worth much in these cold regions, depends on the women. As militarism does not prevail here to any great extent, women are not so much in need of male protection. And village life makes conspiracy of women possible. So among the Aleuts "a religious festival used to be held in December, at which all the women of the village assembled by moonlight, and danced naked with masked faces, the men being excluded under penalty of death" [1]. Last but not least, subsistence here is largely dependent on female labour. Lewis and Clark remark: "Where the women can aid in procuring subsistence for the tribe, they are treated with more equality, and their importance is proportioned to the share which they take in that labour; while in countries where subsistence is chiefly procured by the exertions of the men, the women are considered and treated as burdens. Thus, among the Clatsops and Chinnooks, who live upon fish and roots, which the women are equally expert with the men in procuring, the former have a rank and influence very rarely found among Indians. The females are permitted to speak freely before the men, to whom indeed they sometimes address themselves in a tone of authority. On many subjects their judgments and opinions are respected, and in matters of trade, their advice is generally asked and pursued. The labours of the family too, are shared almost equally" [2].

We have only enumerated some causes tending to bring about a good condition of women. It is not the place here to expatiate upon this point any further. But it is worth while to emphasize the fact itself, that women are on the whole well treated among these tribes. A German writer, Dr. Grosse, has tried to prove, that among the "higher hunters" (*höhere Jäger*) as well as among the "lower hunters" (*niedere Jäger*)

hardly ever allowed to have a fire on the grate during the winter. The cause of this imperious behaviour of Ameland women is not difficult to detect: as the men are at home only in the winter, the women rule for the greater part of the year, and are not inclined to part with their authority in winter-time. Therefore most men, so to speak, board at their wives' houses, and if they want to keep peace, have to put up with female ascendency." Tegenwoordige Staat der Vereenigde Nederlanden, XIV pp. 363, 364.

In the same sense Professor Nieuwenhuis writes about the Kayans on the Mendalam: "As the men are often absent on long journeys, the women get the lead in household affairs" (Door Centraal-Borneo, I p. 77.). — 1) Bancroft, p. 93. — 2) Lewis and Clark, II pp. 334, 335.

woman's state is a bad one. As all our tribes belong to Grosse's "higher hunters" [1]), we shall attempt to find out, why his conclusion is so different from ours. He quotes several ethnographical statements, which are to afford a basis for his inference [2]). We shall examine whether this is a sound basis. Grosse does not always exactly specify which tribe each quotation applies to; but as he most frequently quotes Bancroft, we can easily find it out. He first quotes this statement of Bancroft's about the Shoshones: "The weaker sex of course do the hardest labour, and receive more blows than kind words for their pains" [3]). But the very next sentence: "These people, in common with most nomadic nations, have the barbarous custom of abandoning the old and infirm the moment they find them an incumbrance," shows that these Shoshones are not at all to be compared to the Tlinkits and similar tribes; their mode of life is decidedly rude and little comfortable. Then he refers to some passages of Bancroft's, proving that unfaithfulness of the wife is punished with death, whereas the husband has the right to prostitute his wife to strangers. These passages apply to the Southern and Northern Californians as well as to the Shoshones. But about the former it is also stated: "If a man ill-treated his wife, her relations took her away, after paying back the value of her wedding presents, and then married her to another" [4]). And of the Northern Californians we are told: "Among the Modocs polygamy prevails, and the women have considerable privilege. The Hoopa adulterer loses one eye, the adulteress is exempt from punishment" [5]). Moreover, "although the principal labour falls to the lot of the women, the men sometimes assist in building the wigwam, or even in gathering acorns and roots" [6]). Another statement of Bancroft's, quoted by Grosse, applies to the Chepewyans: "The Northern Indian is master of his household. He marries without ceremony, and divorces his wife at his pleasure. A man of forty buys or fights for a spouse of twelve, and when tired of her whips her and sends her away" [7]). This statement is corroborated by a report of Hearne's. But why Grosse calls

---

1) Grosse, p. 65. — 2) Ibid., pp. 74—78. — 3) Bancroft, p. 437. — 4) Ibid., p. 412. — 5) Powers, as quoted by Bancroft, p. 351. — 6) Bancroft, p. 351. — 7) Ibid., p. 117.

the Chepewyans "higher hunters" we do not understand. "Altogether they are pronounced an inferior race". "The "Chepewyans inhabit huts of brush and portable skin tents". "Their weapons and their utensils are of the most primitive kind" [1]). The next quotation applies to the Kutchins, whose wives "are treated more like dogs than human beings". But this is only stated of the Tenan Kutchin, "people of the mountains," "a wild, ungovernable horde, their territory never yet having been invaded by white people". "The Kutcha Kutchin, "people of the lowland," are cleaner and better mannered". And of these "better mannered" Kutchins Bancroft says: "The women perform all domestic duties, and eat after the husband is satisfied; but the men paddle the boats, and have even been known to carry their wives ashore, so that they might not wet their feet" [2]). As for the Nootkas, women being "somewhat overworked" (Grosse does not mention that among the richer class most female work is done by slaves), and excluded from some public feasts, Grosse concludes that their state is a bad one. We have quoted above some facts tending to prove the contrary. Then Grosse asserts that, according to Bancroft, Haida husbands prostitute their wives for money. Bancroft, however, says literally: "While jealousy is not entirely unknown, chastity appears to be so, as women who can earn the greatest number of blankets win great admiration for themselves and high position for their husbands" [3]); which is not exactly the same. The Tlinkits, according to Grosse, are the only, unaccountable exception to his general rule. Finally he attempts to prove, that the alleged supremacy of women in Kamchatka does not signify so very much; but that Kamchadale women are badly treated, even he does not assert.

What remains now of Grosse's evidence? Tlinkit and Kamchadale women he himself admits not to be badly off. What he says of Nootkas and Haidas proves very little. About the Northern and Southern Californians we have got statements that impair Grosse's argument very much. Only among the Shoshones, Chepewyans, and Tenan Kutchin is the state of women decidedly bad; but these are not on a level with the

---

1) Ibid., pp. 117—119. — 2) Ibid., pp. 131, 132. — 3) Ibid., p. 169.

other tribes; they are migratory and little advanced in the arts of life. And of the Tenan Kutchin we know very little, "their territory never yet having been invaded by white people" [1]).

Grosse derives most of his evidence from Bancroft's book; but he evidently has not paid attention to all the data given by Bancroft, which relate to the condition of women. Sometimes he quotes one sentence, where two successive sentences taken together would give quite another view of the matter. Several statements of Bancroft's (such as about the tribes on Puget Sound, Chinooks, Tacullies) he omits altogether; whereas just the tribes of the N. W. Coast of North America are, according to him, among the most typical "higher hunters" [2]). And he can only give a semblance of truth to his inference by classifying under "higher hunters" Shoshones and similar tribes, which are not more advanced in the arts of life than some Australians, and decidedly much less than the Eskimos and Aleuts whom he calls "lower hunters".

Returning to our chief subject, we may remark, that our survey of slave labour leads to the same conclusion we arrived at before, viz. that the preserving of food, a settled life, and the high development of trade, industry and wealth, are the main causes which have made slavery so largely prevalent here. As additional causes we may now name the high position of women, which induces the men to relieve them of a part of their work by giving them the help of slaves; and, in a few cases, the want of fighting men, who are to strengthen their masters' force in warfare.

We shall now briefly examine, which are the causes of slavery among the slave-keeping hunters and fishers outside the Pacific Coast.

Among the Abipones the function of slavery was beyond any doubt reinforcement of the tribe. The slaves were very leniently treated. "I know of many people" says Dobrizhoffer, "who, being released by their friends and brought back to their native country, voluntarily returned to their masters, the

---

1) Some other writers, however (whom Grosse does not refer to), speaking of the Kutchins in general, state that women are badly treated; see Kirby, p. 419; Hardisty, p. 312; Jones, Kutchin tribes, p. 325. — 2) Grosse, p. 65.

Abipones, whom they follow in their hunting and fighting expeditions; though Spaniards themselves, they do not hesitate to stain their hands with Spanish blood." "The liberty to go where they like, the abundance of food and clothing procured without any labour, the possesion of many horses, the freedom to idle and run into debauchery, the lawless impunity they enjoy, bind the Spanish captives so much to the Abipones, that they prefer their captivity to liberty". "The Abipones, though considering polygamy allowed, very seldom take several wives at a time; the captives do not often content themselves with one wife, but marry as many female prisoners, Spanish or Indian, as they can" [1]).

The reason for taking prisoners here was the same as among the Iroquois and similar tribes, where they were adopted; with this sole difference, that the Abipones seem to have had a sexual aversion (that cannot be accounted for here) to all men and women outside their own nation; therefore they did not adopt their prisoners, nor had they any sexual intercourse with them. Slavery as a system of labour did not exist here.

As for their economic life, this was much inferior to that on the Pacific Coast of North America. They subsisted on the spontaneous products of nature and on game. Food was abundant; yet their mode of life required frequent migrations. All their journeys were performed on horseback [2]).

The information we get about the Tehuelches is very incomplete. Falkner states, that the female relatives of the cacique have slaves, who perform most of their work [3]).

In Kamchatka slaves were employed for various domestic labours, such as fetching wood, feeding the dogs, making axes and knives from stone and bone [4]). The Kamchadales were not so far advanced in the arts of life as the tribes of the Pacific Coast of North America. They think only of the present, says Steller; they are not ambitious to become rich. They do not like to work more than is needed for their own and their families' subsistence. "When they have got as much as they think to be sufficient, they do not collect any more food; they would not even do so, if the fish came on land and the animals into their dwellings". A rather brisk trade was, however, carried on by them and was largely dependent on female labour [1]. They also had fixed habitations [2].

Speaking of the tribes of the Pacific Coast, we concluded that slavery must have already existed among them at a somewhat lower stage of economic life. The Kamchadales afford a proof of this. They were not so far advanced in the arts of life as the tribes of the Pacific Coast; yet slavery already existed among them, though it does not seem to have prevailed here to any great extent.

§ 3. *Experimentum crucis: Australia.*

In the last paragraph we have shown that in the economic and social life of the slave-keeping hunters and fishers (especially those on the Pacific Coast of North America) there are some features which account for the existence of slavery. But there is still something wanting in our argument. It might be that the circumstances which we have called causes of slavery were equally found among the hunting and fishing tribes that do not keep slaves; in that case the foregoing argument would prove insufficient. Therefore we shall apply here the *experimentum crucis;* we shall inquire how much the economic and social life of the slave-keeping tribes differs from that of the other tribes. This investigation may be instructive in various respects. It might be, that of the supposed causes of slavery some were found among non-slave-keeping as well as among slave-keeping tribes, whereas others existed among none but slave-keeping tribes; then the latter causes only would be decisive. Or perhaps we shall find that each of these causes exists among one or more non-slave-keeping tribes; but that the combination of all the causes is found nowhere but among slave-keeping tribes. It were also possible, that a combination of the same causes existed among non-slave-keeping tribes, but that among these there were other circumstances neutralizing the former. Whether any of these possibilities is a reality, will appear from the ensuing investigation.

1) Ibid., pp. 245, 286. 286 note, 317, 318. — 2) Ibid., pp. 210 sqq.

We do not, however, think that it is necessary to give a survey of the economic and social life of all non-slave-keeping hunters and fishers. For we have seen that among the tribes of the Pacific Coast of North America the growth of slavery is much furthered by their forming a somewhat homogeneous group. Accordingly slavery among the few slave-keeping tribes outside the Pacific Coast seems to be little developed. Now there are many non-slave-keeping hunting and fishing tribes, either living quite isolated (*e. g.* Andaman Islanders, Fuegians) or surrounded by more powerful, agricultural or pastoral, tribes (*e. g.* Bushmen, African pigmies). That such a position is very unfavourable to the existence of slavery is evident. We shall therefore confine ourselves to a survey of the three great groups of hunters and fishers outside the Pacific Coast: the Australians, the Indians of Central North America, and the Eskimos. Australia and the regions where the Eskimos live are inhabited by hunters and fishers only. In Central North America a few agricultural tribes of the lowest stage (hunting agriculturists) are found; but these differ so little from hunters proper, that we may speak here of a group of hunters, not inclosed between superior peoples. Perhaps the hunters and hunting agriculturists of Brazil, Paraguay, etc. form a similar group; but the literature on these tribes accessible to us was rather incomplete.

We shall inquire now, whether the several circumstances furthering the growth of slavery on the Pacific Coast, are found among each of these groups.

In the first place we shall regard Australia.

1°. *Abundance of food.* Food in Australia is by no means abundant and often very scarce. The Australians are omnivo-rous in the widest sense of the word; they eat even mice, rats, lizards, beetles, etc. In some parts of Australia, especially on the West Coast and in the interior, the natives are continually suffering from hunger [1]. Thomas remarks: "In few parts of Australia can the native count on anything like regular supplies of food. He is dependent on the course of the seasons for his seeds and fruits; the time of year also affects the supply of fish in many parts; and in Central Australia, perhaps owing

---

[1] Waitz-Gerland, VI pp. 724, 725.

to the barrenness of the land, much time is given up, if our accounts are accurate, to magical ceremonies, whose object is to promote the increase of game and plant life, so difficult does the native find it to obtain sustenance" [1]). We shall soon see that scarcity of food compels them to live in very small groups.

2°. *Variety of food.* There is a great variety. Concerning S. W. Australia Gerland enumerates 6 kinds of kangaroos, 29 of fish, two of seals; and further wild dogs, emus and other birds, tortoises, opossums, frogs, shell-fish, grubs of beetles, bird's eggs, mice, rats, snakes and lizards; roots, mushrooms, resins and various fruits [2]). But this list, including (as Gerland remarks) everything eatable, proves only that they live very poorly. The natives of South Australia also, according to Eylmann, though they have a great many kinds of food, seldom live in abundance. During the frequent times of drought they suffer severely from want of food [3]). In Central Australia "with certain restrictions... everything which is edible is used for food" [4]). And as for fishing, though fish enters for a large part into the subsistence of the coast tribes, there are no fishing tribes in the higher sense in Australia, like those of the Pacific Coast. Their canoes, where they have any, are very primitive; and the principal means of catching fish are by spearing and setting traps [5]).

3°. *Fixed habitations, large groups, preserving of food.* Gerland states that to find sufficient food, the Australians must continually roam over the country. These wandering tribes cannot be large, else food would fail them; so the division of the Australians into numerous small tribes is a consequence of the nature of their country [6]). Spencer and Gillen speak of the natives of Central Australia as living in small local groups [7]). Brough Smyth remarks: "It is necessary for a tribe to move very frequently from place to place, always keeping within the boundaries of the country which it calls its own —, now to the spot where eels can be taken in the creeks; often to the feeding-grounds of the kangaroo; sometimes to the thicker forests to get wood suitable for making weapons; to the sea-

---

1) Thomas, p. 88. — 2) Waitz-Gerland, VI pp. 724, 725. — 3) Eijlmann, p. 293. — 4) Spencer and Gillen, Native tribes, p. 21. — 5) Waitz-Gerland, VI pp. 732, 733, 738. — 6) Ibid., p. 722. — 7) Spencer and Gillen, Native tribes, p. 8.

coast continually for fish of various kinds; and, at the right
season, to the lands where are found the native bread, the yam,
and the acacia gum" [1]). According to Eylmann, the natives of
South Australia, in their barren country, are forced not only
to continually move on, but to live in small hordes [2]). And
Thomas states that "the tribal areas are almost invariably
small" [3]). The writers who describe separate tribes also often
state that these tribes are nomadic and live in small groups.
We shall quote here only the statements of our ethnographers
concerning one significant fact, that presents a striking contrast to the state of things on the Pacific Coast, viz. the improvidence of the Australians. In the Moore River District of
W. Australia food is abundant in the summer; but the natives
are reckless of the future: they consume whatever they have
got. The natives of S. W. Australia preserve no food; if the
game killed is too much for a family to eat in one day, neighbouring families are invited and a feast is given, till nothing
is left. They do, however, store up acacia gum, and carry
roots with them. The Queenslanders on Herbert River think
only of the present moment. The Cammarray of N. S. Wales
eat as long as they have anything; they never lay up provisions, except when a dead whale has been cast on shore. Of
the aborigines of N. S. Wales in general Fraser tells us: "When
the fish are abundant, the fishers cannot use a tithe of the
fish they catch, and so sell them to all comers at a few pence
for a backful. As for themselves, they have a noble feast,
they and all their tribe; and, as is their habit whenever they
have abundance, they gorge themselves so that their bodies
are swollen to unnatural dimensions and seem ready to burst.
When they can hold no more, they go to sleep like snakes,
and sleep for twenty-four hours or more." Similar particulars
are gives by Angas. Spencer and Gillen, in their description
of the natives of Central Australia, remark that "when times
are favourable the black fellow is as lighthearted as possible.
He has not the slightest thought of, or care for, what the
morrow may bring forth, and lives entirely in the present" [4]).

---

1) Brough Smyth, I p. 123. — 2) Eylmann, p. 155. — 3) Thomas, p. 26. — 4) Spencer
and Gillen, Native tribes, p. 53.

As for the Tasmanians: "They lay up no store of provisions, and have been known in winter time to eat kangaroo skins" [1]). Matthews, speaking of several tribes of Queensland and South Australia, states that they "are very improvident, and accumulate no property beyond their weapons and rugs" [2]). And Forrest tells us that the natives of Central and Western Australia "live from hand to mouth, never collect more than enough for the day, and each morning have to look out for their day's food" [3]). Thomas remarks, that it is not true that the Australian does not store food. "Much of his food he must perforce eat quickly, or natural processes would make his labour in vain. But the *bunya-bunya* nut, grass and other seed cakes, and possibly other kinds of food, were certainly put aside for future use" [4]). He evidently means to say, that their preserving relatively little food is not due to improvidence, but to necessity. But however this may be, the fact that most of the collected food is consumed quickly remains, and this fact, not the underlying motives, has important consequences with regard to the economic structure of their society.

4°. *Trade and industry.* Bartering is not at all unknown among the Australians. Fraser, speaking of N. S. Wales, remarks: "I have already spoken of pipe-clay and ruddle as articles of trade; the Mindi-mindi gatherings are the markets at which this trade is carried on. The necessity for these fairs is not far to seek. A black man's own "taurai" does not furnish everything he requires for his daily life. In it there may be food enough, but he wants suitable stone for an axe, wood for his spears, and "bumerangs" and shields and clubs, flint for cutting and skinning, gum to be used as cement, and lumps of gritty sandstone, on which to sharpen his stone-axe; for adornment, the pipe-clay and the red-ochre are much valued, and so are swan-down feathers and the rose-coloured crests of a certain kind of cockatoo; some of these he can

1) Literature. On the Moore River District, Oldfield; on S. W. Australia, Salvado; on the natives on Herbert River, Lumholtz; on the Cammarray, Collins; on N. S. Wales, Fraser and Angas; on Central Australia, Spencer and Gillen, Native tribes, p. 53; on the Tasmanians, Ling Roth. As we had not got all the books at hand, but only some notes which we had previously made, in which the pages were not specified, we could not give all the exact references. — 2) Matthews, in Fraser's Notes, p. 188. — 3) Forrest, p. 318. — 4) Thomas, p. 117.

supply, and for them he gets in barter others that he wants. Then also there are manufactured articles which he can give in exchange, — cloaks, rugs, baskets, knitted bags, nets, weapons, and tools; most of these articles bear the "brand" of the maker. In this way the black man's wants are supplied by the mutual interchange of commodities. I suppose that, at these fairs, the usual amount of haggling goes on in the making of bargains, but there is no quarrelling; for, during the time, universal brotherhood prevails. The fairs are held whenever there is a need for them" [1]). Intertribal commerce is also carried on by the Narrinyeri and Dieri [2]). It seems, indeed, that there is hardly any savage tribe, among which the interchange of commodities is quite unknown. [3]) And in N. S. Wales it is not only the spontaneous products of nature that are exchanged, but manufactured articles, so the trade requires industry. Yet trade and industry are not nearly so fully developed here as on the Pacific Coast. Nowhere are there particulars given, showing that any Australian tribe is, like the Koniagas of the Pacific Coast, "adapted to labour and commerce rather than to war and hunting." On the Pacific Coast the coast tribes exchange their manufactured goods for the raw products of the hinterland; but in Australia there is nothing but hinterland.

That trade and industry do not signify nearly so much as on the Pacific Coast is clearly proved by their not having here the same effect; they have not led in Australia to any development of:

5°. *Property and wealth.* Professor Steinmetz, in his *Entwicklung der Strafe*, has closely studied the forms of government existing among the Australian natives. From the details he gives it appears, that a man's influence depends on his age, his bravery, eloquence, etc., and his having numerous relatives, but not on his wealth. Among the Queenslanders described by Lumholtz the old men have most influence. Among the Kurnai age, rather than bravery, gives influence. In Central Australia a man's power depends chiefly on his age, but also on force, courage, prudence, dexterity, perseverance, and the

---

1) Fraser, p. 67. "Taurai" is the land owned by a tribe or a division of a tribe, see ibid., p. 36. — 2) Steinmetz, Strafe, II pp. 27, 29. — 3) See Schmoller, Grundriss, I p. 333.

number of his relatives. On the Bourke and Darling rivers the council of old men is the only form of government. In Tasmania a man's influence depended on his strength, courage, perseverance, prudence, and dexterity. The old men were highly honoured and had many wives. In the Wellington tribe there is no government whatever; all are equal. Among the Cammarray the old men are chiefs. Among the Narrinyeri chieftainship is elective; wisdom, moderation, and good humour are the qualities most required in a chief. Among the Dieri the oldest man of the clan is chief, but has not always most power. A chief has real power only when, besides his age, he has other valued qualities, such as bravery, eloquence, or a large family. Great warriors, orators and sorcerers have most influence. In the Moore River District there is no government, a perfect equality prevails. The natives of Port Lincoln have no government; old people are held in high esteem. In the Western District of Victoria "the succession to the chiefdom is by inheritance". "The eldest son is appointed, unless there is some good reason for setting him aside." If the heir is weakly in body or mentally unfitted to maintain the position of chief, — which requires to be filled by a man of ability and bravery, — and has a better-qualified brother, he must give way to the latter or fight him in single combat. Among the tribes of Victoria described by Le Souëf government in the true sense does not exist, but the bravest and strongest, and often the most dangerous men, have most influence [1]. Some other statements lead to the same conclusion. In N. W. Central Queensland "a ripe old age constitutes the highest social status in the camp, and the one calling for the greatest respect. There is no single individual chief to direct affairs" [2]. In N. S. Wales, according to Fraser, "there is nothing of the nature of kingly rule in any one of the tribes, nor is there an over-chief for the whole of a tribe; but the affairs of each section of a tribe are administered by a number of elders, among whom one man is considered the leader or chief, because of his superior wisdom and influence". "If there are two rivals competing for the chiefship, they settle the matter by single

1) Steinmetz. Strafe, II pp. 20—34. — 2) Roth, p. 141.

combat". And Wilkes says: "As no system of government
exists, or any acknowledgment of power to enact laws, they
are solely guided by old usage" [1]. Among the Dieri chieftainship
is elective according to the influence of the candidate's clan
and his oratorical power [2]. About Powell's Creek there is no
government whatever; "the oldest man in the tribe would
usually carry most sway in tribal matters" [3]. Matthews, speaking of several tribes of Queensland and South Australia,
remarks: "They have elders or chiefs corresponding with the
Indian Medicine men, who I believe are principally self-con-
stituted, or admitted as such on the score of age or personal
prowess. Great respect is attached to age as a rule, especially
in visiting another tribe" [4]. Among the native tribes of Central
Australia, described by Spencer and Gillen, the chief has "a
position which, if he be a man of personal ability, but only
in that case, enables him to wield considerable power" [5]. In
South Australia the chiefs are either hereditary or elected for
their personal qualities [6]. A describer of the natives of North
Australia tells us: "There are no recognized chiefs in a tribe
in the true sense of the word, as far as I have come in contact
with them; the old men of each tribe form themselves into a
sort of council when anything of importance is to be discussed,
and what they decide upon is generally carried out" [7]. Thomas
remarks that, among the Australians in general, "where there
was a tendency to select the son of the late headman, it was
modified by the rule that he must have shown himself worthy
of the post by attaining distinction as a warrior, orator or
bard" [8], and Brough Smyth has the following statement: "The
government of aboriginal tribes is not a democracy. There are
the doctors or sorcerers who, under some circumstances, have
supreme power; there are the warriors who in time of trouble
are absolute masters; there are the dreamers, who direct and
control the movements of the tribe until their divinations are
fulfilled or forgotten; there are the old men (councillors)

---

1) Fraser, pp. 38, 39; Wilkes, II p. 204. — 2) Gason, in Frazer's Notes, p. 173. — 3) The
Stationmaster, in Frazer's Notes, p. 179. — 4) Matthews, in Frazer's Notes, p. 189. —
5) Spencer and Gillen, Native tribes, p. 10. — 6) Eylmann, p. 172. — 7) Foelsche, in Frazer's
Notes, pp. 196, 197. — 8) Thomas, p. 143; see also Howitt's detailed account of chieftainship
in South East Australia, pp. 296—320.

without whose advice even the warriors are slow to move; and, finally, there are the old women, who noisily intimate their designs and endeavour by clamour and threats to influence the leaders of their tribe" [1]).

We see that influence and power in Australia depend on personal qualities, not on wealth. We have only found two instances on record of men trying to strengthen their influence by means of their property. Gason tells us of a celebrated Dieri chief, who received regular tributes from the hordes under his control. The writer often observed him distributing presents among his personal friends, in order to avoid their jealousy [2]). But this is quite another thing than what we found existing on the Pacific Coast of North America. In the latter group a rich man, by being rich, attains to power; whereas here the chief, elected for his personal qualities, receives tributes, and by distributing what he has received strengthens his influence. Moreover we are told that these Dieri "have no property except a few weapons or ornaments; they are generally buried or destroyed", viz. after their owner's death [3]). Lumholtz speaks of an old man in Queensland who distributed his property among his fellow-tribesmen to attain to greater influence [4]). This looks somewhat like the state of things existing on the Pacific Coast; but as the same writer tells us that there is no government except the council of old men, this may be an isolated case. And even if among one or two tribes wealth gave a certain influence, this would not impair the conclusion we have arrived at, that generally a man's influence and power do not depend upon his wealth, whence we may infer that wealth and property are little developed here.

6°. *Condition of women.* Whereas on the Pacific Coast women are held in rather high esteem, and therefore provided by the men with slaves who help them in their work, the condition of women in Australia is decidedly bad as we have seen in the first chapter of Part I [5]).

---

1) Brough Smyth, I p. 126. The ethnographers give many more details regarding tribal government; but we have only quoted those that bear directly on the question at issue, *i.e.* that show on what qualities influence and power depend. — 2) Steinmetz, Strafe, II p. 28. — 3) Gason, in Frazer's Notes, p. 171. — 4) Steinmetz, Strafe, II p. 20. — 5) See above, pp. 10—23.

7°. *Militarism.* We have shown that slaves are sometimes taken in order to strengthen their masters' force in warfare. On the other hand, where militarism does not prevail to any considerable extent, the tribe can afford the luxury of having male slaves living among them who do not fight. As. for the Australians, their wars generally are not sanguinary, and often settled by single combat [1]).

Our conclusion is that the Australians differ from the tribes of the Pacific Coast of North America in many respects. Food is by no means abundant; the highly developed fishing methods of the Pacific Coast are unknown here; the Australians are migratory and improvident, and live in small groups; though some tribes interchange commodities, trade and industry do not signify nearly so much as on the Pacific Coast; the objects of property are very few and wealth does not exist; the condition of women is a bad one. Only in two respects do both groups agree: there is a great variety of food, and militarism does not prevail to any great extent. We have seen, however, that "variety of food" here means that the Australians must avail themselves of whatever is eatable, *i. e.* that they live in the deepest misery. Therefore henceforth we shall no longer speak of variety of food as a circumstance favourable to the existence of slavery; and in the next paragraphs we shall not inquire whether the Central North Americans and Eskimos have a variety of food.

§ 4. *Experimentum crucis: Central North America.*

This paragraph will contain a survey of the economic state of the group of hunting tribes, extending across North America, from the Montagnais near the Atlantic Coast to the Apaches of Texas. Besides hunters in the proper sense this group includes the Cheyennes and Comanches, who, though slight traces of agriculture were found among them, subsisted almost entirely on the products of the chase.

1° *Abundance of food.* Le Jeune, speaking of the Mon-

---

1) Steinmetz, Strafe, II pp. 3 sqq.

tagnais, says: "The savages are almost always hungry" [1]).
The Chepewyans "are not remarkable for their activity as
hunters, owing to the ease with which they snare deer and
spear fish" [2]). Among the Kutchins a good hunter can always,
except in very unfavourable circumstances, procure sufficient
food [3]). The Beaver Indians, according to Mackenzie, seemed
to live in a state of comparative comfort [4]). The Comanches
in the summer, when the buffaloes remove to the North, often
suffer from want of food [5]). Lewis and Clark tell us, that the
Shoshones "suffer the extremes of want; for two-thirds of the
year they are forced to live in the mountains, passing whole
weeks without meat, and with nothing to eat but a few fish
and roots" [6]). Grinnell, speaking of the inland Indians in general,
remarks: "The life of the Indian was in some respects a hard
one, for the question of food was an ever-present anxiety with
him" [7]).

Considering the foregoing statements, and remembering Tanner's narrative that gives a description of a continual struggle
for mere existence, we may safely conclude that, though a
few of these tribes lived rather comfortably, food, among the
Indians of Central North America in general, was not nearly
so abundant as on the Pacific Coast.

2°. Whereas the tribes of the Pacific Coast subsist chiefly
by *fishing*, the Indians of Central North America are, nearly
all of them, hunters (See § 2 of this chapter).

3°. *Fixed habitations, large groups, preserving of food.* In a
general description of the "vast but thinly populated interior
of Northern America" we read that, with regard to the mode
of living, a distinction is to be made between the thick-wood
Indians and the prairie Indians. The thick-wood Indians consist
of small groups. During the summer they live on waterfowl,
fish, berries, etc. In the winter they often suffer from want of
food. The prairie Indians during the whole year live on the
buffalo. Their groups number on an average 400 people [8]).
The Montagnais, in Le Jeune's time, were wandering and few
in number; their life consisted of feasting as long es they had

1) Jes. Rel., VI p. 277. — 2) Mackenzie, I p. 151. — 3) Hardisty, p. 311. — 4) Mackenzie, II p. 193. — 5) Schoolcraft, I p. 231. — 6) Lewis and Clark, II p. 116. — 7) Grinnell
p. 48. — 8) Further papers, p. 47.

anything; they lived from hand to mouth and did not lay up
any provision [1]). The same writer calls the Algonquins a wandering tribe [2]). The Ojibways, according to Keating, are divided
into small groups, each containing a few families. They do
not lay up any provision for winter use. Jones also remarks,
that they are very improvident. Kohl, however, gives a long
description of the fruits preserved by them. [3]). The Knisteneaux
often, at one feast, consume what would have been enough for
several weeks [4]). The Blackfeet tribes are nomadic in their habits [5]).
Ross tells us, that the Eastern Tinneh "are obliged to lead a
wandering life, in order to procure food either by fishing or
hunting" [6]). The Indians on the Upper Yukon are very improvident. When fish is abundant, they gorge themselves with
it, instead of drying it for winter use [7]). The Kutchins live
in transportable dwellings. According to Kirby they "are
divided into many petty tribes". Hardisty, however, states
that they generally live in large groups [8]). Mackenzie speaks
of a Beaver Indian establishment of about 300 inhabitants [9]).
The Sioux live in small bands, owing to the scarcity of game [10]).
The Osages are nomadic. Our informant speaks of an Osage
town of 1500 inhabitants [11]). Apache tribes of 100—200 people,
of whom 25—50 are warriors, are headed by a captain. They
are "nomadic and roving in [their habits". "Seldom do they
remain more than a week in one locality" [12]). The Comanches
"usually roam in small subdivisions, varying according to ca-
price or the scarcity or abundance of game". These subdivisions consist of 20—110 families. Brancroft remarks about the
Comanches: "No provision is made for a time of scarcity, but
when many buffalo are killed, they cut portions of them into
long strips, which, after being dried in the sun, are pounded
fine. This pemican they carry with them in their hunting
expeditions, and when unsuccessful in the chase, a small
quantity boiled in water or cooked with grease, serves for a

---

1) Jes. Rel., VI pp. 83, 259, 149. — 2) Ibid., p. 133; see also Sagard, p. 78. — 3) Keating,
II pp. 149, 51; Jones, Ojibway Indians, p. 58; Kohl, II pp. 133 sqq. — 4) Mackenzie, I p.
128. — 5) Reports of Expl., I p. 448; XII Part I p. 73. — 6) Ross, p. 310. — 7) Elliott,
p. 417. — 8) Jones, Kutchin tribes, p. 321; Kirby, p. 418; Hardisty, p. 312. — 9) Mackenzie,
II p. 10. — 10) Schoolcraft, II p. 172. — 11) Hunter, Gedenkschriften, pp. 49, 46. — 12) Schoolcraft, V p. 260; Bancroft, p. 485.

meal" [1]). These details do not quite agree with Bancroft's assertion that "no provision is made". Grinnell remarks, that the Indians are often undeservedly taxed with improvidence. "We are told in books much about the Indian's improvidence, and it is frequently stated that however abundant food might be with him to-day, he took no thought for the needs of the morrow. Such statements are untrue and show but superficial observation. The savage does not look so far ahead as does the civilized man, but still the lessons of experience are not wholly lost on him. He remembers past hardships, and endeavours to provide against their recurrence; and these people were rather remarkable for their foresight, and for the provision which they were accustomed to make for the future" [2]).

However this may be, it is evident that the supplies these wandering tribes (as they subsist on hunting, we may safely suppose that they are all of them nomadic, whether this be explicitly stated or not) were able to store for winter's use, cannot compare with those of the tribes of the Pacific Coast.

4°. *Trade and industry.* The Montagnais, in Le Jeune's time, bought maize from the Hurons for elk-skins [3]). The Algonquins, according to the same writer, used to sell furs to the French [4]). The Blackfeet tribes sold peltries which they procured in the Northern part of their country [5]). Jones calls the Kutcha Kutchin traders: "they make very little for themselves, but buy from the other Indians." And Hardisty tells us, that they live by trading; they exchange beads, which are their circulating medium, for the peltries of other tribes [6]). The Osages, too, carried on the fur-trade in Hunter's time [7]).

We see that trade does not hold a large place in the economic life of these Indians, and that only raw products are exchanged.

Grinnell enumerates the branches of industry existing among them. "Food supply and defence against enemies depended on the warrior's weapons. These were his most precious possessions, and he gave much care to their manufacture. Knowing nothing of metals, he made his edge tools of sharpened stones."

---

1) Schoolcraft, I p. 231; Bancroft, p. 492. — 2) Grinnell, p. 48. — 3) Jes. Rel., VI p. 273. — 4) Ibid., p. 19. — 5) Reports of Expl., I p. 444. — 6) Jones, Kutchin tribes, p. 324; Hardisty, p. 311. — 7) Hunter, Gedenkschriften, p. 50.

"The most important part of the warrior's equipment was the bow, and over no part of it was more time and labour spent." "The stone axe, the maul, and the lance were all simple weapons." "A very important part of the warrior's outfit was the shield, with which he stopped or turned aside the arrows of his enemy. It was usually circular in shape, and was made of the thick, shrunken hide of a buffalo bull's neck." "Clothing was made of skins tanned with or without the fur." "Many tribes — especially those to the south — made a simple pottery... Among the northern tribes, where pottery was least known, ladles, spoons, bows, and dishes were usually formed from horn or wood". "The different tribes had but slight knowledge of the textile art, and this knowledge seems to have been greatest in the south and on the coast." "Three vehicles were known to the primitive Indian — the travois in the south and the sledge in the north for land travel, and the canoe wherever there were water ways." "The Indian's ideas of art are rude." "It is in the art of carving, however, that the greatest skill was shown" [1]. So these tribes do not seem to have attained to a high industrial development; the less, as most of the instances Grinnell gives of their skill in carving relate to tribes of the Pacific Coast.

5°. *Property and wealth.* Whereas on the Pacific Coast influence and power depend on wealth, we shall see that in Central North America it is otherwise. Le Jeune, speaking of the Montagnais, remarks: "Rhetoric controls all these tribes, as the captain is elected for his eloquence alone, and is obeyed in proportion to his use of it, for they have no other law than his word" [2]. Roosevelt states that among the Algonquins the war-chief "wielded only the influence that he could secure by his personal prowess and his tact" [3]. The power of an Ojibway chief depended upon his wisdom, courage, and hospitality [4]. Of the Blackfeet we are told: "Chiefs never receive a gift, considering it a degradation to accept anything but what their own prowess or superior qualities of manhood acquire for them. Their hearts are so good and strong that they scorn to take

---

1) Grinnell, pp. 146, 150, 152—156, 160, 161. — 2) Jes. Rel., V p. 195. — 3) Roosevelt, I p. 90. — 4) Jones, Ojibway Indians, p. 108.

anything, and self-denial and the power to resist temptation to luxury or easily acquired property is a boast with them. On these men, in time of peace, when difficulties occur among themselves, the tribe relies, and in time of war they are their leaders to the scene of action". And Schoolcraft states that the chiefs "have little or no power, unless they have distinguished themselves as warriors and are supported by a band of braves" [1]). Among the Kutchins, according to Jones, the chiefs are elected for their wisdom and courage. Hardisty, however, states that the power of the chiefs depends on the number of beads they own; for these afford a means of injuring those who displease them. And Whymper remarks: "The chiefs, who are without exception good hunters or fishers, often procure or strengthen their position by periodical distributions of their chattels. They not seldom have the worst clothing and food of all inhabitants" [2]). Among the Cheyennes generally the bravest and wisest man is elected as a chief [3]). Mrs. Eastman tells us of the Sioux, that formerly "their bravest men, their war chief too, no doubt exercized a control over the rest." The chief lived like the common people and Neill remarks: "The individual who desires to improve his condition is not only laughed at, but maltreated. Moreover, if he acquires any property, there is no law which secures it to him, and it is liable to be taken away at any time by any ill-disposed person" [4]). Among the Apaches, according to Schoolcraft, "the chiefs are the wealthiest men, the most warlike, the first in battle, the wisest in council". According to Ten Kate the power of the chiefs depends on their success in forays. And Bancroft remarks: "Sometimes it happens that one family retains the chieftaincy in a tribe during several generations, because of the bravery or wealth of the sons" [5]). Comanche chiefs, according to Schoolcraft, "are selected for their known or pretended prowess in war". In another place he states, that they

---

1) Reports of Expl., XII Part I p. 76; Schoolcraft, V p. 686. — 2) Jones, Kutchin tribes, p. 325; Hardisty, p. 312; Whymper, p. 280. — 3) Ten Kate, Noord-Amerika, p. 365. — 4) Eastman, Dahcotah, pp. 82—84; Neill, p. 86. — 5) Schoolcraft, V p. 260; Ten Kate, Noord-Amerika, p. 195; Bancroft, p. 508.

are made chiefs for their "superior cunning, knowledge or success in war" [1]).

Influence and power depend thus on bravery, wisdom, eloquence, not on wealth. Only among the Apaches does it depend on wealth, though not on wealth exclusively. The distributions of property among the Kutchins somewhat resemble those on the Pacific Coast, but are not indicative of quite the same development of wealth; for on the Pacific Coast wealth consists to a large extent of more durable goods, such as houses, canoes, etc.

A few other statements also tend to prove, that wealth is not highly developed; the economic life of some tribes shows rather communistic features. Among the Kutchins, "unless he is alone, a hunter cannot take and appropriate the meat of the animal he kills. Should he do so, he would be considered mean. And this feeling is strong. When two good hunters go together, good and well, the one has as good a chance of getting meat as the other; but when one is a bad hunter and the other a good one, the former gets all the meat and the real hunter has nothing, and loses his ammunition into the bargain" [2]). Among the Chepewyans the game is distributed among those who shared in the chase. The game which a man catches in his snare is his private property; "nevertheless any unsuccessful hunter passing by may take a deer so caught, leaving the head, skin, and saddle for the owner" [3]).

Among the Osages, too, wealth was formerly unknown; for in Hunter's time the old men disapproved of the fur-trade, which gave abundance and thereby led to effeminacy [4]).

6°. *Condition of women.* Le Jeune states, that among the Montagnais the sex has great influence. Household affairs are left to the discretion of the women, without any male interference. The women "cut and decide and give away as they please" [5]). Ojibway women, according to Jones, do the hardest work, are slaves of the men, get the worst food and the worst place in the wigwam; and Long states, that the wives are the slaves of their husbands. According to Kohl, nearly all

---

1) Schoolcraft, I p. 231; II p. 132. — 2) Hardisty, p. 314. — 3) Mackenzie, I p. 153. On the Sioux see Neill as quoted on p. 241. — 4) Hunter, Gedenkschriften, p. 50. — 5) Jes. Rel., V p. 181, VI p. 233.

kinds of work, except the chase, fell to the share of the women, who were even obliged to bring home the bears killed by the men [1]). Mackenzie tells us, that among the Knisteneaux women are in the same subjected condition as among other wild tribes [2]). Among the Blackfeet the husband may send his wife away when he likes; she then takes her property with her; the children remain with the father. Many men have 6 or 8 wives; they readily lend them to whites for brandy [3]). Chepewyan wives are subjected to their husbands, who are very jealous and "for very trifling causes treat them with such cruelty as sometimes to occasion their death" [4]). Among the Kutchins, as we have seen in § 2, the condition of women is a rather bad one [5]). Mackenzie speaks of the "extreme subjection and abasement" of Beaver Indian women [6]). Cheyenne women perform all the drudgery. Yet they have some influence in government matters; they do not attend the councils; but their wishes, privately uttered, are not generally disregarded [7]). Among the Sioux women as children and wives are despised, as girls a little more honoured. And Schoolcraft states that they exercise some influence in tribal matters by expressing their desires at home, but are not admitted to the council [8]). Bancroft, speaking of the Apache family in general (including Apaches, Comanches, and several other tribes), remarks: "Womankind as usual is at a discount. The female child receives little care from its mother, being only of collateral advantage to the tribe. Later she becomes the beast of burden and slave of her husband." But another statement of the same writer proves that the women's condition is not so very bad: "The marriage yoke sits lightly; the husband may repudiate his wife and take back the property given for her; the wife may abandon her husband, but by the latter act she covers him with such disgrace that it may only be wiped out by killing somebody — anybody whom he may chance to meet" [9]). The wife may thus with impunity leave her husband, the latter venting his anger upon "some-

---

1) Jones, Ojibway Indians, p. 108; Long, p. 137; Kohl, I p. 8, II p. 252. — 2) Mackenzie, I p. 120. — 3) Zu Wied, Nord-Amerika, I p. 573. — 4) Mackenzie, I p. 147. — 5) See above, p. 224. — 6) Mackenzie, II p. 11. — 7) Dodge, p. 122. — 8) Eastman, Dahcotah, p. XXIV; Schoolcraft, II p. 189. — 9) Bancroft, pp. 511, 513.

body". Schoolcraft states that Comanche women are not thought much of, even by themselves; the husband has unlimited sway over his wife [1]). Among the Shoshones, according to Lewis and Clark, "the man is the sole proprietor of his wives and daughters, and can barter them away, or dispose of them in any manner he may think proper." "The mass of the females are condemned, as among all savage nations, to the lowest and most laborious drudgery" [2]).

Now let us inquire what Grinnell, who is so well acquainted with Indian life, has to say about the treatment of women among the Indians in general. "A word or two with regard to the position of the wife in the household may not be out of place here. The Indian woman, it is usually thought, is a mere drudge and slave, but, so far as my observations extend, this notion is wholly an erroneous one. It is true that the women were the labourers of the camp, that they did all the hard work about which there was no excitement. They cooked, brought wood and water, dried the meat, dressed the robes, made the clothing, collected the lodge poles, packed the horses, cultivated the ground, and generally performed all the tasks which might be called menial, but they were not mere servants. On the contrary, their position was very respectable. They were consulted on many subjects, not only in connection with family affairs, but in more important and general matters. Sometimes women were even admitted to the councils and spoke there, giving their advice. This privilege was very unusual, and was granted only to women who had performed some deed which was worthy of a man. This in practice meant that she had killed or counted *coup* on an enemy, or had been to war. In ordinary family conversation women did not hesitate to interrupt and correct their husbands when the latter made statements with which they did not agree, and the men listened to them with respectful attention, though of course this depended on the standing of the woman, her intelligence, etc. While their lives were hard and full of toil, they yet found time to get together for gossip and for gambling, and on the whole managed to take a good deal of pleasure in

1) Schoolcraft, I p. 235, II p. 132. — 2) Lewis and Clark, II pp. 118, 119.

life" [1]). And Ten Kate, a careful observer, remarks that the Indians do not, as has often been asserted, regard woman as a beast of burden and a drudge. Her condition, as compared with that of the women of the lower classes in civilized countries, is rather better than worse [2]).

So the lot of the Indian woman is not so hard as at first sight it seems. Yet the fact, that several ethnographers picture it in such dark colours, whereas the describers of the tribes of the Pacific Coast agree, that the sex command great respect, tends to prove, that the condition of women is not quite so good here as on the Pacific Coast.

7°. *Militarism.* These tribes are very warlike. Roosevelt states that warfare and hunting were the chief occupations of the Algonquins [3]). Among the Ojibways the end of education is to make good hunters and warriors [4]). According to Mackenzie, warfare and hunting, among the Knisteneaux, are the occupations of the men. They are continually engaged in warfare [5]). The Blackfeet were very warlike, and always fighting with their neighbours [6]). Mackenzie tells us, that it was a custom with Chepewyan chiefs "to go to war after they had shed tears in order to wipe away the disgrace attached to such a feminine weakness" [7]). The Beaver Indians were even more warlike than the Chepewyans [8]). Mrs. Eastman calls the Sioux "brave, daring, revengeful" [9]). The Apaches, according to Bancroft, "are in their industries extremely active, — their industries being theft and murder, to which they are trained by their mothers, and in which they display consummate cunning, treachery, and cruelty" [10]). And the same writer tells us that "the Comanches, who are better warriors than the Apaches, highly honour bravery on the battle-field. From early youth, they are taught the art of war, and the skilful handling of their horses and weapons; and they are not allowed a seat in the council, until their name is garnished by some heroic deed" [11]).

---

1) Grinnell, pp. 46, 47. — 2) Ten Kate, Noord-Amerika, p. 365. — 3) Roosevelt, I p. 82. — 4) Jones, Ojibway Indians, p. 64. — 5) Mackenzie, I pp. 130, 123. — 6) Reports of Expl., I p. 443. — 7) Mackenzie, I p. 271. — 8) Ibid., II p. 33. — 9) Eastman, Dahcotah, p. X. — 10) Bancroft, p. 524. — 11) Ibid., p. 499.

We see that the Indians of Central North America present a strongly marked contrast with such tribes as the Koniagas who are "adapted to labour and commerce rather than to war and hunting" and the Chinooks who "were always a commercial rather than a warlike people". Therefore all available men are wanted in warfare; they cannot afford to have male slaves living among them, who do not share in their military operations. They are very much in need of warriors, and little of labourers. Accordingly among many of these tribes such prisoners of war as are allowed to live, are adopted into the tribe or into some family within the tribe [1]).

Concluding, we may remark, that the Indians of Central North America differ from the tribes of the Pacific Coast in many respects. They have no abundance of food, are hunters and nomadic; wealth does not exist, and militarism prevails to a great extent. The groups in which they live, though larger than in Australia, are smaller than on the Pacific Coast. Food is preserved, but not so systematically as on the Pacific Coast. The condition of women, though not so bad as in Australia, is not quite so good as among the slave-keeping tribes of the North-West Coast of North America. Their trade consists only in exchanging raw products; and industry is little developed.

§ 5. *Experimentum crucis: Eskimos.*

1°. *Abundance of food.* In Greenland vegetable food is very scarce. The flesh of the reindeer is most valued by the Greenlanders, but is not available in large quantities; so they have to live chiefly upon sea-animals, seals, fish and sea-birds [2]). Boas states that "the mode of life of all the Eskimo tribes of North-Eastern America is very uniform." They depend entirely on animal food, especially seals and deer [3]). Bancroft, speaking

---

1) Adoption of captives was very frequent among the Indians of North America. Of the tribes, on which we were able to get information, the following practised this custom: Delawares, Ojibways, Shahnees, Crees, Cheyennes, Abenakies, Iroquois, Hurons, Cherokees, Sioux, Hidatsas, Omahas, Osage and Kansas Indians, Mandans, Comanches, Montagnais. See above, pp. 52—65, 192. — 2) Crantz, I p. 161. — 3) Boas, Central Eskimo, p. 419.

of the Eskimos of Alaska, remarks: "Their substantials comprise the flesh of land and marine animals, fish and birds; venison, and whale and seal blubber being chief" [1]). Though we nowhere find it stated that food is exceedingly scarce, the details given here sufficiently prove that it is not nearly so abundant as on the Pacific Coast. Shell-fish, fruits, roots, and other vegetables, acquired so easily and in large quantities by the tribes of the Pacific Coast, do not enter for any considerable part into the food of the Eskimos.

2°. As for *fishing*, taken in the wider sense (including the killing of water animals besides fish), all Eskimos are fishers.

3°. *Fixed habitations, large groups, preserving of food*. Though the Eskimos move about much for the purpose of obtaining food, they are not quite nomadic. In winter-time they live in solidly constructed dwellings [2]). Rink states that they have their winter-houses on the same place during several generations [3]). Boas remarks: "There is no need of any new buildings, as the Eskimo always locate in the old settlements and the old buildings are quite sufficient to satisfy all their wants" [4]). And Crantz tells us that a Greenlander is not generally much inclined to leave the place where he was born and bred and settle somewhere else; for in nearly every place there is a peculiar method of fishing and seal-hunting, which the newcomer has to learn; and in the meantime, often for several years, he is poorly off [5]). An Eskimo village most often consists of a single house [6]), but Eskimo houses accommodate several (in Greenland from 4 to 10) families [7]). Among the Western Eskimos, however, there are larger villages [8]). Food is preserved for winter use by the Eskimos, though not in such large quantities as on the Pacific Coast. "The Esquimaux" says a writer on British North America "possess a quality which I may say is almost unknown among Indians, namely, providence; thus, in the season, when the animals are plentiful on the shores of the Arctic Sea, they make "caches" of large quantities of meat for winter use" [9]). The Greenlanders, though laying up some provision for the winter, are rather improvident.

---

1) Bancroft, p. 54. — 2) Crantz, I pp. 158 sqq.; Boas, l. c. pp. 540 sqq.; Bancroft, pp. 50 sqq. — 3) Rink, p. 9. — 4) Boas, l. c. p. 547. — 5) Crantz, III p. 147. — 6) Rink, p. 27. — 7) Crantz, I p. 159. — 8) Rink, p. 33. — 9) Further papers, p. 43.

As long as they have abundance of food, they feast and gorge
themselves with it; but in the winter they often live in the
greatest misery [1]). Boas, speaking of Central Eskimo store-
houses, remarks: "In winter, blubber and meat are put away
upon these pillars, which are sufficiently high to keep them
from the dogs." Yet "the house presents a sad and gloomy
appearance if stormy weather prevents the men from hunting.
The stores are quickly consumed, one lamp after another is
extinguished, and everybody sits motionless in the dark hut" [2]).
Among the Eskimos of Alaska "meats are kept in seal-skin
bags for over a year.... Their winter store of oil they secure
in seal-skin bags, which are buried in the frozen ground" [3]).

4°. *Trade and industry.* Rink states that the Eskimos make
long journeys for the purpose of interchanging such commodities, as are found in some districts only and yet are necessary to all the tribes. The trade is carried on from Asia to
Hudson Bay [4]). The Greenlanders mutually exchange the articles they need. With some of them bartering is quite a
passion; they often exchange useful things for worthless trifles.
They have a kind of annual fair, at which the inhabitants of
several districts interchange the products of their country. "A
great article of commerce are vessels made of soapstone, which
are not found in all parts of the country; and, as the Southern
Greenlanders have no whales and the Northern no wood, there
come, all through the summer months, from the South and
even from the East of the country many boats with Greenlanders from 100 to 200 miles, to Disko, bringing new kyaks
and women's boats with the necessary implements. They receive
in exchange horns, teeth, bones, whale-bones and whale-ten-
dons, part of which, on their homeward voyage, they sell
again" [5]). Among the Central Eskimos "two desiderata formed
the principal inducement to long journeys, which sometimes
lasted even several years: wood and soapstone. The shores of
Davis' Strait and Cumberland Sound are almost destitute of
driftwood, and consequently the natives were obliged to visit
distant regions to obtain that necessary material. Tudjaqdjuaq

1) Crantz, I pp. 162—164. — 2) Boas, l. c. pp. 550, 574. — 3) Bancroft, p. 55. —
4) Rink, p. 11. — 5) Crantz, I pp. 195, 196.

in particular was the objective point of their expeditions. Their boats took a southerly course, and, as the wood was gathered, a portion of it was immediately manufactured into boat ribs and sledge runners, which were carried back on the return journey; another portion was used for bows, though these were also made of deer's horns ingeniously lashed together. A portion of the trade in wood seems to have been in the hands of the Nugumiut, who collected it on Tudjaqdjuaq and took it north. Another necessary and important article of trade, soapstone, is manufactured into lamps and pots. It is found in a few places only, and very rarely in pieces large enough for the manufacture of the articles named.... The visitors come from every part of the country, the soapstone being dug or "traded" from the rocks by depositing some trifles in exchange. In addition to wood and soapstone, metals, which were extremely rare in old times, have formed an important object of trade. They were brought to Baffin Bay either by the Aivillirmiut, who had obtained them fom the Hudson Bay Company and the Kinipetu, or by the Akuliarmiut. Even when Frobisher visited the Nugumiut in 1577 he found them in possession of some iron. The occurrence of flint, which was the material for arrow-heads, may have given some importance to places where it occurs. Formerly an important trade existed between the Netchillirmiut and the neighbouring tribes. As the district of the former is destitute of driftwood and potstone, they are compelled to buy both articles from their neighbours. In Ross's time they got the necessary wood from Ugjulik, the potstone from Aivillik. They exchanged these articles for native iron (or pyrite), which they found on the eastern shore of Boothia and which was used for striking fire. After having collected a sufficient stock of it during several years, they travelled to the neighbouring tribes" [1]. The Eskimos of Alaska are also very commercial. "On the shore of Bering Strait the natives have constant commercial intercourse with Asia.... They frequently meet at the Gwosdeff Islands, where the Tschuktschi bring tobacco, iron, tame-reindeer skins, and walrus-ivory; the Eskimos giving in exchange wolf and wolverine

---

1) Boas, l. c. p. 469.

skins, wooden dishes, seal-skins and other peltries. The Eskimos
of the American coast carry on quite an extensive trade with
the Indians of the interior, exchanging with them Asiatic
merchandise for peltries" [1]. We see that most of the Eskimo
trade is bartering of raw products. This agrees with what
Rink remarks, viz. that there is no division of labour; each
group that has a tent or boat is entirely self-dependent [2].

In industry they display much skill. Their boats are ingeniously made and have excited the admiration of all travellers.
"The kajak (qajaq) is almost exclusively used for hunting by
all Eskimo tribes from Greenland to Alaska" [3]. Crantz tells
us that the implements the Greenlanders use for procuring
their subsistence are simple, but so well adapted to their purpose that they are more convenient than the costly implements
of the Europeans. Their harpoons consist of several pieces,
but are so ingeniously made that not a single piece is superfluous. Their boats are also greatly admired by this writer [4].
And Bancroft tells us that "the Hyperboreans surpass all
American nations in their facilities for locomotion, both upon
land and water. In their skin boats, the natives of the Alaskan
seaboard, from Point Barrow to Mount St. Elias, made long
voyages, crossing the strait and sea of Bering, and held commercial intercourse with the people of Asia. Sixty miles is
an ordinary day's journey for sledges, while Indians on snow-
shoes have been known to run down and capture deer". "So
highly were these boats esteemed by the Russians, that they
were at once universally adopted by them in navigating these
waters. They were unable to invent any improvement in either
of them" [5].

5°. *Property and wealth.* It is nowhere stated that a man's
rank or power depends upon his wealth. The Greenlanders
live without any government; the head of each family is independent. When several families live together in one house,
they have no control over each other, but voluntarily obey the
most respected head of a family, *i. e.* the one who is best
acquainted with hunting and the signs of the weather. Yet our

---

1) Bancroft, pp. 63, 64. — 2) Rink, p. 13. — 3) Boas, l. c. p. 486. — 4) Crantz, I pp.
165—168. — 5) Bancroft, pp. 59, 61.

informant also states: "If several Greenlanders live together, they like to keep an *angekok* (priest), to avail themselves of his advice. And if they do not keep one, they are despised or pitied by the others as being poor men" [1]. So poor people are despised, but this applies to villages or settlements rather than individuals. This agrees with what Rink tells us of their communistic *régime*. Only the indispensable implements and utensils are individual property, and also provisions sufficient for less than a year. If an individual or group have got too much, they are compelled by public opinion to give it to those who have too little [2]. Among the Central Eskimos men unable to provide for themselves are employed as servants, but their position "is a voluntary one, and therefore these men are not less esteemed than the self-dependent providers" [3]. Among the Eskimos of Alaska "now or then some ancient or able man gains an ascendency in the tribe, and overawes his fellows." "Caste has been mentioned in connection with tattooing, but, as a rule, social distinctions do not exist" [4].

Though the Eskimos are dependent for their subsistence on the possession of boats, houses and implements, they do not want more property than is needed for procuring their daily food. According to Rink, the benefit of an inheritance is smaller than the duties it involves; for boat and tent continually require so much mending, that a single hunter is hardly able to keep them in order [5]. In Greenland, if a man dies leaving no full-grown son, his goods devolve upon the next of kin, who is obliged to provide for the widow and her children. But if he already possesses a tent and a boat, he will leave the inheritance and the duties connected with it to an alien; for nobody is capable of keeping two tents and two boats in repair [6].

6°. *Condition of women.* Though not quite so bad as in Australia, woman's condition is not so good here as among the Indians of the Pacific Coast. Greenland women lead a hard and almost slave-like life, says Crantz [7]. And Bancroft tells us that among the Eskimos of Alaska "the lot of the women is but little better than slavery" [8]. The principal cause of this

---

1) Crantz, I pp. 201, 202; III p. 180 note. — 8) Rink, pp. 9, 29. — 3) Boas, l. c. p. 581. — 4) Bancroft, p. 65. — 5) Rink, p. 26. — 6) Crantz, I pp. 214, 215. — 7) Crantz, I p. 187. — 8) Bancroft, p. 65.

difference perhaps is, that female labour among the Eskimos is not productive. In Greenland "a man who has two wives is not despised; on the contrary he is looked upon as an able provider" [1]. This proves that subsistence depends upon male, not as in Australia upon female labour. Among the Central Eskimos "the principal part of the man's work is to provide for his family.... The woman has to do the household work, the sewing, and the cooking" [2]. Among the Western Eskimos "polygamy is common, every man being entitled to as many wives, as he can get and maintain" [3]. So the man maintains the family; female labour, however useful, is not so indispensable as male. The men know this quite well. In Greenland "the man hunts and fishes, and having brought the animals ashore he pays no more attention to them; it would even be a disgrace for him to carry the captured seal on land" [4]. This is quite another state of things than what we have seen to exist on the Pacific Coast, where female labour, especially in the preparation of articles of commerce, is highly valued.

7°. *Militarism.* Among the Greenlanders warfare is unknown [5]. Boas, speaking of the Central Eskimos, says: "Real wars or fights between settlements, I believe, have never happened, but contests have always been confined to single families" [6]. In Alaska it is otherwise, for "the Northern Indians are frequently at war with the Eskimos and Southern Indians, for whom they at all times entertain the most inveterate hatred" [7]. This absence of militarism enables the Greenlanders and Central Eskimos to have men performing women's work living among them, as we have seen in § 1 of this chapter [8].

So the Eskimos, like the slave-keeping Indians of the Pacific Coast, are accomplished fishers, have fixed habitations, are industrially highly developed, and generally not warlike. On the other hand there is no abundance of food, wealth does not exist, and woman's condition is not nearly so good as on the Pacific Coast. Also in the size of their groups, the preserving of food, and the development of trade, they are decidedly

---

1) Crantz, I p. 180. — 2) Boas, l. c. pp. 579, 580. — 3) Bancroft, p. 66. — 4) Crantz, I p. 186. — 5) Crantz, I p. 207. — 6) Boas, l. c. p. 465. — 7) Bancroft, p. 120. — 8) See above, p. 200.

inferior to the slave-keeping tribes of the N. W. Coast of North America.

The principal cause why the Eskimos do not keep slaves evidently is the difficulty with which food is procured. We have seen that female labour, being unproductive, is little valued. Male labour only is indispensable, and this is labour of high quality. Navigating in the kyak is a matter of much skill. Crantz tells us that Europeans who tried it, could move about a little in very calm weather; but they were not able to fish while being in the kyak, nor to save themselves when the least danger occurred. This requires peculiar skill, and Eskimos take several years to learn it. There are indeed men unable to capture seals; they are much despised [1]). Bancroft also states that considerable skill is required in taking seals [2]), and Boas describes at great length the ingenious methods used in seal, walrus, and whale hunting [3]). Unskilled labour is not wanted; and widows and orphans who have lost their bread-winner may be glad if any one is willing to receive them into his house [4]).

Sometimes an Eskimo wants labour. In Greenland a married couple having no children at all or no full-grown children, adopt male and female children whom they treat as their own; the adopted son is considered the future head of the family [5]). Among the Central Eskimos too, as to the right of inheritance "an elder adopted son has a preference over a younger son born of the marriage" [6]). Thus we see that a normally constituted family is self-dependent. If there are no children, their place has to be supplied by strangers; boys have to perform the same highly skilled labour as the father, and girls to help the mother in her work that, though less valued, has also to be done. But a further increase of the family by slaves performing menial work is not wanted; the man, if able, would not be willing to maintain them. The only kind of work indispensable here cannot be imposed upon slaves; and the cost of maintaining slaves performing other

---

1) Crantz, I pp. 172, 173, 184, 185. — 2) Bancroft, p. 56. — 3) Boas, l. c. pp. 471 sqq. — 4) See above, pp. 47—48. — 5) Crantz, I p. 186. — 6) Boas, l. c. p. 581. See also Murdoch, p. 419, and Ray, p. 44 on adoption among the Eskimos of Point Barrow.

work would be greater than the profit they would yield. Food is not preserved in such large quantities as on the Pacific Coast; shell-fish and vegetable food are almost entirely unknown here; nor is any fish, oil, etc. prepared for commercial purposes.

There is one more cause at work among the Eskimos, preventing the existence of slavery: the dependence of labour upon capital. Boas, describing the Central Eskimos, states that among the adopted people "who may almost be considered servants" there are "men who have lost their sledges and dogs." Such servants "fulfil minor occupations, mend the hunting implements, fit out the sledges, feed the dogs, etc.; sometimes, however, they join the hunters. They follow the master of the house when he removes from one place to another, make journeys in order to do his commissions, and so on" [1]. And Crantz tells us that among the Greenlanders many boys are neglected in their youth, as the providing of them with kyak and implements is very costly [2]. Among the Indians of the Pacific Coast the possession of capital gives great advantage; thus among the Makah the owner of the canoe receives a proportionate share of the booty from the crew [3]; but it is not indispensable. Here it is. A man destitute of capital cannot provide for himself, and is therefore at the mercy of the capitalist. Now the Eskimo capitalist most often allows such men to share his house and food, and makes them feed the dogs, etc. rather as means of procuring employment for them, than because such work requires hands outside the family. The capitalist does not want labourers; but even if he did, there would always be widows and orphans, and men destitute of capital, who would readily enter into his service. The Eskimos have to struggle with "unemployment" difficulties, not with scarcity of hands; therefore a slave-dealer visiting them would not find a ready sale for his stock-in-trade.

1) Boas, l. c. p. 581. — 2) Crantz, I p. 215. — 3) See above, p. 212.

§ 6. *Conclusion.*

We shall sum up here the conclusions to which the fore-going paragraphs have led us.

1º. *Hunters* hardly ever keep slaves; and when they do slavery is of little moment. But among *fishers* slavery often, though by no means always, exists: of the two large groups of fishing tribes one (the Indians on the Pacific Coast of North America) keeps slaves, the other (the Eskimos) does not.

2º. The living in *fixed habitations* is more favourable to the existence of slavery than *nomadism.*

3º. Slavery is most likely to exist among men who live in rather *large groups.*

4º. Where *food* is *abundant* and easy to procure, slaves can be of more use than where food is scarce; in the latter case the slave, to use Spencer's words, "is not worth his food."

5º. The *preserving of food* furthers the growth of slavery.

6º. *Commercial tribes*, especially those that carry on a trade in manufactured goods, have more use for slaves than others. We must, however, bear in mind that trade, even among savages, does not seem anywhere to be altogether unknown.

7º. A high development of *industry* also tends to further the growth of slavery. The instance of the Eskimos, however, shows that industrial tribes do not always keep slaves.

8º. Where *wealth* exists slaves are more likely to be kept than where wealth is unknown.

9º. Where *subsistence* is *dependent on capital*, slaves are not wanted.

10º. Where only highly *skilled labour* is required, slaves cannot be of any use.

11º. *Female labour* may in some degree serve as a substitute for slave labour (as in Australia). But where women enjoy much consideration, the men sometimes procure slaves in order to relieve the women of a part of their task, especially where the women perform productive labour.

12º. Where *militarism* largely prevails, and warriors are more wanted than labourers, slavery is not likely to exist. Yet in a few cases the same militarism leads to the keeping of slaves, viz. when slaves are kept mainly for military purposes.

13º. Tribes forming a somewhat *homogeneous group*, and maintaining constant relations with each other, are more likely, *ceteris paribus,* to keep slaves, than an isolated tribe.

These conclusions, arrived at by an examination of hunting and fishing tribes, all, except the first, bear a general character. We may therefore suppose that they will equally apply to pastoral and agricultural tribes. Whether this really be the case, will appear from the ensuing chapters. It may, however, be convenient first to simplify and systematically arrange them.

As the *principal factor* we may regard the general economic state of society. Two distinctions are to be made here:

1º. Subsistence either is or is not dependent on capital.

2º. Subsistence is either easy or difficult to acquire.

These two distinctions are independent of each other. For where subsistence depends on capital, it may, with the aid of capital, be easily acquired or not. Similarly, where it does not depend on capital, it may be easy or difficult to procure. Accordingly we find the following forms of economic life:

1º. Subsistence depends on capital. Without capital a man cannot get on. Now, if labourers are wanted, there are likely to be people destitute of capital, who have no other resource left but to offer their labour to the capitalist. But there is a difference, according as subsistence is easily acquired or not.

a. Subsistence, even with the aid of capital, is difficult to procure. The procuring of subsistence requires a combination of capital and skilled labour. Thus among the Eskimos a man unacquainted with their ingenious hunting and fishing methods cannot get on any more than a man destitute of a boat, or of sledges and dogs. Here labourers are not much wanted. Helpless persons are kept as servants, but this is done for pity's sake rather than because they are useful. Slavery does not exist.

b. Subsistence, with the aid of capital, is easy to procure. Unskilled labour, combined with capital, is so productive that it gives a surplus beyond the subsistence of the labourer. In this case the capitalist wants labourers, but there are also labourers who want the capitalist. We have not yet met with any instance of this state of things. Slavery can exist here, if the demand for labour exceeds the supply of labour; but we do not think this will often be the case.

2⁰. Subsistence does not depend on capital. We are, of course, aware that a man, to procure his subsistence, always wants some implements, such as a spear, bow and arrow, etc. But he does not, therefore, depend on capital; for he can always make a spear or bow for himself; so after all, he depends only on his own strength and skill. If an Eskimo loses his boat, he wants a long time to make a new one; in the meantime he has to live, and so is thrown upon the mercy of others. But where the necessary implements can always be procured at a moment's notice, subsistence is not dependent on capital: the man who has broken his spear can immediately make a new one; he need not ask anybody to feed him in the meantime [1]).

Subsistence, where it does not depend on capital, is again either easy or difficult to procure.

a. Subsistence is not easy to procure; it requires much skill. As subsistence does not depend on capital, every skilled labourer is able to provide for himself. Those who are not able providers are dependent on the others; but their labour, being little productive, is not much valued. Such is the state of things among many hunting tribes. As slaves cannot be compelled to perform work that requires the utmost skill and application, slavery cannot exist here.

b. Subsistence is easy to procure. The produce of unskilled labour can exceed the primary wants of the labourer. As subsistence is not dependent on capital, everybody is able to provide for himself; therefore labourers do not voluntarily offer themselves. In such circumstances a man can, it is true, acquire the products of another's labour by producing commodities himself and exchanging them for what another has

---

1) Such a state of things, in Wilkes's time, prevailed in Tahiti. "A native" he remarks "may in the morning be wholly destitute even of implements wherewith to work, and before nightfall he may be found clothed, lodged, and have all the necessaries of life around him in abundance." Wilkes, II p. 17.

produced. He can also, like the Makah boat-owner, produce such things as enhance the productiveness of labour, and lend them to others, stipulating for a part of the profit for himself. But he cannot make others work under his direction. The common labourer of modern European societies, in order to get his subsistence, performs the work which his employer assigns to him. Were he free to choose, he would prefer to work according to his own inclinations. In countries however, where nobody need apply to another for employment, there is little chance of people voluntarily submitting to the orders of employers. In such countries, if there is to be an organization of labour with subordination under the master of the work, some men must be compelled to work for others, and we know that one form of compulsory labour is slavery. Therefore, when subsistence is easy to procure, and not dependent on capital, slave labour can be of much use. Yet even then slavery does not always exist. We shall see that there are disturbing factors. But we may now, at least, say that, generally speaking, *slavery can only exist when subsistence is easy to procure without the aid of capital.*

There are some additional, or *secondary*, *factors* which increase or diminish the use of slave labour.

1°. It may be, that unskilled labour is required, but is sufficiently performed by the women. Thus in Australia women gather vegetable food and perform all the common drudgery; and some Australian tribes subsist mainly on the produce of female labour. In such cases slaves are not wanted. This is a circumstance of much importance; for everywhere women are about half, sometimes more than half, of the population. As in our days, in civilized Europe, the employing of women in factories tends to diminish the want for male labour and so to keep wages low, so *female labour* in Australia makes slavery superfluous. The causes on which the division of labour between the sexes depends cannot be examined here; this would require an investigation of the whole history of marriage. But, though unable to find the causes, we can trace the effects of this division of labour. Where women are looked upon as "beasts of burden" (to use an expression the ethnographers are very fond of), there is not so much use for slave labour as where they hold a high position and the men are desirous of relieving them of a part of their task.

2º. Where *food* is *preserved* in large quantities, more work has to be done at a time, viz. in the season of plenty, than where life is continually a hand-to-mouth proceeding. And the additional work required for preserving food, *e. g.* the drying of fish, is very fit to be imposed upon slaves: it requires little skill and is easy to supervise.

3º. The development of *trade and industry* has a great influence. When the freemen wish to devote themselves to these pursuits, they want others to perform the common drudgery for every-day subsistence. Moreover, the preparing of the articles of commerce may require menial labour: thus on the Pacific Coast slaves are employed in drying fish, preparing oil, etc. And finally, trade and industry lead to the development of wealth. As soon as wealth exists, a man does not only want food and the other necessaries of life, but also luxuries, so his wants may become almost unlimited, and there is much more use for slave labour.

Hitherto we have considered slavery as serving economic purposes. But *slaves* may also be *kept for non-economic purposes*. There is only one such purpose we have as yet met with: the *employing of slaves in warfare*. We have seen that among the Abipones this was the main and almost the only function of slavery.

On the other hand, it may be that *militarism* so largely prevails, that all available men are wanted in warfare. If, then, the military organization is not so highly developed, that slaves can be employed in warfare without any danger, slavery is not likely to exist, though it might be economically of great use.

There are other causes, which we may call *external*. However much slaves are wanted, there must be a coercive power strong enough to make the keeping of slaves possible. The following causes tend to increase this coercive power:

1º. Living in *fixed habitations*. Besides the effect this has on the growth of industry, it makes the escape of slaves more difficult and the surveying of slave labour easier.

2º. Living together in *large groups*. In a small group any

increase in the number of slaves would soon become dangerous to the maintenance of power by the freemen within the group, and an escaping slave would soon be out of reach of the group.

3⁰. The *preserving of food*. Besides having some economic effects of which we have treated above, it makes living in large groups and in fixed habitations possible; moreover it attaches the slave to his master's home; for he knows he will get there sufficient food in the time of scarcity, whereas, if he escaped, he would have to shift for himself.

4⁰. The existence of a somewhat *homogeneous group of tribes* maintaining constant relations with each other greatly accelerates the growth of slavery, especially by means of the *slave trade*. Twenty tribes, living separately, have, each for itself, to invent slavery; but when twenty tribes maintain relations with each other, as soon as one of them has invented slavery, the other 19 have it ready-made before them.

Recapitulation.

	Furthering the growth of slavery.	Hindering the growth of slavery.
I. Internal causes.		
A. General:	1⁰. Subsistence easily acquired and not dependent on capital.	1⁰. Subsistence dependent on capital. 2⁰. Subsistence not dependent on capital, but difficult to acquire.
B. Secondary, economic:	1⁰. Preserving of food. 2⁰. Trade and industry. 3⁰. A high position of women.	1⁰. Female labour making slave labour superfluous.
C. Secondary, non-economic:	1⁰. Slaves wanted for military purposes.	1⁰. Militarism making slavery impossible.

	Furthering the growth of slavery.
II. External causes:	1°. Fixed habitations.
	2°. Living in large groups.
	3°. Preserving of food [1]).
	4°. The existence of a homogeneous group of tribes.

1) "Preserving of food" occurs twice, because it works in different directions.

CHAPTER III.

PASTORAL TRIBES.

§ 1. *Capital and labour among pastoral tribes.*

The number of these tribes is not large, as they are found in a few parts of the world only. Moreover, the descriptions available to us were in many cases too incomplete to justify any inference as to their having or not having slaves.

The clear cases noticed by us are the following.

Positive cases.	Arabia:	Aeneze Bedouins, Larbas.	2
	Caucasus:	Circassians, Kabards.	2
	Bantu tribes:	Ovaherero, Bahima.	2
	Hamitic group:	Beduan, Beni Amer, Somal, Danakil.	4
			10
Negative cases.	India:	Todas.	1
	Central Asia:	Kazak Kirghiz, Altaians, Turkomans.	3
	Siberia:	Samoyedes, Tunguz, Yakuts, nomadic Koryakes.	4

Bantu tribes:	Ama Xosa,	
	Ama-Zulu,	
	some divisions of the Mun-	
	dombe.	3
Hamatic group:	Massai.	1
		12

We see that there are almost as many positive as negative cases. So those theorists are wrong, who hold that the taming of animals naturally leads to the taming of men [1]).

It might, however, be that the non-existence of slavery in our negative cases were due to a special, external cause, viz. that these tribes were so inclosed between more powerful nations as not to be able to procure slaves, though slaves would be of much use to them. A brief survey of the political state of these tribes shows that they are not all in this position. The Kazak Kirghiz, in Levchine's time, kidnapped slaves whom they sold abroad. The Massai are very warlike and adopt captives. The Turkomans are "the intermediate agents for carrying on the slave-trade" [2]). The Ama-Xosa and Ama-Zulu are also very warlike [3]). We see that there are some pastoral tribes that, though able to procure slaves, do not keep any. The non-existence of slavery among them must be due to other, more internal, causes.

It might also be that our positive cases were exceptions to a general rule. For many pastoral tribes, though subsisting mainly by cattle-breeding, carry on agriculture besides. If these only kept slaves, and employed them chiefly in work connected with agriculture, slavery would prove foreign to pastoral nomadism as such; for then these tribes would only keep slaves in their quality as agriculturists.

We shall inquire whether this be so; and for this purpose we shall give a survey of the work imposed upon slaves among pastoral tribes. This survey, besides enabling us to decide upon the question at issue, will show what place slavery occupies in pastoral life.

Among the Larbas the boys (also free boys) guard the cattle

---

1) See above, p. 173. — 2) See above, pp. 127, 128, 131, and Baumann, p. 165. — 3) Fritsch, pp. 79, 80, 135, 136.

on the pasture-ground, whereas the work that requires more skill (the tending of young animals, the breaking of horses, etc.) is equally divided between master and slaves [1].

Circassian slaves, according to Bell, till the soil, tend the cattle and perform domestic labour. Klaproth, however, states that the peasants may only be sold together with the land; so they are rather a kind of serfs. Domestic slaves may be sold separately [2].

According to Roscoe, among the Bahima, "the women's duties are to wash the milk pots, perhaps it would be better to say see the pots are washed, because the work generally falls upon the slaves to perform" [3].

Munzinger speaks of domestic labour being imposed on slaves by the Beduan. Most of these slaves are women [4].

Among the Beni Amer it is considered an honour to have many slaves. "Properly speaking slaves serve their master only when children. Adult female slaves are concubines, live with their master, but are exempt from nearly all labour; adult male slaves generally despise all work, and belong to the retinue of the master. The master derives no real profit from his slaves." According to Von Müller the fabrication of tar falls to the share of the slave, such work being below the dignity of a freeman [5].

Paulitschke tells us that among the nomadic Somal and Danakil slavery is not profitable; for the territories inhabited by them are thinly peopled, agriculture is insignificant, and these cattle-breeders get their subsistence rather easily; moreover they would be unable to support a considerable number of slaves by the produce of their cattle. Therefore among the Danakil on the river Aussa and the Rahanwîn Somal on the lower Wêbi-Schabêli, where slaves are employed in agriculture, there is more use for slave labour. Among the nomadic Somal and Danakil slaves appear also to be employed in warfare. According to Bottego, whose account applies to the Somal of the towns, adult male slaves till the soil, build houses, and perform the rudest and most fatiguing kinds of work. The

---

1) Geoffroy, pp. 430, 431. — 2) Bell, I p. 170; Klaproth, p. 567. — 3) Roscoe, p. 100. —
4) Munzinger, Ostafr. Stud., pp. 154, 155. — 5) Ibid., p. 310; Von Müller, p. 429.

boys lead the cattle to the pasture-ground; the women are employed in household work and often are concubines of their masters [1]).

There are some tribes that subsist mainly on agriculture, but also, to a great extent, on cattle-breeding. It may be of some use to give a survey of the work done by slaves, among them too; it will appear, then, whether they keep their slaves for agricultural purposes only, or employ them also for pastoral work.

Among the Kafirs some slaves are blacksmiths. In war a slave boy beats the drum [2]). Our informant speaks only incidentally of slave labour; he does not mean to say that this is the only work performed by slaves.

Among the Barotse young slaves are given as pages to the children of freemen. Slaves till the soil and tend the cattle; slave boys are employed as herdsmen [3]).

In a description of the Waganda it is said: "One of the principal evils resulting from slavery in Uganda is that it causes all manual labour to be looked upon as derogatory to the dignity of a free man" [4]).

Among the Mandingoes native-born slaves enjoy much liberty; they tend the cattle, and go to war, even without their masters. Freemen work as much as slaves. Every Mandingo, to whatever class he belongs, is occupied in agriculture. The tending of horses is incumbent on slave boys [5]).

Hildebrandt states that the occupations of the Sakalavas are not many. In North Sakalavaland, however, rice is cultivated for export, and so there is more labour wanted here; therefore in this district slavery prevails to a large extent [6]).

Among the Bogos there are hardly 200 slaves (whereas Munzinger estimates the total population at 8400). Slaves are of little use to their owners. Male slaves live separately and generally take to robbery. Female slaves, having no opportunity to marry, become prostitutes and live rather independently [7]).

---

1) Paulitschke, II pp. 138, 139; I pp. 260, 213, 263; Bottego, p. 423. — 2) Robertson, pp. 78, 79. — 3) Holub, Süd-Afrika, II pp. 348, 189, 262. — 4) Wilson and Felkin, I p. 186. — 5) Tautain, Mandingues, pp. 348—350. — 6) Hildebrandt, West-Madagaskar, p. 113. — 7) Munzinger, Bogos, pp. 49, 50, 35.

The Takue have very few slaves. In their laws and customs
they show a close resemblance to the Bogos [1]).

Among the pirate-tribes of Mindanao and Sulu agriculture
is incumbent on slaves. The slaves also share in their masters' slave-raids. Jansen gives some more details about the work
of slaves in the Sulu Islands. The ordinary occupations of slaves
are agriculture, fishing, manufacture of salt, trade, and domestic work [2]).

The slaves of the Geges and Nagos of Porto Novo are
chiefly employed in agriculture [3]).

Among the Ossetes the slaves perform household work; the
peasants are serfs [4]).

The slaves captured and purchased by the Gallas are generally sold to foreign traders; in large households they are
sometimes retained and employed in various kinds of work.
In another place our informant states that most slaves are
employed in agriculture [5]).

Yoruba slaves are employed in trade and warfare [6]).

We see that slaves are employed in agriculture among the
agricultural Somal and Danakil, Fulbe, Barotse, Mandingoes,
Sakalavas, pirate-tribes of Mindanao and Sulu, Geges and
Nagos, Gallas; and very probably also among the Waganda,
where they perform "all manual labour." As the details given
by our ethnographers are not always complete, it is possible
that in some more cases slaves are employed in agriculture.
But it is sufficiently clear, that among the Beni Amer, nomadic
Somal and Danakil, Bogos, and probably also among the
Beduan and Takue, slaves do not till the soil. Among the
Ossetes and Circassians the peasants are serfs, slaves being
employed in household work. What work is incumbent on
slaves among the Aeneze Bedouins we are not told; but agriculture seems to be unknown among them. Among the Larbas
the daily work is equally divided between master and slaves,
agriculture holding a very subordinate place. Hence it appears
that several of these tribes keep slaves, though they do not

---

1) Munzinger, Ostafr. Stud., pp. 207, 206. — 2) Blumentritt, Ethnographie, pp. 54,
53; Jansen, p. 225. — 3) Hagen, p. 97. — 4) Klaproth, II p. 615. — 5) Paulitschke,
I p. 262; II p. 140. — 6) Lander, I pp. 17, 37, 113.

employ them in agriculture; pastoral tribes, as such, sometimes keep slaves.

But another inference we can draw from the foregoing survey of slave labour is this. Where slaves are not employed in agriculture or in such other work as requires a settled life (*e. g.* house-building among the Somal of the towns, fishing and manufacture of salt among the pirate-tribes of Mindanao and Sulu), the use of slave labour is not great. Among the Beni Amer, Bogos, and nomadic Somal and Danakil slave-keeping is stated to be a mere luxury. The Sakalavas, except in the rice-exporting district, do not want much slave labour. And only in one case, viz. among the Larbas, is it clearly stated that the chief business of slaves is pastoral work.

This tends to prove, that *among true pastoral tribes slavery, as a system of labour, is of little moment.* This inference is verified by several statements about slaves being often manumitted or in the course of time becoming practically free.

Burckhardt, speaking of the slaves of the Aeneze Bedouins, says: "After a certain lapse of time they are always emancipated, and married to persons of their own colour" [1]).

Among the Circassians slaves are often manumitted. A slave can also purchase his freedom, and then becomes a member of a Circassian fraternity [2]).

The Beni Amer have two kinds of slaves, newly-purchased and native-born. "Their condition differs so much, that only the former may properly be called slaves; the latter are rather serfs. The newly-purchased slave is treated like every Mohammedan slave, he may be sold and does not yet belong to the family. The native-born slave has only the name, not the state of a slave; this appears from his being allowed to intermarry with the Woreza (subjected class). The children born of such a marriage are considered free, as they descend from a free mother. In Barka the Kishendoa, *i. e.* native-born slaves, who inhabit a camp of tents of their own, are governed by a chief who is one of their own number, and intermarry with the Woreza. Native-born slaves may live where they like and have the same right of inheritance as freemen; only if such

1) Burckhardt, I p. 356. — 2) Bell, I pp. 169, 308.

a slave leaves no relatives does the master succeed to his goods.... In the blood-feud too the native-born slave is in a peculiar condition. If a newly-purchased slave is killed, his price is restored to his owner; for such a slave is looked upon as an article of trade. The native-born slave, however, belongs to the family; therefore his blood requires blood; he is avenged by his relatives if there are such, and otherwise by his master; if this is not practicable because the murderer is a man of power, the matter is hushed up; but a compensation is never given" [1]).

The Somal often buy slaves whom they manumit soon afterwards [2]).

Among the Kafirs of India each tribe is governed by a council. Even slaves can be elected as members of this council [3]).

Our survey of the work done by slaves shows in the third place, that slaves are often employed in warfare. This will be accounted for later on.

Here we have only to emphasize the fact, that to pastoral tribes as such slave labour is of little use. This makes it easy to understand why so many of them dispense with slavery altogether.

Going on to inquire what is the cause of this phenomenon, we may remember the general conclusion we have arrived at in the last paragraph, viz. that slave labour is of little use, where subsistence is either dependent on capital, or very difficult to procure. Now it is easy to see that among pastoral tribes subsistence entirely depends on capital. Among people who live upon the produce of their cattle, a man who owns no cattle, *i. e.* no capital, has no means of subsistence. Accordingly, among pastoral tribes we find rich and poor men; and the poor often offer themselves as labourers to the rich [4]).

Among the Syrian Bedouins "to every tent, or to every two or three tents, there is a shepherd or person to attend the cattle, either a younger son or servant; he receives wages for ten months" [5]).

---

1) Munzinger, Ostafr. Stud., p. 309. — 2) Paulitschke, I p. 260. — 3) Ujfalvy, Les Aryens, p. 352. — 4) See Hildebrand, Recht und Sitte, pp. 35, 36. — 5) Burckhardt, I p. 182.

Among the Larbas alms are given to the poor. The social rank of the head of a family depends on the number of his children, his practical knowledge of the pastoral art, and his wealth. There are free labourers who are paid in kind. Herdsmen have the usufruct of a part of the herds they tend. Generally the labourer takes a tenth in kind at the close of the time agreed upon; moreover he receives his daily food during the time of his engagement [1]).

Levchine, speaking of the Kazak Kirghiz, tells us: "Once I asked a Kirghiz, owner of 8000 horses, why he did not sell every year a part of his stud. He answered: "Why should I sell that which is my pleasure? I want no money; if I had any, I should be obliged to shut it up in a box, where nobody would see it; but when my steeds run over the steppe everybody looks at them; everybody knows that they are mine; and people always remember that I am rich." In this manner is the reputation of being a rich man acquired throughout the hordes; such is the wealth that procures them the regard of their countrymen and the title of *baï* (rich man), which sometimes gives them an ascendency over the offspring of the khans and the most deserving old men." On the other hand the number of beggars is very considerable. Levchine makes no mention of servants; but Radloff, who about thirty years later visited the Kazak Kirghiz, says: "There exists here a class of servants, whom I found in every well-to-do family. The herds are generally tended by hired herdsmen, who are subjected to a kind of supervision." The rich also engage poor families to till their lands. A man who loses all his cattle has no resource left but to offer himself as a labourer [2]).

The same first-rate ethnographer informs us that among the Altaians "rich and poor eat the same kind of food; the difference is only in the size of the kettle and the quantity of food. The poor man eats what he has got, which most frequently is very little; and he would starve but that the rich have such an abundance of food, that in summer they readily entertain whoever comes to their *jurts* (tents)." When a beast

1) Geoffroy, pp. 420, 425, 434. — 2) Levchine, 348, 349, 344 note 1; Radloff, Aus Sibirien, I pp. 462, 463, 416; see also Ujfalvy, Expéd. Scient., p. 112.

is being killed, the poor neighbours in large numbers throng towards the place and try to secure those portions of the bowels that the rich disdain; they have to fight for them with the dogs, who are equally fond of the delicacies. When all guests have been served, pieces of meat are thrown towards the door, where poor men and dogs try to secure them. The picked bones are also thrown to the poor, who clean them so thoroughly that nothing but the bare bone is left to the dogs. The cattle of the rich are generally tended by poor neighbours, who live in the vicinity of the rich, partake of their food, and receive their worn clothes. Young girls often seek employment as servants; orphans of poor men also serve the rich [1]).

Among the Kalmucks there are poor people who serve the rich as herdsmen [2]).

Prschewalsky states that rich Mongols, who own thousands of beasts, employ herdsmen who are poor and have no relations [3]).

The Kurds of Eriwan employ freemen as herdsmen [4]).

Among the Tunguz the poor generally serve the rich, by whom they are badly treated [5]).

Yakuts, who have less than one head of cattle per soul, must hire themselves out for wages [6]).

Pallas says: "Every Samoyede has his reindeer and tends them himself with the help of his family, except the very rich who employ poor men as herdsmen." Von Stenin also states that the poor serve the rich. The following anecdote, given by this writer, shows how strongly the desire of wealth influences psychical life among the Samoyedes. One of them depicted the delight of intoxication in these terms: "Spirits taste better than meat. When a man is drunk, he fancies he has many reindeer and thinks himself a merchant. But on coming to his senses he sees that he is poor and has just spent his last reindeer in drinking" [7]).

Of the Koryakes we are told: "Before they were subjected

---

1) Radloff, Aus Sibirien, pp. 298, 302, 303, 287, 295, 312. — 2) Pallas, as quoted by Hildebrand, Recht und Sitte, p. 36. — 3) Hildebrand, 1. c., p. 36; see also Obrutschew, I p. 37, and Iwanowski, pp. 8, 11. — 4) Von Stenin, Die Kurden, p. 221. — 5) Müller, Unter Tungusen und Jakuten, p. 50. See also Georgi, as quoted by Hildebrand, 1. c. p. 36. — 6) Sumner, p. 66. — 7) Pallas, Reise, III p. 74; Von Stenin, Samojeden, p. 187.

by the Russians, they had neither government nor magistrates; only the rich exercised some authority over the poor." Their greatest pleasure consists in looking at their herds. The poor are employed in tending the herds of the rich for food and clothing; if they have themselves some reindeer, they are allowed to join them to their master's herds and tend them together with the latter [1]).

Among the Tuski, according to Georgi, the poor serve the rich as herdsmen [2]).

In North-East Africa the state of things is not quite the same. The pastoral nomads here form the nobility, and tax subjected tribes with tributes and compulsory labour. Servants are not found here so often as in Asia. Sometimes, however, they are found. Thus among the Beni Amer there are herdsmen, maid-servants etc. who work for wages [3]). The same, perhaps, applies to the Massai, where the man who owns large herds and many wives, enjoys high consideration but a poor man is despised [4]).

"Among all South African natives" says Fritsch "the rich tyrannize over the poor who, in the hope of filling their stomachs, comply with a state of dependence that is not authorized by law" [5]).

Among the Caffres poor men place themselves under the protection of a rich head of a family, build their huts in his *kraal*, and in reward yield their cattle to him [6]).

Kropf tells us that among the Ama-Xosa the consideration a man enjoys depends on the number of cattle he owns. The poor are fed by the chief and in return render him services [7]).

The Ovaherero despise any one who has no cattle. The rich support many people, who become their dependents, and so they acquire distinction and power [8]). The children of impoverished families who, according to Andersson [9]), are kept as slaves, are perhaps rather to be called servants.

Among those tribes which are mainly agricultural, but besides

---

1) Histoire de Kamtschatka, II pp. 239, 243, 233; see also Hildebrand, Recht und Sitte, p. 36 (after Georgi). — 2) Hildebrand, l. c. — 3) Munzinger, Ostafr. Stud., p. 318. — 4) Merker, p. 117. — 5) Fritsch, p. 364. — 6) Tromp, De Kaffers, p. 197. — 7) Kropf, pp. 109, 170, 171. — 8) Hahn, Die Ovaherero, p. 245; Viehe, in Steinmetz's Rechtsverhält- nisse, p. 301. — 9) See above, p. 144.

subsist largely upon the produce of their cattle, similar phenomena present themselves.

Among the Ossetes freemen are often employed as servants [1]).

Among the Bechuanas the possession of cattle and a waggon
is a mark of distinction. They mix their porridge with curdled
milk, and therefore call a poor man a water-porridge man [2]).

Casalis gives an elaborate description of the value which the
Basutos attach to the possession of cattle. Wealth, among them,
consists in cattle, and this wealth is the base of the power of
the chiefs. By means of the produce of their herds they feed
the poor, procure arms for the warriors, support the troops in
war and entertain good relations with neighbouring nations.
Were a chief to lose his cattle, his power would be at an end [3]).

The Barotse employ as herdsmen young slaves and sons of
poor men [4]).

Among the Dinka every man upon an average owns three
head of cattle; but there are also poor men, who are the
slaves or servants of the rich [5]). We may safely infer that
these "slaves or servants" are servants and not slaves.

The sheikh of each Chillook tribe, according to Chaillé Long,
detains as slaves those who do not own even a single cow [6]).
Probably the same state of things prevails here as among the
Caffres: these poor men are not slaves, but compelled by hunger
to seek the protection of a rich man.

In the country of the Gallas the value of labour is very
small [7]).

The Bogos employ freemen as herdsmen and peasants; they
also keep maid-servants [8]).

Among the Amahlubi there are herdsmen, who serve for
wages [9]).

We see that, wherever men subsist by cattle-breeding, a
peculiar characteristic of economic life presents itself. This
characteristic is not the existence of wealth; for wealth also
exists among the tribes of the Pacific Coast of North America;
yet on the Pacific Coast slave labour is of great use. It is the

---

1) Klaproth, II p. 615. — 2) Livingstone, Miss. Trav., pp. 109, 160. — 3) Casalis, pp.
227, 228. — 4) Holub, Süd-Afrika, II p. 348. — 5) Schweinfurth, I p. 164. — 6) Chaillé
Long, p. 29. — 7) Paulitschke, I p. 333. — 8) Munzinger, Bogos, p. 46. — 9) L. Marx,
in Steinmetz's Rechtsverhältnisse, p. 359.

existence of poverty. On the Pacific Coast the "abundant natural supplies in ocean, stream, and forest" enable each man, be he rich or not, to provide for himself; but among pastoral tribes the means of subsistence are the property of individuals; and those who own no cattle have no resource but to apply to the owners for support [1]). Therefore, if labourers are wanted, there are always freemen who readily offer their services; and there is no great use for slave labour [2]).

So there is always a supply of labour. On the other hand, the demand for labour is small. There is but little work to be done. Among some pastoral tribes the men spend a great deal of time in idleness [3]).

Prschewalsky, speaking of the Mongols, remarks: "Unlimited laziness is a main characteristic of the nomads; they spend their whole life in idleness, which is furthered by the character of pastoral nomadism. The tending of the cattle is the sole occupation of the Mongol, and this does not nearly require all his time. The guarding of cows and sheep is the business of the women and grown-up children; milking, creaming, buttermaking and other domestic labour falls almost entirely to the share of the mistress of the house. The men generally do nothing, and from morning till night ride from one *jurt* (tent) to another, drinking *koumiss* and chattering with their neighbours. The chase, which the nomads are passionately fond of, serves mainly as a pastime."

The Altaians have to survey the cattle; this consists only in riding a few times a day to the herds, and driving them together. The milking of the mares during the summer, which requires some courage, is also the men's business.

Among the Aeneze Bedouins the men's sole business is feeding the horses, and in the evening milking the camels [4]).

---

1) The cattle, among pastoral tribes, are the property of individuals, not of the community; see Dargun, pp. 58—69. — 2) Schmoller remarks, that in pastoral life, among the savages of to-day as well as among the ancient nations of Europe and Asia, the contrast of wealth and poverty and the dependence of the poor upon the rich are strongly marked. (Grundriss, I pp. 198, 370, 371). — 3) "It is the nature of pasturage to produce food for a much greater number of people than it can employ. In countries strictly pastoral, therefore, many persons will be idle, or at most be very inadequately occupied." Malthus, Book II Ch. V (Bettany's edition, p. 196). — 4) Hildebrand, Recht und Sitte, first edition, pp. 37, 38 (after Prschewalsky, Radloff and Burckhardt). On the Mongols see also Iwanowski, p. 12.

The Kazak Kirghiz, too, are very lazy. They pass a great part of the summer sleeping because of the warmth; and in winter-time they hardly ever leave their tents, because the snow covers the roads. As they are not acquainted with any arts, and the tending of the cattle is their only occupation, there is no need for much work [1]).

Rowney tells us of the Mairs and Meenas of Rajpootana: "The ostensible occupation followed by them was that of goatherds; but the herds were usually left to the charge of their boys and old men, while the more able-bodied spent their time, mounted on their ponies, in marauding, plundering, and murdering" [2]).

Among the Massai the men despise every kind of work. Only warfare is considered an occupation worthy of a man [3]).

It has to be remarked that most of these tribes do not keep slaves; so it is not by imposing all the work upon slaves that the men are enabled to pass their time in idleness; yet they do almost nothing. "The herdsman is lazy," says Schmoller [4]), and Schurtz speaks of the aversion from all hard and regular work, which characterizes the pastoral nomads [5]). This proves that but little labour is wanted. One might object, that perhaps women and boys are overworked. But the fact that the able-bodied men, who form a considerable part of the community, can afford to take life so very easily, sufficiently proves that the total amount of labour required is rather small.

Here we find one more reason why pastoral tribes have little use for slave labour. The demand for labour is small; therefore, even if free labourers were not available, only a few slaves would be wanted. Capital is here the principal factor of production, labour holding a subordinate place. Among agricultural tribes, when there is a practically unlimited supply of fertile soil, every person whose labour is available to the tribe can cultivate a piece of ground, and so, the more people there are, the more food can be produced. But among pastoral tribes, as soon as there are people enough within the tribe to guard the cattle, milk the cows, and do the other

---

1) Levchine, p. 341. — 2) Rowney, p. 51. — 3) Merker, p. 117. — 4) Schmoller, Grundriss, I p. 197. — 5) Schurtz, Das Afr. Gewerbe, p. 78.

work required, an increase in the number of labourers is not profitable. There is only a limited demand for labour; therefore, though there may be a temporary scarcity of labour which makes strengthening of the labour forces of the tribe by means of slaves desirable, — when a few slaves have been procured, the point at which a further increase in the number of people gives no profit will soon be reached again.

We see that among pastoral tribes little labour is required; and such as is, is easy to procure; for there are always people destitute of capital, who offer themselves as labourers. Therefore slaves are economically of little use.

There is, however, one description of a pastoral tribe, in which it is stated, that men as well as women have to work very hard. This is Geoffroy's capital monography on the Larbas. The head of the family and his sons have to guard the herds, trace and dig pits, share in all operations common to the horsemen of the tribe: raids and battles, the pursuing of thieves, the defense of the pecuniary interests of the family, the depositing of merchandise in the *ksours* (store-houses). The head of the family tends the sick animals, and has the administration of the wool and grain; but practically he will not have much to do with these matters, not considering them worth his attention. But a great part of his time is taken up with keeping watch and marching, and this makes his life a rather hard one. He does not sleep at night; he waters the cattle in the pits or *r'dirs*; he surrounds his tents with a protecting hedge, the *zirba*; he struggles against the elements, which often disperse beasts, tents and men. Daily, from the cradle to the tomb, the nomad's life is a struggle for existence. As a child he already has to look after the cattle; he learns to ride on horseback with his father. When older, whether rich or poor, he has to learn, for several years, to conduct large numbers of cattle, which is a very difficult and dangerous work, to tend the different kinds of animals, to cure them, to sell them, to derive from them as much profit as possible. Pastoral art is more complicated than at first sight it seems, and comprehends a long series of accomplishments. At twenty years the nomad is an accomplished man, thoroughly acquainted with the life he has to lead, enjoying all the physical strength indispensable in the exceptional *milieu* where he has to struggle. The two youngest sons of the head of the family our informant describes, 15 and 13 years of age, now perform in the family the duties of herdsmen. Daily occupations of master and slaves are the driving together of the dispersed animals, the tending of the females that have calved, the preparing of special food for the young animals, the dressing of the stronger ones for the saddle and pack-saddle, and the chase of hares and gazelles [1]).

We see that pastoral life is not so easy here as on the fertile plains of Central Asia. But the work that is most necessary here, and also most difficult, is the care for the security of the tribe and its possessions, or, as Geoffroy very appropriately expresses it, *"c'est un peu toujours comme la guerre"*. And this work cannot be left to slaves; else the slaves would become the masters of the tribe. Warriors are wanted here; labourers not so much.

We have now accounted for the non-existence of slavery among many pastoral tribes, and the little use of slave labour among pastoral tribes in general, by the principle laid down in the last paragraph, that, generally speaking, slaves are not wanted where subsistence depends upon capital.

In North-East Africa, however, there is one more cause at work, making slavery superfluous. This is the existence of a kind of *substitute for slavery*, viz. *subjection of tribes as such*. Pastoral tribes often levy tributes on agricultural tribes, to which they are superior in military strength; the latter cannot easily leave the lands they cultivate and seek a new country; if not too heavily oppressed, they will prefer paying a tribute. And to pastoral nomads the levying of a tax on agricultural tribes brings far more profit than the enslaving of individuals belonging to such tribes, whom they would have to employ either in pastoral labour, which they do not want, or in tilling the soil, which work the nomads would be unable to supervise. There are also pastoral tribes subjected by other pastoral nomads, the latter forming the nobility and the military part of society. Finally we find subjected tribes of hunters, smiths,

---

1) Geoffroy, pp. 429—431.

etc.; here we have sometimes rather to deal with a voluntary division of labour [1]).

The Somal have several pariah castes. Among the Wer-Singellis in North Somaliland we find the following: 1°. Midgân, smiths and traders; these, by acquiring considerable wealth, sometimes win so much regard, that even a Somali noble deigns to marry his daughter to a Midgân. 2°. Tómal, who are employed by Somali nobles as servants, herdsmen and camel-drivers, and are also obliged to go to war. The noble Wer-Singelli carries sword and spear, whereas the Tomali uses bow and arrows; sometimes a Midgân girl is given him as a wife, but never the daughter of a noble Somali. The Tómal, however, belong to the tribe. 3°. Jibbir, who are very much despised. They have no fixed habitations; they roam in families over the country, from tribe to tribe, as jugglers and magic doctors. Everybody, for fear of sorcery, gives them food and presents, and in return receives from them amulets, made of stone and roots. They contract no marriage outside their own caste [2]).

The Massai, true warriors and raiders, "keep a subjected tribe, the Wa-rombutta, who do their hunting and what meagre agriculture they indulge in. This tribe is insignificant in appearance, and although servile and subject to the Massai are not slaves; they present almost the appearance of dwarfs." The Wandorobo too, according to Thomson, are regarded by the Massai as a kind of serfs, and treated accordingly; and Johnston calls them a helot race of hunters and smiths [3]).

Among the Bogos "patronage results from military subjection or from the helpless state of separate immigrants with regard to a strong and closely united nation. As the nobles carefully trace their pedigrees, it is easy to find out the Tigres. Tigre means a man of Ethiopian extraction, who speaks the Tigre language. Some Tigre families, subjected from time immemorial, have immigrated together with the family of Gebre Terke [the legendary ancestor of the Bogos]. Others already lived in

---

1) On the economic function of these pariah tribes of Africa, see Schurtz, Das Afr. Gewerbe, pp. 38—45. — 2) Hildebrandt, Somal, p. 4. — 3) Mrs. French-Sheldon, p. 380; Thomson, Through Masailand, p. 448; Johnston, p. 402.

the country, and unable to withstand the invasion, hastened to submit in order to be tolerated. The Bogos seem to have taken possession of the country in a very pacific and forbearing way, and unlike the Normans and other European invaders, do not interfere with the regulation of landed property, so that the ancient aborigines still own most of the land. The third class is composed of foreign families who, being for some reason unable to agree with their countrymen, settle in the country of the Bogos and place themselves under their protection, which still continually occurs. A member of the Boas family [*i. e.* of the Bogos nobility], however poor and weak, never becomes a Tigre; his origin is a guarantee of his independence. A Tigre, however mighty and rich, cannot become a Schmagilly [noble]; for the Tigres, who are a compound of various elements, cannot trace their origin so far back as the Schmagillies who pretend to spring all from the same ancestor. Moreover, the oppression is so slight, that a revolution is unimaginable" [1].

Among the Takue the state of the Tigres is the same as among the Bogos; formerly they brought beer to their lords; now they pay them a small tribute of corn and fat [2].

Marea Tigres have a harder lot. Two kinds of obligations are incumbent on them: towards their respective masters, and towards the nobility *en bloc*. Even the poorest noble never becomes a Tigre, and does not perform degrading work, such as for instance milking. The Tigre pays his master yearly 8 bottles of fat, a measure of corn, and every week a leathern bag with milk. Of every cow killed by a Tigre the master receives a considerable portion; a cow belonging to a Tigre, which dies a natural death, falls entirely to the master. As for the Tigres' obligations towards the nobility as a whole, on several occasions they have to give up their cattle for the nobility. Among the Black Marea the Tigres own most of the land; among the Red Marea the greater part of the land is in the hands of impoverished nobles, who live chiefly upon the rent of their ⎯ded property. Another class are the Dokono, who are obliged to choose a patron and pay a tribute, but

---

1) Munzinger, Bogos, pp. 48, 49. — 2) Munzinger, Ostafr. Stud., p. 207.

are held in rather high esteem and often marry daughters of the nobles; they own land and herds and are much given to trading [1]).

Among the Beni Amer the same distinction, of nobles and subjects, prevails. The latter are called Woréza. "We shall speak of master and servant," says Munzinger "though the latter term does not quite answer the purpose. The state of things we are going to describe much resembles that which we have met with among the aristocrats of the Anseba; among the Beni Amer, however, the servant is a feoffee rather than a protégé. But as he derives his wealth from his master, to whom he owes what we may call interest, his state is one of much greater dependence.... Among the Beni Amer it is an ancient custom, that a lord distributes his wealth among his servants; e. g. if he receives 100 cows as his portion of the spoils of war, he does not add them to his herd, but leaves them to his servants as a present. When the servant marries, the lord presents him with a camel. In every emergency the servant applies to his lord, who helps him whenever possible. All these presents become the true property of the recipient; the servant may do with them as he likes, sell and even spend them; the lord may upbraid him for it, but legally has nothing to do with it. On the death of the servant the presents devolve upon his heirs. But the lord has a kind of usufruct of these presents; the servant provides him with fat and daily brings him a certain quantity of milk, i. e. he feeds the lord and his family. Often has the lord to wait for his supper till midnight, because the servant provides for himself first. The servant, moreover, has to provide the funeral sacrifice for his lord and for every member of the latter's family; he leaves to the lord every sterile cow, and when he kills a beast he brings him the breast-piece. He stands by his lord in every emergency, and even assists him according to his means towards paying the tribute". The servant is, so to speak, a tenant of his lord. As the Beni Amer are nomads, there is no land to distribute; the pasture has no owner; therefore the fief can only consist in movable property. As most of the wealth of the country is

---

1) Ibid., pp. 235—242.

in the hands of the servants, they have a decisive voice in every public council; they have to find out where the best pastures are, where the camp has to be erected [1]).

Similar phenomena present themselves outside North-East Africa.

In the second chapter of Part I we have met with subjected tribes in South Africa, such as Fengu, Makalahiri, etc., sometimes called slaves by our ethnographers [2]).

Geoffroy speaks of settled tribes being in some way the vassals of the Larbas. The *ksours* are buildings in which the nomads preserve their corn, dates and wool; these stores are guarded by settled tribes, that permanently live there and receive one tenth of the preserved stock yearly. The nomads look upon all settled tribes as degenerate beings and inferiors [3]). Here we have to deal with a voluntary division of labour, rather than with subjection.

In Circassia, according to Bell, the serfs are prisoners of war and the ancient inhabitants of the country. The latter are perhaps the same peasants who, according to Klaproth, may not be sold apart from the land [4]).

It is remarkable, that in Central Asia and Siberia we do not find a single instance of this subjection of tribes as such [5]). This is probably the reason why in these parts members of the tribe are so often employed as servants.

Where nearly all work is left to subjected tribes or castes, and the nobles do nothing but fight, there is not much use for slave labour. The nobles do not want slaves, because all work required by them is performed by their subjects.

We have now found a new cause, from which in some cases slaves are not wanted: the subjection of tribes as such, which serves as a substitute for slavery.

§ 2. *Slavery among pastoral tribes.*

Yet several pastoral tribes keep slaves; this has still to be

---

1) Ibid., pp. 311, 312, 316, 317. — 2) See above, pp. 139—143. — 3) Geoffroy, pp. 412 414, 415. — 4) Bell, I, p. 337; Klaproth, p. 567. — 5) It is stated, that the nomadic Koryakes regard the settled Koryakes as slaves (Histoire de Kamtschatka, II p. 223). But

accounted for. We shall inquire first, whether the *secondary causes* we have found in the last paragraph are at work here.

1°. *Condition of women.* On the Pacific Coast of North America the men sometimes procure slaves, in order to relieve the women of a part of their task. There are some details on record suggestive of the same state of things among some pastoral tribes. Among the Circassians, Bahima and Beduan (pastoral tribes), Waganda, pirate-tribes of Mindanao and Sulu, Ossetes and Gallas (agricultural tribes depending largely on cattle for their subsistence), slaves are employed for household work. The same is the case with female slaves among the Larbas and Somal of the towns. Munzinger states that only few Beduan are rich enough to keep a female slave or a maid-servant; therefore in most families the preparing of food falls to the share of the wife, this being almost her only occupation [1]). Hence we may infer that among the Beduan, and probably among some other tribes, slaves are procured by the men for the benefit of the women.

2°. *Preserving of food.* This does not seem to require much labour among pastoral tribes. On the Pacific Coast of North America the fish have to be prepared for winter use. But where men live upon the products of their cattle, food is not at one time much more abundant than at another.

3°. *Trade and industry.* Household work, sometimes performed by slaves, does not seem to serve the purposes of trade, as on the Pacific Coast; there is not a single detail on record, that would lead us to suppose that it does. We even find particulars tending to prove the contrary. Among the Beni Amer, who have many slaves, the women are continually occupied in making mats, the proceeds of which labour are often sufficient to pay the tribute to the Turks [2]). Slaves do not seem to join in this occupation.

Among the Larbas free women manufacture tissues, which are sold abroad [3]). Probably slaves are not capable of performing such fine work.

Among the Yorubas and pirate-tribes of Mindanao and Sulu

---

we are not told that they require tributes or services from them. Probably our informant only means to say, that the settled Koryakes are despised by the nomads (see p. 222, ibid.). — 1) Munzinger, Ostafr. Stud., pp. 149, 150. — 2) Ibid., p. 327. — 3) Geoffroy, p. 432.

the slaves are occupied in trading. But these tribes are not
nomadic; moreover, these slaves do not, like the slaves on the
Pacific Coast, prepare the articles of commerce, but are themselves the traders, which is quite another thing.

4°. *Slaves wanted as warriors.* Slaves sometimes serve to
augment the military strength of the community. From the
survey of the work done by slaves, given in the beginning of
this chapter, it appears that they are often employed in warfare,
viz. among the nomadic Somal and Danakil, Kafirs, pirate-tribes
of Mindanao and Sulu, Mandingoes and Yorubas; probably also
among the Bogos, where they generally take to robbery. Circassian slaves cannot be compelled to go to war [1]). Hence it
seems to follow that they may go if they like. Among the
Beni Amer native-born slaves are avenged by their own relatives; so these slaves are armed, and probably fight together
with their masters.

The ensuing statement strikingly shows how highly slaves
are valued as warriors among the nomadic Somal and Danakil.
If a slave kills one enemy, he becomes free; if two or more,
he is entitled to being adopted. Having killed ten enemies,
he becomes a person of rank and enjoys many privileges [2]).

In these cases slaves strengthen the military force of the
tribe. But the tribe profits only indirectly by this reinforcement of the family. Most pastoral nomads live in comparatively
small groups, rather independently; there is no strong central
government [3]). And where quarrels between these small groups
are frequent, the more numerous the family (in the wider
sense, the Roman *familia*, including slaves), the better will
the head of the family be able to maintain his position [4]). And
pastoral nomads have always a great motive for fighting: they
can enrich themselves by a successful raid. Among hunting,
fishing, and agricultural tribes, if the conqueror does not want
to keep the vanquished as slaves, war gives little profit [5]). But

---

1) Bell, I p. 170. — 2) Paulitschke, I p. 263. — 3) Several instances of this phenomenon
are on record with Hildebrand, Recht und Sitte, pp. 30, 31, 37, 38. — 4) Malthus, in his
chapter on modern pastoral nations (Bettany's edition, p. 73), remarks: "The power and
riches of a chaik consist in the number of his tribe.... His own consequence greatly depends
on a numerous progeny and kindred; and in a state of society where power generally
procures subsistence, each individual family derives strength and importance from its
numbers." — 5) Viz. as long as the country is thinly peopled. We shall see later on, that
among some savages the desire to occupy land is a great motive for making war.

in the raids pastoral nomads make on each other, the successful raider may acquire numerous herds, *i. e.* great wealth. Therefore it is of the utmost importance for a man to have as numerous a *familia* as possible.

When speaking of the Larbas, we have seen that their mode of life is *un peu toujours comme la guerre.* Their describer states: "Theft is the most threatening evil the nomad has to deal with; he is therefore most severe in suppressing it, the punishment being invariably death." He also speaks of free servants, members of the family, who live under the protection and at the expense of some rich head of a family; they are generally very numerous, and form a body of clients that strengthens their patron's power [1]).

Levchine, speaking of the Kazak Kirghiz, says: "Their feuds are caused by the unrestrained desire for plunder, that ruins and entirely demoralizes them; this plundering is called *baranta*, These *barantas* consist in reciprocal cattle-stealing, from which often sanguinary combats result.... And we must not think that public hatred or contempt falls on those who are addicted to these horrible excesses; on the contrary, they enjoy a reputation for bravery, and are distinguished by the name of *Batyr* or *Boghatyr*, which name spreads through all the hordes the fame of their exploits. Many of these braves, called *Batyr* for their plundering ardour, though many years dead, still live in the remembrance of their countrymen, and their names are celebrated." Accordingly, one of the qualities required in a chief is a large family, that gives him the power to maintain his authority [2]).

Among the Beni Amer, where it seems to be quite an ordinary thing for a noble to receive 100 cows as his portion of the spoils of war, it is a great support for a man to have many children, as in these countries family is opposed to family [3]).

A writer of the 18th century tells us that "the Chukchi who live to the north of the river Anadir, are not subjected to the Russian empire, and often make raids on those brought under Russian control, on the Koryakes as well as on the Chukchi,

1) Geoffroy, pp. 425, 422, 441. — 2) Levchine, pp. 349, 350, 397. — 3) Munzinger, Ostafr. Stud., pp. 311, 327.

killing or making prisoners all they meet, and carrying off
their herds of reindeer" [1])

Among the Somal and Gallas internal wars are very frequent; among the former most wars are marauding expeditions.
And here too the possession of wife and children is indispensable; an unmarried man cannot attain to wealth and
power [2]).

Among the Ama-Xosa and Ovaherero the chief object of
warfare is cattle-stealing. Fugitives from other tribes are never
delivered up by the Ama-Xosa, whatever the reason of their
flight; for they strengthen the chief's power. Another fact,
showing the great importance they attach to the numerical
strength of their tribe, is this, that he who kills a man or
woman bij accident has to pay a fine to the chief, as a compensation for the loss suffered bij the government of the tribe [3]).

We have already seen that the Massai are "true warriors
and raiders" and that the Mairs and Meenas spend their time
in "marauding, plundering and murdering" [4]).

We see that among these tribes everybody is desirous of
having as many people about him as possible for the protection
of his own property and the capturing of his neighbour's. And
a convenient means of procuring such people is the purchase
of slaves.

There is one more secondary cause here, which we have
not met with before. It is sometimes stated that keeping slaves
is a mere *luxury*. Now rich nomads, like all rich people, love
luxury. Like the rich Kazak Kirghiz who told Levchine that
the possession of over 8000 horses procured him a reputation
among his countrymen, many rich nomads will win renown
by possessing a large retinue of slaves. Thus for instance we
know that among the Beni Amer slave labour is of little use;
yet it is stated, that the Beni Amer are ambitious to possess
many slaves [5]). And slaves are preferable, as objects of luxury,
to free servants. For slaves, generally acquired from beyond
the limits of the tribe, are much more apt to gratify the
pride of the rich man by their submission, than poor freemen,

---

1) Histoire de Kamtschatka, II p. 218. — 2) Paulitschke, I pp. 254, 195. — 3) Fritsch,
pp. 79, 226, 93; Kropf, p. 179. — 4) See above, pp. 274, 277. — 5) Munzinger, Ostafr.
Stud., p. 310.

who are always conscious of their memberschip of the tribe and unwilling to be trampled down. The latter fact is proved by several statements of ethnographers.

If a rich Samoyede refuses to give his poor countryman a reindeer for food, the latter has the right to carry off one or more from the rich man's herd; the law does not give the owner any hold upon him [1]).

Among the Yakuts, according to Müller, the rich sustain their poor fellow-tribesmen; if the latter lose their reindeer, they are indemnified by the rich. Another writer tells us that the poor, when dying of hunger, refrain from slaughtering an animal, from fear of losing their independence [2]).

Similarly among the Ostyaks "members of the same tribe, whether large or small, consider themselves as relations, even where the common ancestor is unknown, and where the evidence of consanguinity is wholly wanting. Nevertheless, the feeling of consanguinity, sometimes real, sometimes conventional, is the fundamental principle of the union. The rich, of which there are few, help the poor, who are many. There is not much that can change hands. The little, however, that is wanted by the needy is taken as a right rather than a favour" [3]).

The Altaians are very sensitive about their liberty. "Every poor man who joins a rich family considers himself a member of it. He will perish of hunger, rather than comply with a demand of his rich neighbour made in a commanding tone" [4]).

Licata tells us that hungry Danakil go to their chief and say: "I am hungry, give me something to eat" [5]).

Among the Larbas free labourers "work for one more fortunate than themselves, but not for a superior; for notwithstanding the relation of employer and employed, equality prevails" [6]).

It is easy to understand that slaves are preferred to such servants. Only in one case is this preference mentioned by an ethnographer. Munzinger states that the slaves bought by the rich Beduan for household work are generally more trusted

---

1) Von Stenin, Samojeden, p. 187. — 2) Müller, Unter Tungusen und Jakuten, p. 173; Sumner, p. 67. — 3) Latham, as quoted by Spencer, Descr. Soc., V p. 16. — 4) Radloff, Aus Sibirien, I p. 312. — 5) Licata, as quoted by Paulitschke, I p. 253. — 6) Geoffroy, p. 434.

than ordinary servants, as they are riveted to their position [1]). But we may safely suppose that in other cases also this circumstance has furthered the growth of slavery.

We have explained why pastoral tribes have no great use for slave labour. We have also mentioned some motives that may induce such tribes to keep slaves. But the fact has not yet been accounted for, that some pastoral tribes keep slaves and others do not. Whence this difference? It has been shown that slavery does not only exist among pastoral tribes that till the soil to a limited extent. Among all pastoral tribes subsistence is dependent on capital. Wealth, too, exists among all these tribes [2]); and we cannot see why slaves, as a luxury, would be wanted by one such tribe more than by another. As slaves are sometimes employed as warriors, we might be inclined to suppose that slavery exists among all warlike tribes, and among these only. But there are several pastoral tribes which, though very warlike, do not keep slaves: Kazak Kirghiz, Turkomans, Massai, and some pastoral nomads of South Africa.

That the subjection of tribes as such in stead of individual slaves, of which we have spoken in the last paragraph, cannot account for all cases in which slavery does not exist, becomes evident, if we take into consideration that most of the pastoral tribes of North-East Africa, which keep other tribes in subjection, practise slavery, whereas in Central Asia and Siberia we find neither subjected tribes nor slaves.

Therefore there must be other causes.

In chapter II we have spoken of *external causes*: it may be that slaves would be of great use, and yet cannot be kept, because the coercive power of the tribe is not strong enough. We have also seen that this coercive power is most strongly developed where men have fixed habitations, live in rather large groups and preserve food for the time of scarcity, and where there is a group of somewhat homogeneous tribes maintaining constant relations with each other. Pastoral tribes are nomadic,

---

1) Munzinger, Ostafr. Stud., p. 154. — 2) Even among the simple Todas; for it is stated that the decision of their disputes by the priest is "generally given in favour of the wealthiest of the litigants." Metz, as quoted by Spencer, Descr. Soc., V p. 12.

do not live together in very large groups, and do not want to preserve food, for they have their supply of food always at hand. Yet the fact that several pastoral tribes keep slaves proves that at least among these the coercive power is strong enough. We shall try to find a cause peculiar to these tribes, that enables them to keep slaves. Now it is remarkable that our positive cases are nearly all of them found in a few definite parts of the globe: North-East Africa, the Caucasus, and Arabia; whereas the pastoral nomads of Siberia, Central Asia, India, and South Africa, with one exception (the Ovaherero), do not keep slaves. And the parts where slavery exists are exactly those where the slave-trade has for a long time been carried on on a large scale. Accordingly, the slaves these tribes keep are often purchased from slave-traders and in several cases belong to inferior races.

The slaves of the Aeneze Bedouins are Negroes [1]).

The slaves kept by the Larbas are Negroes purchased from slave-trading caravans [2]).

Although we find no description of slave-trade among the Circassians, slaves in the Caucasus are exported on a large scale [3]).

Most slaves found among the Somal and Danakil are articles of transit trade: they are purchased from interior tribes and intended to be sold to Arabians. A Somali never becomes the slave of a Somali, and prisoners of war are not enslaved [4]).

Many Beduan make it their business to steal slaves, whom they sell in Massowah [5]).

The slaves kept by the Beni Amer are either captured from enemies or purchased abroad; a Beni Amer never loses his freedom. Slaves are not, however, often sold abroad [6]).

On the other hand, the pastoral tribes of Central Asia and Siberia live in secluded parts, far from the centres of the slave-trade.

The slave-trade greatly facilitates the keeping of slaves. Where slaves are brought by slave-dealers from remote parts, it is much easier to keep them than where they have to be

---

1) Burckhardt, I p. 356. — 2) Geoffroy, p. 440. — 3) Chantre, IV pp. 79, 136. — 4) Paulitschke, I p. 260. — 5) Munzinger, Ostafr. Stud., p. 155. — 6) Ibid., pp 308, 311.

captured from enemies, *i. e.* from the neighbours; in the latter case the slaves are very likely to run away and return to their native country; but a purchased slave transported from a great distance cannot so easily return; if he succeeded in escaping, he would be instantly recaptured by one of the foreign tribes whose countries he would have to traverse. Moreover, some tribes may, by their intercourse with slave-traders, have become familiar with the idea of slavery, and so the slave-trade may have suggested to them the keeping of slaves for their own use.

There is another circumstance, which may partially account for the existence of slavery among some of these tribes: the slaves are often Negroes. And Negroes have always and everywhere been enslaved; they seem to be more fit for slaves than most races of mankind. Galton, speaking of the Damaras, says: "These savages court slavery. You engage one of them as a servant, and you find that he considers himself your property, and that you are, in fact, become the owner of a slave. They have no independence about them, generally speaking, but follow a master as spaniels would. Their hero-worship is directed to people who have wit and strength enough to ill-use them. Revenge is a very transient passion in their character, it gives way to admiration of the oppressor. The Damaras seem to me to love nothing; the only strong feelings they possess, which are not utterly gross and sensual, are those of admiration and fear. They seem to be made for slavery, and naturally fall into its ways" [1]). And Hutter, describing the Bali tribes of Cameroon, remarks that the Negro wants to be ruled and patiently endures any amount of oppression [2]). Similar descriptions may undoubtedly be given of many other Negro tribes. Moreover several slave-keeping nomadic tribes are Semites and Hamites, and therefore look upon the Negroes as an inferior race. Now, where slaves are procured mainly for military purposes (and we have seen that this is often the case with pastoral tribes), an absorption of foreigners into the tribe would answer the purpose as well as, and perhaps better than, slavery. But where the foreigners belong to inferior races, the members of the tribe

---

1) Galton, p. 142. — 2) Hutter, p. 343.

are not likely to intermarry with them and look upon them as their equals; they remain slaves, though they are not of great use as such. We must also take into consideration that inferior races are not so much to be dreaded as superior peoples; the latter, if individuals belonging to them were kept as slaves, might retaliate upon the slave-owners. This may have been the reason why the Kazak Kirghiz who, in Levchine's time, kidnapped many Russians, always sold them abroad: it would not have been safe to keep them as slaves. Accordingly, Pallas states that in his time they used to kidnap men on the Russian frontiers towards the time when they were going to remove with their herds, so that they could not be pursued [1]).

In the second chapter of this Part we have remarked that the growth of slavery is furthered by the existence of a group of more or less similar tribes, the slave-trade being in such cases the means of spreading slavery over the group. We may say now that, whether such a group exists or not, the slave-trade facilitates the keeping of slaves. When the coercive power of a tribe is not strong enough for the keeping of prisoners as slaves, the slave-trade may enable such a tribe to keep slaves; for the keeping of purchased slaves, brought from a great distance, does not require so much coercive power.

We see that the difference between the slave-keeping and the other pastoral tribes consists in external circumstances. Pastoral tribes have no strong motives for making slaves, for the use of slave labour is small. On the other hand, there are no causes absolutely preventing them from keeping slaves. These tribes are, so to speak, in a state of equilibrium; a small additional cause on either side turns the balance. One such additional cause is the slave-trade; another is the neighbourhood of inferior races. There may be other small additional causes, peculiar to single tribes. We shall not inquire whether there are, but content ourselves with the foregoing conclusions, of which the principal are these, that the taming of animals does not naturally lead to the taming of men, and that the relation between capital and labour among pastoral tribes renders the economic use of slavery very small.

---

1) Pallas, Reise, I p. 337.

Recapitulating, we may remark that our general theory, that there is no great use for slave labour where subsistence depends on capital, is fully verified by our investigation of economic life among pastoral tribes.

Two secondary internal causes found in the second chapter have been also met with among pastoral tribes: slaves are sometimes employed in warfare, and sometimes for domestic labour to relieve the women of their task. Two new secondary factors have been found in this chapter: slaves are kept as a luxury; and sometimes the subjection of tribes as such, serving as a substitute for slavery, makes slavery proper superfluous.

With regard to the external causes it has been shown that the coercive power of pastoral tribes is not very strong, as they are nomadic and live in rather small groups; but this want is sometimes compensated for by the slave-trade and the neighbourhood of inferior races. The two latter circumstances may therefore rank as new external causes, the slave-trade taking the place of the existence of a homogeneous group. On the Pacific Coast of N. America it is the trade between tribes of the same culture, among pastoral nomads it is the trade with Arabia, etc.; but in either case it is the slave-trade that furthers the growth of slavery.

Recapitulation of the causes we have found up to the present.

	Furthering the growth of slavery.	Hindering the growth of slavery.
I. Internal causes.		
A. General.	1°. Subsistence easily acquired and not dependent on capital.	1°. Subsistence dependent on capital.
		2°. Subsistence not dependent on capital, but difficult to procure.

	Furthering the growth of slavery.	Hindering the growth of slavery.
I. Internal causes.		
B. Secondary economic:	1º. Preserving of food. 2º. Trade and industry. 3º. A high position of women.	1º. Female labour making slave labour superfluous. 2º. Subjection of tribes as such.
C. Secondary non-economic:	1º. Slaves wanted for military purposes. 2º. Slaves kept as a luxury.	1º. Militarism making slavery impossible.
II. External causes:	1º. Fixed habitations. 2º. Living in large groups. 3º. Preserving of food 1). 4º. The slave-trade. 5º. The neighbourhood of inferior races.	

---

1) "Preserving of food" occurs twice, because it works in different directions.

CHAPTER IV.

§ 1. *Numbers of positive and negative cases in the three agricultural groups.*

The list given in § 3 of the first chapter of this second Part contains the following numbers of agricultural tribes with and without slaves, classified according to the division into three groups we have made in § 2 of the same chapter:

First agricultural group [1]).

	a^1		$a^1 + c$		$a^1 + t$		Total.	
	Pos.	Neg.	Pos.	Neg.	Pos.	Neg.	Pos.	Neg.
North America		6						6
South America	6	9					6	9
Melanesia	2	12			3	1	5	13
Polynesia		1						1
Malay Archipelago	11	4			1		12	4
Indo-Chinese Peninsula		1						1
India	2	3				1	2	4
Bantu tribes	4	1		1	3	1	7	3
Soudan Negroes	1			2	1		2	2
	26	37	0	3	8	3	34	43

---

1) In this paragraph we shall use the same abbreviations as in Part II, Chap. I, § 3.

Second agricultural group.

	a²		a²+c		a²+t		a²+c+t		Total.	
	Pos.	Neg.	Pos.	Neg.	Pos.	Neg.	Pos.	Neg.	Pos.	Neg.
N. America		11								11
S. America	1	2							1	2
Melanesia	1	3							1	3
Polynesia	1	6							1	6
Micronesia		5								5
Malay Arch.	29	1	3		7		2		41	1
Indo-Chin. Penins.	5								5	
India	4	4	1						5	4
Bantu tribes	18	6	7	3	12		1		38	9
Soudan Negroes	5	4	4	2	7		4		20	6
Hamitic peoples	2	1	2						4	1
	66	43	17	5	26	0	7	0	116	48

Third agricultural group.

	a³		a³+c		a³+t		a³+c+t		Total.	
	Pos.	Neg.	Pos.	Neg.	Pos	Neg.	Pos.	Neg.	Pos.	Neg.
N. America				1						1
Malay Arch.	9	1							9	1
Indo-Chin. Peninsula					1				1	
Caucasus			1						1	
Bantu tribes	1			1	5				6	1
Soudan Negroes							1		1	
Hamitic peoples			2	1					2	1
	10	1	3	3	6	0	1	0	20	4

§ 2. *Development of agriculture and development of slavery.*

What do these numbers teach us?

In the first place we see that many (170) agricultural tribes keep slaves. Hence it appears that slavery is by no means incompatible with agriculture. But there are also many (95) agricultural tribes without slaves, so the existence of agriculture among savage tribes does not necessarily lead to the keeping of slaves.

In the second place it appears that the more agriculture is developed, the more frequent slavery becomes. Looking at those agricultural tribes among which subsistence does not depend to any considerable extent on cattle-breeding or trade (a^1, a^2, a^3), we find that in the first group there are 26 positive and 37 negative cases, i. e. 41,3 per cent. of these tribes keep slaves. In the second group the corresponding numbers are 66 positive cases, 43 negative cases, and 60,6 per cent.; in the third group 10 positive cases, 1 negative case, and 90,9 per cent. We see that in the second group slavery is more frequent than in the first, whereas in the third group it is almost universal. It has, however, to be taken into consideration, that the great majority (9 out of 10) of the slave-keeping tribes belonging to the third group live in the Malay Archipelago, and 5 out of these 9 are divisions of the Battas. We may not, therefore, attach much importance to the numbers relating to the third group; for they may be strongly influenced bij local circumstances. Taking the second and third group together we find 76 positive and 44 negative cases, i. e. 63,3 per cent. keep slaves, which percentage is considerably higher than that of the first group.

We do not claim mathematical exactness for these numbers. But at any rate we may say that they sufficiently prove, that slavery is considerably more frequent among truly agricultural tribes, which subsist chiefly by agriculture, than among incipient agriculturists, who still depend on hunting or fishing for a large portion of their food.

The total numbers lead to the same conclusion. Looking at these we find in the first group 34 positive and 43 negative cases, i. e. 44,2 per cent. keep slaves. For the second group the corresponding numbers are 116 pos. cases, 48 neg. cases and 70,7 per cent; for the third group 20 pos. cases, 4 neg. cases and 83,3 per cent; for the second and third group taken together 136 pos. cases, 52 neg. cases and 72,3 per cent.

This agrees with what we expected. The tribes belonging to the first group, the "hunting agriculturists" (*Jägerbauern*),

as Dargun calls them, bear a strong resemblance to hunting
tribes. Generally the men's business is hunting and warfare,
whereas the women have to till the soil. The division of labour
between the sexes does not much differ here from that which
exists in Australia, where the men hunt and the women gather
fruits and dig roots. These tribes are also often nomadic: when
the fruits of their fields are scarcely ripe, they reap them and
remove to some other place [1]).

The best specimens of this type are found in South
America.

Azara, speaking of the Indians living in and around Paraguay,
remarks: "Even the agricultural tribes are more or less nomadic.
Wherever the Indians pass they sow something, and later on
return to reap the fruits" [2]).

Lery, a writer of the 16th century, tells us that among the
Tupinambas the principal cultures were two roots, which he
calls *aypi* and *maniot*. They were cultivated by the women. After
being planted the roots needed no further care, and within
2 or 3 months were fit to be dug up. Maize was also cultivated
by the women. The Tupinambas depended on hunting and
fishing for a considerable portion of their food. They did not
generally remain for longer than 5 or 6 months in one place,
but were always removing from one place to another, carrying
their house-building materials with them [3]).

Von den Steinen, describing the tribes on the Upper Schingu
(in Brazil), states that, though largely subsisting on agriculture,
they are psychically hunters rather than agriculturists. Like
everywhere in Brazil, the women not only prepare the food,
but cultivate the manioc. The men cultivate nothing but tobacco,
the smoking of which is their exclusive privilege [4]).

We have seen (in chap. II of this second Part) that hunters hardly ever keep slaves; and as the "hunting agriculturists"
so much resemble true hunters, it is easy to understand why
among the majority of them slavery does not exist. Slaves
cannot be employed for hunting, and the women can easily
perform the small amount of cultivation wanted by these tribes.

---

1) Cunningham (English Industry, I p. 31) remarks that "primitive agriculture is
perfectly consistent with a very migratory life." — 2) Azara, II p. 160. — 3) Lery, pp.
123, 127, 141—175, 312. — 4) Von den Steinen, Unter den Naturvölkern, pp. 201, 214.

Moreover, the men who, as warriors, are able to procure slaves, are not likely to take them for the sole benefit of the women. And where the men are always hunting, the women would have to supervise the slaves and keep them in order, which is not easy for them.

That this lowest stage of agriculture is not favourable to the growth of slavery, is confirmed by what Mr. A. C. Kruyt had the kindness to write us regarding Central Celebes. There is one native tribe, the Topebato, that formerly did not keep slaves, the probable cause being that they had remained hunters longer than the other tribes in the neighbourhood. In a legend, in which it is told that the gods made gifts to the different tribes characterizing their manner of life, the Topebato get a dog allotted to them for the chase, and though now they till the soil, they are still passionate hunters. They now buy a few slaves and so in the course of time a slave class will originate among them.

Yet there are a considerable number of positive cases in our first group (26 out of 63). We will, of course, make due allowance for mistakes; there may be several tribes contained in our first group which on closer scrutiny would prove to be true agriculturists and not *Jägerbauern*. But we cannot think but that among these 26 tribes there are many, which have been justly placed in the first group. The existence of slavery among them will have to be accounted for by secondary causes, internal and external, such as we have found in the foregoing chapters and of which we shall perhaps find some more in the continuation of this chapter.

We must, however, bear in mind that our first group does not only contain "hunting", but also "fishing agriculturists"; and we know that fishers are more likely to keep slaves than hunters. This may perhaps account for the existence of slavery among some of these tribes. But our numbers give us no hint in this direction. We find, indeed, that 11 out of 26 positive cases are afforded by tribes inhabiting the islands of the Malay Archipelago; but among these there are some Dyak tribes living in the interior of Borneo. Moreover, South America affords 6 positive, and the Melanesian islands 12 negative cases. We may suppose that whatever effect this factor has is neutralized by the intervention of other circumstances.

§ 3. *Capital and labour among agricultural tribes.*

We have seen that among the purely agricultural tribes of the second and third stages there are altogether 76 positive and 44 negative cases, *i. e.* more than three-fifths of them keep slaves. These numbers make it probable, that the existence of slavery among agricultural tribes has to be accounted for by general causes, that agricultural life as such is favourable to the growth of slavery. We have to inquire now, whether this supposition is justified by an application of the general principle laid down in § 6 of the second chapter, *i. e.* whether among agricultural tribes subsistence is dependent on capital, and if not, whether it is easy or difficult to procure.

It appears that, where agriculture is carried on without the aid of domestic animals, subsistence does not depend on capital. The savage agriculturist is unacquainted with the more perfect and costly agricultural implements used in Europe, and, where population is scarce (as it is among most savages) cultivates only such grounds as are most fertile and easiest of access. Even the plough is used by very few savages; they most often content themselves with a pointed stick or hoe, wherefore Hahn calls the agriculture carried on by them hoe-culture (*Hackbau*), as distinguished from agriculture proper (*Ackerbau*) [1]). And even where agriculture is carried on in a more skilful manner, *e. g.* by means of irrigation, it is not capital that is wanted, but labour. The construction of the irrigation-works may be a long and laborious task, but the materials cost nothing. There is only one instance in which we have found it stated that agriculture cannot well be carried on without capital. Radloff tells us that the Kazak Kirgbiz, besides rearing cattle, are largely agricultural. Some fields want constant irrigation, and the water is very difficult to procure. The rich use a paddle-wheel; the poor bring the water to their fields in buckets and wooden vessels, but this is of little avail. Therefore it is only the rich who are capable of carrying on agriculture to any considerable extent [2]). But this state of things probably had not yet existed more than some 30 years; for

---

1) Hahn, Die Haustiere, pp. 388 sqq. — 2) Radloff, Aus Sibirien, I pp. 463—465.

Levchine (writing about 30 years earlier than Radloff) states that in his time agriculture was of little importance; and he does not make any mention of irrigation [1]). The introduction of the paddlewheel has therefore probably to be ascribed to the Russians; for the Kazak Kirghiz, in Radloff's time, were already strongly influenced by them; so we may not speak here of a fact belonging to savage life. We have not found any other instance of this dependence of agriculture on capital; but even if there be a few instances, we are justified in concluding that, generally speaking, the savage agriculturist can perfectly well do without capital, except, of course, where he depends on cattle.

Moreover, subsistence is fairly easy to procure. Agriculture, where it is carried on in such simple manner as among most savages, does not require much skill or application. As compared with hunting, seafaring and manufactures, it is rather dull work, requiring patience rather than strength or skill. It is one of the occupations about which there is no excitement, and which in many primitive societies are performed by the women. Hunting requires personal qualities, and a good hunter is held in high esteem; but we have not found it stated in a single instance, that a man's influence or power depends on his ability in agriculture.

Subsistence, therefore, is independent of capital and easy to procure. Every one is able to clear a piece of ground and provide for himself; nobody offers his services to another, and so, if a man wants a labourer, he must compel his fellow-man to work for him. "All freemen in new countries" says Bagehot "must be pretty equal; every one has labour, and every one has land; capital, at least in agricultural countries (for pastoral countries are very different), is of little use; it cannot hire labour; the labourers go and work for themselves. There is a story often told of a great English capitalist who went out to Australia with a shipload of labourers and a carriage; his plan was that the labourers should build a house for him, and that he would keep his carriage, just as in England. But (so the story goes) he had to try to live in his carriage, for

---

1) Levchine, p. 413.

his labourers left him, and went away to work for themselves" [1]. Similarly, Sombart observes: "Colonies, in which there are no labourers to exploit, are like knives without blades" [2]. In such countries, if a man wants others to work in his service and according to his instructions, he must compel them to do so, *i. e.* he must enslave them. And agriculture, requiring little skill and application, is very fit to be imposed upon slaves: compulsory agricultural labour, though not so productive as voluntary labour, can yet yield some profit. Moreover, the agricultural slave is rather easy to control; his work does not require independent action. It is also easy to prevent him from running away. In all this he differs from a hunting slave. And agriculture is also more favourable to the existence of slavery than cattle-breeding; for among pastoral tribes there is but a fixed and rather small amount of work to be done; but where men subsist by agriculture, any increase in the number of slaves brings about an increase of food.

We cannot, therefore, agree with Adam Smith, who asserts that in those countries where slaves are employed, it would be more profitable to employ free labourers, and that it was, in general, pride and love of power in the master that led to the employment of slaves [3]. A free labourer, it is true, is more interested in the work he has to do, and therefore likely to do it better, than a slave; but in those countries where there is an abundance of fertile soil, and capital is of little use, free labourers cannot be had; every freeman prefers working for himself, or perhaps not working at all.

Cairnes, speaking of Negro slavery as it was carried on in the United States, admits that slave labour has sometimes an advantage over free labour, but only where tobacco, cotton and similar crops are raised for industrial purposes, not where cereals are grown. "The economic advantages of slavery" he remarks "are easily stated: they are all comprised in the fact that the employer of slaves has absolute power over his workmen,

---

1) Bagehot, pp. 72, 73. Hutter (pp. 353, 354), speaking of the Bali tribes of Cameroon, remarks that there is a difference between rich and poor, but the poor are not so badly off as in Europe, for the land is open to every one. — 2) Sombart, I p. 342. — 3) Adam Smith as referred to by Ingram, p. 282. Loria (p. 97) also holds that production was decreased by the introduction of slavery.

and enjoys the disposal of the whole fruit of their labours. Slave labour, therefore, admits of the most complete organization; that is to say, it may be combined on an extensive scale, and directed by a controlling mind to a single end, and its cost can never rise above that which is necessary to maintain the slave in health and strength. On the other hand, the economical defects of slave labour are very serious. They may be summed up under the three following heads: — it is given reluctantly; it is unskilful; it is wanting in versatility.... The line dividing the Slave from the Free States marks also an important division in the agricultural capabilities of North America. North of this line, the products for which the soil and climate are best adapted are cereal crops, while south of it the prevailing crops are tobacco, rice, cotton, and sugar; and these two classes of crops are broadly distinguished in the methods of culture suitable to each. The cultivation of the one class, of which cotton may be taken as the type, requires for its efficient conduct that labour should be combined and organized on an extensive scale. On the other hand, for the raising of cereal crops this condition is not so essential. Even where labour is abundant and that labour free, the large capitalist does not in this mode of farming appear on the whole to have any preponderating advantage over the small proprietor, who, with his family, cultivates his own farm, as the example of the best cultivated states in Europe proves. Whatever superiority he may have in the power of combining and directing labour seems to be compensated by the greater energy and spirit which the sense of property gives to the exertions of the small proprietor. But there is another essential circumstance in which these two classes of crops differ. A single labourer, Mr. Russell tells us, can cultivate twenty acres of wheat or Indian corn, while he cannot manage more than two of tobacco, or three of cotton. It appears from this that tobacco and cotton fulfil that condition which we saw was essential to the economical employment of slaves — the possibility of working large numbers within a limited space; while wheat and Indian corn, in the cultivation of which the labourers are dispersed over a wide surface, fail in this respect. We thus find that cotton, and the class of crops of which cotton may be taken as the type, favour the employment of slaves in competition with peasant proprietors in two leading ways: first, they need extensive combination and organization of labour — requirements which slavery is eminently calculated to supply, but in respect to which the labour of peasant proprietors is defective; and secondly, they allow of labour being concentrated, and thus minimize the cardinal evil of slave labour — the reluctance with which it is yielded. On the other hand, the cultivation of cereal crops, in which extensive combination of labour is not important, and in which the operations of industry are widely diffused, offers none of these advantages for the employment of slaves, while it is remarkably fitted to bring out in the highest degree the especial excellencies of the industry of free proprietors. Owing to these causes it has happened that slavery has been maintained in the Southern States [1]), which favour the growth of tobacco, cotton, and analogous products, while, in the Northern States, of which cereal crops are the great staple, it from an early period declined and has ultimately died out. And, in confirmation of this view, it may be added that wherever in the Southern States the external conditions are especially favourable to cereal crops, as in parts of Virginia, Kentucky, and Missouri, and along the slopes of the Alleghanies, there slavery has always failed to maintain itself. It is owing to this cause that there now exists in some parts of the South a considerable element of free labouring population" [2]).

This reasoning is quite correct so far as Negro slavery in the United States is concerned; but it does not hold with regard to primitive slavery or "retail slavery" as Bagehot calls it. The few slaves kept in primitive agricultural societies work together with their masters, who can therefore continually supervise their work and do not want overseers. Moreover, the slave in primitive and simple societies is not looked upon as a piece of machinery; he is, so to speak, an inferior member of the family, sharing in its pleasures, sorrows, and occupations; therefore it is not only the fear of punishment that induces him to work; he is interested in the welfare of the family, and knows

---

1) Cairnes wrote in 1862. — 2) Cairnes, pp. 43, 44, 49—52.

that the better he works, the more he will be valued, and the more food there will be of which he will get his due share [1]). This retail slavery, as Bagehot remarks, "the slavery in which a master owns a few slaves, whom he well knows and daily sees — is not at all an intolerable state; the slaves of Abraham had no doubt a fair life, as things went in that day. But wholesale slavery, where men are but one of the investments of large capital, and where a great owner, so far from knowing each slave, can hardly tell how many gangs of them he works, is an abominable state" [2]). Retail slavery, therefore, can very well exist where cereal crops are raised; it is even the most convenient system of labour in primitive agricultural societies.

We see that the general economic state of truly agricultural tribes may account for the existence of slavery among so many of these tribes. We shall now inquire what secondary causes there are at work among agricultural tribes, and what effect they have. But we shall have to speak first of a great factor in economic life, which we have not met with before.

§ 4. *Land and population.*

The general principle laid down in the last paragraph is that in primitive agricultural societies capital is of little use and subsistence easy to acquire; therefore every able-bodied man can, by taking a piece of land into cultivation, provide for himself. Hence it follows that nobody voluntarily serves another; he who wants a labourer must subject him, and this subjection will often assume the character of slavery.

But this general rule requires an important qualification. Hitherto we have supposed, that there is much more fertile land than is required to be cultivated for the support of the

---

1) Such was the slave system of the ancient Germans described by Tactitus: "You cannot tell master from slave by any distinction in education: they spend their time among the same flocks, upon the same land, until age separates the nobles and their valour causes them to be acknowledged." Tacitus, Germania, 20. On the character of primitive slavery, see also Schmoller, Grundriss, I p. 339. — 2) Bagehot, pp. 73, 74; see also Flügel, p. 96, and Jhering's excellent description of the character of slavery in early Rome (Jhering, II Part I pp. 172 sqq.).

actual population. Such, indeed, is the case among most savages; but it is not always so. And where it is not so, our general rule does not obtain. When all land fit for cultivation has been appropriated, a man, though able-bodied and willing to work, if he owns no land, cannot earn his subsistence independently of a landlord; he has to apply to the owners of the land for employment as a tenant or servant. In such case free labourers are available; therefore slaves are not wanted.

In this and the ensuing paragraphs we shall endeavour to prove by facts the hypothesis arrived at here by a deductive reasoning, which we may express thus: *where all land fit for cultivation has been appropriated, slavery is not likely to exist.*

The same vieuw is held by some theoretical writers.

According to Cairnes "slavery, as a permanent system, has need not merely of a fertile soil, but of a practically unlimited extent of it. This arises from the defect of slave labour in point of versatility. As has been already remarked, the difficulty of teaching the slave anything is so great — the result of the compulsory ignorance in which he is kept, combined with want of intelligent interest in his work — that the only chance of rendering his labour profitable is, when he has once learned a lesson, to keep him to that lesson for life. Accordingly where agricultural operations are carried on by slaves, the business of each gang is always restricted to the raising of a single product.... Whatever crop may be best suited to the character of the soil and the nature of slave industry, whether cotton, tobacco, sugar, or rice, that crop is cultivated, and that alone. Rotation of crops is thus precluded by the conditions of the case. The soil is tasked again and again to yield the same product, and the inevitable result follows. After a short series of years its fertility is completely exhausted, the planter — "land-killer" he is called in the picturesque nomenclature of the South — abandons the ground which he has rendered worthless, and passes on to seek in new soils for that fertility under which alone the agencies at his disposal can be profitably employed.... Slave cultivation, wherever it has been tried in the new world, has issued in the same results. Precluding the conditions of rotation of crops or skilful management, it tends inevitably to exhaust the land of a country and consequently requires for its permanent success not merely a fertile soil but a practically unlimited extent of it." Therefore expansion is a necessity of slave societies [1]).

In the same sense Weber, speaking of the ancient states of Asia and Europe, remarks that slavery is uneconomical, where a dense population and high prices of the land render an intensive cultivation necessary [2]).

It is easy to see that these arguments do not apply to slavery as practised by savages. Rotation of crops and skilful management are wanting among most savage tribes, whether they keep slaves or not. Moreover, as we have already remarked, the slaves kept by them are not pieces of machinery, nor, as in the United States, kept in compulsory ignorance; they are rather regarded as members of the master's family; there is no great difference between master and slave [3]). We may therefore suppose that, whether a savage tribe keeps slaves or not, agriculture is carried on in the same manner.

Loria also holds that slavery requires an abundant supply of ground; but his arguments are quite different from Cairnes'. His reasoning is as follows.

As long as there is land not yet appropriated, which a man destitute of capital can take into cultivation, capitalistic property cannot exist; for nobody is inclined to work for a capitalist, when he can work for his own profit on land that costs him nothing. If, then, the capitalist wants by any means to get a profit, he must violently suppress the free land to which the labourer owes his force and liberty. And as long as the population is scarce and therefore all land cannot possibly be appropriated, the only means of suppressing the free land is by subjugating the labourer. This subjugation assumes at first the form of slavery; afterwards, when the decreasing fertility of the soil has to be made up for by a greater fertility of labour, slavery gives place to serfdom, which is milder and makes labour more productive.

When the population increases, and all land that can be culti-

---

1) Cairnes, pp. 53—56, 62, 179 sqq. — 2) Weber's Article "Agrarverhältnisse im Altertum", in Handwörterbuch der Staatswissenschaften, 3rd edition (1909) I p. 63. — 3) Cairnes is also aware of the difference between ancient and modern slavery (pp. 109 sqq.).

vated by labour without the aid of capital had been appropriated, quite another state of things prevails. The labourer has now no other resource but to sell his labour to the capitalist for such wages as the latter likes to give; he is compelled to yield to the capitalist the greater part of the produce of his labour. Now the latter need no longer use violence to get his profit; for it falls to him by the automatic operation of the social system. Yet, even then the capitalistic *régime* is not absolutely certain to arise, for there is still land not yet appropriated, that can be cultivated with the aid of capital. If, therefore, the labourers could save a portion of their earnings and thus accumulate capital, they would be able to take this land into cultivation and so make themselves independent of their employers. This consideration induces the capitalist to keep wages so low that they cannot exceed the immediate wants of the labourers, which he brings about by various artificial means.

When, finally, a further increase of population makes the total appropriation of the land possible, the mere appropriation of it by the capitalist class renders the labourers for ever subjected. The capitalist need no longer have recourse to artificial methods of reducing wages; the system operates automatically. The capitalists have only to retain the land for themselves; they will then secure a perpetual revenue at the cost of the labouring class.

"The basis of capitalistic property is thus always the same, viz. the suppression of the free land, the exclusion of the labourer from the appropriation of the land. This is brought about by various means, according to the fertility of the land and the extent to which it has already been appropriated. As long as there is free land fit for cultivation by labour without the aid of capital, the only means of suppressing it are slavery and serfdom; afterwards, when the land not yet appropriated can only be cultivated by one who owns capital, it is sufficient systematically to reduce wages to a level that does not enable the labourers to save; when, finally, the population has so far increased as to make the appropriation of all land possible, the capitalists have only to keep the land to themselves" [1]).

---

1) Loria pp. 2—6.

Many objections can be made to Loria's arguments. He is constantly confusing capitalist and landlord. He seems to consider capitalists and labourers as two strictly separated classes, though we see continually people passing from one class to the other. And when he tells us that, if wages were higher, the labourers would save a portion of their earnings and so accumulate capital, but that the employers, wishing to prevent this, keep wages low, — he ascribes to both capitalists and labourers so much forethought and consciousness of class-interest as men scarcely ever have, except in books on political economy [1]. Yet we cannot think but that in the main Loria is right. The gist of his reasoning is what we have already remarked in the beginning of this paragraph. As long as there is an abundance of land not yet appropriated, and therefore at the disposal of whoever may choose to cultivate it, nobody applies to another for employment, and the only labourers a man can procure are forced labourers. But when all land has been appropriated, those who own no land are at the mercy of the landholders, and voluntarily serve them; therefore slaves are not wanted.

Much more fully has the true reason, why in densely peopled countries there is little use for slaves, been recognized by Wakefield in his book on the art of colonization. With him, the theory is not based upon a general conception of society, but upon the facts of the colonial history of his own time.

Wakefield, then, complains that in Australia and other colonies manufactures cannot thrive; the reason for this is, according to him, that there are no labourers to be had; for there is so much free land that every newly-arrived labourer becomes a landowner rather than work for wages. Therefore there are many colonies which would keep slaves if the home government let them. This leads the writer to an investigation of the circumstances which induce men to keep slaves.

"They are not moral, but economical circumstances; they relate not to vice and virtue, but to production. They are the circumstances, in which one man finds it difficult or impossible

---

1) On Loria's incorrect manner of reasoning, see B. Croce's essay on "Le teorie storiche del Prof. Loria", in "Materialismo storico ed economia Marxistica". A much better opinion of Loria is held by Sombart (I p. 358).

to get other men to work under his direction for wages. They are the circumstances .... which stand in the way of combination and constancy of labour, and which all civilized nations, in a certain stage of their advance from barbarism, have endeavoured to counteract, and have in some measure counteracted, by means of some kind of slavery. Hitherto in this world, labour has never been employed on any considerable scale, with constancy and in combination, except by one or other of two means; either by hiring, or by slavery of some kind. What the principle of association may do in the production of wealth, and for the labouring classes, without either slavery or hiring, remains to be seen; but at present we cannot rely upon it ....

Slavery is evidently a make-shift for hiring; a proceeding to which recourse is had, only when hiring is impossible or difficult .... it is adopted because at the time and under the circumstances there is no other way of getting labourers to work with constancy and in combination. What, then, are the circumstances under which this happens?

It happens whenever population is scanty in proportion to land. Slavery .... has been confined to countries of a scanty population, has never existed in very populous countries, and has gradually ceased in the countries whose population gradually increased to the point of density. And the reason is plain enough .... In populous countries, the desire to own land is not easily gratified, because the land is scarce and dear: the plentifulness and cheapness of land in thinly-peopled countries enables almost everybody who wishes it to become a landowner. In thinly-peopled countries, accordingly, the great majority of free people are landowners who cultivate their own land; and labour for hire is necessarily scarce: in densely-peopled countries, on the contrary, the great majority of the people cannot obtain land, and there is plenty of labour for hire. Of plentifulness of labour for hire, the cause is dearness of land: cheapness of land is the cause of scarcity of labour for hire" [1].

---

1) Wakefield, pp. 323—325. Marx (I pp. 795—804) gives a detailed account of the same argument as developed in another book of Wakefield's, and adds that the exclusion of the mass of the people from the soil forms the basis of the capitalistic mode of production (ibid., p, 798).

Wakefield proposed that the government should sell the new land in the colonies at a sufficient price, *i. e.* at a price which would oblige the newly arrived labourers to serve a few years for wages before being able to become landowners [1]).

Another writer on colonial matters of the same period, Merivale, follows quite the same line of argument as Wakefield. The great demand for slaves and the great profitableness of slavery, he says, arise altogether from the scarcity of labour. "When the pressure of population induces the freeman to offer his services, as he does in all old countries, for little more than the natural minimum of wages, those services are very certain to be more productive and less expensive than those of the bondsman, whose support is a charge to the master, and who has nothing to gain by his industry .... This being the case, it is obvious that the limit of the profitable duration of slavery is attained whenever the population has become so dense that it is cheaper to employ the free labourer for hire. Towards this limit every community is approximating, however slowly." That the relation between land and population is indeed the determining factor as regards the system of labour most suitable to a country, is clearly shown by the effect which the emancipation of the slaves had upon the economic development of the different colonies. Merivale then proceeds to divide the British slave colonies, at the time of emancipation, into three classes, as respects their economical situation. First, the oldest settlements, established in the smaller Antilles (Barbadoes, Antigua, etc.). They were those in which the land was nearly all occupied. "They were less injured than any others by the immediate effect of emancipation; for the negroes had no resource except in continuing to work; there was no unoccupied land for them to possess, no independent mode of obtaining a subsistence to which they could resort, still less of obtaining those luxuries which habit had rendered desirable to them." "The next class is that of colonies in which the fertile or advantageously situated soil was all cultivated, and becoming

---

exhausted; but there remained much unoccupied soil, of a less valuable description, and the population was not dense in proportion to the whole surface." This applies especially to Jamaica. Here the colonists "were injured, *perhaps*, by the abolition of the slave trade; and they suffer now, since emancipation, by the difficulty of compelling the negroes to perform hired labour while they have their own provision grounds, and other resources, at their disposal." "Finally, there is a third class of colonies, in some of which the fertility of the cultivated soil is as yet unexhausted, in others there is abundance of fertile and unoccupied land. Such are the Mauritius and Trinidad, and, in a far higher degree, Guiana". In these colonies, after emancipation, "the negroes have found it easy to obtain a subsistence in a country overflowing with natural wealth: they have been rescued from a servitude involving, perhaps, a greater amount of labour than in any other settlements: they have abundance of land to resort to for their maintenance. The accounts, both from Guiana and Trinidad, seem to report the negroes as generally peaceful and well-inclined, but indisposed to labour, to which they can only be tempted by the most exorbitant offers of wages" [1]).

There is one more reason why slaves are of little use in those countries where all land has been appropriated. When there is free land, a man can, by increasing the number of his slaves, to any extent augment his revenue: every slave will take a new patch of land into cultivation; the more slaves a man owns, the more land he will have in tillage. But when the supply of land is limited, each landowner can employ only a definite number of labourers. As soon as there are hands enough to cultivate his grounds, an increase in the number of labourers soon becomes unprofitable. What we have said of pastoral tribes obtains here too: it may be that slaves are wanted, but when they are procured the point will soon be reached at which a further increase in their number yields no longer any profit. Therefore, when all land has been appropriated, even though it be equally divided between the members of the

1) Merivale, pp. 305, 313—317. See also Waltershausen, article "Negerfrage", in Handwörterbuch der Staatswissenschaften, 2nd edition, V p. 973.

community and so a labouring class be wanting, there is little use for slaves.

It must be understood that we speak here of self-dependent agricultural countries. Where manufactures and the trade with foreign parts are highly developed, economic life becomes much more complicated and presents quite another character.

What we want to prove is that in such self-dependent agricultural countries, when all arable land has been appropriated, slavery is not likely to exist.

All land has been appropriated, when every piece of land is claimed by some one as his property. The owner, of course, need not be an individual; land may also be owned by a group of individuals. Yet the statements of our ethnographers concerning tribal property may not be accepted without much caution. They often tell us that a tribe claims the ownership of the territory it inhabits. This so-called right of property held by the tribe often proves to consist in this, that no strangers are admitted to the territory, but every member of the tribe may cultivate as much of the land as he likes. In such case, whether it be the tribe or the king to whom the land is stated to belong, the term "ownership" is very inappropriately used [1]). We shall only speak of appropriation of land when some one claims the use of it to the exclusion of all others, and values his property. Where the so-called owner is always willing to give a piece of it in cultivation to whoever wants to cultivate it, we shall not speak of appropriation; where, however, the land is never (except by way of favour) given in use *gratis*, but a rent is always stipulated, it appears that the owner values it, it has now really been appropriated [2]).

---

1) See Dargun, pp. 49 sqq. Hildebrand (Recht und Sitte, pp. 134 sqq.) rightly remarks that in primitive societies the uncultivated land is not the property of the community, but nobody's property (*res nullius*). — 2) Where the State owns the land and gives it in use gratuitously or at a low rent, the land is practically free. Such was the case in China, in the 5th century of our era, where the State gave allotments to farmers at a definite tax. "It is obvious, that the condition of the free cultivators without land could not become intolerable so long as they were able to rent in on the simple condition of paying the ordinary tax; and as long as the State had land to let on these terms, private agglomerators would be unable to get farmers to pay more to themselves ; so that large estates could only be profitable on condition of evading the land tax, or being tilled for the owner bij servile labour." Simcox, II p. 127.

It is not always clearly stated whether all land has been appropriated. Then we shall have recourse to some criteria from which we may infer whether such be the case.

The principal criterion is the existence of a class of freemen destitute of land [1]. Where such people are found we may be sure that there is no free land; else they would be able to take it into cultivation. It need scarcely be added that even where no such people are found, it may be that all land has been appropriated, everybody sharing in it.

The appropriation of the land does not imply that all land is actually being cultivated. There may be land actually out of tillage and yet valued by the owner. But when it is stated that all land is being cultivated, it must all have been appropriated. This will therefore be our second criterion.

There is another criterion that proves that all land has not yet been appropriated. When we are told that clearing a piece of land is a *modus acquirendi* of landed property, there must still be free land.

The appropriation of all land implies that property in land exists; but the reverse is not true: when we are informed that property in land exists, this does not prove that all land has already been appropriated. For as soon as the population has so far increased as to require the cultivation of land less fertile than that which was at first exclusively cultivated, the more fertile land acquires value. "On the first settling of a country" says Ricardo "in which there is an abundance of rich and fertile land, a very small proportion of which is required to be cultivated for the support of the actual population, or indeed can be cultivated with the capital which the population can command, there will be no rent; for no one would pay for the use of land, when there was an abundant quantity not yet appropriated, and, therefore, at the disposal of whosoever might choose to cultivate it." But "when in the progress

---

1) "Destitute of land" is, not the same as: "who own no land." When the population is so scarce that even the most fertile land has no value, nobody owns land; but there are no men destitute of land, any more than in our countries there are men destitute of air or water; every one has land at his disposal. Only when every piece of land has an owner, can there be people destitute of land, *i. e.* who have no land at their disposal.

of society, land of the second degree of fertility is taken into cultivation, rent immediately commences on that of the first quality, and the amount of that rent will depend on the difference in the quality of these two portions of land" [1]. As soon as land of the second degree of fertility is cultivated, rent commences; but in such cases there is possibly much land of the second degree not yet appropriated, and at any rate land of the 3rd, 4th, etc. degrees. Accordingly we find that among some savage tribes, where there is an abundance of free land, some very fertile or very favourably situated pieces of land are highly valued. We shall give one instance. Among the Sea Dyaks land is so abundant that, if a Dyak, when about to cultivate a piece of land, finds a dead animal lying on it, which he considers a bad omen, he immediately leaves the land, and seeks a new field. Yet among the same Sea Dyaks "parents and children, brothers and sisters, very seldom quarrel; when they do so, it is from having married into a family with whom afterwards they may have disputes about land. One would imagine that was a subject not likely to create dissensions in a country like Borneo; but there are favourite farming-grounds, and boundaries are not very settled. It used to be the practice not to have recourse to arms on those occasions, but the two parties collecting their relatives and friends, would fight with sticks for the coveted spot" [2]. The last sentence proves that these quarrels were rather frequent. When, therefore, it is stated that land has value, or that lands are rented, or that the wealth of individuals consists partly in landed property, this does not prove that all land has already been appropriated.

We have spoken of all land fit for cultivation being appropriated. What land is fit for cultivation in each country depends on the ability of the inhabitants in agriculture. Much will also depend on the character of the individuals. Where these are vigorous and enterprising, the people destitute of arable land will endure many hardships in taking new lands into cultivation, whereas weak and indolent men will prefer being employed by the rich. A good instance of this is furnished by the Bontoc

---

1) Ricardo, pp. 35, 36. — 2) Spenser St. John, I pp. 74, 60.

Igorot of Northern Luzon. Landed property here is highly developed. "It is largely by the possession or nonpossession of real property that a man is considered rich or poor." "Irrigated rice lands are commonly leased." "Unirrigated mountain camote lands are rented outright." Yet there is still unoccupied land. "Public lands and forests extend in an irregular strip around most pueblos ... Public forests surround the outlying private forests. They are usually from three to six hours distant. From them any man gathers what he pleases, but until the American came to Bontoc the Igorot seldom went that far for wood or lumber, as it was unsafe." There are, however, people who do not own land enough to live upon. "It is claimed that each household owns its dwelling and at least two sementeras and one granary, though a man with no more property than this is a poor man and some one in his family must work much of the time for wages, because two average sementeras will not furnish all the rice needed by a family for food" [1]. So the poor work for wages rather than going to settle on the outlying public lands, to which they have free access. Here again we see that economic phenomena have always a psychological basis [2].

We shall not, in order to prove our hypothesis, examine the regulations of landed property among all agricultural savage tribes, but confine ourselves to one geographical group, in which the phenomena we have spoken of in this paragraph most strikingly present themselves. This group is Oceania, comprehending Polynesia, Micronesia, and Melanesia. We shall, however, leave out of regard New Guinea, one of the largest

---

1) Jenks, pp. 160—163. — 2) Dr. Tönnies, in his review of the first edition of this work, remarks that the last sentences contain a most important qualification of our theory of the connection between slavery and land tenure. Every one does not want to take land into cultivation, though he may do so without any payment. On the other hand, where there are people destitute of land, it is not certain that they serve the landowners and so make slavery superfluous. It may be that, though they own no land, they have other resources to live upon, or that they are not apt to perform such work as is most wanted by the rich, etc.

We are well aware of all this. Yet we think we are justified in concluding that, generally speaking, slavery only exists where there is still free land, *i. e.* free land fit for cultivation. That we admit many exceptions to this rule, will appear from the last paragraphs of this chapter.

islands of the world. The rest of Oceania consists chiefly of small islands.

Slavery in Oceania (with the exception of New Guinea) has never prevailed to any great extent. In the second chapter of Part I it has been shown that slavery, so far as we can know, existed only in the N. W. Solomon Islands, on the Gazelle Peninsula of Neu Pommern, and in New Zealand.

We shall try to account for this fact by showing that on most of the Oceanic islands all land had been appropriated, which led to a state of things inconsistent with slavery as a social system.

In the following paragraphs we shall inquire what our ethnographers have to say about landed property in Oceania and the extent to which the land had been appropriated.

§ 5. *Land tenure in Polynesia.*

In this and the following two paragraphs we shall not mention all particulars of land tenure given by the ethnographers, but only those which may enable us to decide whether all land had been appropriated.

Mahler, speaking of Polynesia and Micronesia generally, remarks that on many islands the burial-places occupied large tracts of land; but this does not prove that there was abundance of land, for these places were hardly ever anything but (according to Penny), "barren points where the wind howls and the sea moans, or rocky caverns in which the waves dash with sullen roar" [1]).

Waltershausen tells us that in Polynesia the cultivated land belonged to the king and nobility, to the exclusion of the labouring classes. The upper classes also owned the fruit-trees, the small coral islets surrounding the larger islands, the lakes, the rivers, and those parts of the sea which extended from the land to the reefs. The untilled land was the property of the tribe and, unless the king forbade it, every one might cut the

---

1) Mahler, pp. 58, 59.

wood growing on it for building houses and canoes; but only the ruling classes might take it into cultivation [1]).

Mariner states that in Tonga property principally consists in plantations, canoes and houses. The plantations are owned by the chiefs and the nobles. Agricultural labourers are very much despised; they serve the chiefs on whom they are dependent. West tells us that "the feudal principle, that the whole country belonged exclusively to the king, regulated the disposal and tenure of lands," and so the lower classes were in a slavelike condition. "Lands were held in fief. The great landlords derived them by hereditary right, in conjunction with their chieftainship, but held them at the will of the supreme ruler." These landlords distributed their lands among their relations and followers [2]).

In Niué or Savage Island, "the land belongs to clans represented by their heads". "At present there is land enough for all, and the junior members of the clan come to the headman whenever they want land to plant upon. Titles can be acquired by cultivation" [3]).

"The land in Samoa" says Turner "is owned alike by the chiefs and these heads of families. The land belonging to each family is well known, and the person who, for the time being holds the title of the family head, has the right to dispose of it. It is the same with the chiefs. There are certain tracts of bush or forest land which belong to them. The uncultivated bush is sometimes claimed by those who own the land on its borders. The lagoon also, as far as the reef, is considered the property of those off whose village it is situated." Von Bülow concludes from the legends and traditions of the Samoans that formerly all the land belonged to the chiefs. But now the land is owned by the families [4]).

Gardiner gives an elaborate account of the regulation of landed property in Rotuma: "No private property in land formerly existed, it was all vested in the *pure* for the time

---

1) Waltershausen, pp. 17, 18. — 2) Mariner, II pp. 162, 160; West, p. 262. — 3) Thomson, Savage Island, p. 143. — 4) Turner, Samoa, pp, 176, 177; Von Bülow, p. 192.

being of the *hoag* [1]); the district generally had rights over it. It usually consisted of four kinds: bush, swamp, coast, and proprietary water in the boat channel; common to the *hoag*, too, were wells and graveyards. Every member of the *hoag* knew its boundaries, which consisted of lines between certain trees or prominent rocks, posts, and even stone walls. In the bush land every *hoag* possessed property; it lay on the slopes of hills and in valleys between at some slight distance from the coast, from which it was separated by a stone wall, running round the whole island. On it taro, yams, bananas, plantains, and a few cocoanut trees were grown for food, while the paths into it and through it were planted with the Tahitian chestnut, the fava tree, and the sagopalm. The Tahitian chestnut and fava trees were favourite boundary marks owing to their size and longevity. Swamp land is only possessed by Noatau, Oinafa, Matusa, and Itomotu. It is low-lying land, on extensive beach sand flats, which exist in these districts. The tide always keeps it wet, percolating through the sand, and in it is grown the *papoi*, or *broka*, against famine. The possession of a good-sized strip always caused and gave to the *hoag* a position of importance; its boundaries were stones at the sides. Coast land lay outside the surrounding wall, to which the *hoag* had a strip from and including the foreshore. On it as near as possible to the coast the house or houses of the *hoag* were placed, while the rest of the land was planted with cocoanuts for drinking purposes. Hifo trees are stated to have been planted formerly to show the boundaries, but they more often now consist of stones or cocoanut trees, the ownership of which is a constant source of dispute. Districts and even villages were sharply marked off by walls down to the beach. All had the right of turning out their pigs on this land, and each *hoag* had to keep in proper repair the parts of the wall adjacent to it. Each had, however, usually an enclosure on its own land for its own pigs, when young. The proprietary water ran from the foreshore to the reef, a continuation of the strip on shore. At Noatau and Matusa, where it is very broad, it was to some extent cross-divided. It consists of a sand flat covered by 10—12 feet of

---

[1] *Hoag* is a large family-group of which the *pure* is the head.

water at high-tide. On it fish of all sorts are caught by traps and various devices, and shell-fish are gathered. As these form no inconsiderable portion of the daily food, indeed the principal animal food, the value of this property was always very considerable. The reef — *i. e.* the part on the outside exposed at the low tide — was the common property of all. It was explained to me that fish, crabs, etc., cannot be cultivated there, owing to the heavy breaking seas, but are sent up by the *atua*, or spirits." "Any land, not being planted, is willingly lent to another *hoag* on condition of two baskets of first-fruits of each patch being brought to the *pure*, but cocoanut trees on the land cannot be touched by the tenant, nor is he entitled to their usufruct. If a *hoag* owns land in one district, but lives in another, first-fruits are always paid to the chief of the district, in which its lands lie. Any encroachment on the land was very vigorously resented, it was usually referred to the district chief to settle, and his decision loyally adhered to." "If he [a man] had planted more cocoanuts than required by the *hoag*, he has the entire usufruct of these trees during his lifetime, quite independently of the apportionment of the land below them for planting." We see that the idea of landownership is most fully developed here. During the 19th century the population has much diminished, and so "most of the *hoag* have far more land than they can cultivate." But formerly it was otherwise. "Examining the remains of planting, it appears as if the whole island, wherever practicable, was at one time tilled. The land, where there is a good and deep soil, is, and was, no doubt tilled regularly from year to year, while the rocky country was planted more or less in rotation with yams and kava. Even on the steepest slopes, there are signs of clearing, the summit alone being left crowned by the hifo. The bottoms of the craters of many hills used to be planted too; in the crater of Sol Satarua, the *lulu* as it is termed, there are still bananas growing, but planted so long ago that the fact that it had a *lulu* at all was almost forgotten" [1]). According to Hale, food was not always abundant on this island; therefore the natives liked to engage themselves as sailors on

---

1) Gardiner, pp. 483—485; 497.

whaling-ships, until they had earned enough to buy a piece
of land [1]). In Hale's time land was evidently not so abundant
as it is now that the population is so rapidly declining.

In Tahiti "every portion of land had its respective owner;
and even the distinct trees on the land had sometimes different
proprietors, and a tree, and the land on which it grew, different owners." What our informant further tells us of the
present state of things as compared with that of earlier times,
shows a remarkable likeness to Gardiner's statement about
Rotuma. Ellis states that "an extent of soil capable of cultivation, and other resources, are adequate to the maintenance
of a population tenfold increased above its present numbers."
But a great depopulation has taken place in the course of
years. "In the bottom of every valley, even to the recesses in
the mountains, on the sides of the inferior hills, and on the
brows of almost every promontory, in each of the islands, monu-
ments of former generations are still met with in great abundance. Stone pavements of their dwellings and court-yards,
foundations of houses, and remains of family temples, are numerous. Occasionally they are found in exposed situations, but
generally amidst thickets of brushwood or groves of trees,
some of which are of the largest growth. All these relics are
of the same kind as those observed among the natives at the
time of their discovery, evidently proving that they belong to
the same race, though to a more populous era of their history.
The stone tools occasionally found near these vestiges of anti-
quity demonstrate the same lamentable fact." According to
Moerenhout "landed properties constituted the principal, or
rather the only wealth of these people; therefore the power of
the chiefs always depended on the quantity and quality of
their lands; moreover, the more people they could support,
the more sure they were of having subjects." This writer does
not, however, enter into many details [2]).

In Hawaii four social ranks existed. The members of the
third rank, according to Ellis, "are generally called *haku aina*,
proprietors of the land." "In the fourth rank may be included

---

1) Hale, p. 105. — 2) Ellis, Pol. Res., III p. 116; I pp. 109, 103; Moerenhout, II
p. 12.

.he small farmers, who rent from ten to twenty or thirty acres of land; the mechanics, ... indeed all the labouring classes, those who attach themselves to some chief or farmer, and labour on his land for their food and clothing, as well as those who cultivate small portions of land for their own advantage." "Sometimes the poor people take a piece of land, on condition of cultivating a given portion for the chief, and the remainder for themselves, making a fresh agreement after every crop." Hale states that formerly there were no landed proprietors; all the land was "the property of the king, and leased by him to inferior chiefs (*hatu aina*, landlords), who underlet it to the people; as the king, however, though absolute in theory, was aware that his power depended very much on the co-operation of the high chiefs, they became, to a certain degree, partakers in his authority." Remy tells us that the land belonged exclusively to the great chiefs, who leased it and received considerable rents. Chamisso and Marcuse equally state that the land belonged to the chiefs [1]).

In Rarotonga, according to Gerland, a man's power depends on the quantity of land he owns. Meinicke states that there are four social classes. The third class is composed of the landed proprietors; the lowest class are those who own no land and live as tenants on the estates of the nobles [2]).

On the Marquesas Islands, according to Gerland, three ranks formerly existed: chiefs, landholders, and the common people. The landholders were the most powerful class; the common people were obliged to pay them a tribute. Yet those who owned most land were not always most respected, and even of the common people some owned land. Meinicke, however, states that the whole of the land is the property of the nobles. Hale, after speaking of the nobles, adds that the rest of the people were the landholders and their relatives and tenants [3]).

In Mangarewa (belonging to the Paumotu group) the nobles

1) Ellis, Pol. Res., IV pp. 412, 413, 416; Hale, p. 36; Remy, p. XLVI; Chamisso, in Kotzebue, p. 149; Marcuse, p. 95. — 2) Waitz-Gerland, VI p. 199; Meinicke, Die Inseln des stillen Oceans, II p. 148. — 3) Waitz-Gerland, VI pp. 216, 217; Meinicke, l. c., p. 254; Hale, p. 36.

were the proprietors of the soil; they often let out their lands to the third class, the common people [1]).

Meinicke tells us that in the Manahiki group the cocoanut trees and the lagoons (for fishing purposes) were private property [2]).

In an article, quoted by Schurtz, it is stated that in the Tokelau group the land belongs exclusively to the nobles. Lister, speaking of Fakaofu or Bowditch Island (in the Tokelau group), says: "Two islets belonged ... to the king. Two others were common property, and the rest were divided up as the property of individuals" [3]). So it seems that in this part of the group there was land which had not yet been appropriated.

In the Abgarris, Marqueen and Tasman groups all the land belongs to the chiefs and the nobles, the common people having no landed property [4]).

Tregear has the following notes on landed property in New Zealand: "Land was held primarily by tribal right; but within this tribal right each free warrior of the tribe had particular rights over some portion. He could not part with the land because it was not his to give or sell, but he had better rights to certain portions than others of his tribe. He would claim by having the bones of his father or grandfather there, or that they once rested there; or by the fact of his navel-string having been cut there; or by his blood having been shed on it; or by having been cursed there; or by having helped in the war party which took the land; or by his wife being owner by descent; or by having been invited by the owners to live there." Thomson states that "all free persons, male and female, constituting the nation were proprietors of the soil." The chiefs were the greatest landholders. "Conquest and occupation gave titles to land. The right of fishing in rivers and sea belonged to the adjoining landed proprietor. Amongst the families of each tribe there are also laws regarding landed property. Thus the cultivation of a portion of forest land renders it the property of those who cleared it, and this right descended from generation to generation .... It was illegal for one family to

---

1) Waitz-Gerland, VI p. 219. — 2) Meinicke, l. c., p. 264. — 3) Tutuila, as quoted by Schurtz, Anfänge des Landbesitzes, p. 355; Lister, p. 54. — 4) Parkinson, Dreissig Jahre, p. 535.

plant in another's clearing without permission". "The independence and social happiness of the people were chiefly caused by cultivating their own lands." According to Taylor, each tribe had its own district; "each member can cultivate any portion of it he thinks fit, if unoccupied, or if it has not been previously cultivated by another." Polack says: "Possession is obtained by planting a portion (however small) of the soil, and reaping the same" [1]).

On Easter Island, according to Geiseler, every piece of land has its own name and its owner. The natives attach much value to landed property [2]).

We see that on most Polynesian islands all land has, or had been appropriated. Regarding Rotuma, Tahiti and Easter Island this is explicitly stated; and the same must be the case in Tonga, Hawaii, Rarotonga, the Marquesas Islands, Mangarewa, part of the Tokelau group, and the Abgarris, Marqueen and Tasman groups, where classes destitute of land are found. In Manahiki property in land was strongly developed; but whether there was still free land is not clear. In Samoa there was still unappropriated bush land, though this was already "sometimes claimed by those who own the land on its borders." In New Zealand clearing was still a *modus acquirendi,* which proves that all land had not yet been appropriated. Equally on Savage Island titles can be acquired by cultivation.

§ 6. *Land tenure in Micronesia.*

Kubary tells us that the population of Ebon, and of the whole Rallik group (in the Marshall Islands), consists of four ranks. "The common people are called *armĳ kajur* and form the greater part of the subjects. They have no property, except the land allotted to them by the chief, who can take it from them at his pleasure. Every week they have, each of them, to provide the chief with prepared food, the quantity and quality of which are determined. The next class are the *leotakatak,*

---

1) Tregear, p. 106; Thomson, New Zealand, I pp. 96, 97, 98; Taylor, p. 355; Polack, II p. 69. — 2) Geiseler, p. 42.

who hold their property by hereditary right and not from the chief. The chief cannot take the property of these men unless he kills them first." "The punishments inflicted by the chiefs in former times consisted most often in capital punishment, and more rarely, in less serious cases, in confiscation of land and house" [1]).

Several other writers affirm that in the Marshall group the upper classes are the sole proprietors of the soil and the common people are destitute of land [2]).

Regarding the isle of Nauru we are told that not only every inch of land and every palm, but even the reefs and the sea washing them, are held as property [3]).

On the Pelau Islands the right of disposing of the land of the tribe vests in the *obokúl* (chief of a family-group); but he cannot alienate any land without the consent of his nephews. However, a regular agriculture does not exist, and most of the land remains untilled; therefore the opposition of the nephews generally bears a formal character; they only aim at extorting a present from the *obokúl*. The *obokúl* divides the land among the members of the tribe for cultivation. He may also cede pieces of land to aliens for use without payment; such persons then enter into the position of *kaukáth, i. e.* they are considered as related to the tribe without possessing the same rights, they occasionally provide the *obokúl* with food, and help him in his work. In another place our informant states that there is not often reason for disputes about land, as the population is scarce and large tracts of land are uncultivated [4]).

On the Mortlock Islands the chief of each tribe has an unlimited right to dispose of the land belonging to the tribe. He divides it among the heads of families on condition of their paying a tribute in kind. The latter assign to each member of their groups a piece of land for cultivation. Most land is divided up between the several *keys* (family-groups); the land which is not yet occupied is the property of the principal *key* and thus more directly than the rest at the disposal of the chief [5]).

---

1) Kubary, Die Ebongruppe, pp. 36, 37. — 2) Senfft, in Steinmetz's Rechtsverhältnisse, pp. 448, 452; Steinbach, p. 297; Krämer, Hawaii, etc., pp. 430, 431. — 3) Jung, p. 68. — 4) Kubary, Soc. Einr. der Pelauer, pp. 47, 48; Kubary, Die Verbrechen, p. 85. — 5) Kubary, Mortlock-Inseln, p. 253.

On the isle of Kusaie twelve principal chiefs own all the land; but the chiefs of the second rank administer and cultivate it for them. The common people are obliged to pay a tribute to the chiefs and serve them. The highest mountains are planted up to their summits with bananas, taro, sugarcane, etc [1].

On the Eastern Caroline Islands the land belongs exclusively to the two upper classes; the third class are attached to the soil on which they live [2]).

Hale states that in Ponape or Ascension Island there are three classes. All the land belongs to the two upper classes. The estates are never alienated and pass only by succession [3]).

Gerland tells us that on the Marianne Islands the nobles were hereditary owners of the whole of the land [4]).

As to the Kingsmill Islands, the particulars given bij Wilkes and Parkinson, as quoted in the second chapter of Part I [5] sufficiently prove that all land had been appropriated. According to Wilkes "any one who owns land can always call upon others to provide him with a house, canoe, and the necessaries of life; but one who has none is considered as a slave, and can hold no property whatever." Hale tells us that "the *katoka* are persons not originally of noble birth, who either by the favour of their chief or by good fortune in war, have acquired land and with it freedom" [6]). If in Wilkes' statement we read "proletarian" instead of "slave," and take Hale's "freedom" in an economic, not in a legal sense, we find that here too the lowest class were destitute of landed property.

The conclusion is that on most of the islands of Micronesia all land has been appropriated, most often by the upper classes to the exclusion of the lower. In Pelau, though a vast amount of land is actually out of tillage, the regulation of landed property related by Kubary proves that all land is held as property. Here, as well as in Rotuma and Tahiti, we have to deal with the effects of the depopulation that has taken place in Oceania. In Mortlock there seems to be free land; but Kubary's account is not very clear.

---

1) Waitz-Gerland, V, 2 pp. 120, 121, 78. — 2) Ibid., p. 118. — 3) Hale, p. 83. — 4) Waitz-Gerland, l. c., p. 114. — 5) See above, pp. 107—109. — 6) Wilkes, p. 96; Hale, p. 102.

§ 7. *Land tenure in Melanesia.*

Codrington, in his article "On social regulations in Melanesia," remarks that his observations "are limited to the Northern New Hebrides, the Banks Islands, the Santa Cruz Group, and the South-eastern Solomon Islands" [1]. Of land tenure he says: "Land is everywhere divided into (1) the Town, (2) the Gardens, (3) the Bush. Of these the two first are held as property, the third is unappropriated.... Everywhere, or almost everywhere, the abundance of land makes it of little value. If an individual reclaims for himself a piece of bush land, it becomes his own" [2].

Somerville, speaking of New Georgia (one of the central Solomon Islands, and therefore not included in Codrington's description) remarks: "Property seems to be well recognised: every one of the myriad islets of the great eastern lagoon has its understood owner, no matter if cocoanuts be growing there or not. Groves of cocoanut trees are well protected by *hopes*, as before described, as are also taro patches. Hunting rights over opossums on a man's property are also protected by *hopes*" [3]. Ribbe, however, states that in the New Georgia group, uncultivated land, *i. e.* bush and forest, has no owner, except the parts planted with sago trees and fruit trees. Every one may clear and cultivate this land and so acquire a right of property [4].

On the Shortland Islands, near Bougainville (N. W. Solomon Islands), landed property in the European sense does not exist. Everybody has the right to take a part of the wood into cultivation. By doing so, he acquires a right of property, but only for so long as he has the land in use [5].

Woodford describes the regulation of landed property in the Solomon Islands in general in the following terms: "As to the system of land tenure among them, I believe that to land, *per se,* they attach but little value. Any individual of the tribe appears to be able to select at will a piece of land from the

---

1) Codrington, Soc. Reg., p. 306; see also Codrington, The Melanesians, pp. 59, 60. —
2) Codrington, Soc. Reg., pp. 311, 312. — 3) Somerville, New Georgia, p. 404. —
4) Ribbe, p. 272. — 5) Ribbe, p. 116.

forest, which he clears, fences in, and upon it rears his crop
of yams or bananas. After the crops are taken off, the land
is allowed to relapse again to forest. When, however, a native
plants cocoanuts his property appears to be in the trees themselves, apart altogether from any idea of ownership in the land
upon which they are planted. I do not think that any objection
would be raised to another native utilizing the ground upon
which the cocoanuts were planted for other crops so long as
the trees themselves were in no way damaged or interfered
with. Property in cocoanuts appears to pass, upon a man's death,
to his heirs" [1]).

Of land tenure on the isle of Aneityum, in the New Hebrides, Inglis says: "There is neither a town nor a village in
the whole Island. The system of cottage farming is in a state of
full development there. There is no large proprietor, no powerful
or wealthy chief; every man sits proprietor of his own cottage,
his own garden, and his own cultivated patches — you could
not call them fields. The waste lands and the forests, to the
summits of the mountains, belong to the tribe. They are a
kind of crown lands, but what each man cultivates belongs to
himself" [2]).

In New Caledonia, according to Brainne, a noble's authority
depends on the range of cultivated grounds he owns, and one
who possesses large tracts of cultivated land and large plantations of cocoanut trees is called a great chief. Glaumont tells
us that "property is acquired by purchase or exchange. It
may also be acquired by labour. Thus uncultivated grounds
belong to the tribe, are so to speak common property; but if
a Kanaka clears and cultivates a portion of this bush land it
passes into his property. Property is held sacred (viz. in time
of peace); the chief himself, however powerful, would not dare
to take away the field of taros or ignames from the least of
his subjects." Lambert tells us that individual property in land
is highly developed. The forest land, however, has no owner;
every one may take a portion of it into cultivation and by
doing so acquire a right of property. Meinicke says: "Each
tribe possesses a separate territory in which the land fit for

---

1) Woodford, pp. 32, 33. — 2) Inglis, p. 24.

cultivation is the individual property of the chiefs and nobles, whereas the rest is at the disposal of all." According to Rochas there are two ranks: nobles and common people; but the latter enjoy a rather independent position and always own some land. The rights of property in land are highly respected, even by the chiefs [1].

Williams, describing Fiji, speaks of a feudal government; but he adds that the ancient divisions of landed property are much respected. Seemann states that the "real power of the state resides in the landholders or gentry"; and Hale tells us that the members of the lowest class "work for the chiefs and landholders and are supported by them." The fullest account of land tenure in Fiji is given by Fison. The lands are of three kinds. "1. The *Yavu* or Town-lot; 2. The *Qele*, or Arable Land; and 3. the *Veikau*, or Forest." "The town-lots and the arable lands are divided among the *taukei* (landowners), while the forest lands are held in common by them. Arable land also, which is not in actual use, is in some places common to a certain extent." "The land is vested in — or, at any rate, is held by — certain joint tribal owners who have a common descent. These are called the *Taukei ni vanua* or owners of the land .... Not all the people are landowners." Fison then speaks of some classes destitute of land, of whom it is not quite clear whether they are tenants or serfs. But the following statement of his clearly shows that all land has been appropriated: "In addition to the *koro* [villages] already mentioned, there are others inhabited by tribes who have either migrated from their own lands owing to disagreement with their kinsfolk, or have been driven thence by war. These emigrants beg land from a *taukei* tribe, and settle down upon it. They are not landowners where they are now living, but it does not follow that they are *kaisi* [base-born men, who are very much despised]. If they were *taukei* in their own land they cannot be placed on the level of the people without a father." They pay "rent of produce and service .... Tribes such as these are tenants at will, and the land may be taken from them whenever it

---

1) Brainne, p. 241; Glaumont, p. 75; Lambert, pp. 82, 85; Meinicke, Die Inseln des stillen Oceans, I p. 230; Rochas, pp. 245, 262.

may be required. How long soever their occupation may continue, it does not establish a title. The descendants of the *taukei* can always resume the lands, upon giving formal notice, and presenting some property or other, which is called "the falling back of the soil" [1]. These emigrants are neither slaves nor serfs, but destitute of land; if there were free land fit for cultivation, they would appropriate it instead of becoming tenants at will.

On the Gazelle Peninsula of Neu Pommern, according to Pfeil, uncultivated land as such is not claimed by any one as his property. When a native wants land, he takes some piece which is not in use, without having to ask leave of anybody. Hahl also states that in the Northern part of the Gazelle Peninsula grass or forest land as a rule is at the disposal of whoever wishes to cultivate it. Equally among the Baining of the Gazelle Peninsula, as Parkinson tells us, the land is regarded as private property as long as it is being cultivated [2].

In the Nissan Islands poverty is unknown, as there is an abundance of free land. Private property in land is acquired by taking it into cultivation. Land is sold and leased [3].

Haddon, in his article on the Western Tribes of Torres Straits, remarks: "I have no precise information as to land laws, but I believe that the whole of the land is divided up into properties, certainly the arable land is, the chief sharing like anyone else. There is no one person or class of landowners who possess land to the total exclusion of anyone else. Title to land is derived from inheritance, gift or purchase. I never heard of any means of conveyance" [4].

Hunt, describing the Murray Islands, says: "The chiefs held only their own hereditary lands, but the first fruits of all cultivated lands were presented to them as their share.... Any dispute about land would be settled by the old men who would meet and discuss the point in dispute and then pronounce their decision. Land was never sold, but could be leased, when,

---

1) Williams, pp. 18, 22; Seemann, p. 233; Hale, p. 59; Fison, Land tenure in Fiji, pp. 336, 338, 343. — 2) Pfeil, p. 69; Hahl, p. 82; Parkinson, Dreissig Jahre, p. 158. — 3) Sorge, in Steinmetz's Rechtsverhältnisse, pp. 401, 422. — 4) Haddon, p. 334.

if used for planting, a share in the first fruits would be paid to the owner" [1]).

From the foregoing it appears that in many parts of Melanesia clearing is a *modus acquirendi*, viz. in the Solomon Islands, Northern New Hebrides, Banks Islands, Santa Cruz Group, New Caledonia, Gazelle Peninsula of Neu Pommern and Nissan Islands. Yet the rights of landowners are recognized everywhere in these islands. Here, as Ricardo would say, land of the second degree of fertility has already been taken into cultivation, and so rent has commenced on that of the first; but there is still free land. In Aneityum, too, there seems to be land not yet appropriated. In Fiji people destitute of land are found. Among the Western tribes of Torres Straits all arable land is divided up into properties, as Haddon tells us; but whether the rest of the land is still free is not quite clear. With regard to the Murray Islands we cannot arrive at any definite conclusion.

Generally speaking we may conclude that in Polynesia and Micronesia all land has been appropriated, whereas in the Melanesian Islands free land still exists.

We see further that not only the arable land is held as property, but often also the fruit-trees, lakes and streams, the shore and the lagoon as far as the reef. On most Polynesian and Micronesian islands whatever portion of land or water can yield any profit has been appropriated.

§ 8. *Landlords, tenants and labourers in Oceania.*

It appears from the foregoing paragraphs that in those islands where all land has been appropriated, there are nearly always found people destitute of land. The only exceptions are Rotuma and Pelau. Gardiner, in his very minute article on Rotuma, makes no mention of social ranks; and Kubary, as we have already seen in the second chapter of Part I, states that "among the Pelau islanders there is no question of a division of the people into ranks or classes." But Semper, as has also been shown in the same chapter, speaks of a despised

---

1) Hunt, p. 7.

working class [1]). Regarding the social classes on Easter Island we are not sufficiently informed.

Another state of things would not be inconceivable. It were quite possible that every inhabitant had appropriated a portion of the land, nothing of it remaining unclaimed. Yet it is easy to understand that, when all land has become individual property, a class of people destitute of land is likely soon to arise. In large families the portions falling to each of the children will often become too small to live upon. And where it is customary to buy and sell land, there may be improvident people who squander the land that was to afford them subsistence. But the principal cause probably is the arbitrary conduct of the chiefs and other men of power who appropriate the land of their enemies, and even, under some pretext, that belonging to their own subjects.

In Tahiti the chiefs had "a desire for war, as a means of enlarging their territory, and augmenting their power" [2]).

Regarding Hawaii Ellis tells us: "When Tamehameha had subdued the greater part of the islands, he distributed them among his favourite chiefs and warriors, on condition of their rendering him, not only military service, but a certain proportion of the produce of their lands, This also appears to have been their ancient practice on similar occasions, as the *hoopahora* or *papahora*, division of land among the *ranakira* or victors, invariably followed the conquest of a district or island". Wilkes says: "Any chieftain, who could collect a sufficient number of followers to conquer a district, or an island, and had succeeded in his object, proceeded to divide the spoils, or "cut up the land", as the natives termed it. The king, or principal chief, made his choice from the best of the lands. Afterwards the remaining part of the territory was distributed among the leaders, and these again subdivided their shares to others, who became vassals, owing fealty to the sovereigns of the fee. The king placed some of his own particular servants on his portion as his agents, to superintend the cultivation. The original occupants who were on the land, usually remained

---

1) See above, p. 107. In Tahiti there were also people destitute of land, of whom we shall have to speak in this paragraph. — 2) Ellis, Pol. Res., I p. 107.

under their new conqueror, and by them the lands were cultivated, and rent or taxes paid." Remy equally states that a victorious chief gave the lands of the conquered party to his followers [1]).

On Niué (Savage Island), "in fighting times the braves (*toa*) ignored all rights and seized upon any land that they were strong enough to hold" [2]).

On Nauru the chief had the right to keep all the land his tribe had conquered for himself or distribute it among the other chiefs of the tribe [3]).

In the Kingsmill Islands the *katoka* are persons who "either by the favour of their chief or by good fortune in war, have acquired land" [4]). Hence it appears that, here too, the victors used to occupy the lands of the conquered.

In Fiji, according to Waterhouse, one of the motives of war was the desire for land. Williams also states that each government "seeks aggrandizement at the expense of the rest" by means of conquest, and he adds that the inhabitants of conquered districts were reduced to an abject servitude. According to Wilkes, "the victorious party often requires the conquered to yield the right of soil". Fison says: "It is certain that in former days, when population seems to have been on the increase . . . . tribes were dispossessed of their lands by other tribes who took them into their occupation, and are the *tauke* of the present day" [5]).

We have seen in § 5 that a New Zealander sometimes claimed land "by having helped in the war party which took the land." According to Ellis, a desire to enlarge their territory led to frequent wars. Thomson tells us: "Sometimes whole tribes became nominally slaves, although permitted to live at their usual places of residence, on the condition of catching eels and preparing food for their conquerors at certain seasons" [6]).

In New Caledonia the inhabitants of conquered districts have

---

1) Ibid., IV p. 414; Wilkes, IV p. 36; Remy, p. 155. — 2) Thomson, Savage Island, p. 143. — 3) Jung, p. 67. — 4) Hale, p. 102. — 5) Waterhouse, p. 316; Williams, pp. 43, 54; Wilkes, III p. 85; Fison, Land tenure in Fiji, p. 343. — 6) Ellis, Pol. Res., III pag. 360; Thomson, New-Zealand, p. 148.

to pay a tribute to the conqueror, but generally continue living under their own chiefs [1]).

Von Bülow states that in Samoa conquered lands become the private property of the victorious chief [2]).

It appears that this conquering of land does not always create a class destitute of land; sometimes the inhabitants have only to pay a tribute. But where individuals belonging to the victorious tribe receive portions of the conquered land allotted to them, as in New Zealand and the Kingsmill Islands, or where, as in Samoa, the land becomes the private property of the conquering chief, the original owners consequently are deprived of their property.

It also occurs that within the tribe the land is taken away from its owner.

Williams states that in Fiji an adulterer may be deprived of his land as a punishment; and Fison tells us that the chiefs have overridden the ancient customs regarding land tenure [3]).

In Tahiti, those who resisted the king's authority were banished and deprived of their lands. "Should the offender have been guilty of disobedience to the just demands of the king, though the lands might be his hereditary property, he must leave them, and become, as the people expressed it, a "wanderer upon the road" [4]).

In Niué, widows and orphans "are frequently robbed of the land inherited from their dead husbands and fathers" [5]).

In Ebon, confiscation of land by the chief was formerly a mode of punishment [6]).

On the Kingsmill Islands, if a noble girl were to have connection with a man of the middle class, she would lose her landed property [7]).

On Nauru, according to Krämer, a murderer in most cases has to yield his land to the parents of his victim. Jung tells us that formerly the chiefs often had to settle disputes about land among their subjects. They then generally took the land from the quarelling parties and regarded it as their own [8]).

---

1) Rochas, p. 243. — 2) Von Bülow, p. 193. — 3) Williams, p. 29; Fison, l. c, p. 345; see also Wilkes, III p. 98. — 4) Ellis, Pol. Res., III p. 122. — 5) Thomson, Savage Island p. 143. — 6) See above, p. 322. — 7) Krämer, Hawaii, etc., p. 334. — 8) Ibid, p. 451; Jung, p. 65.

Among the Melanesians described by Codrington the chiefs "often use their power to drive away the owners of gardens they desire to occupy" [1]).

Where land is so highly valued, and wealth and power depend upon the possession of it, the chiefs and other men of power will be inclined to appropriate as much of it as possible. This is not always easy, and sometimes, in democratically organized societies, hardly practicable; but we may be sure that it will be done on the very first opportunity. This is strikingly proved by what Gardiner tells us of Rotuma: "Since the introduction of missionaries, too, much land has been seized by the chiefs, who, as a rule, in each district were its missionaries, as fines for the fornications of individuals. A certain amount of cocoanut oil was then given by the chiefs to the Wesleyan Mission, apparently in payment for their support. The mission in the name of which it was done, though generally without the knowledge of the white teachers, was so powerful that the *hoag* had no redress." Formerly individual rights to land in Rotuma were highly respected: "The victorious side obtained no territorial aggrandisement, as it was to the common interest of all to maintain the integrity of the land, and the victors might on some future occasion be themselves in the positon of the vanquished" [2]). We may suppose that originally the chiefs were not powerful enough to appropriate land belonging to others; but the additional power that the new religion gave them enabled them to seize the lands of their subjects, and they immediately availed themselves of this opportunity.

A similar change has taken place in Samoa. In Turner's time Samoan government had "more of the patriarchal and democratic in it, than of the monarchical." Von Bülow, writing several years later than Turner, states that some chiefs have lately introduced what he calls serfdom. In the villages where this state of things exists the inhabitants live on land belonging to the chief. They pay no rent, but are obliged to stand by the chief in war and peace. They are personnally free and have the right to emigrate, but own no land [3]).

---

1) Codrington, Soc. Reg., p. 311. — 2) Gardiner, pp. 485, 470. — 3) Turner, Samoa, p. 173; Von Bülow, p. 194.

We can now perfectly understand why people destitute of land are found in so many of these islands. And as most often not only the arable land, but fruit-trees, lakes, streams, and the sea adjoining the land are individual property, these people are entirely at the mercy of the landowners. We shall see that they have to perform the drudgery for the landlords, and are sometimes heavily oppressed.

In Tonga, the lowest class were the *tooas*. "The *tooas* can be divided into three categories. A few of them are warriors and form part of the retinue of the chiefs; some are professed cooks in the service of the superior or inferior chiefs; others, and these form the majority, till the soil. The latter are found all over the country and have no other employment" [1]).

"The institutions of Niué seem always to have been republican" says B. Thomson [2]).

In Samoa, in Turner's time, a democratic and even communistic *régime* prevailed. Speaking of the chief, Turner says: "With a few exceptions, he moves about, and shares in everyday employments, just like a common man. He goes out with the fishing party, works in his plantations, helps at house-building, and lends a hand at the native oven." The Samoans were very hospitable: "In addition to their own individual wants, their hospitable custom in supplying, without money and without stint, the wants of visitors from all parts of the group, was a great drain on their plantations." Hale states that "the common people are in general the relatives and dependents of the *tulafales* [landlords] and have no direct influence in the government" [3]). We have seen that recently a class of people destitute of land has been created by some chiefs; but their lot does not seem to be a hard one.

Gardiner, in his description of Rotuma, makes no mention of social classes.

In Tahiti, the lowest class were the *manahune*, including, besides the *titi* or slaves, "the *teuteu* or servants of the chiefs; all who were destitute of any land, and ignorant of the rude

1) Mariner, II p. 350. — 2) Thomson, Savage Island, p. 138. — 3) Turner, Samoa, pp. 175, 171; Hale, p. 28.

arts of carpentering, building, etc., which are respected among
them, and such as were reduced to a state of dependence
upon those in higher stations." Speaking of the great landholders, our informant says: "Possessing at all times the most
ample stores of native provisions, the number of their dependents,
or retainers, was great. The destitute and thoughtless readily
attached themselves to their establishments, for the purpose of
securing the means of subsistence without care or apprehension
of want." That the landholders enjoyed great consideration is
also proved by Wilkes's remark, that the chiefs "find in their
possession [of land] an acknowledged right to rank and
respectability" [1]).

In Hawaii, four social ranks existed. The members of the third
rank held land, "cultivating it either by their own dependents
and domestics, or letting it out in small allotments to tenants. . . .
In the fourth rank may be included the small farmers, who
rent from ten to twenty or thirty acres of land; the mechanics,
namely, canoe and house builders, fishermen, musicians, and
dancers; indeed, all the labouring classes, those who attach
themselves to some chief or farmer, and labour on his land
for their food and clothing, as well as those who cultivate
small portions of land for their own advantage." "Sometimes
the poor people take a piece of land, on condition of cultivating
a given portion for the chief, and the remainder for themselves,
making a fresh agreement after every crop. In addition to
the above demands, the common people are in general obliged
to labour, if required, part of two days out of seven, in
cultivating farms, building houses, etc. for their landlord. A
time is usually appointed for receiving the rent, when the
people repair to the governor's with what they have to pay.
If the required amount is furnished, they return, and, as they
express it (*komo hou*), enter again on their land. But if unable
to pay the required sum, and their landlords are dissatisfied
with the presents they have received, or think the tenants have
neglected their farm, they are forbidden to return, and the
land is offered to another. When, however, the produce brought
is nearly equal to the required rent, and the chiefs think the

---

1) Ellis, Pol. Res., III pp. 96—98; Wilkes, II p. 22.

occupants have exerted themselves to procure it, they remit the deficiency, and allow them to return" [1]). This is quite the reverse of what occurs in slave countries. The slave or serf is prevented from escaping and compelled to remain with his master; the Hawaiian tenant, if the landlord is dissatisfied with the produce brought, is forbidden to return to the land of his employer. In the same sense, Wilkes remarks: "What appears most extraordinary, this bond [*i. e.* the bond between landlord and tenant] was more often severed by the superiors than by their vassals" [2]).

In Rarotonga, the lowest class are the *unga* or servants who have to cultivate the lands of the nobles, build their houses and canoes, make nets for them, pay them tributes, and in general obey all their demands [3]).

In the Marquesas Islands, the *kikinos* (common people) were servants and soldiers of the chiefs. They were always free to leave their employers. The chief, in his turn, if he was not satisfied with a servant, might expel him from his domain [4]). Here again we may mark the great difference between the lower classes of Polynesia and slaves; for the latter are not expelled by way of punishment, but on the contrary forced to remain with their masters.

In Mangarewa, as has been noticed, the whole of the land belonged to the nobility, who often leased their lands to the third class, the common people [5]).

In the Tokelau group, the common people till the lands of the nobles for a payment in kind. A labourer has the right to leave his employer and go into another man's service [6]).

In the Abgarris, Marqueen and Tasman groups, the common people own no land; they serve the members of the upper classes and form their retinue; in reward they are provided with cocoanuts and other fruits and allowed to fish on the reef and in the lagoon [7]).

In New Zealand, as has been shown in § 5, every freeman owned land. Accordingly, we find only a beginning of the

---

I) Ellis, Pol. Res., IV pp. 413, 416, 417. — 2) Wilkes, IV p. 37. — 3) Waitz-Gerland, VI p. 199. — 4) Radiguet, p. 156. — 5) See above, p. 319. — 6) Tutuila, in Schurtz, Anfänge des Landbesitzes, p. 355. — 7) Parkinson, Dreissig Jahre, p. 535.

formation af a class of free labourers. Polack states that "the poorest classes work as freedmen on the farms of their richer relatives" [1]).

On Easter Island, the king formerly held a despotic sway over the common people, *i. e.* those who did not belong to the nobility [2]).

Gerland remarks that the two principal classes, nobles and common people, were nowhere in Polynesia less strictly separated than in Samoa and New Zealand. This strikingly shows that the appropriation of the land was really the basis of Polynesian aristocracy; for Samoa and New Zealand, as we have found, were almost the only Polynesian groups in which there was still free land [3]).

Regarding the condition of the common people in Micronesia we have already mentioned many particulars in § 7 of the second chapter of Part I in inquiring whether they were to be regarded as slaves, and in § 6 of this chapter in order to prove that all land had been appropriated. We shall briefly repeat here what bears on their condition and the work imposed upon them, adding such details as have not yet been mentioned.

Steinbach states that in the Marshall Islands neither the lowest nor the next higher class owns land, "but they are allowed to grow as much produce or catch as much fish as is necessary for their sustenance. They have to perform certain services for the chiefs, such as the cutting of *copra*". And Krämer tells us that the common people are a subjected class without property. The kings have an absolute rule over the people and many islands are their exclusive property. They may take as many women as they like from among the people as wives or concubines. The common man has only one wife and even this one his superiors may take away at their pleasure [4]).

On Nauru, the lower classes (sometimes called "serfs" or "slaves" by the authors) are in the service of the chiefs and nobles.

In Ebon, the common people live on land allotted to them

---

1) Polack, II p. 156. — 2) Geiseler, p. 41. — 3) Waitz-Gerland, VI p. 165. — 4) Steinbach, p. 297; Krämer, Hawaii, etc., pp. 430, 431.

by the chief who can take it from them at his pleasure. Every week they have, each of them, to provide the chief with a fixed quantity of food.

In Mortlock, according to Kubary, social ranks do not exist.

On the isle of Kusaie the chiefs have unlimited power. The common people are obliged to build houses and canoes for them and till their lands; the chiefs may always seize the goods and command the services of the people; the cocoanuts, which are rare, are for the chiefs alone; they receive a certain proportion of all the fish that is caught [1]).

In Yap, the lowest class (whom Gräffe wrongly calls slaves) are obliged daily to provide the upper classes with agricultural produce, and whenever the chiefs require it to aid in constructing houses and canoes. Whatever they possess, even to their wives and daughters, may at any time be required by the upper classes. Yet all labour is not exclusively incumbent on them. They are only bound to definite taxes, viz. to a tribute of victuals, and of mats and other materials for housebuilding; and their "slave-state" consists rather in a low and dependent condition than in being taxed with labour.

On the Marianne Islands there were three classes: nobles, semi-nobles, and common people. The common people were strictly separated from the nobles and entirely subjected to them. They were not allowed to navigate or fish or take part in any other pursuit followed by the nobles. Their principal occupations were tilling the soil, constructing roads, building canoe-houses, making nets, carrying ammunition in war, cooking rice, roots, etc. As they were forbidden to use canoes and fishing implements, the only fish they could procure were eels, which the nobles disdained; and even these they might only catch with the hand, not by means of nets or fish-hooks [2]).

In Pelau, according to Kubary, there are no social classes; but the wants of the chiefs are generally provided for by the work of dependent relatives, who are treated as adopted children and may at any time leave their employers. Semper, however, speaks of a despised working class.

On the Kingsmill Islands, according to Parkinson, there are

---

1) Waitz-Gerland, V, 2, p. 121. — 2) Ibid., p. 112.

two subjected classes. One is the class of the *te torre*, who live as vassals on the lands of the great landholders; they get a small piece of land for their own use; they must provide their lord with men when at war, and bring him the number of cocoanuts he desires, and what he needs for his household. The lowest class are the *te bei* or *kaungo*. They have no property, no land to live upon; they live with the great landholders by whom they are maintained; they on their part must work for their lords, *i. e.* fish, prepare food, etc. The lord, by giving them a piece of land, can raise them to the class of the *te torre*. These two classes have no voice in government matters; they follow their lord without grumbling; his will is their will; an offence against the lord is regarded by them as a personal offence, and avenged as such. Generally no one marries outside his class. In ordinary life there is no difference between master and vassal; they drink, dance, and play together; they wear the same kind of dress.

We shall inquire now what is the condition of the lower classes in Melanesia.

, Rochas states that in New Caledonia the common people enjoy a rather independent position; they have to perform some services for the chiefs, which chiefly consist in cultivating their lands; but they always own a piece of land themselves. They are, however, sometimes killed by the upper chiefs for cannibal purposes. Glaumont enumerates the following classes: sorcerers, warriors, common people, slaves. But he adds that the chief himself, however powerful, would not dare to take away the field of taros or ignames belonging to the least of his subjects. According to Brainne, there are two classes: numerous chiefs of various kinds, and serfs, over whom the former, especially the superior chiefs, have the right of life and death. Lambert, a good authority, remarks that the only division of the people is that between the chiefs and their relatives and the rest of the population, and observes that those writers are wrong who speak of a class of nobles. The chief is not allowed to dispose of the property of his subjects [1]. So it seems that the natives here are rather democratically organized.

In Fiji, according to Williams, the lower classes were for-

1) Rochas, pp. 245, 246; Glaumont, pp. 74, 75; Brainne, p. 246; Lambert, pp. 79, 82, 83.

merly heavily oppressed. The chiefs looked upon them as their property, and took away their goods and often even their lives; this was considered "chief-like." "Subjects" says Williams "do not pay rent for their land, but a kind of tax on all their produce, beside giving their labour occasionally in peace, and their service, when needed, in war, for the benefit of the king or their own chief." Waterhouse states that many poor men could not procure a wife; they then borrowed one from a chief, and so became his retainers. Fison, speaking of the inhabitants of certain villages, says: "These are of the lowest rank, or rather of no rank at all. They are *kaisi*, the descendants of "children without a father." They are *vakatau ni were* (husbandmen), but they are not yeomen like the *taukei*. Neither the lands they cultivate, nor the town lots on which they dwell are their own. They are not even tenants. They are hereditary bondsmen, *adscripti glebae*, whose business it is to raise food for their masters. Their lords may oppress them, and they have no redress. In times of peace they must work for them and in war time they must fight for them to the death". According to Wilkes, "in each tribe great and marked distinctions of rank exist. The classes which are readily distinguished are as follows: 1. kings; 2. chiefs; 3. warriors; 4. landholders (*matanivanua*); 5. slaves (*kai-si*)." In another passage he speaks of "the kai-si or common people". In Jackson's narrative, quoted above, mention is also made of these *kai-si* or inhabitants of "slave lands". [1]).

Codrington remarks: "In the native view of mankind, almost everywhere in the islands which are here under consideration [Solomon Islands, Santa Cruz Group, Banks' Islands, and New Hebrides], nothing seems more fundamental than the division of the people into two or more classes, which are exogamous, and in which descent is counted through the mother .... Generally speaking, it may be said that to a Melanesian man all women, of his own generation at least, are either sisters or wives, to the Melanesian woman all men are either brothers or husbands" [2]) This seems to be sufficient proof that a subjected and despised lowest class does not exist; else the natives would not all be "brothers" and "sisters".

---

1) Williams, pp. 23, 90, 157, 39, 40; Waterhouse, p. 311; Fison, Land tenure in Fiji, p. 342; Wilkes, III pp. 81, 108; see above, pp. 91, 92. — 2) Codrington, The Melanesians, pp. 21, 22.

This conclusion is strengthened by consulting some other writers.

Guppy, describing the Solomon Islands, makes no mention of social ranks. Elton states that the chiefs have little power [1]. Nor have we found in any of the other writers anything tending to prove that the common people are oppressed.

Regarding the New Hebrides, Hagen and Pineau, after speaking of the chiefs, state that the next class are the warriors, which rank can be obtained by a payment of pigs. They make no mention of a despised or oppressed working class. Inglis, as we have seen above, states that in the isle of Aneityum "there is no large proprietor, no powerful or wealthy chief; every man sits proprietor of his own cottage, his own garden, and his own cultivated patches." Turner, speaking of the isle of Tana, says: "The affairs of this little community are regulated by the chiefs and the heads of families"; and in Eromanga, according to the same writer, the chiefs "were numerous, but not powerful". According to Ribbe, in the Shortland Islands (near Bougainville), the chiefs have little power [2]. From all this we may safely conclude that social life in the New Hebrides is democratically organized.

In the Gazelle Peninsula of Neu Pommern wealth gives power; but there is no social or political difference between the rich and the poor [3].

In the Nissan Islands poverty is unknown, as there is an abundance of free land fit for cultivation. Social classes do not exist. There is no nobility, unless the chief and his relatives be regarded as such [4].

Parkinson states that among the Moanus of the Admiralty Islands the power of the chiefs is considerable [5]. We do not, however, hear of a subjection of the common people by the upper classes.

Haddon, speaking of the Western Tribes of Torres Straits, says: "Each household is practically self-sufficient. So far as I could gather there was no division of labour as between man and man, every man made his garden, fished and fought" [6].

---

1) Elton, p. 98. — 2) Hagen and Pineau, p. 335; Turner, Samoa, pp. 315, 328; Ribbe, p. 138. — 3) Hahl, p. 77. — 4) Sorge, in Steinmetz's Rechtsverhältnisse, pp. 401, 414. — 5) Parkinson, Dreissig Jahre, p. 396. — 6) Haddon, p. 342.

Hunt, in his description of the Murray Islands, makes no mention of social ranks.

Generally speaking, we may conclude that in Polynesia and Micronesia there are lower classes destitute of land and entirely at the mercy of the landholders, whereas in Melanesia such classes do not exist. This agrees with our former conclusion, that in the two first-named geographical districts all land has, or had been appropriated, which is not the case in Melanesia. And if we consider the single groups of islands, we find that wherever in Polynesia there is still free land (Samoa, New Zealand), a more or less democratic *régime* prevails, and where in Melanesia all land has been appropriated (Fiji) there is a subjected lower class. In the same sense, Moerenhout, speaking of Polynesia, remarks that, in the sparsely populated islands the chiefs had little power, but wherever there was a dense population, wars were frequent and the chiefs reigned despotically [1]). There are, as we have already remarked, a few exceptions to this general rule (Rotuma, Pelau); but in these cases it is quite possible that a subjected class formerly existed. For a great depopulation has taken place in Oceania, especially in Polynesia and Micronesia [2]); and the value of land must have decreased together with the population. We have seen that in Rotuma all land is still held as property, but large tracts are out of tillage, though there are everywhere traces of former cultivation. In Pelau too, as has been said in § 6, the rights of property are still recognized, though there is but little land actually in cultivation. That the class of people destitute of land tends to disappear when the population decreases, is strikingly shown by the following statement of Ellis's regarding Tahiti: "Although the *manahune* [lowest class] have always included a large number of the inhabitants, they have not in modern times been so numerous as some other ranks. Since the population has been so greatly diminished, the means of subsistence so abundant, and such vast portions of the country uncultivated, an industrious individual has seldom experienced much difficulty in securing at least the occupancy of a piece of land" [3]).

---

1) Moerenhout, II p. 223. — 2) See Gerland, Das Aussterben der Naturvölker, pp. 5, 6; and Mahler's essay, pp. 60, 61. — 3) Ellis, Pol. Res., III p. 96.

This depopulation may perhaps also account for the discrepancy between Semper's and Kubary's accounts of Pelau. Semper spoke of a despised working class; but Kubary, who wrote several years after, stated that there were no social ranks. It is quite possible that in the meantime the population had been so greatly diminished, that every one could obtain possession of a piece of land.

Ellis's above-quoted statement also shows that there is a fundamental difference between such lower classes as were found in Tahiti and slaves. The former were not at all forbidden to provide for themselves, and indeed, when the population had decreased, many of them began to cultivate a piece of land for their own profit. But in former times they were not able to do so, as all land was the property of the upper classes. The lower classes of Oceania were proletarians who wanted employment. The means of subsistence were the exclusive property of the upper classes, and therefore the poor were wholly dependent on them. In slave countries free labourers are not available, and therefore those who want labourers have recourse to slavery; in Oceania the labour market was overstocked, and therefore the poor eagerly asked the landlords for employment even in the meanest work [1]).

There are some more details on record proving that labourers were not wanted.

In Rotuma "Polynesian or Micronesian strangers, *fa helav*, were usually married into different *hoag*, or adopted with the consent of all the members of the *hoag*. A few Fijians and Melanesians have become *fa asoa*, or helping men, of different chiefs; no women would have anything to do with them, and no *hoag* would adopt them. They remained on the island as long as they liked, and transferred their services as they liked; they were treated as inferior members of the *hoag*, to which they gave their services" [2]). In a slave country these Melanesians, looked upon as an inferior race and therefore not adopted, would have been eagerly taken as slaves and prevented from escaping; but here it is quite the reverse: they

---

1) One reason why these islanders wanted little labour may have been that they relied for a considerable portion of their food on the fruits of trees which, when once planted, required little care. — 2) Gardiner, p. 486.

may stay if they like, but they may also go away if they like; nobody wants them.

What Hale tells us of the inhabitants of Ponape is also very remarkable. When it is feared that there will be over-population, some of the lower orders with their wives and children voluntarily go away in their canoes [1]). If these lower classes were slaves, they would not be allowed to emigrate; the masters would value them as their property and prevent them from escaping. Such is not the case here; they remove because there is no room for them.

We see that common labourers are little wanted in Oceania. Some kinds of workmen, however, are much in request in some of these islands.

Mariner states that in Tonga the esteem in which the different trades are held depends on their utility. Most people pursue the same trade as their fathers did before them, because they have learned it in their youth. This especially applies to those trades which are considered most difficult and therefore highly honoured. There is no law obliging a son to follow his father's trade; but it is the custom; and the hope of a high profit stimulates the energy of those who pursue a difficult trade. The noblest trades are those of canoe-builder and undertaker of funerals. They are followed by none but *mataboles* and *mooas* (2nd and 3rd classes), the *tooas* (4th class) being excluded from them. All other trades are followed by *mooas* and *tooas* alike, except three which the *mooas* consider beneath their dignity and therefore leave to the *tooas*: those of barber, cook, and agriculturist. The latter two, the most depised trades, are hereditary. Neither cooking nor cultivating requires any particular capacities, everybody is capable of following these pursuits, and those whose fathers were engaged in either of them have no alternative but to continue in the same way. The esteem, however, in which an individual is held, does not only depend on the trade he follows, but on his ability in it. He who distinguishes himself in a lower trade enjoys more consideration than he who following a higher trade proves to be unqualified for it [2]).

---

1) Hale, p. 85. — 2) Mariner, II pp. 159—162.

We see that those trades which require no particular abilities are most despised here, whereas skilled labour is highly honoured and performed even by the higher classes.

In some more cases it is stated that skilled workmen are better paid and more highly valued than unskilled.

In Tahiti the lowest class included those "who were destitute of any land, and ignorant of the rude arts of carpentering, building, etc., which were respected among them . . . . The fishermen and artisans (sometimes ranking with this class, but more frequently with that immediately above it) may be said to have constituted the connecting link between the two" [1]).

Wilkes states that in the Kingsmill Islands "the trade of carpenter is held in great repute." Professed tattooers are also highly esteemed and well paid [2]).

In Fiji the carpenters formed a separate caste, called King's carpenters, having chiefs of their own, for whom and their work they showed respect. Among the social ranks the 4th were distinguished warriors of low birth, chiefs of the carpenters, and chiefs of the fishers for turtle, the 5th were the common people [3]). We see that here too skilled workmen rank above the bulk of the people.

Skilled labour is thus highly valued in some of these islands. The skilled workmen, so far from being slaves, are held in high esteem; but those who have no peculiar accomplishments are obliged to perform the rudest and most despised work. This applies especially to the agricultural labourers. These are entirely dependent on the landowners, and there are more of them than can be profitably employed. They much resemble the proletarians of modern European countries.

The great significance of the appropriation of the land clearly appears, when we consider a phenomenon frequently occurring among savages: debt-slavery. Among some savage tribes there are rich and poor as well as in Polynesia; the poor, however, do not apply to the rich for employment, but are enslaved by them. Thus among the Tagals and Visayas, in the time of the conquista, most slaves had become such by being unable to pay debts they had contracted. If, in a time of famine, a poor man

1) Ellis, Pol. Res., III p. 96. — 2) Wilkes, pp. 99, 108. — 3) Williams, pp. 71, 32.

had been fed for some days by his rich neighbour, he became his slave. Sometimes the rich even placed a quantity of rice in some conspicuous place and lay on the look-out; if then a poor man came and ate of the rice, he was seized and enslaved [1] Such a thing would never have happened in Polynesia, and the reason why is evident. Among the Tagals and Visayas the poor were able, in ordinary times, to provide for themselves they did not offer their services to the rich; the latter had to avail themselves of such an opportunity as a famine, to lay hands on them and compel them to work for them, not only during the famine, but afterwards when, if free, they would have been able to subsist independently of the rich. But in Polynesia the means of subsistence are permanently in the hands of the rich to the exclusion of the poor; therefore the rich need not compel the poor to work for them, for they are always at their mercy. Among the Tagals and Visayas the poor, though destitute of wealth, were not without resources: they had the free land always at their disposal; and it was only in extraordinary circumstances (*e. g.* when the harvest had failed) that they were temporarily dependent on the rich. In Polynesia the poor are destitute of land, and therefore permanently dependent on the landlords.

Their state would even be worse than it actually is, were it not that they are useful in another, non-economic way: they strengthen their employers' force in warfare.

In Tahiti "in times of war, all capable of bearing arms were called upon to join the forces of the chieftain to whom they belonged, and the farmers, who held their lands partly by feudal tenure, were obliged to render military service whenever their landlord required it. There were, besides these, a number of men celebrated for their valour, strength, or address in war, who were called *aito*, fighting-men or warriors. This title, the result of achievements in battle, was highly respected, and proportionably sought by the daring and ambitious. It was not, like the chieftainship and other prevailing distinctions, confined to any class, but open to all; and many from the lower ranks have risen, as warriors, to a high station in the community" [2]).

In Hawaii, "when war was declared, the king and warrior

---

[1] Blumentritt, Conquista, pp. 56, 57. — [2] Ellis, Pol. Res., l. p. 296.

chiefs, together with the priests, fixed the time and place for commencing, and the manner of carrying it on. In the meantime, the *Runapai* (messengers of war) were sent to the districts and villages under their authority, to require the services of their tenants, in numbers proportionate to the magnitude of the expedition" [1]).

In Samoa, as we have seen, those residing on land belonging to the chief were obliged to stand by him in war and peace [2]).

In Tonga, according to Mariner, "the retinue of the upper chiefs consists of *mataboles* or inferior chiefs (2nd class), and each of these has under his command a number of *mooas* (3rd class), who constitute the army of the upper chiefs. Some *tooas* (4th class) are also admitted into this army, if they have given proofs of bravery" [3]).

In the Marquesas Islands the rank of a noble could be acquired through acts of bravery [4]).

On the Kingsmill Islands the tenants must provide their lord with men when at war [5]).

In Fiji, according to Williams, all men capable of bearing arms, of all classes, took part in military operations; and Fison, as we have seen above, states that the people of the lowest rank in war time had to fight for their lords to the death [6]).

Concluding, we may remark that the facts observed in Oceania fully justify our theory, that slavery is inconsistent with a state of society in which all land is held as property.

§ 9. *Transition from serfdom to freedom in Western Europe.*

The conclusion we have arrived at is that the appropriation of the soil is a factor of great importance in shaping the social life of agricultural peoples [7]). When all land is held as prop-

---

1) Ibid., IV p. 152. — 2) See above, p. 332. — 3) Mariner, II p. 349. — 4) Radiguet p. 156. — 5) See above, p. 338. — 6) Williams, p. 45, and see above, p. 339. — 7) We have not spoken of landed property among hunters, because there are reasons enough to be found, apart from the appropriation of the land, why slavery is not likely to exist among them. We will only remark here that among many Australian tribes property in land is stated to exist (see Dargun, pp. 49, 50). Sometimes even the whole of the land seems to be held as property. "It seems curious" says Macgillivray "to find at Cape York and the

erty, a class of people destitute of the means of subsistence is likely soon to arise; such people must seek employment and live on the wages they can earn. But in countries where there in still free land, a class of free agricultural labourers dependent on wages does not exist; therefore in such countries the landowners often resort to slavery as a means of procuring labourers. *Generally speaking, slavery as an industrial system can only exist where there is still free land.*

If this theory is correct, it must hold not only with regard to the simply organized societies of Polynesia and Micronesia, but also with regard to civilized nations. Among such nations too slavery must disappear as soon as all land has been appropriated. And as we know that in Western Europe all land is now held as property and everybody is personally free, whereas in former times, when these countries were far less densely peopled than now, slavery and serfdom existed, it does not seem unreasonable to suppose that the appropriation of the soil has had much to do with the disappearance of servile labour. This opinion is also held by Wakefield. "The serfdom of the middle-ages was for all Europe, what it is for Poland and Russia still [1]), a kind of slavery required by the small proportion of people to land; a substitute for hired labour, which gradually expired with the increase of population, as it will expire in Poland and Russia when land shall, in those countries, become as scarce and dear as it became in England some time after the conquest" [2]). We think Wakefield is quite right here, and we shall adduce some facts in corroboration of this view.

But we must first remind the reader of what we have already said in the Introduction. We confine ourselves in this book to an investigation of the facts of savage life. The study of these facts leads us to conclusions, some of which (and among these the conclusion we are now dealing with) have a wider bearing and can further our understanding of the history of civilized

---

Prince of Wales' Islands a recognised division and ownership of land, seeing that none of it by cultivation has been rendered fit for the permanent support of man. According to Gi'om, there are laws regulating the ownership of every inch of ground on Muralug and the neighbouring possessions of the Kowraregas and I am led to believe such is likewise the case at Cape York." Macgillivray, as quoted by Haddon, p 432.— 1) Wakefield wrote in 1849. — 2) Wakefield, p. 326.

nations. But the scope of the present volume does not allow
us to make any special investigation of this history and inquire
whether the same causes can be seen at work here that have
been found to shape the social life of savage tribes. Accordingly, we shall not try to prove that the appropriation of the
soil has really been the main cause of the disappearance of
slavery and serfdom in Western Europe. We only intend to
show that the matter can be viewed from this side. We wish
to claim attention for this important factor, that is commonly
overlooked, and thus clear the way for future research. This
and the next two paragraphs have to be regarded as a digression,
standing apart from the main body of our book.

The character of these paragraphs may justify us in limiting
our remarks to two countries, the economic history of which
has of late years been the subject of thorough study by eminent
writers, viz. England and Germany, and using only a small part
of the literature existing on this matter. We have, however,
taken care to consult none but first-rate authorities.

We have spoken of the disappearance of *slavery and serfdom*.
In connection with this two remarks have to be made.

First. Slavery in the strict sense existed for a long time in
both England and Germany. In England, shortly after the
Norman Conquest, slaves were still rather numerous. "The *servi*
or slaves" says Ashley "whose average percentage for the whole
land is 9, and who in some of the eastern and midland shires
do not appear at all, or fall to a percentage of 4 or 5, rise
in the country on the Welsh border and in the south-west to
17, 18, 21, and 24 per cent." A century later, however, absolute
slavery had disappeared [1]). And in Germany there was also a
class of *servi*, who had to perform whatever services the lords
might require, and even in the 11th century, though their
condition had already much improved, were sometimes sold
apart from the land [2]).

Secondly. The argument that leads us to conclude that slavery
is inconsistent with a state of society in which all land is held
as property, equally applies to serfdom. For the serf, as well
as the slave, was compelled to work. There is a great difference
between slaves and serfs on one side, and modern labourers

[1] Ashley, I pp. 17, 18. — [2] Inama-Sternegg, II pp. 73, 74.

and tenants on the other. The labourer has to work for his employer, and the tenant has to pay rent; but both can always declare the contract off and so put an end to their obligations. And even as long as the contract lasts, if they do not discharge their duties, they can only be condemned to pay damages; but the labourer cannot be compelled to work, nor the tenant to remain on the farm. The slaves and serfs of early times, however, were under personal compulsion. The slave was the property of his master, whom he was not allowed to leave. And the serf, as we so often read, was "bound to the soil", "astricted to the estate", *"an die Scholle gefesselt"*, which means that he was forbidden to remove from the spot assigned to him. Professor Cunningham states that in England, in the 11th century "a very large proportion of the population were serfs who could not move to other estates or to towns" [1]), and Amira tells us that in Germany, in the Middle Ages, the villeins (*Grundhörigen*) were not allowed to remove from the land which they cultivated [2]). Therefore our argument holds with regard to serfdom as well as slavery. For when all land has been appropriated, a landlord can always find free tenants who are willing to pay him a rent, and free labourers who are willing to work for him, and so he wants neither serfs nor slaves. We may quote here Oppenheimer's remark that, as soon as all land has been appropriated, "serfdom in the proper sense, implying the astriction of the labourer to the soil, has become superfluous. The labourer can safely be allowed personal freedom, and it is allowed him. The produce of his labour can now be taken from him, in the form of rent, though he may be personally free. For he is excluded from the means of production, as far as they could be accessible to him, and so he has to accept the terms of the proprietor or to starve" [3]).

It is of some interest to emphasize what we have said concerning the difference between serfs and free tenants. A free tenant, whatever be the conditions of his tenure, can always remove from the land and cannot be compelled to cultivate it. A serf, whatever be the extent of his obligations, is bound to the

---

1) Cunningham, English Industry, I p. 5. — 2) Amira, p. 138. — 3) Oppenheimer, David Ricardos Grundrententheorie, pp. 152, 153.

soil; if he escapes the lord can bring him back and set him
to work again. The right of emigrating (German "*Freizügigkeit*")
is the true mark of freedom. And therefore, as soon as the
obligations which were personal have become territorial, *i. e.*
as soon as the services and payments which formerly were
exacted from definite persons, are exacted from the cultivators
of definite pieces of land as such, nobody being any longer
obliged to become or remain the cultivator of any definite
piece of land, — serfdom has ceased to exist, even though the
services and payments have remained exactly the same.

The line of demarcation between free and unfree cultivators
has not, however, always been drawn in a strict, scientific
manner. Ashley, speaking of the 11th—14th centuries, says:
"The term *libere tenentes* is elastic enough to cover men in
very different positions.... But the larger number of those
known by that name were, clearly, virgate-holding villeins or
the descendants of such, who had commuted their more oner-
ous labour services of two or three days a week for a money
or corn payment, and had been freed from what were regarded
as the more servile "incidents" of their position. What these
exactly were, or, indeed, what was understood by free tenure,
it is difficult now to determine, precisely because the lawyers
and landlords of the time did not themselves know. The most
widely spread idea was that inability to give a daughter in
marriage or to sell an ox or a horse without the lord's consent,
for which a fine had to be paid, was the certain mark of
servile tenure" [1].

Now we cannot wonder that the lawyers and landlords of the
Middle Ages had no very clear ideas about serfdom and freedom. But modern writers on economic history should have the
true distinction always before their minds. Some of them, however, we think fail in this respect.

In order to demonstrate this we must speak of a change
which, in the later Middle Ages, took place in the manorial
economy. The land belonging to each landlord had always been
divided into two parts, viz. "that part cultivated for the immediate benefit of the lord, the *demesne* or *inland*, and that

---

1) Ashley, I p. 21.

held of him by tenants, the land *in villenage"* [1]). These tenants were not, however, free tenants, but villeins bound to the soil and obliged to work on the demesne. "The whole of the land of the manor, both demesne and villenage, was cultivated on an elaborate system of joint labour. The only permanent labourers upon the demesne itself were a few slaves; all or almost all the labour there necessary was furnished by the villeins and cotters, as the condition on which they held their holdings, and under the supervision of the lord's bailiff". The labour dues of the villeins consisted of *week work, i. e.* a man's labour for two or three days a week throughout the year, *precariae, i. e.* additional labour at ploughing and at harvest time, and miscellaneous services [2]).

But in the course of time money payments were largely substituted for these labour dues. Commutation of the *week work* went on extensively shortly after the Norman Conquest, and commutation of the whole of the services occurs occasionally as early as 1240. "With the reign of Edward II complete commutation became general" [3]) The cultivators had now to pay money to the lord instead of working on the demesne.

Though the change occurred at a time when personal serfdom was gradually declining, it is easy to see that this commutation is not identical with the transition from serfdom to freedom. A free tenant may by contract take upon himself to perform some kind of work for the landlord. This was the case in England where "the rendering of services reappeared in the seventeenth and eighteenth centuries, not as the incidents of villanage, but as a form of agreement which proved more or less convenient to one party and perhaps to both" [4]). On the other hand, it is quite possible that a cultivator who pays money instead of rendering services, is yet bound to the soil and devoid of personal freedom. Ashley, speaking of the 13th century, states that most of the cultivators "had continued to hold by servile tenure, as villeins or customary tenants, even when they had commuted all or most of their services.... There can be no doubt that.... they were bound to the soil;

---

1) Ibid., p. 7. — 2) Ibid., pp. 8, 9. — 3) Ibid., pp. 22, 31. — 4) Cunningham, English Industry, I p. 476.

in the sense, at any rate, that the lord would demand a heavy fine before he would give one of them permission to leave the manor" [1]).

Now, though none of our writers on economic history explicitly say that these two things, the commutation of labour dues for money and the transition from serfdom to freedom, are identical, we think some of them do not sufficiently keep in view the difference existing between the two. Thus only can we account for the prevalence of a theory which seems to be the current mode of explaining the fall of serfdom and rise of freedom.

This theory has been introduced by a German writer, Professor Hildebrand. He distinguishes three stages of economic development: natural economy, money economy, and credit economy.

In the system of natural economy goods are exchanged directly for goods; when money economy prevails use is made of a means of exchange, money; and when credit economy has been developed goods are exchanged for a promise in the future to give back the same or a like value, *i. e.* on credit. Every nation begins with natural economy, for the use of money as a means of exchange supposes an abundance of labour or products of labour which enables people to procure the precious metals. As long as natural economy prevails capital does not exist: the soil and human labour are the only productive agencies. There are, therefore, two classes of people only; labourers and landowners. Sometimes every landowner is at the same time a labourer; in such cases democracy prevails. But it often occurs that labourers and landowners form separate classes. These are then mutually dependent on each other; for the labourer wants a landlord to give him employment and so enable him to earn his subsistence, and the landlord wants labourers to cultivate his lands. This interdependence effects that the relations existing between the two classes assume a durable character. The labour contracts are made to last for the life of the labourer or even become hereditary. The labourer is bound to the soil and forbidden to leave the manor.

---

1) Ashley, I p. 37.

As soon as money economy exists, capital arises and takes its place as the third factor of production. The owning classes comprise now both capitalists and landlords. The labourer has no longer to apply to the landlord for employment, but can leave him and work for the capitalist; he is therefore no longer astricted to the soil. The wages he receives from the capitalist are paid in the form of money, and so the labourer is much freer than before, for this money can be turned to various purposes. Moreover, capital (as opposed to land) can be augmented to any extent, and this enables the labourer to become a capitalist himself.

The position of the labourers who remain on the land also undergoes a change. The landlord who brings the agricultural produce to the market can pay wages in money and therefore hire able and dismiss incompetent labourers. His lands, worked with free labourers who serve for wages, yield him a far greater income than formerly when they were cultivated by serfs. Moreover, the fixed labour dues of the serfs do not answer the purposes of an improved economy. It is thus the interest of the landlord to put an end to his fixed and hereditary contracts and loosen the ties with which natural economy had bound the agricultural labourer. The dues in kind and services are commuted for money payments. The labourer, who was a serf, becomes now either a free peasant or a free servant and day-wage worker who is no longer astricted to the soil, but can leave his employer whenever he likes and seek such work as most agrees with his capacity and inclination.

On the other hand, the employers have become independent of the labourers. In the system of natural economy the landlord took care not to lose his labourers, whom he wanted to cultivate his land; but now landlords and capitalists can always get as many labourers as they like and dismiss them as soon as they are no longer of any use. This leads to an oppression of the poor by the rich [1].

This is Hildebrand's theory, so far as the condition of the labouring classes is concerned. Natural economy, according to him, leads to serfdom, money economy leads to freedom.

---

[1] Hildebrand, Natural-, Geld- und Creditwirthschaft, pp. 4, 8, 9, 14, 15, 18.

We think this theory is erroneous.

It would perhaps be better not to speak of "natural economy" and "money economy"; for these terms are likely to lead to misunderstanding. The mere existence of money is of comparatively little consequence. A circulating medium arises as soon as it is wanted; and where the precious metals are unknown something else will do, as in Melanesia and among many Negro tribes, where shells are used for money. The existence of a circulating medium denotes a development of commerce; for barter on any extensive scale is hardly possible. Therefore we had better speak of self-sufficing and commercial communities. As long as each village is practically self-dependent money is not wanted; but as soon as the interchange of commodities takes any considerable dimensions the need for a means of exchange becomes pressing. And there is, indeed, a great difference in social structure between self-sufficing and commercial communities [1]); but if we ascribe this difference to the existence of gold and silver coins we arrive at false conclusions. A proof of this is the fact that Hildebrand thinks capital can only exist when there is money. Yet we know that the Germans have kept cattle from early times, long before money economy prevailed; and cattle are decidedly to be called capital; they cannot be classified under either of the only two means of production which, according to Hildebrand, exist in a system of natural economy: land and human labour; and in our chapter on pastoral tribes we have seen that cattle-keepers form strongly marked capitalistic communities.

But even if we speak of self-dependent and commercial communities, we cannot admit that in the former labour must necessarily be servile and in the latter free.

First. How can natural economy, *i. e.* the absence of commerce, lead to serfdom? Hildebrand says: landlords and labourers are mutually dependent on each other, and so their relations assume a durable character, and the labourer is astricted to the soil.

---

1) Absolute self-sufficiency does not appear to exist anywhere, not even among savage tribes, see above, p. 255. But there certainly is a great difference between those countries which get their chief necessaries directly by their own labour, and those which produce mainly for export.

We think his meaning is the following. In self-sufficing communities the fluidity of labour which exists in modern society, is wanting. In such countries there can be famine in one district, whilst in a contiguous district there is plenty of food; similarly labour can be scarce in one place whilst it is abundant in a neighbouring place. Therefore a landlord cannot afford to let his labourers leave the manor; for as there is little intercourse between the different villages and districts it is difficult for him to procure other labourers. It is thus most convenient for him to bind his labourers to the soil and forbid them to leave him.

This may at first sight seem a reasonable explanation of the origin of serfdom. But on closer scrutiny it will be seen that this argument does not hold. When there is little intercourse, each landlord is dependent on the labourers of his own district; and there must be a great stability in the relations of the two classes. But this need not bring about an astriction of the labourers to the soil. The landlord cannot easily procure labourers from other districts; but it is even more difficult for the labourers to find employment in foreign parts; for such intercourse as there is, is kept by the ruling, not by the labouring classes. Therefore it is not necessary to bind the labourers to the soil; for they are already naturally dependent on the landlords of their own district. We think slavery and serfdom can only be accounted for by a general scarcity of labour. When labour is everywhere scarce a labourer who leaves his employer can everywhere find employment, whereas an employer cannot easily procure labourers; it is then the interest of the employer to prevent his labourers from leaving him. But the mere lack of intercourse limits the labourer in his choice of employment even more than it limits the employer in his choice of labourers.

Nor do the facts agree with this theory. We have seen that among pastoral tribes free labourers are frequently found, though labour is by no means fluid and the labourers are paid in kind, not in money. Among the natives of Hawaii, who lived under a system of natural economy, labour was also free. The passage in which Ellis describes the relation between landlords and cultivators has already been quoted by us, but it is remarkable enough to repeat here. "Sometimes the poor people take a piece of land, on condition of cultivating a given portion for the chief, and the remainder for themselves, making a fresh agreement after every crop. In addition to the above demands, the common people are in general obliged to labour if required, part of two days out of seven, in cultivating farms, building houses, etc. for their landlord. A time is usually appointed for receiving the rent, when the people repair to the governor's with what they have to pay. If the required amount is furnished, they return, and, as they call it (*komo hou*) enter again on their land. But if unable to pay the required sum, and their landlords are dissatisfied with the presents they have received, or think the tenants have neglected their farm, they are forbidden to return, and the land is offered to another. When, however, the produce brought is nearly equal to the required rent, and the chiefs think the occupants have exerted themselves to procure it, they remit the deficiency, and allow them to return" [1]). These cultivators are by no means astricted to the soil. They make a fresh agreement after every crop. If the produce brought is insufficient, they are either removed or by way of favour allowed to return [2]).

Our conclusion is that, though in medieval Western Europe serfdom and natural economy existed at the same time, the former is not a necessary consequence of the latter.

Secondly. Does money economy, *i. e.* commerce, always lead to freedom? We know now that serfdom is not invariably connected with natural economy. Yet it might be that, wherever both natural economy and serfdom exist (as it was the case in the early Middle Ages) the rise of money economy always brought serfdom to a close.

The argument by which Hildebrand attempts to prove this is rather strange. The development of town life and manufactures, according to him, enables the labourers to find employment in manufactures; they are now no longer dependent on the landlords. The manufacturing capitalists pay them money-

---

1) Ellis, Pol. Res., IV pp. 416, 417. — 2) Among many hunters, fishers and hunting agriculturists slavery and serfdom are also wanting. But among these there are no labouring classes (as opposed to owning classes) at all, whether free or otherwise. Only the Eskimos have free servants.

wages which they can spend in whatever way they like, and so they become more free than they were before.

We think this argument is quite insufficient. The labourers find employment in manufactures, says Hildebrand. But he had told us before that they were astricted to the soil. What enables them now to leave the landlords? Further: why do not the town labourers become slaves or serfs? Here Hildebrand's reasoning is very strange. They receive money-wages which they can spend in whatever way they like. Now one who receives money with which he can buy all kinds of commodities is in a certain sense more free than one who, under a system of natural economy, receives bread and meat which he cannot sell. But this has nothing to do with the legal status of the labourer. A slave who receives pocket-money from his master is free to buy with it what he likes, yet he remains a slave.

But the condition of those of the labouring classes who remain on the land also undergoes a change, according to Hildebrand. The landlord can now sell the produce of his land for money, and this money enables him to hire free labourers.

We cannot see why this should be so, why the mere possibility of paying money-wages (all other circumstances having remained the same) should lead to free labour contracts. We should rather think that the afflux of labourers to the towns of which Hildebrand speaks would make agricultural labour scarce, and each landlord would be most anxious to retain those labourers that had not yet escaped to the towns; they would now, more than ever before, be astricted to the soil.

Hildebrand, however, thinks it will be the interest of the landlord to put an end to the hereditary tenures of his serfs and work his lands with free labourers. And he adds that the dues in kind and services are commuted for money payments. The cultivator who was a serf becomes now either a free landholder or a free labourer.

Whether Hildebrand means to say that the commutation of dues in kind and services for money payments is identical with the transition from serfdom to freedom, does not clearly appear.

We think that the regarding of this commutation as the main fact in the economic history of the later Middle Ages lies at the root of the evil and has given rise to this theory. Money economy, according to Hildebrand, leads to commutation, and commutation is the same as, or at any rate leads to, the disappearance of serfdom.

What does this commutation mean? Formerly the peasants had to work on the demesne which was cultivated for the immediate benefit of the lord; in later times they paid money instead. What was the reason of this change? It must have been that the demesne was cultivated in some other way so that their services were no longer wanted. Sometimes free labourers were employed. "It is evident" says Ashley "that the lord would not have consented, first to partial and then to complete commutation, had he not been able to hire labourers" [1]. But the main reason was that portions of the demesne were let for rents. "If the lord found it his interest to let portions of the demesne instead of cultivating it through his bailiff or reeve, his need for the services of the villeins would be *pro tanto* diminished, and he would be readier to accept commutation" [2]. The same was the case in Germany, where between the 10th and 13th centuries the extent of the land which the landlords kept in their own hands was continually diminishing, so that there was less and less use for the services of the villeins, and commutation took place on a great scale. The landlords, who formerly had taken the lead of agricultural operations, became now mere receivers of rent [3].

Now we must admit that commutation of labour dues for money payments was not possible before money was used. Yet the fact that commutation of services for payments in kind, which does not suppose money economy, also occured [4], shows that the rise of money economy cannot have been the sole cause of this change. We may even go farther and say: if it has been a cause at all, it has not certainly been one of the principal causes. The commutation of the labour dues means that the demesne was thenceforth either worked with free labourers or let for rent. The existence of a class of freemen dependent on wages cannot, however, be accounted for by

---

1) Ashley, I p. 31. — 2) Ibid., p. 27. — 3) Inama-Sternegg, II pp. 167—177. — 4) See Inama-Sternegg, II p. 283.

money economy. Nor can we see how money economy can have led to the letting of the demesnes which the landlords had formerly kept in their own hands. Ochenkowski supposes that in England, after the Norman Conquest, the need of the landlords for money led to commutation [1]). But there is no reason why the landlords could not, instead of receiving money payments, obtain money by selling the produce of their lands. As long as there was no market for agricultural products the landlord, whether he himself had the lead of agricultural operations or let the demesne on condition of receiving a payment in kind, could not obtain money. As soon as there was a market he could make money in three ways: by working the demesne himself and selling the produce, by letting it on condition of receiving part of the produce, which he could bring to the market [2]), and by letting it for a rent in money. Money economy seems to have had little to do with the commutation.

Hildebrand's theory is: money economy led to commutation and commutation led to freedom. We have seen that the first half of this does not hold. What about the second half? Can the commutation have loosened the ties which bound the cultivator to the soil? We think not. For if the landlord could not let the villein who worked on the demesne leave the manor, because he was difficult to replace, he had exactly the same reason for keeping the villein who paid money astricted to the soil. The use of money and the rise of commerce had not augmented the number of agricultural labourers; they had even decreased, as many of them had gone to the towns. And it was even more difficult to replace the money-paying than the labouring villein; for the former had to be a fit person who could conduct his business well enough to be able at the end of the year to furnish the required sum, whereas any able-bodied man could perform agricultural labour under the supervision of the lord's bailiff. Our conclusion is that money economy did not lead to commutation, and that commutation did not lead to freedom.

Yet money economy, taken in the sense of town life and

1) Ochenkowski, p. 11. — 2) This was done on a large scale by the German landlords towards the end of the Middle Ages, see Inama-Sternegg, III Part I p. 384.

commerce, did sometimes affect the condition of the rural classes. Such was the case in Italy where, in the 13th century, the wealthy commercial cities took an active part in the emancipation of the serfs. Florence especially strongly encouraged their enfranchisement. In 1257 this city even went so far as to set free all the serfs in the surrounding country, indemnifying the lords. The city government pretended to act from Christian and philanthropic motives. "But" adds our informant "though the city governments of Central Italy were the first to pronounce themselves in favour of the personal freedom of the peasants, they by no means countenanced the idea of leaving the land to those who had held it for centuries. On the contrary, the citizens endeavour to acquire landed properties, and when they have got them they put an end to the hereditary tenures and replace them by tenancies." Many of the former serfs had to leave the lands of their ancestors and augmented the number of proletarians in the towns. They were replaced by leaseholders [1]).

The disappearance of serfdom was thus accelerated by the measures of the Italian cities. How much of sentiment there was in these measures, and how much of self-interest, we do not know. But at any rate serfdom must already have been drawing to an end before the cities meddled with it. For a firmly established system that discharges an important economic function is not uprooted by mere sentiment. And so far as the self-interest of the citizens induced them to replace the serfs by free tenants, the latter system must have been economically more useful than the former, which was probably only kept up by the landlords because they were accustomed to it. Times had changed and the old system of cultivation had become obsolete; and the citizens of the towns, whom no personal relation bound to the serfs, expelled them and let the land to free tenants. Before their intervention there must adready have been at work an internal cause, which effected that cultivation by serfs was no longer the most profitable mode of managing landed properties.

We do not mean to say that there was no internal connec-

---

1) Kovalewsky, Régime économique moderne, pp. 358—362.

tion between the transition from serfdom to freedom and the simultaneous rise of town life, commerce and manufactures. We think there was such a connection. But we cannot agree with the theory that the disappearance of serfdom was a consequence of the commercial development of Western Europe. It seems to us that the rise of commerce was not the cause of the decline of serfdom, but that both were effects of the same principal cause, the relative scarcity of land which made itself felt towards the end of the Middle Ages. As soon as people had to shift on a limited area, the use of commerce, which enables each district to produce what it is most fit to, and so enhances the productiveness of labour, became more apparent than it had been at a time when there was plenty of land. In the same sense, Malthus remarks: "The great cause which fills towns and manufactories is an insufficiency of employment, and consequently the means of support in the country; and if each labourer, in the parish where he was born, could command food, clothing, and lodging for ten children, the population of the towns would soon bear but a small proportion to the population of the country" [1]. Lange also says that poverty of the masses is a condition of the rise of manufactures [2]. Besides these economists, we may quote the eminent geographist Ratzel, who observes, that in a country with a growing population the soil finally cannot any longer feed the whole of the people and so an ever increasing part of the population devote themselves to manufactures and commerce [3]. That this occurs even in primitive civilization, follows from what Krieger tells us about the natives inhabiting the small islands adjoining New Guinea, especially Berlin Harbour and Dallmann Harbour. The goad of necessity, he remarks, has urged them to a progress in the arts of life. The want of room rendered extension of the plantations on their islets impossible and so they began to manufacture carved work and pottery, which they exported to the continent in exchange for food [4].

As for the medieval history of Europe, Inama-Sternegg observes that the increase of the population, requiring an

---

1) Malthus, p. 438, note 1. — 2) Lange, Die Arbeiterfrage, p. 227. — 3) Ratzel, Anthropogeographie, II p. 242. — 4) Krieger, p. 225.

extension of the means of subsistence, led to the rise of towns and manufactures [1]).

But however this may be, we are certain that the rise of money economy cannot have been the sole, or even the chief cause of the disappearance of servile labour. This is sufficiently shown by the fact that before the emancipation of the Negroes a system of servile labour on a large scale prevailed in the United States and the West Indies, *i. e.* in countries working for export.

Hildebrand's theory has been accepted by some writers on economic history. Ochenkowski repeatedly asserts that the change in the condition of the rural population was the effect of money economy. Inama-Sternegg, in one passage of his excellent book on the economic history of Germany, expresses the opinion that in the early Middle Ages natural economy, defined by him as the absence of regular commercial intercourse, made astriction of the labourers to the soil necessary. Professor Cunningham, in his book on Western Civilization, ascribes the changes which in the history of ancient Greece and Rome took place in the status of the labouring classes to the prevalence of natural economy and money economy respectively [2]). But none of these writers give any new argument in favour of the theory.

Our conclusion is that the rise of money economy was not the cause of the disappearance of serfdom. We shall inquire now whether Wakefield's theory, with which we agree, can further our understanding of the economic history of England and Germany.

§ 10. *The rural classes of medieval England.*

Of land tenure in England before the 11th century we do not know very much [3]).

---

1) Inama-Sternegg, I p. 382. — 2) See Ochenkowski, pp. 11, 15, 21; Inama-Sternegg, I pp. 236, 237; Cunningham, Western Civilization, pp. 73, 74, 95, 108, 192. According to Marx (Vol. III Part II pp. 332, 333), the substitution of money payments for dues in kind necessarily leads to free contracts between landlords and cultivators.

Grupp (Zeitschrift für Kulturgeschichte, IV p. 242) asserts that the rise of money economy caused the transition from slavery to serfdom. We shall not discuss this point, as it is not directly connected with the subject of this paragraph. — 3) Ashley, I p. 13.

The first detailed account of the economic condition of the country is contained in Domesday Book, in which William of Normandy embodied the results of an inquiry into the state of the kingdom he had secured.

"When Domesday Survey was compiled" says Cunningham, "every yard of English soil was as really, if not as definitely, subject to proprietary rights as it is now" [1]. We do not, however, think that much importance has to be attached to this statement; for there was still much uncultivated land and, though the king claimed a right of property over this land, it was not yet held as property in the strict sense of the word, which means that all except the owner are excluded from its use. This appears from what took place in 1305, under Edward I. "By an adjustment of boundaries considerable portions of the Crown forest were given over to certain barons, who gained personally; but the position of the tenants was so much altered for the worse that their case obtained special attention in the *Ordinance of the Forest,* by which their rights of pasture and common were secured" [2]. We see that these Crown forests had been open to the use of the peasants, so that practically there was still free land. And in this time of extensive tillage the common pasture played a great part in the rural economy [3].

Accordingly, rent in the modern sense did not yet exist. The landlords had abundance of land; but the land was worth little if it was not provided with people to cultivate it. "The rent of the proprietor now is directly connected with the physical character of his estate, its productiveness and its situation. The income of the lord of a Domesday Manor depended on the tolls he received, and the payments of his dependents: and thus was based on the way in which his estates were stocked with meat and men, rather than on the physical condition of the land. His income was a very different thing from modern rent" [4]. Even in later centuries "a fertile estate would have yielded but little annual income, unless the necessary labour was attached to it" [5].

In this time the whole of Central England was covered with

1) Cunningham, English Industry, I p. 95. — 2) Ibid., p. 251. — 3) Ochenkowski, p. 7. — 4) Cunningham, l. c. p. 5. — 5) Ibid., p. 407.

manors, and the mass of the rural population consisted of two classes: landlords and villeins; the latter were not all of the same condition, but none of them enjoyed entire personal freedom [1]). Of those cultivators who are described as *freemen* and *socmen* some could "sell their lands without leave asked or given, but others could only do so on obtaining licence from the lord" [2]). Finally there were some slaves [3]). Every freeman was a landholder, therefore there was no class of free labourers. "The labourer, as a man who depended on some employer for the opportunity and means of doing his work, seems to have been almost unknown in the eleventh century" [4]).

All this agrees with our theory. All land had not yet practically been appropriated; therefore people could not be got to cultivate the land for the benefit of the landlords, unless they were deprived of personal freedom.

During the two following centuries population increased and land became more scarce. In the 13th century some lords already began to inclose portions of the waste, which had always been used for common pasturage, and "it was necessary to limit by the statute of Merton, in 1236, the lord's "right of approver" or improvement, by the condition that he should not take away so much as not to leave enough for the purpose of pasture" [5]). Forests were often fenced off and the rights of common pasture restricted [6]). We have already mentioned an instance in which the condition of the peasants was much altered for the worse by such measures.

The changes which, during the same period, took place in the condition of the rural classes, are grouped by Ashley under four heads: "1. the growth of a large class of free tenants; 2. the commutation of the week work for money or corn payments; 3. the commutation of the boon-days and other special services; and 4. the appearance of a class of men dependent wholly or in part on the wages they received for agricultural labour" [7]).

In a passage quoted in the last paragraph Ashley states that

---

1) Ashley, I p. 13; Cunningham, l. c. I pp. 95, 96. — 2) Cunningham, l. c. pp. 158, 159. — 3) Ashley, I p. 17; Cunningham, l. c. p. 160. — 4) Cunningham, l. c. p. 5. — 5) Ashley, I p. 26. — 6) Ochenkowski, pp. 33, 34. — 7) Ashley, I p. 20.

most of the "free tenants" were villeins who had commuted their labour services for a money or corn payment, and had been freed from the more servile "incidents" of their position, such as inability to sell a horse without the lord's consent [1]). Hence it follows that personal freedom, i. e. the right to leave the manor, was not regarded as characteristic of free tenure. Yet at the end of the 13th century every tenant was already permitted to sell his lands or parts of them [2]). This transition from personal to territorial obligations was certainly due to the increase of population and consequent enhanced value of land. In early times labour was scarce and therefore the landlord could not let a cultivator leave the manor. But now land, or at least some pieces of land, had already acquired so much value that there were always people to be found ready to cultivate them on condition of paying certain dues to the lord.

The principal cause of the commutation of labour dues for money was that the lord let portions of the demesne instead of cultivating it through his bailiff or reeve. He had now less need for the services of the villeins; for these services had consisted mainly in working on the demesne [3]). This change in the mode of cultivation was perhaps due partly to political circumstances (absence of the lord at court or in war), as in Germany it certainly was. But we think there were economic causes also at work. In early times, when land was abundant, it was necessary for the lord to keep the cultivators he wanted in personal subjection; he therefore made them work in his presence and under the supervision of his bailiff. But now the villeins had come to attach value to their holdings, they were no longer inclined to run away, for it would have been difficult for them to find land to live upon. The villein claimed an hereditary right to the land he cultivated, and the question as to whether he had any such right already began to be discussed by the lawyers [4]).

At the beginning of the 14th century most of the cultivators were still bound to the soil [5]), but the first germs of a tho-

---

1) See above, p. 350. — 2) Cunningham, l. c. p. 253. — 3) See Ashley, I. p. 27. — 4) Ibid., pp. 38—40. — 5) Ibid., p. 37.

rough change were already present. There were free tenants
who could sell their lands; tenancies at will already occurred,
though not frequently [1]); and a class of free labourers arose.
In Grossteste's rules, dating from 1240 or 1241, it is said that
servants and retainers "are to do what they are bid immediately without any grumbling or contradiction; if they show
any such disloyal spirit they must be dismissed, for many can
be had to fill their places" [2]). And there were also agricultural
labourers who, though holding small pieces of land, had not
enough land to live upon, and were partially dependent on
wages. Even where the peasants were still obliged to cultivate
the demesne, they did not usually perform such work themselves, but hired labourers to do it; the usual phrase is that
they have to "find" a man for the work [3]).

Here again our theory holds. Population had increased, land
became scarce, and the transition from serfdom to freedom
commenced. If the population of England had continued increasing, most of the villeins would probably have become
freeholders or copyholders, whereas the lands that the lords
had kept in their own hands would have been leased. And
poor people who had neither land of their own nor capital
enough to become farmers would have served for wages.

But an unexpected event entirely changed the economic condition of England. The Black Death, which made its first
appearance in 1349, swept away a large part of the population.
Whole villages were practically annihilated and large tracts of
land went out of tillage. The economic consequences were such
as we should expect. "As one immediate result there was
great difficulty in getting labourers; the difficulty was aggra-
vated in those cases where the tenants had died off and the
lords were left with large holdings on their hands and no
means of working them; while they lost the predial services
of these deceased tenants on the home farm. There was consequently an immensely increased demand for hired labourers
at the very time when their numbers were so much thinned, and
it seemed as if the agriculture of the country was completely

---

1) Ibid., p. 29. — 2) Cunningham, l. c. p. 225. — 3) Ashley, I p. 32.

ruined" [1]). Land was now again abundant, and so "instead of ousting tenants, lords of land found it hard enough to retain them even with lightened services" [2]). And the natural consequence was that the landlords attempted to re-attach tenants and labourers to the soil. Whether, as Professor Thorold Rogers asserts, the customary tenants, who had commuted their labour dues for money, were forced back into the servile position of their ancestors, is not certain [3]). At any rate "we may grant that, now that labour had become so costly, the lords would insist on the exact performance of such labour dues as had not yet been commuted, and on the punctual payment of all money rents. There is much reason to believe, moreover, that they abused their power of imposing "amercements" on their tenants in the manor courts for trivial breaches of duty" [4]). This severe and unaccustomed pressure on the villeins, who were becoming comfortable copyholders, resulted in Wat Tyler's revolt of 1381 [5]).

Nor were the labourers any longer allowed to dispose freely of their labour power. "While the plague was actually raging parliament could not meet, but a proclamation was at once issued by the king with the advice of certain prelates and nobles, of which the preamble states that, "many seeing the necessity of masters and great scarcity of servants will not serve unless they get excessive wages", and that consequently the land can be scarcely tilled. Everyone, free or villan, who can work and has no other means of livelihood, is not to refuse to do so for anyone who offers the accustomed wages; each lord is to have the preference in hiring the men on his own estate, but none is to have too many men for his work; no labourer is to leave his employment before the specified time; nor to receive more rations or wages than he did in the twentieth year of the king and the common years before that; none are to give or take more wages in town or country" [6]).

---

1) Cunningham, l. c. p. 305. — 2) Ashley, II p. 277. — 3) See Ashley, II pp. 264—267, and Ochenkowski, pp. 18—20. — 4) Ashley, II p. 265. — 5) Cunningham, l. c. pp. 356, 357. On the Black Death and its effects, see also Thorold Rogers, Work and Wages, pp. 5—26, and The Economic Interpretation of History by the same author, pp. 24 sqq. — 6) Cunningham, l. c. p. 306.

The depopulation of this time caused a reappearance of free land, *i. e.* of land which had practically no value, and so agricultural labourers were scarcely to be had. Therefore the lords to some extent reattached the cultivators to the soil.

These measures, however, were of little avail. It was not easy to prevent an employer from secretly giving more than the statutory wages. The penalties for infraction of the regulation were rendered more severe, the fines being replaced by imprisonment; yet the whole legislation proved a failure [1]).

And even if the statutes of labourers had been everywhere enforced, "many landowners would have been left in a position of great difficulty; if there was no one to do the work it did not much matter what they were to be paid, and in not a few villages scarcely any one was left to carry on the ordinary agricultural operations." Therefore new expedients had to be devised, of which the most general appears to have been the stock and land lease; "the new tenant took the land and the stock off the lord's hands and made in return a definite annual payment." These tenants "probably sprang from the class of free labourers, as the surviving villans who already had their own holdings, would not be so easily able to offer for a portion of the domain land which the lord desired to let" [2]).

Here again we see the consequences of the abundance of land. The land alone could not fetch a reasonable price; stock and land had to be leased together.

As these leaseholders were taken from the labouring class, this measure, of course, still further diminished the supply of labour.

All these palliatives could not, indeed, better the postion of the landlords to any considerable extent. They had to wait for an increase of population which would render to the land the value that it had before the Black Death. As, however, the plague recurred several times, the population appears to have scarcely increased [3]).

The landlords remained in this difficult position till about 1450 [4]), when a new and very efficacious remedy was suggested

---

1) Ibid., pp. 307, 308. — 2) Ibid., pp. 355, 356. — 3) See Ochenkowski, p. 37. — 4) This date is given by Ashley, II p. 264.

to them: they applied a new mode of working their estates, which rendered them the practical command over the land, without need of a denser population. The extension of the wool trade and the dearth of labour made it far more profitable to keep large flocks of sheep than to grow corn. Consequently much land was laid down in pasture; there was a steady increase of sheep farming during the 15th century and a corresponding decrease of corn growing [1]).

In our chapter on pastoral tribes it has been shown that the care of flocks and herds does not require much labour. We can, therefore, easily understand that after the rise of sheep farming there was far less need for agricultural labour than before. There had been scarcity of labour; now there was over-population and many people were thrown out of employment; for over-population exists, not only when there are more people than the land can support, but when there are more people dependent on wages than can be profitably employed by the owners of land and capital [2]).

Sheep farming was introduced in the first place on the manorial demesnes, of which the lords had the free disposal. The demesne usually formed from one-third to a half of the whole arable area of a manor. Since the labour services of the villeins had been commuted, the tillage of the demesne had furnished employment to many small tenants and landless cottagers who, partly or entirely, depended on wages. The substitution of pasture for tillage on the demesne, therefore, brought many of them to ruin; for none but a few shepherds could thenceforth be employed [3]).

But far graver evils resulted from the appropriation by the lords of the commons and the land held by villeins or customary tenants.

The commons, i. e. the common pasture and waste, had always been used jointly by the lord and villeins. Whether the latter had any legal right to them is not certain; probably they had not; but they had always been accustomed to have the

---

1) Cunningham, l. c., p. 361. — 2) Lange (Die Arbeiterfrage, p. 241) also remarks that in England the transition from agriculture to sheep breeding engendered a relative over-population. On relative and absolute over-population, see further Oppenheimer, Das Bevölkerungsgesetz, etc., pp. 79—84. — 3) Ashley, II p. 267.

free use of them. Now the lords began to inclose large parts of these commons for the formation of sheep runs. The consequence was that many of the customary tenants, who had relied on the commons for pasturing their cattle, could no longer keep the cattle necessary for the cultivation of their holding. Their farming became unprofitable, and they had to leave their lands, which were instantly occupied by the lords and laid down in pasture [1]).

Even when the cultivator had not left his tenement, the lord sometimes appropriated and "inclosed" it.

The inclosures which took place, especially in the 16th century, are a fact of foremost importance in the history of English agriculture. The term "inclosure" has two different meanings. In medieval England the lands of the villeins, with those of the lord interspersed between them, lay scattered in a number of acre or half-acre strips, no two strips held by one man being contiguous. This system, dating from a time of extensive tillage, fell short of the exigencies of advanced culture, and had to be removed before any improvement in the mode of cultivation could be made. Therefore inclosures have often, especially in the reign of Elizabeth, been made with the common consent of all the landholders concerned, the result being that every tenant, instead of many scattered strips, obtained one or a few fields lying together. "But in the earlier part of the same movement, during the period which may be roughly defined as from 1450 to 1550, inclosure meant to a large extent the actual dispossession of the customary tenants by their manorial lords. This took place either in the form of the violent ousting of the sitting tenant, or of a refusal on the death of one tenant to admit the son who in earlier centuries would have been treated as his natural successor" [2]). It was this latter kind of inclosure that was condemned by several writers of the 16th century, for instance by Hales, who by inclosure did not mean "where a man doth enclose and hedge in his own proper grounds where no man hath commons. For such enclosure is very benificial to the commonwealth; it is a cause of great encrease of wood; but it is meant thereby when any man hath taken away and enclosed any other men's com-

1) Ashley, II pp. 270—272; Cunningham, l. c., p. 362. — 2) Ashley, II pp. 272, 273.

mons, or hath pulled down houses of husbandry and converted the lands from tillage to pasture" [1]).

Ashley, discussing the question as to whether the lords had a right to turn out the villeins, arrives at the conclusion that "during historical times and until comparatively modern days, the cultivators of the soil were always in a condition of dependence, and held their lands at the arbitrary will of their lords. For centuries the lord knew no other way of getting his land cultivated, and had no wish to get rid of a tenant; whenever he did so, it was altogether exceptional. But with the tendency to limitation and definition so characteristic of the feudal period, custom tended to harden into law, and it would seem to have been on the point of becoming law when a change in the economic situation, — the increasing advantage of pasture over tillage, — prompted the lords to fall back on their old rights. Then followed a struggle between *a legal theory becoming obsolete*, but backed by the influence of the landowners, and *a custom on its way to become law*, backed by public sentiment and by the policy of the government" [2]).

This is in perfect keeping with our theory. In former times land was abundant, and therefore the lord "had no wish to get rid of a tenant," for he "knew no other way of getting his land cultivated". But now sheep farming made appropriation of the whole of the land possible, and so the lord was no longer in need of the villeins; he even went so far as to evict those whom his ancestors had attached to the soil. And even where the cultivators remained on the land, they often, and not always voluntarily, became leaseholders instead of copyholders; and "in many cases a lease was but a stepping-stone to tenure at will" [3]). The lords no longer contented themselves with the customary payments; instead of villeins they wanted leaseholders, whose rents they could raise at the end of each term, according as the value of the land had increased. "Rents were raised with great rapidity as the tenant had to pay a sum equivalent to the utility of his holding as part of a large pasture farm." [4]).

There was also far less need for agricultural labourers than

1) Cunningham, l. c., p. 474. — 2) Ashley, II p. 281. — 3) Ibid., p. 284. — 4) Cunningham, l. c., p. 408.

before. "The decay of tillage and lack of rural employment, during this century," says Professor Cunningham "rest on unimpeachable evidence" [1]. In the 14th century "the problem of the unemployed, as it now presents itself, had not yet arisen." But the agrarian changes "deprived great numbers of the agricultural labouring class, — small customary tenants and cottagers, — of the means of support in their old places of abode, and sent them wandering over the country" [2].

The appropriation of the whole of the land had thus given to the rural economy of England a new and essentially modern character: tnere were now leaseholders and tenants at will, labouring poor and unemployed. And the ancient institution of serfdom could not hold its own in the presence of such thorough changes. "The slow agricultural revolution which rendered their services less useful to the manorial lords, gradually set the villans free by removing the interest their masters had in retaining a hold upon them." "In some instances the exaction of predial services from villans by manorial lords can be traced as late as the time of Elizabeth; but though no change was made in the law, the lords seem to have found that it was not worth their while to assert their rights over the persons of their bondmen" [3].

There were, however, many parts of England in which scarcely any inclosures took place [4]. Here the villeins remained on their lands and gradually became copyholders. They were still bound to services, which, however, were generally commuted for small money payments, so the conditions of their tenure were annoying rather than oppressive. Moreover, their obligations were no longer personal, but territorial; they were not astricted to the soil. And as they had an hereditary right to their holdings, they differed but little from freeholders. The "innocuous curiosities of copyhold," survivals of ancient serfdom, have lasted up to modern times [5].

Our theory can thus be of much use in accounting for the

---

1) Ibid., p. 393. — 2) Ashley, II pp. 336, 352. — 3) Cunningham, l. c., pp. 361, 476. — 4) See Ashley, II pp. 286—288. — 5) See Gonner, Article "Bauernbefreiung in Grossbritannien" in Handwörterbuch, 2nd edition, II pp. 593, 594.

changes which have taken place in the rural economy of England. As long as there was still free land, *i. e.* land which, though sometimes claimed by an owner, could not fetch any reasonable price, the cultivators were astricted to the soil; but as soon as the proprietors had got the practical command over the whole of the land, many of the villeins were evicted and replaced by leaseholders or tenants at will or became such themselves; and the remainder became copyholders, *i. e.* proprietors obliged to some services or payments without being personally unfree.

We shall inquire now whether in Germany too the appropriation of the whole of the land coincided with the transition from serfdom to freedom.

§ 11. *The rural classes of medieval Germany.*

In the time of the Merovingians the greater part of the country was covered with forests and people relied on the products of the forests for a considerable portion of their subsistence. Land was abundant, and even the cultivated land had hardly any exchange value [1]).

Much new land was, however, already being taken into cultivation. The village communities, consisting of free peasants, as well as separate members of these communities, cleared considerable portions of the waste land lying round the villages. In the 8th century some communities already forbade individuals to reclaim land; but this was still of rare occurrence; generally speaking the waste could be appropriated by whoever chose to take it into cultivation [2]).

The bulk of the population consisted of free peasants. There were two unfree classes: slaves and *lites* (a kind of serfs); but these were not numerous [3]).

The free peasant, though he had plenty of land, was rather poorly off; he had no slaves and so could only dispose of the labour power of himself and his family; and in this

---

1) Inama-Sternegg, I pp. 110, 111, 163—165. — 2) Ibid., pp. 81—83. — 3) Ibid., pp. 72, 60, 70.

time of extensive tillage the produce of each man's labour was small [1]).

Great proprietors were still rare. They worked their own lands with slaves. Sometimes, however, they gave pieces of land in use, generally to slaves; for, says our informant, the free peasants did not like to take the land of the nobles and so make themselves dependent on them [2]). And when land was given in use to free peasants (especially by the church) this was done on very advantageous terms, often at a nominal rent [3]).

Land was thus abundant, slavery existed, and tenant farmers and free labourers were absent.

In the Carolingian period the clearing of forests went on continually. Some land was still reclaimed by free peasants, but much more by the great proprietors who controlled abundant labour forces [4]). The lords were already beginning to claim much uncultivated land, the reclaimiug of which they only allowed on condition of the cultivator subjecting himself to them. There was far less unappropriated land than in the foregoing period, and such as there was was claimed by the king [5]). Yet we cannot speak of an appropriation of the whole of the land; for we know that a claim of the king to large tracts of uninhabited land is practically of little consequence. Accordingly our informant states that land was still abundant. The free peasants were already in a difficult position, not, however, because land was scarce, but because they could not provide the labour necessary to convert woods and marshes into arable land [6]).

In this period the free peasants began to be absorbed by the great proprietors. The latter wanted labourers and did their utmost to astrict the common freemen to their estates. Many people placed themselves under the protection of nobles; others, being reduced to poverty (especially through the institution of the *wergild,* and the compulsory military service which interfered with the cultivation of the land) fell into the hands of the lords; and some were straightway made serfs by violence. As the landlords had the right of jurisdiction and

---

1) Ibid., pp. 147, 148, 165. — 2) Ibid., pp. 119, 120. — 3) Ibid., pp. 123, 124. — 4) Ibid., pp. 207— 217. — 5) Ibid., pp. 220, 221, 279—281. — 6) Ibib., pp. 382, 235, 236.

other public rights, they could easily subject the small land-holders under some pretext or even without any. Former free peasants, *lites*, and such slaves as had received a piece of land in use, though designated by different names, came to form practically one class, the labouring as opposed to the ruling class [1]). A manorial organization arose similar to that which existed in England. There were some slaves for personal service and agricultural labour and a great number of dependent peasants of various kinds, who had to cultivate the demesne of the lord and yield him part of the produce of their own holdings [2]).

Free labourers were found rarely if at all [3]).

Our informant in several passages speaks of freemen destitute of land [4]). But these people are not in any way to be identified with the poor of modern times who depend on wages. They were generally foreigners who had no rights in any village community; but the lords were always ready to receive them and give them a piece of land in use on condition of their rendering services and paying tributes. The natural increase of the labouring population and immigration of foreign labour did not yet cause any difficulty [5]).

Most of the cultivators of this time had not the right of leaving the manors to which their holdings belonged [6]).

We see that in this period there was still much free land; slavery existed and serfdom was on the increase; leaseholders, tenants at will and free labourers were wanting. All this agrees with our theory.

In the next period colonization and reclaiming of waste land went on on a large scale. But at the same time the population increased and the value of the land increased with it. Lamprecht, speaking of the 13th century, writes: "Colonization and reclaiming of land had entirely changed the condition of the rural population between the 10th and the 13th century. In the time of the Carolingians wood and land had

---

1) Ibid., pp. 226—257. — 2) Ibid., pp. 237, 367—371, 381. — 3) Ibid., pp. 236, 367. — 4) Ibid., pp., 240, 241, 319, 355. Even in the Merovingian period there were already such people, according to him, see pp. 122, 124, 163. — 5) Ibid., pp. 241, 382. — 6) Ibid., p. 367.

still been regarded as inexhaustible goods of the nation, like the sun, air and water; but now the limitations of the geographical basis of national life appeared more and more clearly. There had been an immense range of land to grow food upon; but now the supply of land became limited, chiefly and first on the Rhine, in Suabia and Franconia, afterwards in Saxony, and finally in Bavaria, the Tyrol, and Styria; people had to shift on a limited area. The soil became, more than before, an object of economic value; its price kept continually increasing. In the 12th century, in some prosperous districts, land seems to have attained twelve times the value it had in the 9th; and even afterwards, down to the second half of the 13th century, an increase of about 50 per cent. is to be observed. Taking into consideration that land was still regarded, especially by the ruling classes, as the only basis of social and political influence (though already other sources of large incomes were gradually arising), we may understand how intense the struggle for the possession of the soil must have been at this period" [1]).

The right of the king to unappropriated land was now enforced more strictly than before, and the lords began to claim a right of property over the commons surrounding the villages, which, however, were often still left to the use of the peasants [2]).

However, there was no over-population as yet. The proprietors did their best to attract people to the vast newly colonized districts, especially to the eastern parts of Germany [3]).

During the whole of this period the landlords went on subjugating the rural population, so that at the end of it the peasant proprietors, who had once formed the bulk of the population, had almost entirely disappeared, and most of the land was taken up with the estates of the great proprietors [4]).

But the increase in the value of land already made itself

---

1) Lamprecht, III pp. 56, 57. See also Inama-Sternegg, II pp. 70, 164, 285. — 2) Inama-Sternegg, II pp. 115, 145, 84, 85, 207, 209. — 3) Ibid., pp. 4—27. Similarly in France, in the 12th century, the landlords encouraged emigration to the outlying, newly reclaimed districts. Villeins who were willing to settle in these parts were granted special privileges, a house and land were given them at a nominal rent (Luchaire, in Lavisse, Vol. II Part. II p., 336.) — 4) Inama-Sternegg, II pp. 36—38.

felt in the way in which the lords managed their estates. They less and less frequently worked their own lands; their chief aim was no longer the disposal of the labour of their dependents, but the receiving of rent. The labour dues were often commuted for money payments [1]).

Labour was not worth so much to the lords as it had been. They sometimes emancipated their slaves, retaining the land which they had given them in use [2]).

At the same time a class of free tenants arose. Lamprecht remarks that while the value of land had considerably increased the tributes which the villeins had to pay had remained unchanged for several centuries. In an economic sense the landlords had been dispossessed of a large proportion of their property in the land. Therefore it was not their interest to let serfdom continue.

"At this time, especialy since the middle of the 12th century, the villeins and landlords of the most progressive districts settled their mutual relations by free contract. Serfdom was abolished, sometimes entirely, sometimes for the greater part, some formalities only subsisting. The former villein acquired the right to emigrate, and remained as a free tenant on the land he had till then occupied. Thus, by leasing his lands for terms of years, and sometimes for life or on hereditary tenancy, the landlord got back the full rent of his property; and this system, especially the lease for years, enabled him to raise the rent at the end of each term, according as the value of the land had increased in the meantime" [3]).

Inama-Sternegg does not quite agree with this view of Lamprecht's. Even where the rent was higher than the former customary payment, he says, the leaseholder was free from the labour dues and additional payments to which the villein had been bound, so the transition from fixed payment to rent did not always mean an enhancement of the obligation of the peasant [4]). Yet this writer too states that the leasing of land became more and more frequent. There were free contracts between proprietor and tenant, which did not interfere with the

1) Ibid., pp. 70, 71, 63. — 2) Ibid., p. 64. — 3) Lamprecht, III p. 63. — 4) Inama-Sternegg, III Part I pp. 394, 395.

personal liberty of the latter; even non-fulfilment of his obligations by the tenant had only pecuniary consequences [1]).

We cannot but think that the reason given by Lamprecht
for the transition from servile to free tenure is true. For even
when the original rent was not higher than the former customary payment plus the value of the labour dues, the possibility of raising the rent after each term remained.

We hear of free tenants in this period, but not yet of free
labourers. This is exactly what our theory teaches us to expect.
Land, in some parts of Germany, had already acquired a high
value; such land must have been very renumerative, and so
people were ready to pay a rent for its use, even though there
was still land to be had gratis or at a nominal rent, but far
from the market and therefore less profitable. But the country
was not yet so densely peopled that there were men who could
not secure the use of any piece of land; therefore a class of
people dependent on wages did not yet exist.

In the 13th century much new land was still taken into
cultivation, in Western as well as Eastern Germany; but in
the following centuries very little land was added to the arable
area. The woods, which had formerly been regarded as inexhaustible, were no longer present in great abundance, and the
rulers of the German states as well as the landlords exerted
themselves to preserve the remainder and forbade the peasants
to clear them. From the middle of the 14th century these
prohibitive measures became general [2]).

As the population continued to increase, land became
scarce. In many parts of Southern and Western Germany
the lords parcelled out their lands in small portions, and
farms of the size which had been customary for centuries
became rare [3]).

The rights of the peasants to the use of the commons, on
which they had always relied for a considerable portion of
their subsistence, were now restricted, and the lords asserted
their claims to the commons more strictly than before [4]).

---

1) Ibid., II pp. 203, 204. — 2) Ibid., III Part I pp. 1—13. — 3) Lamprecht, V Part I p.
82; Inama-Sternegg, l. c., p. 212. — 4) Inama-Sternegg, l. c., pp. 38, 214, 237, 285 sqq.

Another consequence of the increase of population was that cattle-keeping was no longer possible on such a large scale as formerly when the common pasture occupied a great part of the land. At the end of the Middle Ages there was a scarcity of meat, and people had to rely, more than before, on vegetable food [1]).

The need of the landlords for the services of the peasants went on diminishing. They no longer worked their own estates; nearly the whole of their income consisted of the payments in kind and in money which they received from their dependents [2]).

In Lower Saxony and part of Westphalia the lords, as early as the 13th century, emancipated considerable numbers of villeins in their own interest. For the villeins had gradually acquired some right to their holdings, and the landlords, by setting them free, got back the free disposal of the land, which they thenceforth let out to free tenants [3]).

In the 14th century the lords began to turn out peasants (*Bauernlegen*) and lease the land of which they thus re-acquired the free disposal [4]).

Free tenancies became now general, parts of the demesne, as well as lands which had been held in servile tenure, being leased. The increased demand for land enabled the lords to let small allotments at extravagant prices [5]).

Even where the customary tenures remained, the obligations of the peasants, which had been personal, in many cases became territorial, the holder of the land as such being subject to payments. And the conditions of this tenure were so little servile that sometimes nobles and knights received such land in use and took the obligations on themselves [6]).

The difference between farmers and agricultural labourers now first came into existence. The latter most often held a small patch of land, but this was not sufficient to live upon; they depended on wages. Besides agricultural labourers there were male and female servants for household labour. The regu-

---

1) Ibid., pp. 366, 367. — 2) Ibid., pp. 261—265. — 3) Ibid., p. 220. — 4) Ibid., pp. 176, 201, 249. — 5) Ibid., pp. 202—205, 208—210, 225, 251, 255, 256, 277; Lamprecht, l. c., p. 82. — 6) Inama-Sternegg, l. c., pp. 46, 174, 175.

lation of wages by law, which occurred especially after the
ravages of the great plague, proves that in the southern and
western parts of Germany free labour had become general.
Such servile work as still remained was often done by labourers
hired by the peasant to whose duty the work fell, just as in
the case of the English peasant who "found" a man [1]).

All land was now held as property; consequently the land
was more and more held by free tenants and worked with
free labourers dependent on wages, whereas serfdom gradually
died out.

In the 15th century, however, according to both Lamprecht
and Inama-Sternegg, serfdom and even slavery reappeared.

Lamprecht, after speaking of the raising of rents by the
landlords, adds: "But more disastrous in its consequences than
all this was the manner in which the landlords dealt with
the increasing surplus population of the farms occupied by
their villeins. Formerly, younger sons of villeins, as well as
children of free parents, had removed to the woods for the
purpose of clearing them; and it was with their help that
the landlords had in the course of the 12th and 13th centuries
extended their landed properties. In later times such younger
sons had often gone to the towns or the newly colonized
districts of Eastern Germany. Now there was a stagnation
among them as well as among the small remainder of the
free population. There remained no other alternative but to
divide the farms of the villeins. But the interest of the landlord was opposed to this. He had no security of receiving
rent and services from farms parcelled out into small allotments.
Therefore he did not, as a rule, divide the farms into more
than four parts; and those of the servile population who could
not secure the use of such a small holding were regarded as
slaves. This institution, the origin of which went back to
the first half of the 12th century, had till then been almost
entirely foreign to the development of Germany. Together
with a rural proletariat destitute of nearly everything, a real
slavery came now for the first time into existence on German
ground.... And this new slave class went on continually

---

[1] Ibid., pp. 48, 50, 51, 213, 223, 241, 282, 303—309, 314, 408, 413.

increasing; in the first half of the 15th century they already
formed a considerable number, about whose fate patriots were
very uneasy.... Nor did the evil stop here. The term slavery,
used first with regard to villeins who occupied no farm, was
soon applied to all villeins, in order to tax them more and
more heavily and dispute their right of succeeding to the
farms of their parents, which had been established at least
since the end of the 12th century. Finally the landlords came
to regard even free tenants as slaves and slavery as the only
status of the rural population" [1]).

We can easily understand that the lords designated these
proletarians by the most contemptuous name they could devise.
But were they really slaves? A slave, as opposed to a free
labourer, is not allowed to leave his master. Now it is remarkable that Inama-Sternegg, describing the condition of the
rural population in the different states of Germany, though
he states that in the newly colonized eastern parts of Germany the peasants, who had been free, were restricted in their
right of leaving their lords, mentions no such particulars of
Western Germany [2]). And the chief aim of the peasants, in
their revolts at the end of the 15th century, was not to acquire
personal freedom, but to retain the use of the commons,
which the lords were appropriating [3]).

The peasants were, indeed, obliged to more services in the
15th than in the 13th and 14th centuries. But we cannot regard
this as a mark of returning serfdom or slavery; for Inama-
Sternegg explicitly states that the greater oppression of the
rural classes in the 15th century was chiefly due to the increase
of the services required by the rulers of the several German
states. The services exacted by the landlords had rather
diminished [4]).

The same writer, recapitulating his conclusions as to the con-
of the rural population at the end of the Middle Ages,
begins by saying that the cultivators, who formerly had had
an hereditary right to the land on condition of paying a fixed
sum, were now far more heavily taxed and had little security

---

1) Lamprecht, l. c., p. 83; see also Inama-Sternegg, l. c., pp. 54, 55, 420. — 2) Inama-
Sternegg, l. c., pp. 56—61. — 3) Ibid., p. 67. — 4) Ibid., pp. 54, 398, 417, 419, 411.

of remaining on the land [1]). We think that this is what the statements of our informants about the reappearance of slavery mean. The cultivators were not slaves, but impoverished and despised tenants at will and agricultural labourers.

At any rate, in the 16th century eviction of peasants, which is the reverse of astriction to the soil, became of frequent occurrence. Ashley, who has consulted some of the best literature, states that "the Bavarian code of 1518 laid down that the peasant had no hereditary right to his holding, and not even a life interest unless he could show some documentary evidence. In Mecklenburg a decree of 1606 declared that the peasants were not *emphyteutae* but *coloni*, whom their lords could compel to give up the lands allotted to them, and who could claim no right of inheritance even when their ancestors had held the land from time immemorial. In Holstein, again, a great number of the peasants were expelled from their holdings, and such as remained became tenants at will" [2]).

Serfdom, in Southern and Western Germany, thus died out towards the end of the Middle Ages, at a time when population had become numerous and land scarce.

The eastern parts of Germany had quite another agrarian history. Here serfdom was not common before the 16th century. From this time, however, and especially after the Thirty Years' War, it became more and more general. As this is quite a separate history we shall not speak of it any further [3]).

---

1) Ibid., p. 420; see also p. 311. — 2) Ashley, II pp. 281, 282; see also Inama-Sternegg, III Part II p. 201. — 3) On the history of the rural classes in Eastern Germany, see Knapp, Die Bauernbefreiung.

It may be of some interest to point out the great resemblance between the rise of Roman *colonatus* as described by Max Weber and the rise of serfdom in Eastern Germany. In both countries most of the peasants were originally free (Weber, Römische Agrargeschichte, p. 244; Knapp, I p. 32). The landlords, who formerly had passed most of their time outside their properties, when they lost their military function took the cultivation of their manors into their own hands (Weber, l. c., pp. 243, 244; Knapp, I p. 37). They soon acqui? d rights of jurisdiction over the peasants (Weber, l. c., p. 260; Knapp, I p. 33), and began to compel them to work on the demesne (Weber, l. c., p. 244; Knapp, I p. 40). The cultivators lost the right of emigrating (Weber, l. c., pp. 256—258; Knapp, I p. 42). Even the *Bauernlegen, i. e.* the joining of a peasant's holding to the demesne, occurred in Rome as well as in Eastern Germany (Weber, l. c., p. 247; Knapp, I pp. 50, 55). And it is most remarkable that in both countries the rise of serfdom took place at an advanced period of their history.

This proves once more that the institutions of different countries may closely resemble

We think the above remarks on England and the older parts of Germany may suffice to show that our theory can throw some light on the agrarian history of Western Europe.

We are fully aware that the condition of the rural classes must have been determined by many more circumstances of greater and lesser importance. But it seems to us that the general cause of which we have spoken in these paragraphs is second to no other in its operation [1]).

§ 12. *Open and closed resources.*

We have said that among agricultural peoples slavery, as an industrial system, only exists where there is still free land; it disappears as soon as all land has been appropiated. We have also seen that slavery does not prevail to any considerable extent where subsistence is dependent on capital [2]). We may

---

each other, even in many details, without the one country having derived its institutions from the other. For even the influence of Roman law cannot serve as an explanation of this resemblance, as Roman law takes little notice of *colonatus* (Weber l. c., p. 259).

[1]) We must admit that we are not sure whether the facts of Roman agrarian history agree with our theory. In Rome slavery prevailed to a large extent at a time when the relative scarcity of land gave rise to the difficulties about the *ager publicus*.

We shall not attempt to solve this question. We will only mention our impression, on reading Weber's *Römische Agrargeschichte*, viz. that, even in the time of the Empire, though some land fetched a high price, all disposable land had not yet been appropriated, and therefore the want of servile labour remained. At the beginning of the Empire free labourers were very scarce, and could only be got to help the landlords in sowing and at harvest time on condition of receiving a pretty considerable part of the harvest (Weber, l. c., pp. 236—238). Under Augustus and Tiberius the procuring of slaves from abroad became very difficult, and this led to kidnapping of men by the landlords (Ibid., p. 242). In the boundary provinces, even in later centuries, barbarians were imported and became *coloni* attached to the soil (Ibid., pp. 259, 260).

Slavery proper declined from the beginning of the Empire (Meyer, Altertum, p. 71); but the *coloni*, who originally seem to have been free tenants, gradually lost the right of removing from the manor they inhabited (Weber, l. c., pp. 242, 248—250, 256—258).

We must, however, bear in mind that the writers on the economic history of Rome still disagree very much, not only as to the explanation of the facts, but as to the facts themselves. See Max Weber's article on "Agrarverhältnisse im Altertum", in Handwörterbuch der Staatswissenschaften, 3rd edition, Vol. I. — [2]) The reader will remember that there are tribes among which land is abundant, but nobody can live upon land and human labour only: the possession of capital is necessary, and those destitute of capital have to apply to the owners for employment. The best instance is furnished by the pastoral tribes.

We have purposely avoided speaking of countries in which all land has been appro-

now combine these two conclusions into this general rule: *slavery, as an industrial system, is not likely to exist where subsistence depends on material resources which are present in limited quantity.*

A tribe or nation cannot subsist without labour (though the amount of labour required is sometimes small); but, besides this, material resources are always necessary. The resources which man uses to procure his subsistence are of two kinds: gifts of nature, and products of human labour. The latter are commonly termed capital; their supply is always limited. Most of the former (air, water, the heat of the sun, etc.) exist in unlimited quantity, *i. e.* there is so much of them that nobody wants to appropriate them. Land is also a gift of nature, and in some very thinly peopled countries, where there is much more fertile ground than can be cultivated, it has not any more value than air and water. But as all land has not the same properties, it soon comes to pass that the most fertile and most favourably situated land is appropriated by some men to the exclusion of others. This is the origin of rent. Finally, when the less valuable grounds have also been appropriated, free land no longer exists; there is no piece of land but has its definite owner [1]. This last state of things has social consequences very similar to those which exist where subsistence depends on capital. In both cases indispensable means of production are in the hands of definite persons; therefore a man destitute either of land or of capital (according as subsistence depends on the former or the latter), cannot subsist independently of the owners, but has to apply to them for employment. More-

---

priated and capital also plays a great part, as it is the case in the manufacturing countries of modern Europe. Here the structure of society is very complicated and difficult to disentangle. We think, however, that here also the most important fact is the appropriation of the soil.

1) "The earth, as we have already seen, is not the only agent of nature, which has a productive power; but it is the only one, or nearly so, that one set of men take to themselves, to the exclusion of others; and of which, consequently, they can appropriate the benefits. The waters of rivers, and of the sea, by the power which they have of giving movement to our machines, carrying our boats, nourishing our fish, have also a productive power; the wind which turns our mills, and even the heat of the sun, work for us; but happily no one has yet been able to say, the wind and the sun are mine, and the service which they render must be paid for." J. B. Say, Économie Politique, as quoted by Ricardo, p. 35.

over, in both cases more than a limited quantity of labour cannot be profitably employed: the owner of capital, or of a limited space of land, cannot derive any profit from employing more than a certain number of labourers. Therefore in either case slavery, as an industrial system, is not likely to exist.

These considerations lead us to an important conclusion. All the peoples of the earth, whether they subsist by hunting, fishing, cattle-breeding, agriculture, trade or manufactures, may be divided into two categories. Among the peoples of the first category the means of subsistence are open to all; every one who is able-bodied and not defective in mind can provide for himself independently of any capitalist or landlord. Among some of these peoples capital is of some use, and some valuable lands are already held as property; but those who are destitute of such advantages can perfectly well do without them, for there are still abundant natural supplies open to them. Among the peoples of the other category subsistence depends on resources of which the supply is limited, and therefore people destitute of these resources are dependent on the owners. It may be convenient to suggest technical names for these two categories. We shall speak of *peoples with open resources* and *peoples with closed resources.* We think the meaning of these terms is clear, and they may be convenient for use. The distinction is an important one. We suppose we have sufficiently proved that the relations between the social classes differ largely, according as resources are open or closed: only among peoples with open resources can slavery and serfdom exist, whereas free labourers dependent on wages are only found among peoples with closed resources [1]. Our distinction may prove valuable in other respects also, *e. g.* over-population and lack of employment are unknown among peoples with open resources; war, which, when resources are open, has sometimes rather the character of a sport, becomes more serious when resources have become closed, for then its object is to extend the supply

---

1) This is the general rule. We are fully aware that there are exceptions due to secondary causes, internal and external. Moreover, open resources do not necessarily lead to slavery or serfdom: there are many simple societies in which there are no labouring, as opposed to ruling classes, everybody, or nearly everybody, working for his own wants (*e. g.* among many hunters, fishers, and hunting agriculturists).

of land or capital at the cost of the enemy [1]); pessimism is more likely to prevail among peoples with closed than among peoples with open resources, etc. [2]). We shall not, however, enlarge upon these points any further.

Most savage tribes have open resources. All hunters have (with the exception, perhaps, of some Australians): neither the game nor the hunting territories are held as property. Further, most fishers: fishing is carried on in a simple manner and does not yet require capital. And finally, most agricultural tribes; among them *superest ager*, as Tacitus says of the ancient Germans [3]).

Savage tribes with closed resources are: 1° possibly some Australian hunters, if it is true that among them every inch of ground is held as property, 2° the Eskimos (fishers), who cannot get on without a boat, or a sledge and dogs, 3° all pastoral tribes, 4° the agricultural tribes inhabiting most of the Polynesian and Micronesian islands, the Fijians and perhaps a few agricultural tribes outside Oceania.

We shall not inquire whether the civilized nations of ancient and modern times have, or had, open or closed resources. We will only remark that in Western Europe resources, from open, have become closed. Yet they are not altogether closed, as long as there are still thinly peopled countries open for emigration. Whether the white races will still have room for expansion for a considerable time, we cannot know.

When we were preparing the first edition of this work, we thought the distinction between countries with open and with closed resources had not been made before. Since we read Lange's book on the labour problem and saw that the author speaks in the same sense of open and closed countries or open and closed economy. We give here the passages of most interest, bearing on the subject. "There is a great difference between

---

1) Malthus (p. 453), speaking of war, says: "One of its first causes and most powerful impulses was undoubtedly an insufficiency of room and food". — 2) See Wakefield, pp. 126—134, on the happiness of settlers in new countries. — 3) A good instance is afforded by the Angoni as described bij Wiese. Their king, he tells us, subjected neighbouring tribes and brought them to his own country. "He did not care for the territory deserted by these tribes. It was his chief aim to have the people; to landed property he attached little value" (Wiese, p. 197).

the economy of open and closed civilized countries. In the former there is still an abundance of land fit for cultivation, of which every labourer has the free use; in the latter all land has been taken into cultivation and appropriated. This difference is so fundamental, that it would be best to formulate a separate economic theory for either of the two cases and then, in applying the theory to the facts, to examine how far, in every instance, the characteristics of open or closed economy are present. The latter proceeding is always necessary; for the important distinction we have made is a relative one, no country presenting exclusively the conditions of either open or closed culture." In another chapter the author dwells more at length on the idea, laid down in the last sentence. "The earth still contains large territories, not yet taken into cultivation, which in a certain sense are open to every one; but there are such factors as habits, prejudices, etc., which bind people to their own country, and there are further material impediments to emigration from old civilized countries, which are so great, that the economy of such countries may practically be regarded as closed, without being such in an absolute sense. On the other hand, even in the most open colonial country there are always circumstances which make the occupation of uncultivated land difficult and so the economy of such a country presents some characteristics of a closed economy. Between these two types there are numberless intermediate stages and therefore economic life is in reality subject to the influences of both open and closed economy. But in theory a sharp line of demarcation must be drawn between these two states of society; for only so can we attain to a right understanding of real economic life" [1]).

In the following paragraphs we shall speak of the effect of secondary causes among agricultural tribes. We shall not, however, enter into many details. The difficulty, in our branch of science, is always, that we have so few works of predecessors to rely upon. For instance, we shall speak of the influence of trade among agricultural tribes. Now, if any accurate re-

---

[1]) Lange, Die Arbeiterfrage, pp. 199, 334.

searches had been made into the general effects of trade, we should be able to conclude that trade having been proved to have such general effects, it must have such an influence on slavery. But as such is not the case, we should be obliged, if we were thoroughly to investigate the subject, to inquire what are the general effects of trade. An equally close study of militarism, of the condition of women, etc., would be required. And as in this way our book would never come to an end, we shall content ourselves with giving a few outlines, which we hope may turn the attention of other ethnologists to the important problems which the ensuing paragraphs will contain.

§ 13. Condition of women.

As we have remarked before, the position held by the women of a tribe determines to some extent whether or not slaves are wanted. Where all the drudgery is performed, and can be performed, by the women, and the men do not want to relieve them of it, there is no great use for slave labour. But where women enjoy high consideration, the men are more likely to procure slaves who are to assist the women in their work.

We shall speak first of the latter fact, of slaves performing female labour. It is very often stated that slaves are employed for domestic labour. And as, in countries where slavery does not exist, domestic labour is nearly always incumbent on the women, slaves who perform such work alleviate the women's task. Where slavery prevails to a great extent it even occurs that slave-owners, female as well as male, have scarcely anything to do, all work falling to the share of the slaves. The slave-owners, in such case, form the aristocracy; the slaves, and the poor freemen unable to purchase slaves, are the labouring classes. We may remind the reader of ancient Rome, where the domestic slaves, the *familia urbana*, performed all domestic services required by the rich, and of the women of the upper classes in Mohammedan countries, who spend their time in idleness in the harems.

We have seen that among some pastoral tribes domestic labour is the chief occupation of the slaves. We do not recollect having found any instance of a similar state of things among any agricultural tribe, and cannot think that such will anywhere be the case. A rich cattle-keeper can easily support, by the produce of his cattle, some domestic slaves who perform no productive labour. But among agricultural tribes it is otherwise: subsistence here depends almost entirely on labour; therefore slaves performing unproductive labour can only be kept if there are other slaves who till the soil and procure food for the family. It is not probable that the master will himself undertake the cultivation required to feed the slaves who assist his wife in her work; nor would the wife be glad to receive slaves from her husband, if she had to provide for them by working on the field. The Romans would not have kept a *familia urbana*, if there had not also been a *familia rustica*.

Hitherto we have spoken of unproductive female labour. But women, in primitive agricultural societies, often perform productive labour also: in many cases the tilling of the soil is incumbent on them. We may suppose that the introduction of slaves has often served to free the women from this task. We shall not, however, proceed to a closer examination of this point; for this would require a digression on the division of labour between the sexes, which falls beyond the scope of the present volume.

On the other hand, the place of slaves is often supplied by wives. We have seen that among the Australian hunters polygamy widely prevails and serves economic purposes. The same is the case among some agricultural tribes.

In § 8 the non-existence of slavery in most of the Melanesian islands has been left unexplained. We shall see now that in several of these islands a "slavery of women" prevails which bears much resemblance to slavery proper. Purchase of wives is in vogue; and most of the women are bought by the rich, many of whom possess a large number of wives. And the women must work hard to increase the income of their owners [1]).

Guppy, in his description of the Solomon Islands, states: "The powerful chiefs of the islands of Bougainville Straits

[1]) See Melching, p. 19.

usually possess a large number of wives of whom only the few that retain their youth and comeliness enjoy much of the society of their lord. The majority, having been supplanted in the esteem of their common husband, have sunk into a condition of drudgery, finding their employment and their livelihood in toiling for the master whose affections they once possessed. I learned from Gorai, the Shortland chief, who has between eighty and a hundred wives, that the main objection he has against missionaries settling on his islands is, that they would insist on his giving up nearly all his wives, thereby depriving him of those by whose labour his plantations are cultivated and his household supplied with food. A great chief, he remarked, required a large staff of workers to cultivate his extensive lands, or, in other words, numerous women to work in his plantations and to bring the produce home" [1]).

This statement is very remarkable. In the second chapter of Part I we have seen that in these same islands of Bougainville Straits boys are captured from the neighbouring islands. Guppy calls them slaves, but at the same time tells us that they "enjoy most of the rights of a native of the common class" [2]). There is thus no difficulty in obtaining slaves; yet slavery is little developed, for the simple reason that polygamy perfectly serves the purposes of slavery.

Ribbe equally remarks that on Bougainville polygamy is common. The wife is the slave of her husband: she has to till the fields, to perform most of the domestic work and to take care of the children. In the Shortland Islands (near Bougainville) the wife is the slave and beast of burden of her husband, rather than his companion [3]).

In the Nissan Islands, according to Sorge, most of the work is done by the women [4]).

In the New Hebrides polygamy also prevails. The price paid for a wife varies from 10 tot 20 pigs, "according to her capabilities as a worker in the yam-patch." "They [the women] learn in their girlhood all that fits them to be man's slave and

1) Guppy, pp. 44, 45. — 2) See above, p. 90. — 3) Ribbe, pp. 100, 141. — 4) Sorge, in Steinmetz's Rechtsverhältnisse, p. 399.

toiler in the fields". "Women are degraded to the level of brute beasts, doing all the hard field work, and being made to carry loads which appear quite disproportionate to their ugly-shaped bodies and thin legs" [1]. Hagen and Pineau give a similar account of female labour, and add that a man's wealth depends on the number of his wives [2].

De Vaux, speaking of the women of New Caledonia, says: "All the drudgery is incumbent on them. They perform the clearing and digging of the soil, carry on their backs crushing loads of ignames and taros to the village, and, if a chief has promised you assistance in some fatiguing work that you want to have quickly done, he will send you a gang of these miserable beings who may scarcely be called women." Turner remarks: "Chiefs had ten, twenty, and thirty wives. The more wives the better plantations and the more food." "If a wife misbehaved, the chief did not divorce her, but made her work all the harder". And Rochas tells us that the New Caledonians keep no servants, but have many wives instead; rich men have as many wives as they want for the cultivation of their fields [3].

In Neu Pommern, according to Parkinson, "every man who can afford it buys many wives. For a wife is a capital that yields a fair interest; she works from an early age till her strength is spent; and when, from age or by being overtaxed with labour, she grows sickly and decrepit, she perishes unheeded by anybody. The wife is nothing but the beast of burden of her husband; she performs all labour, tills the soil, cleans the dwelling, prepares the food, and carries the reaped produce in heavy baskets far away to the market. The husband therefore regards his wife as a valuable property." "The husband continually urges his wives to work, that they may earn much *dewarra* [shell-money] for him; for the more *dewarra* he owns the greater is the consideration and influence he enjoys. But the lot of the wives is not bettered by an increase in the wealth of the husband. The wives of a man who owns thousands of coils of *dewarra* have no better life and are no

1) Somerville, New Hebrides, pp. 3, 5, 7, 4. — 2) Hagen and Pineau, p. 331; see also Meinicke, Neue Hebriden, p. 340. — 3) De Vaux, p. 330; Turner, Samoa, p. 341; Rochas, p. 229; see also Brainne, p. 248.

less overworked than the wife of a very poor man who has no property except his only wife." And Danks states that "a man may have as many wives as he can afford to purchase. If he cannot afford to purchase one, and his credit is low, he may have to remain single. The headmen are generally rich men, hence they invariably have a number of wives, ranging from three to six". "Married life in New Britain is a hard one for the women. They are beaten and ill-treated by their husbands as occasion may arise" [1]).

In New Mecklenburg the condition of the women is equally bad [2]).

In Fiji, according to Williams, "polygamy is looked upon as a principal source of a chief's power and wealth." And Pritchard says: "The greater the number of wives a man had, the better his social position .... Besides the acknowledged wives, there were attached to the household of the chiefs slave-women, who, though performing the most menial services, were at the same time nothing else than what the odalisques are in the Turkish harem" [3]).

We see that these Melanesian wives supply the place of slaves. They are bought like slaves; they have to work for their owners like slaves; and their labour, like that of slaves, increases the wealth of their lords. Another point of resemblance is this. In slave countries it is generally the rich only who are able to procure slaves; poor freemen have to work for themselves. Here it is the rich who appropriate the women; and many of the poor have to remain single. Here, as in all countries where polygamy is practised, it is only the minority of the men who can live in polygamy; for everywhere the number of women is nearly equal to that of men. And as in Melanesia the rich, who otherwise would want slaves, have many wives to work for them, slaves are not required.

We cannot explain here why in Melanesia womankind is so much at a discount, whereas among some other savage tribes (*e. g.* on the North Pacific Coast of North America) the sex

---

1) Parkinson, Im Bismarck-Archipel, pp. 98, 99, 101; Danks, pp. 294, 292, 293; see also Melching, pp. 43, 44. — 2) Parkinson, Dreissig Jahre, p. 269. — 3) Williams, p. 178; Pritchard, p. 372.

commands such respect [1]). But we clearly see what is the effect of this state of things. Much labour is wanted; otherwise the women would not have to work so hard, and the rich would not keep so many female labourers. Yet slaves are not kept in any considerable number, because the women supply the place of slaves.

One might object, that possibly the women are held in such a slavelike state because male slaves are impossible or very difficult to procure, or because the coercive power of these tribes is not strong enough to admit of the keeping of slaves, or because male captives, where they are introduced into the tribe (as in the islands Bougainville Straits), are wanted for warriors. Shortly expressed the objection is, that slavery is not wanting because there exists a "slavery of women," but "slavery of women" exists because slavery proper is wanting. We must own that this is quite possible. But, whatever be the cause of this "slavery of women," as soon as it exists it renders slavery less necessary than it would otherwise be. War is frequent in Melanesia [2]), so there is no physical impossibility of procuring captives. And though it may be difficult to keep male slaves subjected, — if the men were unable to impose all work on the women and obliged to perform their due share of it themselves, they would decidedly take more pains to procure slaves and set them to work. A low condition of women, though only a secundary factor, certainly is a factor which tends to make slavery proper superfluous.

§ 14. Commerce.

In § 1 of this chapter we have found the following numbers of positive and negative cases among commercial agricultural tribes:

---

1) The condition of women is not, however, equally bad in all Melanesian islands. Among the Western Tribes of Torres Straits "the women appear to have had a good deal to say on most questions, and were by no means down-trodden or ill-used" (Haddon, p. 357; see also Meinicke, Die Torrestrasse, p. 115). And Somerville, speaking of New Georgia in the Solomon Islands, says: "In the eastern part the treatment of women is notably good. I have but rarely seen them at work" (Somerville, New Georgia, pp. 405, 406). — 2) See the details given in Part I Chap. II § 5.

	Positive.	Negative.
$a^1 + t$	8	3
$a^2 + t$	26	
$a^2 + c + t$	7	
$a^3 + t$	6	
$a^3 + c + t$	1	
Total	48	3

We use the term "commercial tribes" in a wide sense, as including not only those tribes among which many people subsist by trading, but those that exchange a considerable part of their produce for foreign merchandise. For instance, a tribe that grows corn for export is a commercial tribe in the sense we attach to the word.

We see that, with very few exceptions, all commercial agricultural tribes keep slaves. This proves that among agricultural tribes the development of trade greatly furthers the growth of slavery.

We have not much to say in explanation of this fact. When speaking of the slave-keeping tribes of the Pacific Coast of North America, we have already remarked that the development of trade tends to further slavery in various ways. Commercial tribes are likely to carry on a trade in slaves, and this makes the keeping of slaves very easy. Where the freemen take to commercial pursuits, they want others to perform the common drudgery for every-day subsistence. The trade itself may also require menial work: the articles of commerce have to be prepared and transported, trading vessels have to be rowed, etc. And finally, commerce often leads to a development of wealth and luxury; a man can now, by the labour of his slaves, acquire not only the necessaries, but the refinements of life [1]).

The last point is an important one. In self-dependent agricultural countries the main use of slave labour consists in

---

1) Cunningham (English Industry, I p. 77) justly remarks: "While there is no opportunity for exchange, it is not so well worth while for anyone to preserve a surplus; a very abundant harvest is more likely to be prodigally used within the year, and so with all other supplies; but the existence of opportunities for trade makes it well worth while to gather a store that far exceeds any prospective need and to stow in warehouses for sale all that need not be used by the producers to satisfy their immediate wants; the conditions are present which stil further favour the accumulation of wealth."

providing the master with food. If, then, a man keeps a large number of slaves who work for him, he is able to entertain his friends, or to keep a retinue of unproductive slaves or servants, whose wants are provided for by the work of the soil-tilling slaves. But where this is the sole profit one can derive from one's slaves, an owner who keeps a considerable number of them does not want to make them work very hard; he often contents himself with receiving a tribute, and so the slaves become serfs. In this way the slave-owner gets less out of his slaves than would otherwise be the case; but he does not want more, and he need not now continually supervise their work. Slavery is not likely to exist on a large scale.

Where commercial relations with foreign parts are maintained, it is otherwise. A slave-owner who receives large quantities of agricultural produce from his slaves can now exchange them for foreign merchandise. Retaining for himself as much food as he wants, he exchanges the rest for such objects as are either useful and agreeable in themselves, or give him distinction among his countrymen. The use of slave labour becomes thus practically unlimited. Kohler rightly remarks that only where the economic instinct is awake, can slavery attain to a full development, and Schmoller observes that, when the patriarchal family began to produce for the market, covetousness and pursuit of gain arose and the treatment of slaves became worse [1]).

We must further take into consideration that slavery on a very large scale is only possible, where industrial crops are raised. "Tobacco and cotton" says Cairnes, "fulfil that condition which we saw was essential to the economical employment of slaves — the possibility of working large numbers within a limited space; while wheat and Indian corn, in the cultivation of which the labourers are dispersed over a wide surface, fail in this respect" [2]). And cotton and similar crops are only cultivated in large quantity where they are exported.

---

1) Kohler, Das Recht der Papuas, p. 364; Schmoller, Grundriss, I p. 243. — 2) Cairnes, p. 50. In ancient Rome, at the end of the Republic, plantations of olives and vines were worked with slaves, whereas cereal crops were raised on lands leased to *coloni*; see Weber, Article "Agrarverhältnisse im Altertum", in Handwörterbuch der Staatswissenschaften, 3rd edition, vol. I p. 166.

Of such "wholesale slavery", as Bagehot terms it, we find a few instances among savage tribes.

Köler tells us that in Bonny the great majority of the inhabitants are slaves. The keeping of slaves is very expensive, as agriculture and industry scarcely exist; all food has to be imported. The freemen are traders in palm-oil, and want large numbers of slaves to row the canoes in which this oil is transported [1]).

Among the Ewe of the Slave Coast slavery is practised on a very large scale. Some men keep 200—300 slaves, who form their capital. The slaves are generally employed in carrying oil from the inland to the coast for sale to Europeans. The maintaining of order among such great numbers of slaves requires great severity. Slavery marks all their institutions. It is a common saying with them that "the large water-tub does not go to the spring", whereby they mean that freemen must not do such work as is only fit for slaves and boys [2]).

Miss Kingsley, speaking of the social classes among the tribes, inhabiting the territory of the Oil Rivers on the Western Coast of Africa, says: "The third and fourth classes are true slave classes, the higher one in rank being what is called the Winnaboes or Trade boys, the lower the pull-away boys and the plantation hands. The best point in it, as a system, is that it gives to the poorest boy who paddles an oil canoe a chance of becoming a king" [3]).

Among the Garos, where cotton is the principal culture, two-fifths of the population are slaves. "The distinction [between freemen and slaves] is jealously preserved.... It is from the possession of a large number of them [slaves] that a man obtains influence amongst his tribe" [4]).

It is clear that among these tribes slavery would not prevail to such a great extent, if the preparing and transporting of the articles of export did not require so much labour.

In these cases trade is the cause of "wholesale slavery", not necessarily of slavery in general. "Retail slavery" may have

---

1) Köler, pp. 84, 154. — 2) Zündel, pp. 408, 409, 387. — 3) Kingsley, West African studies, p. 427; see also De Cardi's description of the slave system of Bonny, ibid., pp. 516 sqq. — 4) Dalton, p. 58.

existed among these tribes before they became so largely commercial. But, seeing that among them the extension of commercial relations has so greatly increased the use of slave labour, we may safely suppose that in several cases the development of trade has given rise to slavery among tribes which did not practise it before. This is also made probable by the list given at the beginning of this paragraph.

We shall not proceed to a closer investigation of this subject. We have already remarked that as yet we know very little about the general effects of trade and the place it occupies in social life among savages. And we must know more of this, before we can arrive at any accurate conclusion with regard to the influence of trade on the rise and growth of slavery.

When speaking of hunters and fishers, we have found that the influence of trade is more considerable where manufactured goods, than where raw products are exported. This will probably also apply to agricultural tribes, viz. if we take the term "manufactured goods" in a wide sense, as including agricultural produce. Raw products in our sense means articles which can be exported without any labour being previously applied to them, e. g. the various kinds of stone and earth exchanged by Eskimos and Australians. The articles exported by commercial agricultural tribes are nearly always manufactured goods in this wider sense.

It might be interesting to divide the commercial tribes (in the wider sense) into three categories, according as they export agricultural produce, manufactured goods in the common, restricted sense, or articles purchased abroad (articles of transit trade), the last category comprising the commercial tribes in the restricted sense, and inquire what are the social effects of commerce in each case. But such a subject wants separate treatment; we cannot deal with it here. We will only express our opinion, that the significance of trade and industry among savages is commonly underrated. Whether we are right here will appear when these points have been more closely studied than they are now.

In another paragraph we shall have to speak of a peculiar branch of trade, the trade in slaves.

§ 15. *Slaves employed in warfare.*

In several cases it is stated that slaves are employed in warfare. Leaving out of regard the cattle-breeding agricultural tribes, of which we have already spoken in chapter III, we find the following instances.

Thomson tells us that in New Zealand slaves accompanied their masters on fishing and fighting expeditions; and in another place he states that women and slaves accompanied the warriors to carry burdens [1]). Polack says: "Slaves are permitted to take part in a war", and Brown, speaking of slaves in New Zealand, remarks: "If any of them show superior talents for war, they are duly appreciated, and many slaves by this means raise themselves to the chieftainship of the tribe" [2]).

Dalton, speaking of the slaves kept by the Garos, says: "It is from the possession of a large number of them that a man obtains influence amongst his tribe. Each great chief can go to war with a body-guard of 60 such followers entirely devoted to him" [3]).

Among the Lawas too, according to Colquhoun, slaves are employed as warriors [4]).

In Nias slaves are often compelled to go to war with their masters, except when war is made upon the native village of the slaves. The slaves fight bravely, and in war bear arms like the freemen, but are never set at liberty for their bravery [5]).

Among the Kayans slaves serve as warriors and can even become war-chiefs [6]).

Among the natives of Central Celebes, slaves who excel in those qualities which are highly valued in freemen, *i, e,* bravery or oratorical power, are practically no longer regarded as slaves [7]).

Among the Tagals and Visayas, in the time of the conquista, generally freemen and vassals only took part in military

---

1) Thomson, New Zealand, pp. 150, 125. — 2) Polack, II p. 53; Brown, New Zealand, p. 30. — 3) Dalton, p. 58. — 4) Colquhoun, p. 54. — 5) Modigliani, Nias, p. 525. — 6) Nieuwenhuis, Quer durch Borneo. I p. 66; II p. 96. — 7) See above, p. 197, note 1.

operations; but sometimes slaves too, especially in naval wars: the slaves were then employed for rowing the boats [1]).

The forces sent out by Lunda chiefs on marauding expeditions consist of freemen and slaves [2]).

Among the Angoni the domestic slaves join their masters in the slave-raids [3]).

Bérenger-Féraud tells us that among the Wolofs the slaves of the king are soldiers and form his body-guard; they also collect taxes for him [4]).

Among the Barea and Kunama the spoils taken in war by a native-born slave belong to his master [5]). Hence it appears that these slaves are employed in warfare.

In the French Soudan the master provides his domestic slaves with arms and takes them with him to the battlefield [6]).

Among the Soninkays and Malinkays of French Guinea, one class of warriors is composed of the slaves of the chiefs. At the close of a war they return to their agricultural pursuits; but they are always ready to take arms again [7]).

These are the only instances we have noticed, of purely agricultural tribes among which slaves perform a military function. There may be some more cases. Our informants do not always enter into many details; therefore, when they are silent on the subject, this does not always prove that slaves are not allowed to fight. Yet, considering the small number of instances we have been able to collect, we may safely conclude that among most agricultural tribes slaves do not share in military operations.

This is what we expected. Slaves are not allowed to follow the noble military art, which is the privilege of freemen [8]). A slave is not a warrior for the same reason that he is not a hunter. Moreover, it were too dangerous to trust him with weapons; he might be inclined to rise against his oppressors. And finally, when slaves are procured by capture in war or kidnapping, they would often have to fight against their own

---

1) Blumentritt, Conquista, p. 65. — 2) Pogge, Muata Jamwo, p. 232. — 3) Kerr, II p. 129. — 4) Bérenger-Féraud, p. 59. — 5) Munzinger, Ostafr. Stud., p. 484. — 6) Madrolle, p. 92. — 7) Arcin, p. 275. — 8) Among the ancient Germans the bearing of arms was a sign of freedom (Amira, p. 129).

tribe, and would be very likely to go over to the enemies of
their masters.

It is further remarkable that the tribes we have enumerated
in this paragraph are all in the higher stages of agriculture,
as may be seen from chapter I. We have not found a single
instance of hunting agriculturists employing their slaves in
warfare. There are even hunting agriculturists of the lowest
type, of whom it is explicitly stated that they do not allow
their slaves to fight. Martius tells us that several wild tribes
of Brazil keep slaves. The slaves are differently treated by the
different tribes; but it is a general characteristic of slavery,
that slaves are not allowed to bear arms [1]). And Azara states
that in his time the Mbayas subsisted on hunting and fishing,
and on the produce of the soil that was tilled to a small extent
by their slaves and by a neighbouring tribe, the Guanas. Here
too, warfare was the business of the freemen to the exclusion
of the slaves [2]).

This may, at first sight, seem strange. If it is true, as Powell
asserts, (and it does not seem to us improbable) that slavery
originated from the adoption of captives [3]), we should expect to
find an intermediate stage, in which the captives, though already enslaved instead of adopted, still shared in military
operations, the differentiation of the "regulative part of society"
from the "operative part" (to borrow Spencer's words) not yet
being complete. The existence of slavery, mainly for military
purposes, among the hunting Abipones and some pastoral tribes,
seems to indicate such a stage. But among agricultural tribes
we find no trace of it. Some agricultural tribes (of which
the Iroquois are the classical instance) adopt their captives;
then there are many which keep slaves who are not allowed
to fight; and, finally, in the higher stages of agriculture, we
find a few tribes among which slaves share in military operations.

Yet the cause of this seeming incongruity is not difficult to
detect. Pastoral tribes are always stronger, from a military
point of view, than primitive agricultural tribes. In chapter
III we have seen that the former often keep their agricultural

---

1) Martius, p. 71. — 2) Azara, II pp. 109, 110. — 3) Powell, On regimentation, p. CXII

neighbours in a state of subjection. Therefore it is much easier for them to employ their slaves in warfare than for hunting agriculturists; the latter, if they are to keep slaves at all, must take care to disarm them and so prevent them from doing harm.

Among agriculturists in the higher stages it is otherwise. There is often an elaborate division of labour; the governing classes are differentiated from the labouring classes, and the army is regularly constituted. Now it is not at all dangerous to enlist the slaves into the inferior ranks of the army, under the lead of the governing classes. The slaves, generally brought by traders from a far distance, have no longer to fight against their native tribe, but against strangers. And where slavery prevails to a great extent, the owners of numerous slaves, who form the aristocracy, will often be inclined to rely on their slaves for the maintenance of their power over the common freemen; whereas the slaves, who are no longer on the same footing of familiarity with the freemen as in primitive slavery, but despised and hated for being the tools of the aristocracy, regard their master as their natural protector and are willing to stand bij him [1]).

Such was the course of evolution in ancient Rome. In the old times the slaves were not allowed to fight. "For entering the military service or taking on him any state office, a slave was punished with death" [2]). But later on a change took place. Speaking of the last days of the republic, Ingram remarks: "In the subsequent civil conflicts the aid of slaves was sought by both parties, even by Marius himself, and afterwards by Catiline, though he finally rejected their services. Clodius and Milo employed bands of gladiators in their city riots, and this action on the part of the latter was approved by Cicero. In the First Civil War they were to be found in both camps, and the murderers of Caesar, those *soi-disant* vindicators of liberty, were escorted to the Capitol by gladiators. Antony, Octavius, and Sextus Pompeius employed them in the Second Civil War" [3]). But the slaves soon began to take arms against

---

1) Among the Soninkays and Malinkays of French Guinea the slave warriors are the only force on which the chiefs can rely; for the freemen would not always readily answer to the appeal of their lords. Arcin, p. 275. — 2) Ingram, p. 44. — 3) Ibid., pp. 51, 52.

those who had taught them to fight. "It is recorded bij Augustus on the Monumentum Ancyranum that he gave back to their masters for punishment about 30,000 slaves who had absconded and borne arms against the state. Under Tiberius, at the death of Caligula, and in the reign of Nero, there were threatening movements of the slaves. Nor did the danger of servile insurrection disappear in the later stages of the Empire. The armies of the invading Goths were swelled by their countrymen who had been captured or bought by Romans The slaves of Gaul almost *en masse* took part in the revolt of the Bagaudae, and forty thousand slaves joined Alaric at the siege of Rome" [1]).

The last passage shows that even in a state where the power of the government and the military art are highly developed it is not safe to employ slaves in warfare. They may actually be the ready tools of the aristocracy; but in the long run they will come to form a dangerous element in the state. Yet, as it may be momentarily convenient to an ambitious statesman to employ them, it will sometimes be done; whereas among hunting agriculturists the danger is so obvious that it is not even attempted.

As it is only among a few agricultural tribes, and these in the higher stages, that slaves perform a military function, we cannot think that this has been an important factor in the rise of slavery; and it has probably been nowhere the only motive for making slaves.

Something analogous to the employment of slaves in warfare is their holding high offices of state. This occurs in some despotically governed African countries. Goldstein remarks that in the Soudan states the numerous court and state offices are generally held by slaves. The king prefers them as public officers to royal princes, who might be inclined to rise against him [2]). Among the Bayanzi, according to Torday and Joyce, "the great chief usually has a confidential adviser, who, in all cases observed, was a slave; such slaves have great influence, and receive numerous presents from their masters; they often impersonate the chief before strangers, while their master keeps

---

1) Ibid., pp. 52, 53. — 2) Goldstein, p. 362.

in the background" [1]). In imperial Rome freedmen were appointed to high offices [2]).

§ 16. *Slaves kept as a luxury.*

Sometimes we are told that it is considered an honour to possess many slaves. We shall give a few instances.

Among the Lampongs the keeping of slaves is indicative of wealth and power [3]).

Among the Tagals and Visayas, in the time of the conquista, a man's influence, power and reputation depended on the number of his slaves [4]).

Among the Ininga and Galloa it is the ambition of a freeman to have as many slaves as possible [5]).

Compiègne states that a Mpongwe asked him to give him a portion of his wages in advance, in order to buy a slave. "He will work for me and my wife" said the man, "and I shall be a person of rank" [6]).

Among the Bambala, "when a man buys a new slave, he ornaments him on the first day with his best clothes and ornaments, and walks round the village with him to show him to his friends" [7]).

We have only taken a few instances at random. It cannot be interesting to the reader to know how often the same fact has been noticed by ethnographers. For we may suppose that wherever slavery exists, the possession of a great number of slaves is a mark of distinction. The possession of slaves, like other property, is indicative of wealth; and where slaves are acquired by capture in war it shows the bravery of the captor. Moreover, among agricultural tribes the labour of the slaves augments the revenue of their owner, and so the keeping of slaves is not only a sign but a source of wealth; therefore the slave-owner is looked upon as one who has at his disposal a means of acquiring wealth. Martius, speaking of the wild tribes of Brazil, remarks that a chief who keeps many slaves can

---

1) Torday and Joyce, Congo Free State, p. 139. — 2) Ingram, pp. 58, 59. — 3) De Groot, p. 455. — 4) Blumentritt, Conquista, p. 53. — 5) Lenz, p. 59. — 6) Compiègne, Okanda, pp. 194, 195. — 7) Torday and Joyce, Ba-Mbala, p. 411.

take more land into cultivation than other people. He has therefore always an abundant supply of food, which tends to increase the esteem in which he is held [1]).

Where industry and art are little developed, slaves, besides wives and domestic animals, are almost the only luxury that is to be had. The reader will remember Levchine's statement about a rich Kazak Kirghiz, whose numerous horses gave him no profit, but great renown [2]). In the lower stages of culture a rich man cannot build a palace, or keep a motor-car, or buy pictures; he can only show his wealth to the public by keeping a large number of men or domestic animals continually running about him. Leroy-Beaulieu justly remarks: "The luxury of primitive times is very simple; it consists mainly in the grouping about the rich man (who most often is at the same time a man of high birth) of a large body of servants maintained by him, and in practising hospitality on a large scale. Among patriarchal peoples there is almost perfect equality of material life between men of different stations. Food, clothing, furniture even, differs but little" [3]).

But, though a rich man may display his wealth by keeping a great number of slaves, we do not mean to say that among any agricultural tribe all slaves are kept as a mere luxury. This seems improbable. Among pastoral tribes, as we have seen before, it sometimes occurs. The owner of numerous herds may support a large body of slaves, who have scarcely anything to do. But among agricultural tribes it is quite otherwise. Subsistence here is largely dependent on labour; much labour is required to provide for the slaves, and the master will not choose to work for them himself. The slaves, therefore, must perform at least as much productive labour as is required to provide for their own wants; and there is no reason why the master should not make them work somewhat more, to receive a surplus; the more so, as he is thus enabled to display his wealth in the other manner mentioned by Leroy-Beaulieu, viz. by practising hospitality on a large scale.

It is, of course, perfectly possible, and indeed it often occurs,

---

1) Martius, p. 63. — 2) See above. p. 269. — 3) Leroy-Beaulieu, p.80. See also Malthus (Bettany's edition, pp. 423, 424): "In the feudal times, the landlords could in no other way spend their incomes than by maintaining a great number of idle followers."

that *some* slaves are kept as a mere luxury, either doing nothing at all, or performing personal services. But then there must be other slaves who, by performing productive labour, provide for their master, their fellow-slaves, and themselves. There cannot be a class of unproductive labourers, without there being a class of productive labourers too. We can only imagine one case, in which all slaves might be kept as a mere luxury. It might be, that there were a class of productive labourers consisting of freemen, who provided for the slave-owners and their unproductive slaves. There might, for instance, be an aristocracy, levying taxes on the common people and keeping slaves as a luxury. Such is indeed the case among the pastoral Beni Amer. It might also occur among agricultural tribes; but we have not found any instance of it.

Only in two cases have we found it stated that slaves are not productive.

Coquilhat tells us that on the Upper Congo the keeping of slaves does not increase the master's income; for agriculture is insignificant, and these tribes are not commercial. But he also states that the soil is tilled by old women and male slaves, so slaves do not seem to be kept as a mere luxury [1]).

Among the Fanti, according to Finsch, slaves are articles of luxury; they are as lazy as their masters. They are acquired as prisoners of war or by purchase. Every noble Fanti owns numerous slaves; for it is a mark of distinction to keep many of them. Some slaves carry parasols or fans; others by trumpeting announce the arrival of the patrician. Most of them do nothing at all. But the same writer states that the condition of the pawns (who, as has been shown in the first chapter of Part I, are a kind of slaves) is much worse than that of the slaves in the restricted sense [2]). We may therefore suppose that these pawns are the productive labourers.

We have never found it explicitly stated that among any agricultural tribe slaves are not employed in agriculture.

Our conclusion is that luxury has not probably been among any agricultural tribe the only motive for keeping slaves.

---

1) Coquilhat, pp. 365, 265. — 2) Finsch, Die Goldküste, pp. 359, 360.

Yet many slaves are kept as a mere luxury, and consequently among some tribes slaves are far more numerous than they would be if all of them were engaged in productive pursuits.

§ 17. *Other secondary internal causes.*

We have seen that among the tribes of the Pacific Coast of North America the growth of slavery is furthered by their preserving food for the time of scarcity, whereas hunters who live from hand to mouth have less use for slave labour.

Hunting agriculturists much resemble true hunters: subsistence depends largely on the vicissitudes of the chase. But where a tribe lives principally on the produce of the soil, it is necessary to preserve the reaped fruits until the following harvest.

This leads to the same conclusion we had already arrived at, that slavery is more likely to exist among agriculturists of the higher stages than among hunting agriculturists [1]. We do not think that anything more need be said on this subject.

In our chapter on pastoral tribes we have found that subjection of tribes as such sometimes serves as a substitute for slavery, making slavery proper superfluous. The same proved to be the case among agriculturists who depend on cattle for a large portion of their subsistence. Something analogous to this is the levying of tributes on conquered districts that so often occurs in Oceania, as we have found in § 8. Outside Oceania we have found only one instance among agriculturists who do not depend on cattle, and even this is a doubtful one. Morgan states that among the Iroquois the council "regulated the affairs of subjugated tribes" [2]; but he does not enter into more details, so we cannot exactly know what he means.

It is easy to understand, why subjection of tribes so seldom occurs among agriculturists. Hunting agriculturists, like true

---

1) Among hunting agriculturists we have found 34 positive and 43 negative cases; among agriculturists of the higher stages 136 positive and 52 negative cases. — 2) Morgan, Anc. Soc., p. 136.

hunters, generally live in small groups and therefore cannot keep other tribes in a state of subjection. And among agricultural tribes of the higher stages men as well as women are continually engaged in agricultural labour; they are attached to the spot on which they live and, unlike nomadic cattle-keepers [1]), cannot easily control a neighbouring tribe. The vanquished tribe, by retreating a little, can place itself out of reach of the conquering tribe. Only where, as on the small Polynesian islands, escape is not practicable, can a vanquished district be kept in a state of subjection. The Iroquois were an exceptional case. They were hunting agriculturists in this sense, that agricultural labour was performed by the women only; but at the same time they had a strong military organization: the five nations formed a powerful union.

In the higher stages of culture the growth of militarism enables strong agricultural peoples to subject their weaker neighbours; and the growth of population prevents the latter from receding. But among agricultural savages subjugation of tribes is rarely found.

§ 18. *External causes, especially the slave-trade. Recapitulation.*

In the second and third chapters we have spoken of external causes. We have seen that for slavery to exist it is not sufficient that there should be some use for slave labour; it must also be possible to keep slaves; the freemen of the tribe must have a coercive power strong enough to keep the slaves subjected and prevent them from escaping. It has been shown that this coercive power is most strongly developed, where men have fixed habitations, live in large groups, and preserve food; and further, that the slave-trade greatly facilitates the keeping of slaves.

As for the first three points, it is easy to see that agricultural tribes of the higher stages are more settled, live in larger groups, and are more likely to preserve food than hunting

---

1) See Salvioli's article on the struggles between pastoral and agricultural peoples.

agriculturists [1]), so here again we find a reason why slavery is so much more frequent among the former than among the latter.

The slave-trade is of more interest to us here. It has been shown that among the tribes of the Pacific Coast of North America a brisk trade in slaves was carried on, which must have greatly accelerated the growth of slavery; for it made the keeping of slaves much easier than it would have been if each of these tribes had had to procure its slaves by capture in war. It has also been remarked that among pastoral tribes slavery exists almost exclusively in those parts, were a trade in slaves with civilized or semi-civilized peoples is or was carried on, viz. in Arabia, the Caucasus, North-east and North-west Africa; whereas the pastoral tribes that live in outlying regions (Siberia, South Africa) with the only exception of the Ovaherero, do not keep slaves. We shall inquire now whether the same is the case with agricultural tribes, whether among them too slavery is of rare occurrence in those parts where the slave-trade has never been carried on.

In North America, at the time of its discovery, slavery did not exist among any agricultural tribe. Negro slavery, practised by a few of them in later times, was derived from the whites.

In South America we have found only a few slave-keeping agricultural tribes; and the slave-trade formerly carried on by the whites may go far to explain the existence of slavery in these few cases. "The Brazilian native" says Martius "sometimes sells his children to people of white races, much oftener than to those of his own colour." The principal object of warfare among the natives, in Martius' time, was to capture slaves, whom they sold either to other tribes or to colonists of Portuguese extraction. The custom of selling prisoners to white colonists has strongly influenced the native character. It was already practised very shortly after the discovery of America. Many Indians were transported to Spain and Portugal. The Mamelucos, living in San Paolo, made long and sanguinary wars upon the Indians. They are said during 130 years to have killed

---

[1] See above, p. 295, and Grosse, p. 134.

and enslaved more than two millions of Indians. Pedro de Avila, governor of Buenos Ayres, complained that the Paulistas carried on this trade in public and from 1628 to 1630 had brought 60,000 Indians to the market at Rio Janeiro. The whites continually availed themselves of the quarrels of the several Indian tribes, to procure such Indians as had been made prisoners. Even in Martius' time this trade went on, especially in thinly peopled, outlying districts, where the Brazilian government could not prevent it. The wars of the Indians were simply marauding expeditions; their object was to procure prisoners for sale to Brazilian whites [1]).

In Oceania, slavery was an aboriginal institution in New Zealand and part of the Solomon group and the Bismarck Archipelago. From the lack of details concerning a system of slave labour, we must conclude that in these islands the economic use of slaves was small. Slavery further existed in the western part of New Guinea, where it probably still exists. Here foreign influence clearly appears. In the eastern part of the island, that till quite recently had not been visited by foreigners (British and German New Guinea), slavery is unknown; and the western part (Dutch New Guinea), where slavery exists, was for a long time under the rule of the sultan of Tidore [2]). The tribute which the inhabitants of New Guinea had to pay to the sultan consisted partly of slaves; moreover, many Papuans were captured as slaves in the *hongi* raids [3]). This, however, is not sufficient to account for the keeping of slaves by Papuans themselves. But we may consider, first that several districts on the coast are inhabited by a mongrel race of Papuans and Malays (*e. g.* on the Gulf of Macluer), and secondly that the trade with Tidore, Serang, and other Malay countries must have thoroughly changed the natives' mode of life. Thus we are told that the Dorey people have become somewhat civilized by their intercourse with traders from the Moluccas [4]). We may notice here that all districts where slavery is carried on lie on the coast, and are therefore easiest of access to foreigners. And those districts of Dutch New Guinea of which it is stated

---

1) Martius, pp. 123, 131, 131 note, 154 note, 531—533, 772. — 2) Robidé, pp. 345 sqq. — 3) Ibid., pp. 53, 218, 221, 288, 289, 232, 255, 317. See also "Nieuw Guinea", pp. 186—192. — 4) Robidé, p. 227.

that there are no slaves, Humboldt Bay and Hattam, have
never been visited by *hongi* fleets [1]). Accordingly, Ottow and
Geissler remark that the mountain tribes do not keep slaves,
but kill all their prisoners, for fear they might escape. The
coast tribes, however, being able to procure slaves from a great
distance, who are less likely to escape, practise slavery [2]).

In the Malay Archipelago Mohammedanism already prevailed
to a great extent before the conquista, and had even advanced
as far as the Philippines [3]). Wherever slavery exists in the
Archipelago, we are not certain that we have to deal with a
phenomenon of unadulterated savage life. The influence of
semi-civilized Mohammedans spreads over nearly the whole of
the Archipelago.

In India the slave-trade with semi-civilized countries is, or
was, also carried on by the natives. Cooper states that the
Meshmees sell slaves to Tibet [4]). According to Colquhoun the
Karen-nee sell many slaves to the Shans of Zimmé and these
again to the Siamese [5]). And Rousselet tells us that among the
Kafirs "slavery exists within certain limits, but this criminal
commerce would cease altogether if there were not such a ready
sale for slaves at Djalalabad, Kounar, Asmar and Tchitral" [6]).

From the Caucasus, as we have already seen, slaves are
exported to Turkey on a large scale [7]).

Africa is the classical country of the slave-trade. Egypt and
Ethiopia furnished a certain number of slaves to ancient
Greece, and at Rome there was a regular importation of slaves,
some of whom were brought from Africa [8]). Herodotus speaks
of slaves sent to ancient Egypt as tribute from Ethiopia [9]).
That in later times the African slave-trade, carried on by
Arabs in East Africa and by Europeans in West Africa, assumed
enormous proportions, need scarcely be said. In the later half
of the 19th century the Mohammedan East still received a large
supply of slaves from Africa. Ingram remarks: "The principal
centres from which in recent times the supply has been furnished to Egypt, Morocco, Turkey, Arabia, and Persia, are
three in number. 1. The Soudan, south of the Great Sahara,

---

1) Ibid., pp. 277, 242. — 2) Ottow and Geissler, pp. 152, 153. — 3) See Blumentritt,
Conquista. — 4) Cooper, p. 183. — 5) Colquhoun, p. 70. — 6) Rousselet, p. 223. — 7)
See above, p. 287. — 8) Ingram, pp. 19, 38. — 9) Ibid., p. 268.

appears to be one vast hunting-ground. Captives are brought thence to the slave-market of Kuka in Bornu .... Negroes are also brought to Morocco from the Western Soudan, and from Timbuktu .... 2. The basin of the Nile, extending to the great lakes, is another region infested by the slave trade ... 3. There has long been a slave-trade from the East African coast. The stream of supply came mainly from the southern Nyassa districts by three or four routes to Ibo, Mozambique, Angoche, and Kilimane. Madagascar and the Comoro Islands obtained most of their slaves from the Mozambique coast .... There are other minor branches of the trade elsewhere in Africa. Thus from Harar in Somáliland caravans are sent to Berberah on the coast, where there is a great annual fair. The slaves are collected from the inland Galla countries, from Gurágwe, and from Abyssinia, the Abyssinians being the most highly esteemed" [1]).

We see that in most parts of the world inhabited by slave-keeping agricultural savages, slaves are, or were, purchased or captured by civilized or semi-civilized peoples; whereas in those parts where the slave-trade has always been unknown, slavery has never prevailed to any considerable extent.

We shall try to account for this fact. But we must first reply to a question which the reader may perhaps have asked, viz. why we have not at the beginning of this second Part discussed the question as to whether slavery is ever a phenomenon of genuine savage life, or has always been due to intercourse with higher races. We have not done so, because it seems to us that this question is one of secondary interest. When we see that among a savage tribe slavery is an institution playing a great part in native life and slave labour is of much use, we must come to the conclusion that slavery is perfectly consistent with the economic and social state in which this tribe lives, whether intercourse with superior races gave rise to it or it already existed before any such intercourse had taken place. And the conclusions we have arrived at in this and the foregoing chapters, as to the various circumstances

---

1) Ibid., 224, 225, 230—233. On the African slave-trade, see also Ratzel, Anthropogeo-graphie II (1891), pp. 386, 387.

which further or prevent slavery, remain the same in both cases. Moreover, there are some savage tribes which at the time of their discovery kept slaves without, so far as we know, having had any intercourse with superior races: the New Zealanders and the fishing tribes of Kamchatka and the North Pacific Coast of North America.

Yet, as we have already said, those parts of the world where we have found most of our positive cases are exactly those where the slave-trade has been carried on by civilized and semi-civilized peoples. Going on to account for this fact, we may remark first that it need not have been the slave-trade only that furthered the growth of slavery. The general inter-course with superior races may go far to account for the rise of slavery, irrespectively of the slave-trade. We have seen that commercial tribes are more likely to keep slaves than others; and a savage tribe can engage in commerce with superior peoples, who buy large quantities of native produce and introduce foreign manufactures, to a far greater extent than with neighbouring savages who have not much to ex-change, as their own and their neighbours' mode of life and industrial development are nearly the same. A remarkable in-stance of the influence of commercial intercourse with Europeans on the slave system of a savage race is afforded by Polack's description of the Maori. Formerly, he says, "for a chief to enter his new abode [in the world of spirits], without being ushered by a number of slaves and wives [who were sacrificed], was accounted the greatest indecorum that could possibly exist, but from the scarcity of slaves during late years [Polack wrote in 1840], or rather from the profits accruing from their employment in rearing pigs, and planting provisions, cutting timber, and cleaning flax for their numerous European visitors (their services being at a premium), these butcheries..... have ceased" [1]). Something similar to this may often have taken place.

Probably, however, the slave-trade has also had consider-able influence. The mere fact that foreigners purchase or capture slaves from savage tribes cannot, of course, account

---

1) Polack, I pp. 78, 79.

for the existence of slavery among these savages; it may even result in the disappearance of slavery among them, if they find it more profitable to sell their slaves than retain them. But the slave-trade will often augment the opportunities of acquiring slaves. Slave-traders generally trade in other articles besides slaves; therefore they will often exchange some of the slaves they may have procured for something else. If some slaves are too weak to perform the journey to the coast, it is more profitable to sell them in the interior than to leave them behind. Moreover, the slave-traders often induce savages to make raids upon their neighbours and sell the captives they may secure; and if a savage chief has once learned in this way to kidnap slaves, he will perhaps continue to do so though there be not always a ready sale for them. In a word, the procuring of slaves becomes much easier.

Now we must bear in mind that an institution does not always exist in all countries where it would be economically useful. Not only is an institution which would further the public welfare often wanting, because the immediate interests of individuals are not concerned, but the individuals are not always aware even of their own immediate interests. Such may also be the case with slavery. It may be that, if slavery were introduced into some savage tribe, the tribe, or at least some members of the tribe, would profit by it, and that yet no slaves are made because there are not sufficiently strong motives for doing so, or because there are stronger motives working in the opposite direction. Tribes which have never kept slaves and are unacquainted with slave-keeping tribes, do not know the use of slavery; therefore they have to come to it gradually. Taking for granted that the first source of slavery, as seems very likely, was captivity in war, and that the captives, at first adopted, were afterwards differentiated from the main body of citizens, we can understand why slavery does not exist in all countries where the keeping of slaves would be profitable. It may be that it is the custom to eat the prisoners, or to sacrifice them, or to restore them when peace is concluded. It may also be that the adopted prisoners have from times immemorial been regarded as the equals of the tribesmen. In all these cases the new motive, the want of slaves, must be strong if it is to break through the established custom. The *vis inertiae* plays a great part in the history of mankind.

Returning to the slave-trade, we may remark that this entirely overturns the existing state of things. It enables the tribe to procure slaves who are not captives, and regarding whom therefore no custom has been established. Moreover, the tribe becomes acquainted with the institution of slavery, which it had not seen practised before. Now there is no longer any reason why the members of such a tribe should not purchase the slaves offered to them and set them to work. An external cause has sufficed to disturb the former equilibrium.

We have remarked before that the slave-trade facilitates the keeping of slaves, because purchased slaves are less likely to escape than captives [1]. Here too we have to deal with the *vis inertiae* rather than with an impossibility in the strict sense of keeping slaves. It will not, probably, often be the case that agricultural savages would be quite unable to retain their slaves, if they were really very anxious to keep them; but it may often occur that they are not yet fully aware of the use of slaves, and therefore do not want to take the pains of supervising them, though, if slavery were thoroughly established, it would prove very profitable; in such case the objective want exists, but the subjective want is not yet felt. In this case, too, the slave-trade, by rendering escape of the slaves more difficult, will tend to establish the custom of keeping slaves.

Our conclusion is that slavery existed among some savages who had never had any intercourse with superior races, but that this intercourse, especially where the slave-trade was carried on, has often greatly furthered the growth of slavery.

In our chapter on pastoral tribes we have remarked that a tribe living in the vicinity of inferior races is more likely to keep slaves than one surrounded by tribes of the same or a higher level of culture. Enslavement of lower races also fre-

---

1) In ancient Wales "the price of a slave was one pound, but of one brought across the sea, a pound and a half. The slave who was brought from a distance was much less likely to escape, or even to attempt it, and was therefore a more valuable property; this principle still holds good among slave-owners." Cunningham, English Industry, I p. 117 note 6.

quently occurs among agriculturists; but the agriculturists of the higher races (*e. g.* Malays in the restricted sense, inhabitants of North Africa, etc.) are to be called barbarians rather than savages and have therefore been excluded from the survey of slavery given in our first Part.

Briefly recapitulating the conclusions we have arrived at with regard to agricultural tribes, we have to remark that the general character of their economic and social life is favourable to the existence of slavery: subsistence is easy to procure, and independent of capital, except where cattle are kept.

This applies especially to true agriculturists (agriculturists of the higher stages) as opposed to hunting agriculturists. The latter bear much resemblance to true hunters, who hardly ever keep slaves, accordingly slavery is not so frequent among them as among true agriculturists.

Our general rule, however, requires an important qualification. Where all land has been appropriated, a class of free labourers commonly exists, and slaves are not wanted.

We have not entered into a thorough investigation of the influence of secondary or additional causes. A closer study of this matter will perhaps yield important results. What we have found with regard to these secondary causes is the following.

Slaves often perform female labour; on the other hand female labour sometimes serves as a substitute for slave labour.

Commercial agricultural tribes are far more likely to keep slaves than agricultural tribes among which commerce holds a very subordinate place.

Slaves are sometimes kept for military purposes, or as a mere luxury. These two circumstances, however, though they often lead to the keeping of a larger number of slaves than would otherwise be required, have not probably ever given rise to slavery.

Subjection of tribes as such, which among some pastoral tribes serves as a substitute for slavery, hardly ever occurs among agricultural tribes, except in Oceania, where slavery is already absent for the general cause mentioned above, the non-existence of free land.

Some external causes we had found before: fixed habitations, living in large groups, preserving of food, and the neighbour-hood of inferior races, call for no special notice here.

Intercourse with superior races, especially where these carry on the slave-trade, proves to be a factor greatly furthering the growth of slavery.

We shall not give here a list of the causes found up to the present. We think it more convenient to place such a list at the end of our general survey.

CHAPTER V.

CONCLUSION.

---

§ 1. *General survey.*

The causes which lead to the keeping of slaves, and those which prevent it, have been divided by us into *internal and external causes*. These terms do not perhaps quite answer the purpose, but we cannot find other terms which would express our meaning better, without requiring a prolix circumlocution. We think, however, that it is clear what we mean by these terms. Slavery cannot exist, where there are no internal causes requiring it, *i. e.* where there is no use, economic or non-economic, for slave labour. A tribe will not keep slaves, even though its coercive power would enable it to do so, if there is no employment for them; in such case positive internal causes fail. The same obtains, where definite internal causes are found, which make slave labour useless [1]). The positive internal causes may also be called motive-forces. Slaves will not be kept, even where the best opportunities of procuring them exist, if there is no motive-force which requires the keeping of slaves, *i. e.* if they are not wanted.

But though, where motives for keeping slaves fail, no external causes will give rise to slavery, — even when there are such motives, slavery will not exist, if there are no external causes rendering it possible, *i. e.* if there is no opportunity of procuring and retaining slaves. Where neither capture

---

1) In the first edition we had spoken of *negative* internal causes. Dr. Tönnies, in his review, rightly remarks that this expression is not quite correct.

or purchase of aliens, nor enslavement of members of the tribe is practicable, or where the slaves can very easily escape, slaves cannot be kept, though there might be much use for them [1]).

The principal internal cause which prevents the rise of slavery, or where slavery exists, tends to make it disappear, is the dependence of subsistence upon closed resources. The most important result of our investigation seems to us the division, not only of all savage tribes, but of all peoples of the earth, into peoples with *open*, and with *closed resources*. Among the former labour is the principal factor of production, and a man who does not possess anything but his own strength and skill, is able to provide for himself independently of any capitalist or landlord. There may be capital which enhances the productiveness of labour, and particularly fertile or favourably situated grounds the ownership of which gives great advantage; but a man can do without these advantages. Among peoples with closed resources it is otherwise. Here subsistence is dependent upon material resources of which there is only a limited supply, and which accordingly have all been appropriated. These resources can consist in capital, the supply of which is always limited; then those who own no capital are dependent on the capitalists. They can also consist in land. Such is the case when all land has been appropriated; then people destitute of land are dependent on the landowners.

Where subsistence depends on closed resources, slaves may occasionally be kept, but slavery as an industrial system is not likely to exist. There are generally poor people who voluntarily offer themselves as labourers; therefore slavery, *i. e.* a system of compulsory labour, is not wanted. And even where there are no poor men, because all share in the closed resources, the use of slaves cannot be great. Where there are practically unlimited resources, a man can, by increasing the number of his slaves, increase his income to any extent; but a man who owns a limited capital, or a limited quantity of land, can only employ a limited number of labourers. Moreover, as soon as in a country with closed resources slaves are kept, they form a class destitute of capital, or land, as the case may be;

1) Our "external causes" correspond with what has sometimes been called *condiciones*, as opposed to *causae* proper.

therefore, even when they are set free, they will remain in the service of the rich, as they are unable to provide for themselves [1]). The rich have no interest to keep the labourers in a slave-like state. It may even be their interest to set them free, either in order to deprive them of such rights over the land as they may have acquired in the course of time, or to bring about a determination of the wages of labour by the law of supply and demand, instead of by custom. They will thus, without any compulsion except that exercized by the automatic working of the social system, secure a larger share in the produce of labour than they got before by compulsion.

Among peoples with open resources everybody is able to provide for himself; therefore free labourers do not offer themselves, at least not for employment in the common drudgery, the rudest and most despised work. There may be, and indeed there often are, skilled labourers whose work is highly valued and well paid; such people think it more profitable to earn their livelihood by means of their peculiar talents, than in the common way. A striking instance of this is the priest, whom we may call a skilled labourer performing non-economic labour; his renumeration, both in material goods and in influence and consideration, is greater than the income of a common agriculturist. But there are no labourers in the modern sense of proletarians, destitute of everything and obliged to seek employment in whatever work they can find. If therefore a man wants others to perform the necessary drudgery for him, and cannot impose it upon his wife, or wives, or other female dependents (either because women hold a high position, or because there is more mean work to be done than the women can possibly manage), he must compel other men to serve him; and this compulsion will often assume the form of slavery.

In the first Part we have said that a slave is a man who is the property of another. We can now see the practical meaning of this definition. In slave countries labourers are held as property, and valued as such. If an employer loses a labourer, his income is lessened by it; if his labourer runs away, he eagerly tries to recover him. In countries with closed resources it is

---

1) Viz. if they have no opportunity to emigrate to countries with open resources.

quite the reverse [1]). The labourers are not held as property, because they are not valued. If a labourer leaves his service, the employer knows that there are many others ready to take his place. Here it is not the employer who prevents his labourers from escaping, but the employed who try to prevent the employer from dismissing his workmen. We are, of course, aware that labour is always an indispensable factor of production; yet in many countries, e. g. in modern Western Europe, an employer does not care to keep a particular labourer in his service [2]). We must, however, bear in mind that this rule, in its strictest sense, applies only to unskilled labour. Qualified labourers are often highly valued and able to secure great advantage, because their number is limited. It is therefore that the helpless state of people destitute of material resources appears more clearly in agricultural than in manufacturing countries.

This difference between countries with open and with closed resources goes far to explain why slavery (and serfdom, which is also a form of compulsory labour) has gradually disappeared in civilized Europe, whereas in thinly peopled countries it maintained itself much longer, and even now is sometimes introduced under some disguise ("labour trade", convict labour and similar expedients used in the tropics). In Western Europe unskilled labourers can always be had without compulsion, whereas the qualities required in skilled labourers cannot develop under a compulsory *régime*.

Always and everywhere have men been inclined to burden their fellow-men with heavy and disagreeable work rather than

---

1) Viz. generally speaking. Peculiar circumstances (e. g. a rapid development of industry) may bring about a temporary scarcity of labour. But the growth of population in most cases will soon bring this state of things to an end. — 2) We have repeatedly remarked that the condition of countries with open resources is quite different: land is abundant, but the supply of labour is limited; therefore the ruling classes attach little value to land as such, but their chief aim is to people the land with men who enter into their service. A good instance is given by Junod in his account of the Baronga (near Delagoa Bay): "According to their laws, the soil belongs exclusively to the chief. But practically it belongs to every one. Nobody buys land. It is given gratuitously to whosoever wants to settle in the country. By simply declaring himself a subject of the chief, a native may acquire as much land as he wants for his subsistence." (Junod, pp. 186, 187).

perform it themselves; and the strong have succeeded in imposing this work on the weak. Among some savage tribes it is the weaker sex who perform the drudgery; but in the course of progress the work that has to be done soon becomes too much for the women to manage. Then subjection of males arises, which presents itself in various forms, as subjugation of conquered tribes, or of the common people by the king and nobility, but often also as slavery or serfdom. Finally, when indispensable resources have been appropriated, the meanest labour is imposed upon those who are destitute of land and capital.*There is now no longer a personal, but an impersonal compulsion.* Lange remarks: "In former times the marauding minority of mankind, by means of physical violence, compelled the working majority to render feudal services, or reduced them to a state of slavery or serfdom, or at least made them pay a tribute. Nowadays the dependence of the working classes is secured in a less direct but equally efficacious manner, viz. by means of the superior power of capital; the labourer being forced, in order to get his subsistence, to place his labour power entirely at the disposal of the capitalist. So there is a semblance of liberty; but in reality the labourer is exploited and subjected, because, all the land having been appropriated, he cannot procure his subsistence directly from nature, and, goods being produced for the market and not for the producer's own use, he cannot subsist without capital. Wages will rise above what is wanted for the necessaries of life, where the labourer is able to earn his subsistence on free land, which has not yet become private property. But wherever, in an old and totally occupied country, a body of labouring poor is employed in manufactures, the same law, which we see at work in the struggle for life throughout the organized world, will keep wages at the absolute minimum" [1]).

Little credit is given at present to the opinion expressed in the last sentence, all economists being aware that the wages, not only of the skilled, but even of the unskilled workmen are in many cases above the bare minimum. But this much seems true, that in countries, where all the land is held as private

---

[1]) Lange, Die Arbeiterfrage, pp. 12, 13.

property, labour is at a discount. We may even say, though it sounds strange, that generally labour is much more at a disadvantage in countries where slavery does not exist, than in slave countries. In slave countries labourers are naturally independent; therefore he who wants to make another work for him, must enslave him and resort to all possible means of retaining him in his service. Hence the strange compound of severity and indulgence that has so often been observed among slave-owners. In countries with closed resources the landlord or capitalist has a natural advantage over his labourers; he need neither use severity nor indulgence to maintain his position.

The condition of the working classes in modern Europe in many respects certainly is not better than that of the slaves in countries of lower civilization. We cannot deny the truth of the remark made by the intelligent chief of the Fulbe, whom Hecquard met on his travels in West Africa. "We often" says Hecquard "talked about our mode of government and the relation of the different classes in European society. He did not attach any value to the legal equality of the citizens and asked me how my countrymen got on without slaves. His conclusion was that with us the domestics and the poor classes in general were the slaves of the rich, because the latter could, by refusing to give them work, reduce them to starvation in a country, where nothing is given gratuitously" [1]).

We have seen that slavery cannot exist to any considerable extent among peoples with closed resources. But even among peoples with open resources it is not always found. Slaves perform the drudgery for their masters; therefore they are not wanted where little drudgery has to be done, or in other terms, slavery is not likely to exist where *subsistence* is *difficult to acquire.* Where men subsist by highly skilled labour, there can be little use for slaves; for the slaves cannot be made to perform such labour; and the little unskilled labour that is wanted is not profitable enough to admit of the keeping of slaves, who would have to be fed by the produce of their

---

1) Hecquard, p. 313.

masters' work. This is the principal reason why slavery hardly ever occurs among hunters, and one of the reasons why the Eskimos do not keep slaves.

We find thus that, generally speaking, the keeping of slaves is economically profitable to peoples with open resources among which subsistence is easily acquired, and to such peoples only. But there are several *secondary causes*, internal and external, which bring about that slaves are sometimes kept by peoples with closed resources, or by peoples among which subsistence is difficult to procure, and that on the other hand slavery is sometimes absent where resources are open and subsistence is easy to acquire.

Among the *secondary internal causes* we have noted in the first place the *condition of women*. There is no use for slaves, where all disagreeable work can be, and is performed by the weaker sex; Australian and Melanesian women supply the place of slaves. On the other hand, where the women hold a high position, and the men are desirous of relieving them of a part of their task, slavery is likely to arise sooner than otherwise would be the case.

Commerce probably exists among all savages. Even the Australian tribes mutually exchange rare kinds of earth for painting their bodies, and similar objects. But commerce has only a social importance, where the articles exchanged are manufactured goods in the widest sense, including *e. g.* fish and agricultural products, in a word all articles the production of which requires a considerable amount of labour. Then the freemen who devote themselves to commercial pursuits want others to perform the common labour for every-day subsistence; moreover the preparing of the articles of trade requires more labour than would otherwise be wanted. And last, but not least, commerce leads to the development of wealth and luxury; slave labour is now wanted to provide the owner not only with the necessaries, but with the comforts of life. Commercial tribes in the widest sense, — including 1° tribes which exchange native produce for foreign manufactures, 2° tribes which themselves produce and export manufactured goods in the common, restricted. sense, 3° tribes which carry on a transit-trade, — are therefore far more likely to keep slaves than selfsufficing tribes.

We have seen that subjection of women is sometimes a substitute for slavery. Another substitute is *subjection of tribes*
as such. This subjection occurs only, so far as savages are
concerned, where peculiar circumstances render it possible:
among pastoral tribes, which subject their neighbours to whom
they are superior in military qualities, and in Oceania, where
the limited area prevents the conquered from receding. Where
a tribe subjected as such pays a tribute to the conquerors
and performs services for them, there is not so much need
for enslavement of individuals belonging to the vanquished tribe.

People who live from hand to mouth have less use for
slaves than those who *preserve food* for the time of scarcity.
The preparing of this food may require much labour which
is very fit to be performed by slaves. We have seen that
such is especially the case on the North Pacific Coast of North
America.

Slaves are sometimes kept for *non-economic purposes*.

Warfare plays a great part in savage life, and we have
found that the requirements of warfare sometimes prevent, but
in other cases further the rise of slavery. Many savage tribes
increase their population by introduction of foreign elements.
This may be done for two reasons: men are wanted either for
labourers or for warriors [1]). In the former case the introduction of aliens leads to slavery in its most general form of
extratribal slavery. When warriors are wanted, slavery is not
the most appropriate form; adoption of foreigners, such as was
for instance practised by the Iroquois, answers the purpose
better, because a man who enjoys the common privileges of a
member of the tribe is more reliable in war than a slave. In
such case militarism may prevent the rise of slavery, because all
available men are wanted in war and have therefore to be placed
on a level with the tribesmen. But where superior military
qualities of a tribe render the employment of slaves in warfare (most often in the lower ranks of the army) possible,
slaves are sometimes kept mainly for military purposes, espe-

---

1) There is another reason: foreign women are sometimes procured for wives. But we
may leave this case out of consideration as being foreign to our subject.

cially where prejudices of race or colour prevent the tribe from adopting the foreigners. Then militarism furthers the growth of slavery; for slaves would perhaps not be wanted, if they did not serve as warriors.

Slaves may also be kept as a mere *luxury*. The possession of many slaves, like other property, everywhere tends to give the owner influence and reputation. Yet he most often also derives material profit from his slaves, namely from the total number of them, even where some of them do not perform productive labour. Only in a few cases does the sole use of slaves appear to consist in augmenting their owners' influence and reputation. This occurs among some pastoral tribes, where the rich are able to support a large number of unproductive labourers. But here the military use of slaves has perhaps co-operated in establishing slavery.

In the beginning of this paragraph we have spoken of *external causes*.

It is quite possible that a tribe does not keep slaves, though they would be very useful. The non-existence of slavery in such cases is due to external circumstances. It may be that the coercive power of the tribe is not sufficiently developed to admit of the keeping of slaves. It may also be that slavery does not exist, because it has not yet been invented: people may have always been accustomed to deal otherwise with their prisoners than by enslaving them, and so the idea of making slaves may never have entered their minds. The coercive power is strongest where men live in *fixed habitations* (though several tribes of pastoral nomads also keep slaves), and in *large groups*, and are accustomed to *preserve food*. The *slave-trade* has considerable influence. It increases the coercive power by rendering escape of slaves more difficult; and by making a tribe acquainted with the institution of slavery and providing it with an easy means of acquiring slaves it often overcomes the *vis inertiae*. The slave-trade may go far to account for the very frequent occurence of slavery among savages who have long maintained relations with superior races, though due allowance must be made for the influence of the general intercourse with such races, especially in furthering the commercial development. Another external cause is the *neighbourhood of inferior races,* the influence of which, as we have seen, clearly appears among pastoral tribes. It is easier for Hamitic and Semitic nations to keep Negroes in a state of subjection than people of their own race.

General recapitulation.

	Furthering the growth of slavery.	Hindering the growth of slavery.
I. Internal causes.		
A. General:	1. Open resources and subsistence easy to acquire.	1. Closed resources. 2. Subsistence difficult to acquire.
B. Secondary, economic:	1. A high position of women. 2. Commerce. 3. Preserving of food.	1. Female labour serving as a substitute for slave labour. 2. Subjection of tribes as such.
C. Secondary, non-economic:	1. Militarism (where slaves are employed in warfare). 2. Slaves kept as a luxury.	1. Militarism (especially where foreigners are adopted).
II. External causes:	1. Fixed habitations. 2. Living in large groups. 3. Preserving of food. 4. The slave-trade. 5. The neighbourhood of inferior races.	

Preserving of food and militarism occur twice, because they work in different directions.

We have arranged the separate causes within each group

in the order in which we have found them. If we had arranged them according to their relative importance, they would have been enumerated in another order. Thus among the external causes the slave-trade comes last, though its influence is greater than that of the other external causes [1]).

§ 2. *Outlines of a further investigation of the early history of slavery.*

We have viewed slavery as an industrial system, and inquired under what economic and social conditions this system can exist. This investigation we believe has led to valuable conclusions. But slavery (even if we confine ourselves to slavery among savages) may be viewed under many more aspects. We have not made any further study of the subject: but having collected many ethnographical materials, we have become acquainted with a great number of details which may afford subjects of further investigation. We shall give here an enumeration of various points connected with slavery, though we do not claim that it is in any way complete: it would probably appear on closer scrutiny that many additions could be made to it. We shall mention the various points in short sentences, often in the form of inquiries.

---

1) Dr. Vierkandt, reviewing the first edition of this work, remarks that there is no internal connection between the results of the investigation and the distinction of economic groups, as the existence or non-existence of slavery appears to depend not only on the economic state of society, but on many causes which have little to do with this state.

Though we fully admit this last, we think our division of the savage tribes into economic groups is justified by the results of our investigation. This division has led us to the following conclusions. Hunters and fishers, and equally the lowest agricultural group, as Dr. Vierkandt himself observes, generally do not keep slaves. The state of pastoral nomadism is also unfavourable to the growth of slavery. On the other hand, agriculturists of the higher stages are very likely to keep slaves.

Having arrived at these preliminary results, we have inquired which causes engender this connection between slavery and the economic state of society. We have also asked for the causes of the exceptions to the rules above mentioned. So we have come to an understanding of the internal connection between slavery and the other factors of social life. We cannot think our final results would have been obtained as well in any other way.

I. The different ways in which people become slaves.

There are:

1° Slaves by birth;

2° Free-born people who become slaves.

In connection with the former point it may be inquired what is in each case the status of children born of two slaves, of a male slave and a free woman, of a female slave and a free man, and especially of a female slave and her master. This inquiry will enable us to find, whether and to what extent slaves are merged in the general population. [1]

The manners in which free-born people become slaves may be distinguished according as slaves are acquired from without or within the limits of the tribe. This reminds us of the distinction we have made between extratribal and intratribal slavery. We may inquire then which of these two forms of slavery appears first. If we should find that extratribal is older than intratribal slavery (which does not seem unlikely), we might examine the economic and social conditions under which intratribal slavery can exist.

Extratribal slaves become such by:

1° Capture in war or kidnapping. Here a wide field of research opens itself. Captives, when they are not enslaved, are killed (eaten, sacrificed), or exchanged after peace has been concluded, or ransomed by their countrymen, or adopted into the tribe of the captors. It may be inquired whether any of these modes of treatment can have gradually led to enslavement of the captives (e. g. captives are first adopted, and gradually differentiated from the born members of the tribe; or they are first eaten, then preserved to be eaten later on and in the meantime set to work, and finally employed as slaves and no longer eaten) [2]. Several of these modes of treatment

---

[1] In the Shortland Islands (Solomon group) many of the common people are children of slave parents. Ribbe, p. 138.

[2] Among the Tlinkits, in Holmberg's time, it was the custom to sacrifice slaves at some great feasts; but the master often gave a good slave the opportunity of hiding

coexist with slavery (*e. g.* some captives are sacrificed and the rest kept as slaves; or slaves are occasionally sacrificed); does this only occur in the early stages of slavery, and indicate that slavery has not yet fully developed? When is slavery an object, and when is it only an incident of warfare? A remarkable phenomenon, worth a close investigation, is the occurrence of extratribal slavery or adoption of aliens together with a preventive check on population (infanticide, abortion) [2]). When captives are enslaved, it is worth inquiring in what manner they are distributed among the captors; this will have a strong influence on the division of wealth.

2° Purchase. The prices paid for different classes of slaves show what slaves are most desired (men or women, people of different ages or nationalities). The slaves sold have often been captured by the sellers; but it also occurs that people are sold by their countrymen, especially criminals. Here we may notice the influence of the slave-trade on penal law; people are probably often sold abroad, who otherwise would have been killed or expelled from the community.

Intratribal slaves become such (so far as we know) in the following ways:

‘ 1° For non-payment of a debt. Here the general treatment of debtors and the extent to which the rights of creditors are acknowledged by the community are worth examining. Debtor-slaves have often, but not always, a right to become free by paying off the debt [3]). In some cases the creditor

---

during the feast; he could then return afterwards with impunity. Generally speaking, no slaves were sacrificed but the old and sickly and those who, being defective in some way or other, caused their master more trouble than profit. Except at the great feasts slaves were scarcely ever killed; for they were valuable and difficult to replace. (Holmberg, I p. 51). We see that the keeping of slaves had become profitable and so the old custom of sacrificing slaves was going out of practice. — 2) To give one instance, Guppy states that in Ugi, in the Solomon Islands, "infanticide is the prevailing custom. When a man needs assistance in his declining years, his props are not his own sons but youths obtained by purchase from the St. Christoval natives who, as they attain to manhood, acquire a virtual independence, passing almost beyond the control of their original owner. It is from this cause that but a small proportion of the Ugi natives have been born on the island, three-fourths of them having been brought as youths to supply the place of offspring killed in infancy". Guppy, p. 42. — 3) See Post, Ethn. Jur., I p. 366.

does not keep the debtor as a slave, but recovers his money by selling him abroad [1]).

2° As a punishment, either directly, or when the *wergild* is not paid. This subject might be treated in connection with Professor Steinmetz's investigations of early penal law. Criminals often become slaves of the chief or king; a study of this matter would lead to an inquiry into political institutions at large.

3° By marrying a male or female slave. Here we may inquire where and to what extent *connubium* between free people and slaves exists.

4° By offering themselves as slaves, or selling themselves. In the former case it has always carefully to be inquired whether such persons become slaves or voluntary servants; the latter is quite possible, and the terminology of our informants not always reliable, as we have seen when speaking of Oceania. When they really become slaves, there are probably open resources. It is then worth inquiring what can be the reason why, while resources are open and so everybody is able to provide for himself, there are people who throw themselves upon the mercy of men of power.

5° Finally, orphans and other helpless persons are sometimes enslaved.

II. The different ways in which people cease to be slaves.

1° Redemption. Here the question presents itself, where slaves, or certain categories of slaves, have a right to be redeemed. [2])

2° Emancipation. Where, and under what social conditions does this custom prevail, and where is it of frequent occurrence? What are the motives that induce the master to set his slave free? Emancipation as a substitute for sacrifice [3]).

---

1) Post, l. c. — 2) Among the Chingpaws of Upper Burma slaves can always be liberated by their parents by means of a payment (Wehrli, p. 37). — 3) Among the Tlinkits at the feast held in commemoration of the deceased, the man who gave the feast used to part with some of his slaves, whether by sacrificing or emancipating them was left to the decision of the priest. Erman, p. 382.

3° Adoption. Connected with this is the fact, that in some countries slaves sometimes succeed to their masters' goods [1]). Here we may ask whether or not such adoption and right of inheritance are only found in early stages and have to be regarded as survivals of adoption of aliens.

4° Marriage of a slave with a free person, especially of a female slave with her master.

5° Dedication to a god. Slaves can sometimes become free by devoting themselves to some deity [2]). Further details; power of the priesthood; compare the influence of the church in the Middle Ages.

In whatever way slaves become free, the position of the *liberti* deserves a separate consideration. Are they on a level with free-born men, or do they form a separate class? Do their descendants gradually become merged in the general population?

III. Treatment of slaves by their masters.

1° Is the general treatment stated to be good or bad? Where the former and where the latter?

2° Slaves are often stated to be looked upon and treated as members of the master's family. What does this mean? Where does it occur?

3° Difference between freemen and slaves in food, clothing, etc. Slaves forbidden to wear the same dress and ornaments as freemen [3]).

---

1) Among the Bayaka "if the deceased leaves no heir, his wives and goods pass into the possession of one of his slaves, who thus becomes a free man." Torday and Joyce, Ba-Yaka, p. 44. — 2) Among the Ewe-speaking peoples of the Slave Coast "according to custom, any slave who takes refuge in a temple and dedicates himself to the service of the god, cannot be reclaimed by his owner; but as by paying a fee to the priest the owner can close the doors of all the temples in the neighbourhood to his fugitive slaves, this provision of an asylum for an ill-treated slave is more apparent than real". Ellis, Ewe-speaking peoples, p. 220. — 3) Among the Chinooks, the flattening of the head, "appears to be a sort of mark of royalty or badge of aristocracy, for their slaves are not permitted to treat their children thus". (Swan, The Northwest Coast, p. 168). Among the Malays of Menangkabao slaves were not allowed to dress in the same manner as free people or live in houses like those of the free or wear gold or silver ornaments or silks. (Willinck, p. 141).

IV. Legal status of slaves[1]).

1° Is the master's power over his slave unlimited? Very often it is not. Connection with the development of the power of government.

2° Rights of the slaves with regard to marriage and family. *Connubium* with freemen: see above. Are slave-marriages legally acknowledged, or do they entirely depend on the master's pleasure? Do the masters apply any principles of selection in mating the slaves? When the parents are slaves belonging to different masters, to which master do the children belong? Has the master full rights over his female slaves in a sexual respect?

3° Right of property. Are the rights of slaves to their earnings (*peculium*) recognized? When the slave dies, who succeeds to the *peculium?*

4° Have contracts made by slaves legal force?

5° Punishment of slaves by their masters [2]).

6° Protection of slaves by penal law. When a slave has been killed, is a *wergild* paid as for a freeman, or is only the price of the slave restored to the master? Similarly with regard to lesser injuries. Are those who commit any offence against the slave punished by the government? If so, is any exception made for the master? Is the master responsible for any damages caused by his slave?

7° Sometimes the master may not sell the slave without his consent.

8° It may also be that the slave, if ill-treated by his master, has a right to be sold. In some cases the slave can change his master by causing some slight damage to the new master or his goods. This formality has probably originated from the delivering up of the slave to the injured person for some real damage [3]).

9° Has the slave any public rights, does he share in government matters?

---

1) See also Post, Ethn. Jur., I pp. 370 sqq. — 2) See Steinmetz, Strafe, II pp. 306—315. — 3) See Post, Ethn. Jur., I. p. 377.

V. The attitude of public opinion towards slaves.

1º Are slaves despised? Details. Do the slaves receive a regular burial, or are their corpses thrown away?

2° External signs of slavery (mutilations, dress different from that of freemen) [1]. Are these signs only intended clearly to show the difference of status, or to make fugitive slaves easy to recognize?

3° Are ill-treatment and sale of slaves discountenanced by public opinion? [2]

4º Is there any instance among savages of slavery being considered a *status contra naturam?*

VI. Different kinds of slaves.

Slaves can be distinguished according to
1º their nationality,

2º the manner in which they have become slaves (difference between extratribal and intratribal slaves, between native-born and newly-acquired slaves) [3],

3º the work imposed upon them (outdoor and indoor slaves, *familia rustica* and *familia urbana*).

What are the practical consequences of these distinctions? [4].

VII. Slave labour.

Slaves sometimes perform
1º the same work as freemen,
or 2º the same as free women,
or 3º the same as the lower classes.

---

1) Among the ancient Germans, slaves were obliged to wear their hair short (Amira, p. 139). Similarly in Dorey (New-Guinea); see "Nieuw-Guinea", p. 149. — 2) The facts do not seem to justify Déniker's conclusion that the moral code of savages disapproves of compassion with slaves, because it is not profitable to the tribe. (Déniker, Races et peuples, p. 299.) — 3) On the favourable position of native-born slaves in North-eastern Africa, see above, p. 267. — 4) Déniker remarks that, together with the formation of social classes, a distinction between the different kinds of unfree arises. "The lowest grade are the slaves in the proper sense, who are not even regarded as human beings, whereas, at the top of the scale, we find people, unfree by birth, but able to arrive at a position not very different from that of the free citizens of the upper-classes." Déniker, Races et peuples, p. 296.

4º If some kind of work is performed by slaves only, what is its character? (Drudgery as opposed to noble work).

5º Is the work for which slaves are employed despised [1])?

6º Amount of work. Are the slaves over-worked? Are they supervised? Are they kept at work by any compulsory means (flogging, etc.)?

7º Do the slaves live in their master's house?

VIII. Serfdom.

Does it ever exist among savages? Are there instances of the coexistence of slavery and serfdom? In what manner do people become serfs?

IX. Number of slaves.

1º What is, in each case, the number of the slaves, and their proportion to the general population?

2º What is, in each case, the numerical proportion of the sexes among the slaves?

3º Do the slaves form a separate class of people?

4º Are the slaves an integral part of the wealth of their owners?

5º In some cases only certain classes (e. g. the nobility) are entitled to keep slaves [2]).

X. Happiness or unhappiness of slaves.

Is it considered a great evil for one's self or one's friends to fall into slavery? [3]) Instances of suicide to escape from

---

1) In Dahomey "agriculture is despised, because slaves are employed in it." Burton, II p. 248. — 2) Among the Battas of Mandheling and Pertibie only the nobles are allowed to keep slaves. The higher nobles may keep as many slaves as they like, the lower only two or three (Willer, p. 43). — 3) Among the Ewe it occurs that a slave is emancipated by his master. "But, generally speaking, slaves do not care to be free, for they are treated as members of the family and are so contented that they do not long for a change in their condition." Herold, p. 170. The slaves, formerly kept by the Koniagas, evidently thought otherwise of their servile state: for on the arrival of the Russians, many slaves took refuge to them (Holmberg I p. 79).

slave.'y [1]). In many cases it is not slavery as such, but sale to distant regions that is felt as a great calamity. We may mention here the curious phenomenon of people captured and enslaved by the enemy or sold abroad, being on their return despised or even repelled by their former countrymen [2]).

XI. Consequences of slavery.

1° Influence of slavery on the social organization of the tribe. A slave-owner, having labour forces at his command and being supported by a body of followers, is more likely to attain wealth and consideration than the other freemen. And as in those countries, where the slave trade is developed, the keeping of slaves may soon become a privilege of the rich [3]), slavery furthers the divergence of the rich and the poor, of the nobles and the common people.

2° Connected with this is the influence of slavery on the development of the military principle. The ruling classes, having learned to command their slaves, are more capable of commanding the people.

3° Influence of slavery on the laws and customs regulating marriage, and on sexual morality at large. Female slaves serving as concubines. [4]).

4° Influence of slavery on the condition of free women. When there are many domestic slaves, free women are no longer overtaxed with work. [5]).

---

1) The Athka Aleuts sometimes preferred suicide to captivity in war or slavery (Petroff, p. 158). — 2) "In the district of Allas [in Sumatra] a custom prevails, by which, if a man has been sold to the hill people, however unfairly, he is restricted on his return from associating with his countrymen as their equal, unless he brings with him a sum of money, and pays a fine for his re-enfranchisement to his kalippah or chief. This regulation has taken its rise from an idea of contamination among the people, and from art and avarice among the chiefs." Marsden, p. 255. Similarly, among the Maori, according to Polack (II p. 55), "chiefs who have tasted of slavery are often taunted by their friends, by whom they may have been ransomed, as having been slaves." Brown (New Zealand, p. 62) remarks: "They attach great importance to the circumstance of never having been taken in war." — 3) Among the Ewe, the price of a slave is 140—200 shilling, so the relatively rich only are able to purchase slaves (Herold, p. 168). — 4) On the West African coast, from Lagos to Cameroon, the master of the house has over his wives a limited, over his male and female slaves an unlimited power (Kingsley, West African studies, p. 439). Among the Bali tribes of Cameroon, female slaves are concubines without any recognized rights. — 5) See Schmoller, Grundriss, I p. 339.

5⁰ Influence of slavery on warfare. As soon as captives are regularly enslaved, the cruel modes of treating captives which may have formerly existed disappear. On the other hand, when the procuring of slaves becomes an object of warfare, war becomes much more frequent than before [1]).

6⁰ Influence of slavery on the development of the political power of the tribe. Slavery "creates a set of persons born to work that others may not work, and not to think in order that others may think. Therefore slave-owning nations, having time to think, are likely to be more shrewd in policy, and more crafty in strategy" [2]).

7⁰ Slavery has a great influence on morality at large, in a good as well as in a bad sense.

Slavery has played a great part in the education of mankind. Ingram rightly remarks that "slavery discharged important offices .... by forcing the captives, who with their descendants came to form the majority of the conquering community, to a life of industry in spite of the antipathy to regular and sustained labour which is deeply rooted in human nature, especially in the earlier stages of the social movement, when insouciance is so common a trait, and irresponsibility is hailed as a welcome relief" [3]).

Moreover, slavery affords to the higher classes a leisure, that enables them to reach the higher grades of culture, which would be inaccessible to them, if they had to work for their daily wants [4]).

A bad effect of slavery is that manual labour is identified with slave labour and so discredited [5]).

Other bad effects of slavery are mentioned by Ingram. The habit of absolute rule corrupts the masters. Slavery often

---

1) Winwood Reade, speaking of the coast tribes of West Africa, from Senegambia to Angola, remarks: "In those places where the slave-buying still goes on, the people are more disposed to go to war, to convict criminals, and to make use of any pretence to procure slaves. And it is also certain that there are regions where an almost constant war is carried on for the purpose of obtaining slaves" (Winwood Reade, p. 291). — 2) Bagehot, p. 73; see also Ingram, pp. 5, 6. — 3) Ingram, p. 5; see also Schmoller, Grundriss, I p. 338. — 4) See Lange, Die Arbeiterfrage, p. 63. — 5) Such is the case for instance in Cameroon (Hutter, p. 36). Among the Bali tribes of Cameroon the nobles wear their nails long, in order to show that they are not slaves (Ibid., p. 385). See also Westermarck, Moral Ideas, II pp. 272, 273.

engenders cruelty, or at least harshness. The slaves are demoralized, because their education is neglected and they do not
live in normal family relations. Slavery moreover prevents "the
development of the sense of human dignity, which lies at the
foundation of morals" [1]).

8° Influence of slavery on the intermingling of races. "The
blending of types" says Brinton "was greatly accelerated in
early days by the institution or human slavery" [2]).

9° Selective influence of slavery. Ferrero's theory: slavery
has greatly furthered the survival of the industrious type of
man [3]). Ripley, speaking of colonial slavery, remarks: "Such
an institution exercises a selective choice upon the negro; for
the survivors of such severe treatment will generally be a
picked lot, which ought to exhibit vitality to a marked degree,
all the weaklings having been removed" [4]). High death-rate
among slaves, even in primitive culture [5]).

XII. Development of slavery.

Though we have not systematically investigated this subject,
our studies have brought us into closer connection with this
than with any of the points mentioned above. We shall therefore briefly state our impressions on the development of slavery,
without, of course, claiming for the following remarks the
value of a theory.

Slavery very probably first appears in the form of extratribal slavery, and originates from the adoption of captives,
especially captive children. This is also Powell's opinion. According to him captive children were originally adopted and
treated by the captors entirely as their own children. "This

---

1) See Ingram, pp. 9—11. All this applies much less to early slavery than to slavery
in its more advanced stages. Yet even the patriarchal slave system of primitive societies
sometimes has a bad influence on the slaves. Polack, speaking of the New Zealand slaves,
remarks: "Debarred from the sight of their relatives, they become reckless of moral feeling ...
Obscenity and lying are among the practices most persisted in by the slaves, and to their
demoralized state may be attributed the greater part of the wars and dissensions of this
irritable people; they may be justly regarded as the greatest drawback to the prosperity
and civilization hitherto of the New Zealanders" (Polack, II pp. 58, 59). — 2) Brinton,
Races and peoples, p. 46. — 3) Ferrero, La morale primitiva, etc. — 4) Ripley, p. 564. —
5) Ratzel, Authropogeographie, II pp. 387, 388.

is not yet slavery. If the captive belongs to a tribe of hereditary enemies who have from time immemorial been designated by some opprobrious term, as cannibals, liars, snakes,
etc. — then it may be that the captive is doomed to perpetual younger brotherhood, and can never exercise authority
over any person within the tribe, though such person may
be born after the new birth of the captive. This is the first
form of slavery. Usually, though not invariably, the captives
adopted are children" [1]). Whether the first slaves were really
captives belonging to a tribe of hereditary enemies, we do not
know; but Powell expresses himself very appropriately, when
he says that the slaves are "doomed to perpetual younger
brotherhood". In the early stages of culture slaves are on the
whole leniently treated, and there is little difference between
young slaves and free children. But the slave always remains
a "younger brother". He never becomes the head of a family;
and when the master who educated him dies, he becomes the
subject of the master's child, who has been the companion of his
childhood. The slave does not count among the full-grown men
of the tribe; he is not allowed to bear arms, he has no voice
in government matters; though a member, he is an inferior
member of the household in which he lives.

This is the first stage of differentiation between freemen
and slaves.

The slaves are children captured in war [2]), their number
is small. The slave, who is nearly on a level with the children, is wanted for much the same reason why children are
so eagerly desired among most agricultural savage tribes: the
larger the family, the more food can be produced; for land
is still abundant. Slaves and freemen perform the same kind
of work, with the exception perhaps of some domestic occupations, which are more and more left to the slaves.

Gradually the number of slaves increases. The slave-trade
greatly furthers the growth of slavery. The keeping of slaves

---

1) Powell, On Regimentation, p. CXII. — 2) Adult males are not desired for slaves,
because they are very difficult to manage. This is the case even among the semi-civilized
Mohammedans of Baghirmi; see Nachtigal, II p. 615. The North African slave-hunters,
according to Goldstein (p. 367), have a preference for girls, but also capture boys; full-
grown men, however, are generally killed.

is more and more confined to the chiefs and principal men. Where slaves are captured in war it is the leading men who secure most of the spoils; and where slaves are purchased it is only the rich who can give a good price for them. The ruling classes are the great slave-owners, and these men are naturally inclined to leave all the common work to their slaves, reserving for themselves only the noble pursuits of warfare and government. The difference between the slaves and their owners becomes thus greater than it was before. The common people come to distrust and hate the slaves, whom they regard as the tools of the aristocracy. And the differentiating process we have described here is always going on: the more slaves a man owns, the greater his wealth; and the greater a man's wealth the better will he be able to procure slaves. The common people are continually sinking in the social scale, and in the course of time many of them are reduced to slavery for non-payment of money they have borrowed from the rich.

The further development of slavery can proceed in two different ways.

In some countries, where oil, cotton, and similar products are exported, slavery assumes enormous proportions. The large plantations can best be worked with slaves; and as manufactured goods are imported, slave labour serves not only to feed the master, but to provide him with the luxuries of life; the wants of the slave-owners, and accordingly the possible extent of slavery, become practically unlimited. This slave system, as we have seen, exists in some parts of the West Coast of Africa, and bears a close resemblance to that which till far into the 19th century was carried on in the Southern States of North America.

Where cereals are grown and agricultural produce is not exported on a very large scale, the course of things is different. An increase of slaves above a certain number is of little use to the owner. When he has slaves enough to provide him with a large quantity of food and other necessaries for the use of himself and his family and personal servants, he does not want more slaves. The agricultural produce they could furnish would not be worth the pains of supervising them.

The slaves (except a few who are kept for domestic services) are soon allowed to live rather independently, bound only to provide fixed quantities of agricultural produce and perform occasional services. And when the use of money becomes general, these slaves often contract with their masters to pay a yearly tribute in money instead of the services and payments in kind. The slaves become serfs. And gradually the whole of the lower orders are merged in this servile class. Ancient slaves, members of subjected communities, helpless persons who seek the protection of a powerful chief, all become the subjects and dependents of the ruling nobles. Such was the social system of the early Middle Ages, that in the course of time was entirely overturned through the progress of manufactures and commerce and the gradual appropriation of the whole of the land [1]).

---

1) Slaves have also sometimes been employed in manufactures. Such, according to Cunningham, was the case in ancient Tyre. Slaves also "worked as artisans in the factories of Athens". Cunningham, Western Civilization, pp. 66, 110. But we think such an employment of slaves is rather an exception.

LIST OF AUTHORITIES.

Abbreviations.

A. R. B. E. = Annual report of the Bureau of Ethnology to the secretary of the Smithsonian Institution.

Bijdr. = Bijdragen tot de Taal-, Land- en Volkenkunde van Nederlandsch-Indië, uitgegeven door het Koninklijk Instituut voor de Taal-, Land- en Volkenkunde van Nederlandsch-Indië.

I. A. E. = Internationales Archiv für Ethnographie.

J. A. I. = Journal of the Anthropological Institute of Great Britain and Ireland.

M. D. S. = Mitteilungen aus den deutschen Schutzgebieten.

N. Z. G. = Mededeelingen van wege het Nederlandsch Zendeling-genootschap.

Pet. = Dr. A. Petermann's Mitteilungen aus Justus Perthes' Geographischer Anstalt.

R. E. = Revue d' Ethnographie.

Smithson. Rep. = Annual report of the board of regents of the Smithsonian Institution.

T. A. G. = Tijdschrift van het Koninklijk Nederlandsch Aardrijkskundig Genootschap.

Tijds. = Tijdschrift voor Indische Taal-, Land- en Volkenkunde. Uitgegeven door het Bataviaasch Genootschap van Kunsten en Wetenschappen.

Z. E. = Zeitschrift für Ethnologie.

Z. Erd. = Zeitschrift für allgemeine Erdkunde (Berlin).

Z. G. Erd. = Zeitschrift der Gesellschaft für Erdkunde zu Berlin (Fortsetzung der Z. Erd.).

Z. V. R. = Zeitschrift für vergleichende Rechtswissenschaft.

Adair, J., Geschichte der Amerikanischen Indianer. 1782.

Adriani, N., Mededeelingen omtrent de Toradja's van Midden-Celebes. Tijds. XLIV.

d'Albertis, New Guinea. 1880.

Allison, Mrs. S. S., Account of the Similkameem Indians of British Columbia. J. A. I. XXI (1892).

Amira, K. von, Recht, in Paul's Grundriss der Germanischen Philologie. Vol. III.

Andersson, Ch. J., Reisen in Südwest-Afrika bis zum See Ngami. 1858.

Andree, R., Die Anthropophagie. 1887.

Angas, J. F., Savage Life and Scenes in Australia and New Zealand. 1847.

Angus, H. C., A year in Azimba and Chipitaland. J. A. I. XXVII (1897).

Arcin, A., La Guinée française. 1907.

Ashley, W. J., Economic history and theory. Vol. I 1888, Vol. II 1893.

Azara, F. de, Voyages dans l'Amérique méridionale. 1809.

Bagehot, W., Physics and politics. New edition. 1896.

Bakkers, J. A., De eilanden Bonerate en Kalao. Tijds. XI.

—— De afdeeling Sandjai. Tijds. XI.

—— Het leenvorstendom Boni. Tijds. XV.

—— Tanette en Barroe (Celebes). Tijds. XII.

Bancroft, H. H., The native races of the Pacific States of North America. Vol. I Wild tribes. 1875.

Bartram, W., The Creek and Cherokee Indians, 1789, ed. by Squier in Transact. of the American Ethnol. Society. 1853.

Bas, F. de, Een Nederlandsch reiziger aan den Congo. T. A. G. 2nd series IV.

Bastian, A., Die Rechtsverhältnisse bei verschiedenen Völkern der Erde. 1872.

—— Geographische und ethnologische Bilder. 1873.

Batchelor, J., The Ainu of Japan. 1892.

Baumann, O., Durch Massailand zur Nilquelle. 1894.

Baumstark, Die Warangi. M. D. S. XIII.

Beardmore, E., The natives of Mowat, Daudai, New Guinea. J. A. I. XIX (1890).

Bell, J. S., Journal d'une résidence en Circassie, trad. p. Louis Vivien. 1841.

Bennett, A. L., Ethnographical notes on the Fang. J. A. I. XXIX.

Bérenger-Féraud, L. J. B., Les peuplades de la Sénégambie. 1879.

Beschrijving van het landschap Pasir. Bijdr. LVIII.

Beuster, Das Volk der Vawenda. Z. G. Erd. XIV (1879).

Bibra, E. von, Reise in Süd-Amerika. 1854.

Bieger, Ph., Een doodenfeest te Rendé, op Soemba. N. Z. G. XXXIV.

Bink, Tocht van den zendeling — naar de Humboldtsbaai. T. A. G. 2nd Series XI.

Blumentritt, F., Begleitworte zu meiner Karte der Insel Mindanao. Z. G. Erd. XIX (1884).

—— Beiträge zur Kenntnis der Negritos. Z. G. Erd. XXVII (1892).

—— Die Bungianen. Ausland 1893.

—— Die Kianganen. Ausland 1891.

—— Die Maguindanaos. Ausland 1891.

—— Die Sitten und Bräuche der alten Tagalen. Manuscript des P. Juan de Plasencia. 1589. Z. E. XXV.

—— Über die Staaten der philippinischen Eingeborenen in den Zeiten der Conquista. Mitteilungen der Geogr. Gesellschaft in Wien 1885.

—— Versuch einer Ethnographie der Philippinen. Ergänzungsheft 67 zu Pet. 1882.

Boas, F., Die Tsimschian. Z. E. XX.

—— The Central Eskimo. A. R. B. E. VI.

—— The social organisation and the secret societies of the Kwakiutl Indians (From the report of the U. S. National Museum for 1895). 1897.

Bodenstedt, Die Völker des Kaukasus. 1885.

Boers, J. W., De Koeboes. Tijdschrift voor Nederlandsch-Indië 1838.

Boggiani, G., I Caduvei. 1895.

Bonaparte, Prince Roland, Les habitants de Suriname. 1884.

Bonney, F., On some customs of the aborigines of the Darling River. J. A. I. XIII (1884).

Bonwick, Daily life and origin of the Tasmanians. 1870.

Boot, J., Korte schets der noordkust van Ceram. T. A. G. 2nd Series X.

Bor, A. C. van den, Bijdragen tot de kennis van Sumatras Noord-Oostkust. Tijds. XVII.

Borde, de la, Description des Caraïbes, in Hennepin's Voyage curieux.

Borie, Notice sur les Mantras, tribu sauvage de la péninsule Malaise. Tijds. X.

Bos, P. R., Jagd, Viehzucht und Ackerbau als Culturstufen. I. A. E. X.

Bosman, W., Nauwkeurige beschrijving van de Guinese Goud-, Tand- en Slavenkust. 1709.

Bossu, M., Nouveaux voyages dans l' Amérique septentrionale. 1777.

Bottego, V., Il Giuba esplorato. 1895.

Boudin, Du nègre esclave chez les Peaux-Rouges. Bulletin de la société d'anthropologie V (1864).

Bourke, J. G., On the border with Crook. 1892.

Boutakoff, A., Über den untern Teil des Syr Dariah (Jaxartes) zwischen dem Fort Petroffsky und seiner Mündung. Z. Erd. Neue Folge IV (1858).

Bowdich, T. E., Geschiedenis van het Britsche gezantschap in het jaar 1817, aan den koning van Ashantee. 1820.

Brainne, Ch., La Nouvelle Calédonie. 1854.

Brenner, J. von, Besuch bei den Kannibalen Sumatras. 1894.

Brett, W. H., The Indian Tribes of Guiana. 1868.

Brettes, J. de, Six ans d'exploration chez les Indiens du nord de la Colombie. Tour du monde 1898.

Brinton, D. G., The Lenape and their legends, in Brinton's Library of aboriginal American Literature.

—— Races and peoples. 1890.

Brough Smyth, R., The aborigines of Victoria. 1878.

Brown, Robert, The adventures of John Jewitt. 1896.

Brown, W., New Zealand and its aborigines. 1845.

Browne, J., Die Eingebornen Australiens. Pet. 1856.

Bruijn, A. A., Het land der Karons. T. A. G. III (1878).

Brunner, H., Deutsche Rechtsgeschichte.

Bücher, K., Die Wirtschaft der Naturvölker. 1898.

Buchholz, R., Reisen in West-Afrika. 1880.

Bülow, W. von, Das ungeschriebene Gesetz der Samoaner. Globus LXIX (1896).

Burckhardt, J. L., Notes on the Bedouins and Wahabys. 1831.

Burrows, Guy, On the natives of the Upper Welle District of the Belgian Congo. J. A. I. New series I.

Burton, R. F., A mission to Gelele, king of Dahome. 1864.

Büttikofer, J. Einiges über die Eingebornen von Liberia. I. A. E. I.

—— Mededeelingen over Liberia. T. A. G. Bijblad 12.

Cairnes, J. E., The slave power. Second edition. 1863.

Cameron, V. L., Across Africa. 1877.

Campen, C. F. H., Beschrijving van het district Kau. T. A. G. 2nd series I.

Campbell, J., Wild tribes of Khondistan. 1864.

Capello, H., and R. Ivens, From Benguella to the Territory of Yacca. I 1882.

Cardi, Le Comte C. N. de, Ju-Ju Laws and Customs in the Niger Delta. J. A. I. XXIX.

Carey, H. C., The past, the present and the future. 1848.

Carver, J., Travels through the interior parts of North America in the years 1766, 1767 and 1768. 1779.

Casalis, E, Les Bassoutos ou vingt-trois années de séjour et d'observation au sud de l'Afrique. 1859.

Castro, A. de, Résumé historique de l'établissement portugais à Timor. Tijds. XI.

Cessac, Léon de, Renseignements ethnographiques sur les Comanches. R. E. I.

Chaillé Long, C., Central Africa. Naked truths of naked people. 1876.

Chalmers, J., Toaripi. J. A. I. XXVII (1898).

Chamberlain, A. F., The child and childhood in folk-thought. 1896.

Chantre, E., Recherches anthropologiques dans le Caucase. IV 1887.

Charlevoix, De, Histoire de la Nouvelle France. 1744.

Christian, F. W., Exploration in the Caroline Islands. The Geographical Journal, Vol. 13 (1899).

Clercq, F. S. A. de, Bijdragen tot de kennis der residentie Ternate. 1890.
—— De West- en Noordkust van Nederlandsch Nieuw-Guinea. T. A. G. 2nd series X.

Codrington, R. H., On social regulations in Melanesia. J. A. I. XVIII (1889).
—— The Melanesians. 1891.

Coll, C. van, Gegevens over land en volk van Suriname. Bijdr. LV.

Collins, D., An account of the English Colony in New South Wales. 1798.

Colquhoun, Among the Shans. 1885.

Compiègne, De, L'Afrique équatoriale: Gabonais, Pahouins, Gallois. 1875.
—— L'Afrique équatoriale: Okanda, Bangouens, Osyeba. 1875.

Conder, C. R., The present condition of the native tribes in Bechuanaland. J. A. I. XVI (1887).

Cooper, T. T., The Mishmee Hills. 1873.

Copway. G., The traditional history of the Ojibway nation. 1850.

Coquilhat, C., Sur le Haut Congo. 1888.

Corre, A., Les Sérères de Joal et de Portadal. R. E. II.

Coudreau, H., Chez nos Indiens: quatre années dans la Guyane française (1887—1891). 1893.

Crantz, D., Historie van Groenland. 1767.

Croce, B., Materialismo storico ed economia Marxistica. 1900.

Cunningham, W., The growth of English industry and commerce. I Early and Middle Ages. 1890. II Modern times. 1892.
—— Western Civilization in its economic aspects (Ancient times). 1898.

Curr, E. M., The Australian race.

Dale, G., An account of the principal customs and habits of the Natives inhabiting the Bondei country. J. A. I. XXV (1896).

Dall, W. H., Alaska and its resources. 1870.

Dalton, E. T., Descriptive ethnology of Bengal. 1872.

Danks, B., Marriage Customs of the New Britain Group. J. A. I. XVIII (1889).

Dargun, L., Ursprung und Entwicklungsgeschichte des Eigenthums. Z. V. R. V.

Darwin, Ch., Journal of a voyage round the world. 1889.
—— The Descent of Man and Selection in Relation to Sex. Revised edition. Chicago and New York.

Dawson, J., Australian aborigines. 1881.

Delden, E. Th. van, Verslag over den toestand van het landschap Gloegoer VI Kota. Tijds. XXVII.

Déniker, J., Les Ghiliaks. R. E. II.

—— Les races et les peuples de la terre. 1900.

Dewall, H. von, Matan, Simpang, Soekadana, de Karimata-eilanden en Koeboe. Tijds. XI.

Die Bewohner des schwarzen Irtyschthales. Z. E. VIII.

Dimitroff, Z., Die Geringschätzung des menschlichen Lebens. 1891.

Dinter, B. C. A. J. van, Eenige geographische en ethnographische aanteekeningen betreffende het eiland Siaoe. Tijds. XLI (1899).

Dobrizhoffer, M., Historia de Abiponibus. 1784.

Dodge, R. I., Die heutigen Indianer des fernen Westens. 1884.

Donselaar, W. M., Aanteekeningen over het eiland Saleijer. N. Z. G. I.

—— Aanteekeningen over het eiland Savoe. N. Z. G. XVI.

Doughty, Ch. M., Travels in Arabia Deserta. 1888.

Duloup, G., Huit jours chez les M'Bengas. R. E. II.

Dupont, E., Lettres sur le Congo. 1889.

Dijk, P. A. L. E. van, Nota over de landstreek in de Toba-landen, bekend onder den naam van Habinsaran. T. A. G. 2nd series IX.

—— Rapport betreffende de Si Baloengoensche landschappen. Tijds. XXXVII.

—— Rapport over de Loeboe-bevolking in de onderafdeeling Groot-Mandheling en Batang Natal. Bijdr. XXXVIII.

Eastman, Mrs. E. G., Indian Wars and Warriors. The Cosmopolitan, New York. February 1894.

Eastman, Mrs. M., Dahcotah. 1849.

Eck, R. van, Schets van het eiland Lombok. Tijds. XXII.

Ehrenreich, P., Beiträge zur Völkerkunde Brasiliens. Veröffentlichungen aus dem königlichen Museum für Völkerkunde II (1891).

—— Über die Botocudos der brasilianischen Provinzen Espiritu santo und Minas Geraes. Z. E. XIX.

Eliot, J., Asiatick Researches III. 1807.

Elliott, H. W., An arctic Province. Alaska and the Seal Islands. 1886.

Ellis, A. B., The Ewe-speaking peoples of the Slave Coast of West Africa. 1890.

—— The Tshi-speaking peoples of the Gold Coast of West Africa. 1887.

—— The Yoruba-speaking peoples of the Slave Coast of West Africa. 1894.

Ellis, W., Polynesian researches. Second edition.

—— Three visits to Madagascar. 1859.

Elton, F., Notes on the natives of the Solomon Islands. J. A. I. XVII (1888).

Emin Bey, Sur les Akkas et les Baris. Z. E. XVIII.

Encyclopaedie van Nederlandsch-Indie.

Engelhard, H. E. D., Aanteekeningen betreffende de Kindjin Dajaks in het landschap Baloengan. Tijds. XXIX.

Erman, A., Ethnographische Wahrnehmungen und Erfahrungen an den Küsten des Berings-Meeres. Z. E. II.

Erskine, J. E., Journal of a cruise among the islands of the Western Pacific. 1858.

Evreux, Père Yves D', Voyage dans le nord du Brésil, fait durant les années 1613 et 1614, publié par F. Denis. 1864.

Eyre, E. J., Journal of Expeditions of Discovery into Central Australia. 1845.

Falkner, Th., A description of Patagonia. 1774.

Favre, P., An account of the wild tribes inhabiting the Malayan Peninsula. Journ. of the Indian Archipelago II.

Felix, L., Entwicklungsgeschichte des Eigenthums.

Ferrero, G., La morale primitiva e l'atavismo del delitto. Archivio di psichiatria, scienze penali ed antropologia criminale. Vol XVI (1895).

Finsch, O., Die Goldküste und ihre Bewohner in ihrem heutigen Zustande. Z. Erd. Neue Folge XVII (1864).

—— Reise nach West-Sibirien im Jahre 1876. 1879.

—— Samoafahrten. 1890.

Fison, L., Land tenure in Fiji. J. A. I. X (1881).

Fison and Howitt, Kamilaroi and Kurnai.

Flügel, O., Das Ich und die sittlichen Ideen im Leben der Völker. Zweite Auflage. 1889.

Forbes, H. O, On the ethnology of Timorlaut. J. A. I. XIII (1884).

—— On the Kubus of Sumatra. J. A. I. XIV (1885).

—— On some of the tribes of the island of Timor. J. A. I. XIII (1884).

Forrest, John, On the natives of Central and Western Australia. J. A. I. V (1876).

Forster's J. R., Bemerkungen aus seiner Reise um die Welt. 1783.

Fraser, J., The aborigines of New South Wales. 1892.

Frazer, J. G., Notes on the Aborigines of Australia. J. A. I. XXIV (1895).

Fremont and Emory, Notes of travel in California. 1849.

French-Sheldon, Mrs., Customs among the natives of East Africa from Teita to Kilimegalia. J. A. I. XXI (1892).

Fritsch, G., Die Eingeborenen Süd-Afrika's. 1872.

Fülleborn, F., Ueber seine Reisen im Nyassa-Gebiet. Verhandlungen der Gesellschaft für Erdkunde zu Berlin. 1900.

Further papers relative to the exploration of British North America.

Gabb, Indian tribes and languages of Costa Rica. Proc. of the Amer. Philos. Soc. at Philadelphia XIV (1875).

Galton, F., Narrative of an explorer in tropical South Africa, being an account of a visit to Damaraland in 1851. Edited by G. T. Bettany. 1889.

Gardiner, J. Stanley, The natives of Rotuma. J. A. I. XXVII.

Gasquet, A., Précis des institutions politiques et sociales de l'ancienne France. 1885.

Gatschet, A. S., The Klamath Indians of South-western Oregon. Contrib. to N. Amer. Ethnology Vol. II Part I.

Geiseler, Die Oster-Insel, Eine Stätte prähistorischer Kultur in der Südsee. 1883.

Geoffroy, A., Arabes pasteurs nomades de la tribu des Larbas, in: Les ouvriers des deux mondes, publiés par la société d'économie sociale. Nouvelle Série, 8ième fascicule. 1887.

Gerland, G., Ueber das Aussterben der Naturvölker. 1868.

Gersen, G. J., Oendang-oendang, of verzameling van voorschriften in de Lematang-Oeloe en Ilir en de Pasemah-landen. Tijds. XX.

Gibbs, G., Tribes of Western Washington and Northwestern Oregon. Contrib. to N. Amer. Ethnology I 1877.

Glaumont, Usages, moeurs et coutumes des Néo-Calédoniens. R. E. VII.

Godden, Gertrude M., Naga and other frontier tribes of North-East India. J. A. I. XXVI and XXVII.

Goldstein, F., Die Sklaverei in Nord Afrika und im Sudan. Zeitschrift für Sozialwissenschaft XI (1908).

Goudswaard, A., De Papoewa's van de Geelvinksbaai. 1863.

Graafland, N., De Minahassa. 1867.

—— Eenige aanteekeningen op ethnographisch gebied ten aanzien van het eiland Rote. N. Z. G. XXXIII.

Grabowsky, F., Der Tod, das Begräbnis, das Tiwah oder Todtenfest. I. A. E. II.

Gräffe, E., nach Alf. Tetens und J. Kubary, Die Carolineninsel Yap oder Guap. Journal des Museum Godeffroy I.

Gramberg, J. S. G., Schets der Kesam, Semendo, Makakauw en Blalauw. Tijds. XV.

Grandidier, A., Des rites funéraires chez les Malgaches. R E. V.

Granville, K., and Felix N. Roth, Notes on the Jekris, Sobos and Ijos of the Niger Coast Protectorate. J. A. I. XXVIII.

Gregg, J., Karawanenzüge durch die westlichen Prairieen und Wanderungen in Nord-Mejico. 1845.

Grey, G., Journal of an Expedition of Discovery in North-Western and Western Australia. 1844.

Grinnell, G. B., The story of the Indian. 1896.

Groot, H. F. W. Cornets de, Nota over de slavernij en het pandelingschap in de residentie Lampongsche Districten. Tijds. XXVII.

Grosse, E., Die Formen der Familie und die Formen der Wirtschaft. 1896.

Grupp, G., Die Anfänge der Geldwirtschaft. Zeitschrift für Kulturgeschichte IV and V.

Guiral, L., Les Batékés. R. E. V.

Guise, R. E., On the tribes inhabiting the mouth of the Wanigela River. J. A. I. XXVIII.

Gumilla, J., Histoire naturelle, civile et géographique de l'Orénoque. 1758.

Guppy, H. B., The Solomon Islands and their natives. 1887.

Haarhoff, B. J., Die Bantu-Stämme Süd-Afrikas. 1890.

Haddon, A. C., The ethnography of the Western Tribes of Torres Straits. J. A. I. XIX (1890).

Hagen, La colonie de Porto-Novo et le Roi Toffa. R. E. VI.

Hagen et A. Pineau, Les Nouvelles-Hébrides. R. E. VII.

Hagen, B., Unter den Papuas in Deutsch-Neu-Guinea. 1899.

—— Die Orang Kubu auf Sumatra. 1908.

Hager, C., Die Marshall-Inseln. 1886.

Hahl, Ueber die Rechtsanschauungen der Eingeborenen eines Theiles der Blanchebucht und des Innern der Gazelle Halbinsel. Nachrichten über Kaiser Wilhelms-Land und den Bismarck-Archipel XIII (1897).

Hahn, E., Die Haustiere und ihre Beziehungen zur Wirtschaft des Menschen. 1896.

—— Die Entstehung der wirtschaftlichen Arbeit. 1908.

Hahn, J., Die Ovahereró. Z. G. Erd. IV (1869).

Hale, H., Ethnography and Philology. United States Exploring Expedition. 1846.

Hall, C. F., Life with the Esquimaux. 1864.

Handwörterbuch der Staatswissenschaften. Second and third edition.

Hanoteau, A., et A. Letourneux, La Kabylie et les coutumes Kabyles. 1872—3.

Hardisty, W. L., The Loucheux Indians. Smithson. Rep. 1866.

Harper Parker, E., The Burmo-Chinese Frontier and the Kakhyen tribes. Fortnightly Review, July 1897.

Harris, J. M., Some remarks on the Origin, Manners, Customs and Superstitions of the Gallinas. Memoirs Anthrop. Soc. of London II (1865—6).

Hartmann, R., Madagaskar. 1886.

Hasselt, A. L. van, Volksbeschrijving van Midden-Sumatra. 1882.

Hasselt, J. C. van, De onderafdeeling Bangkala. T. A. G. IV (1880).

Hasselt, J. L. van, Die Noeforezen. Z. E. VIII.

—— Eenige aanteekeningen aangaande de bewoners der N. Westkust van Nieuw-Guinea, meer bepaaldelijk de stam der Noefooreezen. Tijds. XXXI and XXXII.

Haxthausen, von, Transkaukasia. 1856.

Hearne, S., Landreis naar den Noorder-Oceaan. 1798.

Hecquard, H., Voyage sur la côte et dans l'intérieur de l'Afrique occidentale. 1853.

Hensel, R., Die Coroados der brasilianischen Provinz Rio Grande do Sul. Z. E. I.

Hernsheim, F., Südsee-Erinnerungen.

Herold, Bericht betreffend Rechtsgewohnheiten und Palaver der deutschen Ewe-Neger. M. D. S. V.

Herrmann, Die Wasiba und ihr Land. M. D. S. VII.

Hervey, The Endau and its Tributaries. Journ. of the Straits Branch of the R. Asiat. Soc. 1881.

Het landschap Donggala of Banawa. Bijdr. LVIII.

Heusser, J. Ch., und G. Claraz, Auszug aus Don J. M. de la Sota's Geschichte des Territorio Oriental del Uruguay. Z. Erd. Neue Folge X (1861).

Heijting, Th. A. L., Beschrijving der onderafdeeling Groot-Mandeling en Batang-Natal. T. A. G. 2nd series XIV.

Hickson, S. J., Notes on the Sengirese. J. A. I. XVI (1887).

Hildebrand, B., Natural-, Geld- und Creditwirthschaft. Jahrbücher für Nationalökonomie und Statistik II (1864).

Hildebrand, R., Recht und Sitte auf den primitiveren wirtschaftlichen Kulturstufen. Zweite Auflage. 1907.

Hildebrandt, J. M., Ausflug zum Ambergebirge in Nord-Madagaskar. Z. G. Erd. XV (1880).

—— Vorläufige Bemerkungen über die Sómal. Z. E. VII.

—— West-Madagaskar. Z. G. Erd. XV (1880).

Histoire de Kamtschatka. 1767.

Histoire de la Virginie. 1707.

Hoesemann, Ethnologisches aus Kamerun. M. D. S. XVI.

Hoëvell, G. W. W. C. van, Ambon en meer bepaaldelijk de Oeliassers. 1875.

—— De Kei-eilanden. Tijds. XXXIII.

—— Leti-eilanden. Tijds. XXXIII.

—— Tanimbar en Timor-laoet-eilanden. Tijds. XXXIII.

Hoffman, W. J., The Menomini Indians. A. R. B. E. XIV.

Höhnel, L. von, Zum Rudolph See und Stephanie See. 1892.

Holland, The Ainos. J. A. I. III (1874).

Hollander, J. J. de, Handleiding bij de beoefening der Land- en Volken-kunde van Nederlandsch Oost-Indië.

Holle, G. du Rij van Beest, Aanteekeningen betreffende de landschappen VI Kotta Pangkallan en XII Kotta Kampar. Tijds. XXIV.

Holmberg, H. J., Ethnographische Skizzen über die Völker des russischen Amerika. I 1855, II 1862.

Holub, E., On the Central South African tribes from the South Coast to the Zambesi. J. A. I. X (1881).

—— Sieben Jahre in Süd-Afrika. 1881.

Hooper, W. H., Ten months among the tents of the Tuski. 1856.

Hore, E. C., On the twelve tribes of Tanganyika. J. A. I. XII (1883).

Howitt, A. W., The native tribes of South-East Australia. 1904.

Hunt, A. E., Ethnographical notes on the Murray Islands, Torres Straits. J. A. I. XXVIII.

Hunter, J. D., Gedenkschriften eener gevangenschap onder de wilden van Noord-Amerika. 1824.

Hunter, W. W., The annals of rural Bengal. 1868.

Hutchinson, Th. J., Impressions of Western Africa. 1858.

Hutter, F., Wanderungen und Forschungen im Nord-Hinterland von Kamerun. 1902.

Hyades, P., and J. Déniker, Mission scientifique du Cap Horn, 1882—1883. Tome VII, Anthropologie, Ethnographie. 1891.

Im Thurn, E. F., Among the Indians of Guiana. 1883.

Inama-Sternegg, K. Th. von, Deutsche Wirtschaftsgeschichte.

Inglis, J., In the New Hebrides. 1887.

Ingram, J. K., A history of slavery and serfdom. 1895.

Islawin, W., Das Hauswesen, die Rennthierzucht und die Gewerbsthätigkeit der Samojeden der Mesen'schen Tundra. Z. Erd. Neue Folge X (1861).

Iwanowski, A., Die Mongolei. Ethnograpische Skizze. 1895.

Jagor, F., Travels in the Philippines. 1875.

James, E., Account of an Expedition from Pittsburgh to the Rocky Mountains. 1823.

Jansen, A. J. F., Aanteekeningen omtrent Sollok en de Solloksche zee-roovers. Tijds. VII.

Jenks, A. E., The Bontoc Igorot. Department of the Interior. Ethnological Survey Publications. Vol. I (1905).

Jesuit Relations, The, and allied documents.

Jhering, R. von, Geist des römischen Rechts. Dritte Auflage.

Joest, W., Ethnographisches und Verwandtes aus Guyana. I. A. E. Supplement zu Band V.

Joest, W., Weltfahrten.

John, H. C. St., The Ainos: aborigines of Yeso. J. A. I. II (1873).

John, R. St. A. St., Account of the Hill tribes of North Aracan. J. A. I. II (1873).

Johnston, H. H., The Kilima-Njaro Expedition. 1886.

Jones, P., History of the Ojibway Indians. 1861.

Jones, Strachan, The Kutchin Tribes. Smithson. Rep. 1866.

Jung, Aufzeichnungen über die Rechtsanschauungen der Eingeborenen von Nauru. M. D. S. X (1897).

Junghuhn, F., Die Battaländer auf Sumatra. 1847.

Junker, W., Reisen in Afrika. 1875—1886.

Junod, H. A., Les Baronga, Etude ethnographique sur les indigènes de la baie de Délagoa. 1898.

Kallenberg, F., Auf dem Kriegspfad gegen die Massai. 1892.

Kandt, Bericht über meine Reisen und gesammte Thätigkeit in Deutsch Ost-Afrika. M. D. S. XIII.

Kane, Paul, Wanderings of an artist among the Indians of North America. 1859.

Kannenberg, Reise durch die hamitischen Sprachgebiete um Kondoa. M. D. S. XIII.

Kate, H. F. C. ten, Reizen en onderzoekingen in Noord-Amerika. 1885.

—— Verslag eener reis in de Timorgroep en Polynesie. T. A. G. 1894.

Keane, A. H., On the Botocudos. J. A. I. XIII (1884).

Keating, W. H., Narrative of an Expedition to the Source of the St. Peters River in 1823 under the command of Major Stephen H. Long. 1825.

Kennan, J., Tent life in Siberia. 1871.

Kerr, W. M., The far interior. 1886.

Kingsley, Mary H., West African studies. 1899.

Kingsley, Miss, Discussion, in J. A. I. XXIX.

Kinzie, Mrs. John H., Wau-bun, the early day in the northwest. 1873.

Kirby, W. W., A journey to the Youcan, Russian America. Smithson. Rep. 1864.

Klaproth, J. von, Reise in den Kaukasus und nach Georgien. 1812.

Klerks, E. A., Geographisch en ethnographisch opstel over de landschappen Karintji, Serampas en Soengai Tenang. Tijds. XXXIX.

Klutschak, Als Eskimo unter den Eskimos. 1881.

Knapp, G. F., Die Bauernbefreiung und der Ursprung der Landarbeiter in den älteren Theilen Preussens. 1887.

Koehne, C., Das Recht der Kalmücken. Z. V. R. IX.

Kohl, J. G., Kitschi-Gami oder Erzählungen vom Obern See. 1859.

Kohler, J., Das Recht der Marshall-Insulaner. Z. V. R. XII and XIV.

—— Über das Negerrecht namentlich in Kamerun. Separat-Abdruck aus der Z. V. R. 1895.

—— Das Recht der Herero. Z. V. R. XIV.

—— Das Recht der Papuas. Z. V. R. XIV.

—— Das Recht der Hottentotten. Z. V. R. XV.

—— Das Banturecht in Ost-afrika. Z. V. R. XV.

Köler, H., Einige Notizen über Bonny an der Küste von Guinea, seine Sprache und seine Bewohner. 1848.

Koning, D. A. P., Eenige gegevens omtrent land en volk der Noordoost-kust van Ned. Nieuw-Guinea, genaamd Papoea Telandjang. Bijdr. LV.

Korte Beschrijving van het landschap Bila. Bijdr. LVI.

Kotzebue, Otto von, Entdeckungs-Reise in die Südsee und nach der Berings-Strasse. 1821.

Kovalewsky, M., Coutume contemporaine et loi ancienne. 1893.

—— L'avènement du régime économique moderne au sein des campagnes. Revue internationale de sociologie. 1896.

Krämer, A., Die Samoa-Inseln. 1902—03.

—— Studienreise nach den Zentral- und West-Karolinen. M. D. S. XXI.

—— Hawaii, Ostmikronesien und Samoa. 1906.

Krause, A., Die Tlinkit-Indianer. 1885.

Krieger, M., Neu Guinea.

Kroesen, J. A., Nota omtrent de Bataklanden (speciaal Simeloengoen). Tijds. XLI.

Kroesen, R. C., Aanteekeningen over de Anambas-, Natoena- en Tambelan-eilanden. Tijds. XXI.

Kropf, A., Das Volk der Xosa-Kaffern im östlichen Südafrika nach seiner Geschichte, Eigenart, Verfassung und Religion. 1889.

Kruijt, A. C., Een en ander aangaande het geestelijk en maatschappelijk leven van den Poso-Alfoer. N. Z. G. XXXIX and XL.

—— Eenige ethnographische aanteekeningen omtrent de Toboengkoe en de Tomori. N. Z. G. XLIV.

Kubary, J., Die Bewohner der Mortlock- Inseln. Mittheilungen der geographischen Gesellschaft in Hamburg. 1878—9.

—— Die Ebongruppe im Marshall's Archipel. Journal des Museum Godeffroy I.

—— Die Industrie der Pelau-Insulaner. 1892.

—— Die Palau-Inseln in der Südsee. Journal des Museum Godeffroy I.

—— Die socialen Einrichtungen der Pelauer. 1885.

—— Die Verbrechen und das Strafverfahren auf den Pelau-Inseln. Original-Mittheilungen aus der ethnologischen Abtheilung der königlichen Museen zu Berlin. Erster Jahrgang (1886), Heft 2—3.

Kunze, G., Im Dienst des Kreuzes auf ungebahnten Pfaden. Drittes Heft. Allerlei Bilder aus dem Leben der Papua. Zweite Auflage. 1901.

Lafitau, Moeurs des sauvages amériquains. 1764.

Lambert, Le père, Moeurs et superstitions des Néo-Calédoniens. 1900.

Lamprecht, K., Deutsche Geschichte.

Lang, J. D., Queensland. 1861.

Lange, F. A., Die Arbeiterfrage. Ihre Bedeutung für Gegenwart und Zukunft. Vierte Auflage. 1879.

Langen, K. F. H. van, Atjeh's Westkust. T. A. G. 2nd series V.

Laufer, Berthold, Preliminary notes on explorations among the Amoor tribus. American Anthropologist New Series Vol. 2. 1900.

Lavisse, E., Histoire de France. Vol. II Part II. 1901.

Lean, J. Mc., The Indians of Canada, their manners and customs. Third edition. 1892.

Legrand, A., La Nouvelle-Calédonie et ses habitants en 1890. 1893.

Lenz, O., Skizzen aus West-Afrika. 1878.

Leroy-Beaulieu, P., Le luxe, la fonction de la richesse. Revue des deux mondes, Novembre—Décembre 1894.

Lery, J. de, Histoire d'un voyage fait en la terre du Bresil, autrement dite Amérique. Troisième édition. 1585.

Letourneau, Ch., L'évolution de l'esclavage. 1897.

Lettres édifiantes et curieuses.

Levchine, A. de, Description des hordes et des steppes des Kirghiz-Kazaks. 1840.

Lewin, Th., Wild races of South Eastern India. 1870.

Lewis and Clark, Expedition up the Missouri. 1902. (Reprint of the edition of 1814).

Liefrinck, F. A., Nota betreffende den economischen toestand van het rijk Bangli (Bali). Tijds. XXIV.

—— Slavernij op Lombok. Tijds. XLII.

Life in California, by an American. 1846.

Ligtvoet, A., Aanteekeningen betreffende den economischen toestand en de ethnographie van het rijk van Sumbawa. Tijds. XXIII.

Ling Roth, H., The aborigines of Hispaniola. J. A. I. XVI (1887).

—— The aborigines of Tasmania. 1890.

—— The natives of Sarawak and British Northern Borneo. 1896.

Lippert, J., Kulturgeschichte der Menschheit.

Lister, J. J., Notes on the natives of Fakaofu (Bowditch Island), Union Group. J. A. I. XXI.

Livingstone, D., Missionary travels and researches in South Africa. 1857.

—— The last journals of ——, in Central Africa, from 1865 to his death. 1874.

Livingstone, D. and C., Narrative of an expedition to the Zambesi and its tributaries. 1865.

Long, J., Voyages and travels of an Indian interpreter and trader. 1791.

Loria, A., Les bases économiques de la constitution sociale. 1893.

Loskiel, G. H., Geschichte der Mission der evangelischen Brüder unter den Indianern in Nordamerika. 1789.

Low, H., Sarawak. 1848.

Lumholtz, Among cannibals. 1889.

Maass, A., Reise nach den Mentawei-Inseln. Verhandlungen der Gesellschaft für Erdkunde zu Berlin XXV (1898).

Maccauley, Clay, The Seminole Indians of Florida. A. R. B. E. V.

Macdonald, J., East Central African Customs. J. A. I. XXII (1893).

—— Manners, Customs, Superstitions and Religions of South African tribes. J. A. I. XIX and XX (1890 and 1891).

Mackenzie, A., Voyages from Montreal through the continent of North America. 1802.

Maclay, N. von Miklucho, Ethnologische Bemerkungen über die Papuas der Maclay-Küste in Neu-Guinea. Natuurkundig tijdschrift voor Nederlandsch-Indie XXXV and XXXVI.

Macrae, J., Asiatick researches VII. 1807.

Madrolle, C., En Guinée. 1895.

Magyar, L., Reisen in Süd-Afrika in den Jahren 1849—1857. 1859.

Mahler, R., Siedelungsgebiet und Siedelungslage in Oceanien. I. A. E. Supplement zu Band XI (1898).

Mallat, Les Philippines.

Malthus, T. R., An essay on the principle of population. Edited by G. T. Bettany. 1890.

Man, E. H., The aboriginal inhabitants of the Andaman Islands. J. A. I. XII (1883).

Marcuse, A., Die Hawaiischen Inseln. 1894.

Mariner, Histoire des naturels des Iles Tonga ou des Amis. 1817.

Marsden, W., The history of Sumatra. Third edition. 1811.

Martens, E. von, Banda, Timor und Flores. Z. G. Erd. XXIV (1889).

Martius, von, Zur Ethnographie Amerika's, zumal Brasiliens. 1867.

Marx, K., Das Kapital. Vol. I Second edition. 1872, Vol. III 1894.

Mason, Religion etc. among the Karens. Journ. Asiat. Soc. 1865, 1868.

Mathews, W., Ethnography and philology of the Hidatsa Indians. 1877.

Matthes, B. F., Bijdragen tot de Ethnologie van Zuid-Celebes. 1875.

Mauch, C., Reisen im Inneren von Süd-Afrika. Pet. Ergänzungsheft XXXVII.

Maurault, J. A., Histoire des Abénakis depuis 1605 jusqu' à nos jours. 1866.

Mayne, R. C., Four years in British Columbia. 1862.

Mededeelingen betreffende het landschap Panei en het Rajahgebied. Bijdr. LVI.

Meerwaldt, J. H., Aanteekeningen betreffende de Battaklanden. Tijds. XXXVII.

Meinicke, C. E., Der Archipel der Neuen Hebriden. Z. G. Erd. IX (1874).

—— Die Gilbert- und Marshall-Inseln. Z. Erd. Neue Folge XV (1863).

—— Die Inseln des stillen Oceans. 1875—6.

—— Die Torresstrasse, ihre Gefahren und Inseln. Z. Erd. Neue Folge III (1857).

Melching, K., Staatenbildung in Melanesien. 1897.

Meline, J. F., Two thousand miles on horseback. Santa Fé and back. 1867.

Melnikow, N., Die Burjaten des Irkutskischen Gouvernements. I. A. E. XII.

Merivale, H., Lectures on colonization and colonies. New edition. 1861.

Merker, M., Die Masai. Ethnographische Monographie eines ostafrikanischen Semitenvolkes. 1904.

Mess, H. A., De Mentawei-eilanden. Tijds. XXVI.

Metz, F., The tribes inhabiting the Neilgherry hills. Second edition. 1864.

Meyer, E., Die wirtschaftliche Entwickelung des Altertums. 1895.

—— Die Sklaverei im Altertum. 1898.

Meijer, H., Die Igorroten von Luzon. Verhandlungen der Berliner Ges. f. Anthr., Ethn. und Urgeschichte. 1883.

Miesen, J. H. W. van der, Een en ander over Boeroe. N. Z. G. XLVI.

Mill, J. Stuart, Principles of political economy. Fifth edition.

Miller, E. Y., The Bataks of Palawan. Department of the Interior. Ethnological Survey Publications. Vol. II Part III (1905).

Mitchell, Three expeditions into the Interior of Eastern Australia. 1839.

Modigliani, E., L'Isola delle Donne. Viaggio ad Engano. 1894.

—— Un viaggio a Nias. 1890.

Moerenhout, J. A., Voyage aux îles du Grand Océan. 1837.

Mohnicke, Bangka und Palembang. 1874.

Molina, G. I., Saggio sulla Storia civile del Chili. 1787.

Möllhausen, B., Tagebuch einer Reise vom Mississippi nach den Küsten der Süd-See. 1858.

Mommsen, Th. Römische Geschichte. Siebente Auflage.

Montaigne, M. de, Essais.

Montano, Quelques jours chez les indigènes de la province de Malacca. R. E. I.

Moolenburgh, P. E., Extract uit een verslag der Noord-Nieuw-Guinea-Expeditie. Tijds. XLVII.

Morgan, Delmar, The customs of the Ossetes. Journal Royal Asiat. Soc. 1888.

Morgan. L. H., Ancient society. 1877.

Morgan, J. de, Exploration dans la presqu'île malaise. 1886.

Müller, F., Unter Tungusen und Jakuten. 1882.

Müller, F. W. K., Batak-Sammlung. Veröffentlichungen aus dem königlichen Museum für Völkerkunde III (1893).

Müller, J. von, Reise durch das Gebiet des Habäs und Beni-Amer. Z. G. Erd. XVIlI (1883).

Munzinger, W., Ostafrikanische Studien. 1864.

—— Ueber die Sitte und das Recht der Bogos. 1859.

Muratori, M., Relation des missions du Paraguai. 1826.

Murdoch, J., Ethnological Results of the Point Barrow Expedition. A. R. B. E. IX.

Musters, Unter den Patagoniern. 1877.

Nachtigal, G., Sahara und Sûdan.

Nansen, F., The first crossing of Greenland. 1890.

Neill, E.D., The history of Minnesota: from the earliest French explorations to the present time. 1873.

Neumann, J. B., Het Pane- en Bila-stroomgebied. T. A. G. 2nd series III and IV (1887).

—— Schets der afdeeling Laboean-Batoe, residentie Sumatra's Oostkust. Tijds. XXVI.

Newbold, F. J., British Settlements in the Straits of Malacca. 1839.

Niblack, A. P., The Coast Indians of Southern Alaska and Northern British Columbia. Smithson. Rep. 1888.

Nieuwenhuis, A. W., Quer durch Borneo. Vol. I 1904. Vol. II 1907.

—— In Centraal Borneo. Reis van Pontianak naar Samarinda. 1900.

Nieuwenhuijzen, F. N., Het rijk Siak Sri Indrapoera. Tijds. VII.

Nieuw-Guinea ethnografisch en natuurkundig onderzocht en beschreven in 1858. Bijdr. 1862.

Nordenskiöld, A. E. von, Die Umsegelung Asiens und Europas auf der Vega. 1882.

Nys, E., Recherches sur l'histoire de l'economie politique. 1898.

Obrutschew, W., Aus China. 1896.

Ochenkowski, W. von, Englands wirtschaftliche Entwickelung im Ausgange des Mittelalters. 1879.

Ochsenius, C., Chili, Land und Leute. 1884.

Oldfield, A., On the aborigines of Australia. Transact. of the Ethnol. Soc. of London. 1865.

Ophuijsen, C. A. van, De Loeboes. Tijds. XXIX.

Oppenheimer, F., Das Bevölkerungsgesetz des T. R. Malthus und der neueren Nationalökonomie. Darstellung und Kritik. 1901.

—— David Ricardos Grundentheorie. Darstellung und Kritik. 1909.

Orbigny, A. d', L'homme américain. 1839.

Ordinaire, O., Les sauvages du Pérou. R. E. VI.

Ottow en Geissler, Kort overzigt van het land en de bewoners der kust van Noord-Oostelijk Nieuw Guinea (overgedrukt uit de Christelijke Stemmen). 1857.

Oudemans, A. C., Engano, zijne geschiedenis, bewoners en voortbrengselen. T. A. G. 2nd series VI.

Owen Dorsey, J., Omaha Sociology. A. R. B. E. III.

—— Siouan Sociology. A. R. B. E. XV.

Pallas, P. S., Neue nordische Beiträge. 1796.

—— Reise durch verschiedene Provinzen des Russischen Reichs. 1776—8.

Parker Winship, G., The Coronado Expedition 1540—1542. A. R. B. E. XIV.

Parkinson, R., Beiträge zur Ethnologie der Gilbertinsulaner. I. A. E. II.

—— Dreissig Jahre in der Südsee. 1907.

—— Zur Ethnographie der nordwestlichen Salomo Inseln. 1899.

—— Im Bismarck-Archipel. 1887.

Passarge, S., Das Okawangosumpfland und seine Bewohner. Z. E. XXXVII.

—— Die Buschmänner der Kalahari. M. D. S. XVIII.

Paulitschke, Ph., Etnographie Nord-Ost-Afrikas. 1893—6.

Pauw ten Cate, H., Rapport van de Marga Semindo Darat. Tijds. XVII.

Perelaer, T. H., Ethnographische Beschrijving der Dajaks. 1870.

Peschel, O., Völkerkunde. Sechste Auflage.

Peters, W., Der Muata Cazembe und die Völkerstämme der Maravis, Muizas, Muembas, Lundas und andere von Süd-Afrika. Z. Erd. VI (1856).

Petitot, Les Grands Esquimaux.

Petroff, L., Report on the Population, Industries and Resources of Alaska. Tenth census of the United States VIII (1884).

Pfeil, J. Graf, Studien und Beobachtungen aus der Südsee. 1899.

Phillips, R. C., The Lower Congo, a sociological study. J. A. I. XVII (1888).

Pinart, A. Les Indiens de l'état de Panama. R. E. VI.

Pleijte, C. M., Ethnographische beschrijving der Kei-eilanden. T. A. G. 2nd series X.

Ploss, H., Das Kind in Brauch und Sitte der Völker.

Pogge, P., Beiträge zur Entdeckungsgeschichte Afrika's. III Im Reiche des Muata Jamwo. 1880.

Pogge's Aufenthalt in Lubuku, Rückkehr und Tod. Appendix to Wissmann, Unter deutscher Flagge quer durch Afrika von West nach Ost. 1889.

Pohl, J. E., Reisen im Inneren von Brasilien. 1837.

Pokalowsky, H., Die erste Eroberung von Costa-Rica durch die Spanier in den Jahren 1562—1564. Z. G. Erd. XIX (1884).

Polack, J. S., Manners and customs of the New Zealanders. 1840.

Post, A. H., Grundriss der ethnologischen Jurisprudenz.

Powell, J. W., On regimentation. A. R. B. E. XV.

—— Wyandot Government: a short study of tribal society. A. R. B. E. I.

Powers, S., Tribes of California. U. S. Geogr. and Geol. Survey of the Rocky Mountains Region. Contrib. to N. Amer. Ethnology III (1876).

Prehn, R. C. von, Aanteekeningen betreffende Borneo's Westkust. Tijds. VII.

Pritchard, W. T., Polynesian Reminiscences; or, Life in the South Pacific Islands. 1866.

Puchta, G. F., Cursus der Institutionen. Neunte Auflage. 1881.

Quast, H. C. E., Verslag nopens den politieken toestand in de Rokan staatjes. Tijds. XLVIII.

Quatrefages, A. de, L'espèce humaine. 1877.

Radde, G., Reisen an der persisch-russischen Grenze. Talysch und seine Bewohner. 1886.

Radiguet, M., Les derniers sauvages. Souvenirs de l'occupation française aux îles marquises. 1842—1859.

Radloff, W., Aus Sibirien. 1884.

—— Beobachtungen über die Kirgisen. Pet. 1864.

Ratzel, Völkerkunde.

—— Anthropogeographie. II, 1891.

Ray, Report on the Intern. Polar Expedition to Point-Barrow. 1885.

Reclus, E., Voyage à la Sierra Nevada de Sainte Marthe. 1881.

Reed, W. A., Negritos of Zambales. Department of the Interior. Ethnological Survey Publications. Vol. II Part I (1904).

Remy, J., Ka Mooalelo Hawaii. Histoire de l'archipel Hawaien. 1862.

Reports of Explorations and Surveys for a railroad route from the Mississippi River to the Pacific Ocean.

Résumé's van het onderzoek naar de rechten welke in de Gouvernementslanden op Sumatra op de onbebouwde gronden worden uitgeoefend. Second edition. 1896.

Ribbach, C. A., Labrador. T. A. G. I (1876).

Ribbe, C., Zwei Jahre unter den Kannibalen der Salomo-Inseln. 1903.

Ricardo, D., Works. Edited by Mc. Culloch. 1876.

Richter, Der Bezirk Bukoba. M. D. S. XII.

—— Einige weitere ethnographische Notizen über den Bezirk Bukoba. M. D. S. XIII.

—— Notizen über Lebensweisen, Zeitrechnung, Industrie und Handwerk der Bewohner des Bezirks Bukoba. M. D. S. XIII.

Riedel, J. G. F., De landschappen Holontalo, Limoeto, Bone, Boalemo en Katinggola, of Adangile. Tijds. XIX.

Riedel, J. G. F., De Minahasse in 1825. Tijds. XVIII.

—— De sluik- en kroesharige rassen tusschen Selebes en Papua. 1886.

—— De Topantunuazu of oorspronkelijke volksstammen in Centraal-Selebes. Bijdr. 1886.

—— Galela und Tobeloresen. Z. E. XVII.

—— Het landschap Boeool. Tijds. XVIII.

Rink, H., Tales and traditions of the Eskimo. 1875.

Ripley, William Z., The races of Europe. A sociological study. 1899.

Robertson, G. S., Kafiristan and its people. J. A. I. XXVII (1897).

Robidé van der Aa., P. J. B. C., Reizen naar Nederlandsch Nieuw-Guinea. 1879.

Rochas, V. de, La Nouvelle Calédonie. 1862.

Rochefort, de, Histoire naturelle et morale des Iles Antilles. 1641.

Roest, J. L. D. van der, Uit het leven der bevolking van Windessi. Tijds. XL.

Rogers, J. E. Thorold, The economic interpretation of history. 1888.

—— Work and wages. 1885.

Romilly, H. H., From my verandah in New Guinea. 1889.

—— The Western Pacific and New Guinea. Second edition. 1887.

Roo van Alderwerelt, J. de, Eenige mededeelingen over Soemba. Tijds. XXXIII.

Roos, S., Iets over Endeh. Tijds. XXIV.

Roosevelt, Th., The Winning of the West.

Roscoe, J., The Bahima: A Cow Tribe in the Uganda Protectorate. J. A. I. XXXVII.

Rosenberg, H. von, Beschrijving van Engano en deszelfs bewoners. Tijds. III.

—— De Mentawei-eilanden en hunne bewoners. Tijds. I.

—— Der malayische Archipel. 1878.

—— Geografische en ethnografische beschrijving van het district Singkel. Tijds. III.

—— Reistochten naar de Geelvinkbaai op Nieuw-Guinea. 1875.

Ross, B. R., Notes on the Tinneh or Chepewyan Indians of British and Russian America. Smithson. Rep. 1866.

Roth, W. E., Ethnological studies among the North-West-Central Queensland Aborigines. 1897.

Rousselet, L., Le Kafiristan et les Kafirs. R. E. III.

Rowney, H. B., The wild tribes of India. 1882.

Russell, F., Explorations in the Far North. 1898.

Sagard, Fr. Gabriel, Voyage au pays des Hurons. 1632.

Saleeby, N. J., Studies in Moro history, law, and religion. Department of the Interior. Ethnological Survey Publications. Vol. IV Part I (1905).

Salvado, R., Memorie storiche dell'Australia. 1851.

Salvioli, G., Le lotte fra pastori e agricoltori nella storia della civiltà. Rivista Italiana di Sociologia. Anno II.

Sarasin, P. and F., Die Weddas von Ceylon. 1893.

Savage Landor, A. H., Alone with the hairy Ainu. 1893.

Schadenberg, A., Beiträge zur Kenntniss der im Innern Nordluzons lebenden Stämme. Verhandl. der Berliner. Ges, f. Anthrop., Ethnol. und Urgeschichte. 1888.

—— Die Bewohner von Süd-Mindanao und der Insel Samal. Z. E. XVII.

—— Über die Negritos der Philippinen. Z. E. XII.

Scheemaker, L. de, Nota betreffende het landschap Batoebarah. Tijds. XVII.

Schele, von, Uhehe. M. D. S. IX.

Schmeltz., J. D. E., und R. Krause, Die ethnographisch-anthropologische Abtheilung des Museum Godeffroy in Hamburg. 1881.

Schmoller, G., Die Thatsachen der Arbeitsteilung. Jahrbuch für Gesetzgebung, Verwaltung und Volkswirtschaft im Deutschen Reich. 1889.

—— Grundriss der allgemeinen Volkswirtschaftslehre I 1900.

Schomburgk, R., Reisen in British Guiana. 1847.

Schomburgk, R. H., Reisen in Guiana und am Orinoko. 1839.

Schoolcraft, H. R., History, Condition, and Prospects of the Indian Tribes of the United States. 1851.

Schröder, R., Lehrbuch der deutschen Rechtsgeschichte. 1889.

Schurtz, H. Katechismus der Völkerkunde. 1893.

—— Das Afrikanische Gewerbe. 1900.

—— Die Anfänge des Landbesitzes. Zeitschrift für Socialwissenschaft III (1900).

Schütt, O. H., Reisen im Südwestlichen Becken des Congo. 1881.

Schwaner, Borneo. 1853.

Schweinfurth, G., Au coeur de l'Afrique.

Seemann, B., Viti: an account of a Government Mission. 1861.

Semper, Karl, Die Pelau-Inseln im stillen Ocean. 1873.

—— Die Philippinen und ihre Bewohner. 1869.

Senfft, Die Insel Nauru. M. D. S. 1896.

Serpa Pinto, How I crossed Africa. 1881.

Severijn, P., Verslag van een in 1854 bewerkstelligd onderzoek op het eiland Engano. Tijds. III.

—— Verslag van een onderzoek der Poggi-eilanden. Tijds. III.

Shaw, Th., Asiatick Researches IV (1807).

Sibree, J., The great African Island. 1880.

Siegel, H., Deutsche Rechtsgeschichte. Zweite Auflage. 1889.

Sievers, W., Des Grafen Josef de Brettes Reisen im nördlichen Colombia. Globus LXXIII.

—— Reise in der Sierra Nevada de Santa Marta. 1887.

Simcox, E. J., Primitive Civilizations. 1894.

Simons, The Goajiro-Peninsula. Proc. Royal Geogr. Soc. 1885.

Simson, Alfred, Notes on the Zaparos. J. A. I. VII (1878).

Skeat, W. W., and Ch. O. Blagden, Pagan races of the Malay Peninsula. 1906.

Skinner, J., Voyages au Pérou, faits dans les années 1791 à 1794, par les pp. Manuel Sobreviela et Narcisso y Barcelo. 1809.

Smith, E. R., The Araucanians. 1855.

Smyth, W., and. F. Lowe, Narrative of a journey from Lima to Para. 1836.

Snouck Hurgronje, C., De Atjehers. 1893—4.

—— Het Gajoland en zijne bewoners. 1903.

Snow, Parker W., Tierra del Fuego. 1857.

Sohm, R., Institutionen des Römischen Rechts. Vierte Auflage. 1891.

Sombart, W., Der Moderne Kapitalismus. 1902.

Somerville, B. T., Ethnographical notes on New Georgia, Solomon Islands. J. A. I. XXVI (1897).

—— Notes on some islands of the New Hebrides. J. A. I. XXIII (1894).

Sonnenschein, Aufzeichnungen über die Insel Nauru (Pleasant Island). M. D. S. II (1889).

Southey, R., History of Brazil. 1822.

Spencer, H., Descriptive Sociology.

—— Industrial institutions.

—— Political institutions.

Spenser St. John, Life in the forests of the far East. Second edition. 1863.

Sproat, J. M., Scenes and Studies of Savage Life. 1868.

Staudinger, P., Im Herzen der Haussa-Länder. 1889.

Stein, Die Turkmenen. Pet. 1880.

Steinbach, The Marshall Islands. The Geographical Journal, Vol. 7 (1896).

Steinen, K. von den, Unter den Naturvölkern Central-Brasiliens. 1894.

—— Durch Central-Brasilien. 1886.

Steinmetz, S. R., Das Verhältnis zwischen Eltern und Kindern bei den Naturvölkern. Zeitschrift für Socialwissenschaft I.

—— Endokannibalismus. 1896.

—— Ethnologische Studien zur ersten Entwicklung der Strafe. 1894.

—— Rechtsverhältnisse von eingeborenen Völkern in Afrika und Ozeanien. 1903.

—— Classification des types sociaux et catalogue des peuples. L'année sociologique 1898—99.

Steller, G. W., Beschreibung von dem Lande Kamtschatka. 1774.

Stenin, P. von, Die Kurden des Gouvernements Eriwan. Globus LXX (1896).

—— Das Gewohnheitsrecht der Samojeden. Globus LX (1891).

Stokes, J., Discoveries in Australia. 1846.

Storch, Sitten, Gebräuche und Rechtspflege bei den Bewohnern Usambaras und Pares. M. D. S. VIII.

Strachey, The history of Travaile into Virginia Brittannia (1610—1612), printed for the Hackluyt Society. 1849.

Strauch, H., Allgemeine Bemerkungen ethnologischen Inhalts über Neu-Guinea, etc. Z. E. IX.

Stuhlmann, Mit Emin-Pascha ins Herz von Afrika. 1894.

Sullivan, O', Tierra del Fuego. Fortnightly Review. 1893.

Sumner, W. G., The Yakuts. Abridged from the Russian of Sieroshevski. J. A. I. XXXI.

Sutherland, A., The origin and growth of the moral instinct. 1898.

Svoboda, W., Die Bewohner des Nikobaren-Archipels. I. A. E. V.

Swan, J. G., Haidah Indians of Queen Charlotte Islands. Smithson. Contrib. to Knowledge 1874.

—— The Northwest Coast; or, three years residence in Washington territory. 1857.

Tacitus, Germania.

Tanner, J., Denkwürdigkeiten über seinen dreissigjährigen Aufenthalt unter den Indianern Nord-Amerika's. 1840.

Tautain, L., Études critiques sur l'ethnologie et l'ethnographie des peuples du bassin du Sénégal. R. E. IV.

—— Notes sur les castes chez les Mandingues et en particulier chez les Banmanas. R. E. III.

—— Quelques renseignements sur les Bobo. R. E. VI.

Taylor, R., Te Ika á Maui; or, New Zealand and its inhabitants. Second edition. 1870.

Tegenwoordige Staat der Vereenigde Nederlanden.

Telfer, The Crimea and Transcaucasia. 1876.

Tellier, G., Autour de Kita. Etude soudanaise. 1902.

Theal, M. G., The Portuguese in South Africa. 1896.

Thomas, N. W., Natives of Australia. 1906.

Thomson, A. S., The Story of New Zealand. 1857.

Thomson, B., Note upon the natives of Savage Island, or Niué. J. A. I. XXXI.

Thomson, J., To the Central African lakes and back. 1881.

—— Through Massailand. 1885.

Thomson, J. P., British New Guinea. 1892.

Thouar, A., Explorations dans l'Amérique du Sud. 1891.

Tonkes, H., Volkskunde von Bali. 1888.

Torday, E. and T. A. Joyce, Notes on the Ethnography of the Ba-Mbala. J. A. I. XXXV.

—— Notes on the Ethnography of the Ba-Yaka. J. A. I. XXXVI.

Torday, E. and T. A. Joyce, Notes on the Ethnography of the Ba-Huana. J. A. I. XXXVI.
—— On the Ethnology of the South-Western Congo Free State. J. A. I. XXXVII.
Tourmagne, A., Histoire de l'esclavage ancien et moderne. 1880.
Tregear, E., The Maoris of New Zealand. J. A. I. XIX (1890).
Tromp, J. C. E., De Rambai en Sebroeang Dajaks. Tijds. XXV.
Tromp, Th. M., De Kaffers. T. A. G. V (1881).
Tschudi, J. J. von, Reisen durch Süd-Amerika. 1869.
Turner, G., Samoa. 1884.
Turner, L. M., Ethnology of the Ungava District. A. R. B. E. XI.
Turner, W. Y., On the ethnology of the Motu. J. A. I. VII (1878).
Tylor, E. B. Anthropology.
—— On a method of investigating the development of institutions. J. A. I. XVIII (1889).
—— Primitive Culture.

Ujfalvy, Ch. de, Les Aryens au nord et au sud de l'Hindou-Kouch. 1896.
—— Expédition scientifique française en Russie, en Sibérie et dans le Turkestan. 1878.

Vallentin, W., Kaiser Wilhelmsland. Neue deutsche Rundschau, Juni 1897.
Vambéry, H., Das Türkenvolk. 1885.
—— Skizzen aus Mittelasien. 1868.
Vaughan Stevens, H., Materialien zur Kenntniss der wilden Stämme auf der Halbinsel Malâka. Veröffentlichungen aus dem königlichen Museum für Völkerkunde II and III.
Vaux, L. de, Les Canaques de la Nouvelle Calédonie. R. E. II.
Venturillo, M. H., The "Batacs" of the Island of Palawan, Phil. Islds. I. A. E. XVIII.
Verguet, L., Arossi ou San-Christoval et ses habitants. R. E. IV.
Verslag eener reis van den Assistent-resident van Benkoelen naar het eiland Engano. Tijds. XIX.
Veth, P. J., Java. Second edition (by J. F. Snelleman and J. F. Niermeyer).
Vetter, K., Bericht über papuanische Rechtsverhältnisse. Nachrichten über Kaiser Wilhelms-land und den Bismarck-Archipel. 1897.
Vidal, M., Voyage d'exploration dans le haut Maroni, Guyane française. 1862.
Vierkandt, A., Die Culturtypen der Menschheit. Archiv für Anthropologie XXV.
—— Die Verbreitung der Sklaverei und ihre Ursachen. Zeitschrift für Socialwissenschaft 1901.
Vincent, Around and about South America. 1890.

Vink, J. A., Eenige curiosa betreffende de Wadjoreezen, Soembaneezen en Bimaneezen. Tijdschrift voor Nederlandsch-Indië, Mei 1901.

Volkens, G., Ueber die Karolinen-Insel Yap. Verhandlungen der Gesellschaft für Erdkunde zu Berlin. 1901.

Waanders, P. L. van Bloemen, Aanteekeningen omtrent de zeden en gebruiken der Balineezen, inzonderheid die van Boeleleng. Tijds. VIII.

Wagner, A., Grundlegung. Erster Teil des ersten Bandes von: Lehrbuch der politischen Oekonomie von A. Wagner und E. Nasse.

Waitz-Gerland, Anthropologie der Naturvölker.

Wakefield, E. G., A view of the art of colonization. 1849.

Walker, J. B., Notes on the Politics, Religion and Commerce of Old Calabar. J. A. I. VI (1877).

Walland, J., Het eiland Engano. Tijds. XIV.

Waltershausen, A. Sartorius Freiherr von, Die Entstehung des Tauschhandels in Polynesien. Zeitschrift für Social- und Wirtschaftsgeschichte IV.

Ward, H., Ethnographical notes relating to the Congo tribes. J. A. I. XXIV (1895).

—— Five years with the Congo Cannibals. 1890.

Waterhouse, J., The King and People of Fiji. 1865.

Watt, G., The aboriginal tribes of Manipur. J. A. I. XVI (1887).

Weber, Max, Die römische Agrargeschichte. 1891.

Wehrli, H. J., Beitrag zur Ethnologie der Chingpaw (Kachin) von Ober-Burma. I. A. E. Supplement to Vol. XVI.

Weil, La Tourkménie et les Tourkmènes. 1880.

Weisz, Bruno, Mehr als fünfzig Jahre auf Chatham Island. 1901.

Wemiaminow, Charakterzüge der Aleuten von den Fuchsinseln, in Von Baer und Von Helmersen's Beitr. z. Kenntniss des russischen Reiches. 1834.

West, Th., Ten years in South Central Polynesia. 1865.

Westenberg, C. J., Nota over de onafhankelijke Bataklanden. Tijds. XXXIV.

—— Verslag eener reis naar de onafhankelijke Bataklanden ten noorden van het Toba-meer. T. A. G. 2nd series XIV.

Westermarck, E., The history of human marriage. 1891.

—— The origin and development of the moral ideas. 1906—08.

Weule, K., Wissenschaftliche Ergebnisse meiner ethnographischen Forschungsreise in den Südosten Deutsch-Ostafrikas (M. D. S. Erganzungsheft No. 1) 1908.

Whymper, F., Alaska. 1869.

Wickham, A. H., Notes on the Soumoo or Woolwa Indians, of Blewfields River, Mosquito Territory. J. A. I. XXIV (1895).

Wied, Prinz Max zu, Reise in Brasilien. 1819.

Wied, Prinz Max zu, Reise in das Innere Nord-Amerika's. 1832.

Wiese, Carl, Beiträge zur Geschichte der Zulu im Norden des Zambesi, namentlich der Angoni. Z. E. XXXII (1900).

Wilken, G. A., Bijdrage tot de kennis der Alfoeren van het eiland Boeroe. Verhand. v. h. Bat. Genootsch. v. K. en W. XXXVIII (1875).

—— Het pandrecht bij de volken van den Indischen Archipel. 1888.

Wilken, N. P., and J. A., Schwarz, Allerlei over het land en volk van Bolaäng Mongondou. N. Z. G. XI.

Wilkes, Narrative of the United States Exploring Expedition. 1845.

Willer, T. J., Verzameling van Battahsche wetten en instellingen in Mandheling en Pertibie. 1846.

Williams, Th., The Fiji Islands and their inhabitants. 1858.

Willinck, G. D., Het rechtsleven bij de Minangkabausche Maleiers. 1909.

Wilson, James, Zendelingsreis naar den Stillen Oceaan (Dutch translation). 1801—02.

Wilson and Felkin, Uganda and the Egyptian Soudan. 1882.

Winwood Reade, W., Savage Africa. 1864.

Wissmann, H., Im Inneren Afrikas. 1888.

—— Meine zweite Durchquerung Äquatorial-Afrikas, 1886—1887. 1890.

—— Unter deutscher Flagge quer durch Afrika von West nach Ost. 1889.

Wolff, W., Von Banano zum Kiamwo. 1889.

Woodford, C. M., A naturalist among the head-hunters. 1890.

Woods, J., The native tribes of South Australia. 1879.

Yate, W., An account of New Zealand and of the formation and progress of the Church Missionary Society's Mission in the Northern Island. Second edition. 1835.

Ypes, W. K. H., Nota omtrent Singkel en de Pak-paklanden. Tijds. XLIX.

Zenker, G., Yaunde. M. D. S. VIII.

Zondervan, H., Timor en de Timoreezen. T. A. G. 2nd series V.

Zündel, G., Land und Volk der Eweer auf der Sklavenküste in West-Afrika. Z. G. Erd. XII (1877).

SUBJECT-INDEX.